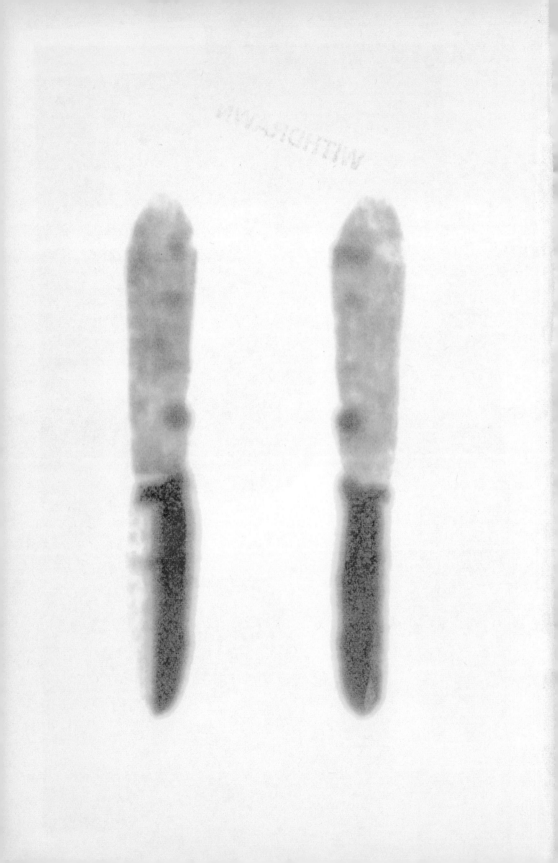

PERGAMON INTERNATIONAL LIBRARY
of Science, Technology, Engineering and Social Studies

*The 1000-volume original paperback library in aid of education,
industrial training and the enjoyment of leisure*

Publisher: Robert Maxwell, M.C.

Experimental Methods
For Social Policy Research

PGPS—69

THE PERGAMON TEXTBOOK
INSPECTION COPY SERVICE

An inspection copy of any book published in the Pergamon International Library
will gladly be sent to academic staff without obligation for their consideration for
course adoption or recommendation. Copies may be retained for a period of 60 days
from receipt and returned if not suitable. When a particular title is adopted or
recommended for adoption for class use and the recommendation results in a sale
of 12 or more copies, the inspection copy may be retained with our compliments.
The Publishers will be pleased to receive suggestions for revised editions and new
titles to be published in this important International Library.

PERGAMON GENERAL PSYCHOLOGY SERIES

Editor: Arnold P. Goldstein, *Syracuse University*
Leonard Krasner, *SUNY, Stony Brook*

The terms of our inspection copy service apply to all the above books. A complete catalogue of all books in the Pergamon International Library is available on request.

The Publisher will be pleased to receive suggestions for revised editions and new titles.

The above list of titles is continued on page 421

Experimental Methods
For Social Policy Research

by
GEORGE W. FAIRWEATHER

and

LOUIS G. TORNATZKY

PERGAMON PRESS
OXFORD   NEW YORK   TORONTO
SYDNEY   PARIS   FRANKFURT

U.K.	Pergamon Press Ltd., Headington Hill Hall, Oxford OX3 0BW, England
U.S.A.	Pergamon Press Inc., Maxwell House, Fairview Park, Elmsford, New York 10523, U.S.A.
CANADA	Pergamon of Canada Ltd., 75, The East Mall, Toronto, Ontario, Canada
AUSTRALIA	Pergamon Press (Aust.) Pty. Ltd., 19a Boundary Street, Rushcutters Bay, N.S.W. 2011, Australia
FRANCE	Pergamon Press SARL, 24 rue des Ecoles, 75240 Paris, Cedex 05, France
WEST GERMANY	Pergamon Press GmbH, 6242 Kronberg-Taunus, Pferdstrasse 1, West Germany

First Edition 1977

Library of Congress Cataloging in Publication Data

Fairweather, George William
Experimental methods for social policy research.

(Pergamon general psychology series; 69)
1. Social policy—Research—Methodology.   2. Social science research—Methodology.   3. Decision-making.
I. Tornatzky, Louis G., joint author.   II. Title.
H62.F278   1977   300'.1'8   76–25590
ISBN 0 08 021237 9 (Hardcover)
ISBN 0 08 021236 0 (Flexicover)

Printed in Great Britain by Western Printing Services Ltd, Bristol

Contents

Preface

There is an urgent need in contemporary societies for social decisions and actions to be taken that are aimed at improving the quality of human life. Correspondingly, the overpopulation of the planet along with its resulting energy and environmental problems, intermingled as they are with human relations crises, present an extremely complex picture of the human condition which societies need constant information and action to correct.

Yet, it is one of the perplexing paradoxes of our time that scientific methodology is rarely used by democratic societies in appraising alternative courses of social action to meet pressing human needs. Whether this is the result of fear by social decision makers that if truth is known their political power will be diminished or a fear by social scientists that to "get into the act" is to tarnish their scientific purity is not clear. What is clear is that contemporary human problems are so real and the future is so threatened that it is absolutely essential for all persons in the society—scientists, politicians, and citizens alike—to work together to preserve and improve the physical and social climates on this planet.

The authors of this book believe that social scientists can make a major contribution to the solution of contemporary problems by aiding the society in incorporating scientific methods into the social decision-making process. This means a more active and involved role for scientists and a more fully appreciative knowledge of the role science can play in decision making on the part of the government and the public. It is our contention that some scientists must become experts in the humane use of scientific methodology to aid in this problem-solving process. In a broader context, it is an attempt to provide society with a social change mechanism and with the personnel to man it that is badly needed in contemporary life.

The title of this book is meant to express its main purpose. It is to provide actual *experimental methods* for those scientists, public officials, and citizens who are committed to the improvement of living conditions for all members

vii

of society. In this sense the book represents not only a "how it can be done" approach but a social philosophy as well.

From an experimental point of view, the book attempts to deal with the two major methodological facets required for social problem solution. They are the methods to evaluate newly created social models aimed at solving particular problems and the methods needed to disseminate those models that are beneficial to the state, the region, and the nation. Each chapter therefore, addresses the methodological questions raised by these two processes which result in experimental methods for social models and for dissemination.

This book springs mainly from our experiences in social experimental work, covering 7 years for the junior author and about 25 years for the senior author, and from the experiences of several students who have themselves been trained in the use of such methods—mainly in the Ecological Psychology Program at Michigan State University. We are thankful to all these students for their special contributions. We are particularly grateful to Amanda Beck, Esther Fergus, Robert Harris, Susan Hedrick, William Ives, Kent Jamison, Lynn Keith, John Lounsbury, Jeffrey Taylor, Charles Tucker, and Monty Whitney. Throughout this book, the examples from the authors' experience and those of these students is given to illustrate particular experimental points. Constantly helpful in the preparation of this book has been the untiring assistance of JoAnn Ohm.

The general plan of the book is first to present the authors' argument that contemporary social policy decision making is inadequate for the late 20th and 21st centuries. The book then proceeds to define the basic ingredients for an adequate social policy decision-making apparatus and to describe how it can be accomplished. The third chapter in the book is devoted to an exploration of the basic parameters of social models and dissemination processes from a conceptual point of view. The remainder of the book gives general experimental procedures from the inception of the ideas to the implementation of social models found to be beneficial. Special emphasis is given to areas of research that are typically not presented in other research books —how to assemble the needed research team, how to obtain the needed administrative agreements from the involved social agencies, how to sample in community settings, how to administer the social action research program, and how traditional scientific techniques can be modified to make the most accurate inferences possible from such naturalistic research data. The techniques are an intertwining of logical thought, social action, and traditional scientific and experimental methods. The final chapter is reserved for a discussion of a proposed center for research and training. It is our belief that the methods presented in this book and the social philosophy it espouses are essential ingredients to the improvement of the living situation of persons in our society, and indeed societies everywhere. It is our hope that they will be widely and wisely used by that echelon of scientists who perceive the end product of science as an improvement in the quality of life.

CHAPTER 1

The Basic Ingredients of an Adequate Social Policy

Any attempt at experimental endeavors in the area of social policy decisions and actions must necessarily be based upon the assumption that such efforts can, in fact, make a vital contribution to the social policy process. Unlike the usual rhetoric of science, social policy experimental endeavors are not value free, nor do they assume that the involved scientists should observe but not act. Since experimental methods in social policy research are intertwined with a philosophy espousing a more active and socially responsible role for social scientists, it is important that the *need* for such a new role be made explicit. We shall elaborate some of the deficiencies inherent in the current political decision-making process and show how these inadequacies can be corrected by a judicious integration of socially conscious scientific thought and action.

As any concerned citizen now knows, contemporary societies are faced with a number of emerging crises that must be solved if people are to survive in a livable environment. Population throughout the world grows out of control and many have predicted that this rapid growth will reduce the quality of life as we now know it (Borgstrom, 1969; National Academy of Sciences, 1969). Industrial excesses continue to pour poisons into the air, streams, rivers, and oceans, further degrading man's environment at an ever-increasing rate (American Association for the Advancement of Science, 1965; Commoner, 1963; Dubos, 1970). Human conflicts exist all over the planet, with social class and caste serving as the framework out of which guerrilla warfare and revolutions grow (Bienen, 1968; Knowles & Prewitt, 1969).

What is so disturbing about this situation is that man has not developed decision-making techniques that solve emergent problems before they become crises. This is a particularly disturbing prospect in modern technological societies because once highly complex problems generate crises, the crises themselves seem impervious to all but major efforts at solution. Equally distressing is the prediction of some scientists that certain

1

environmental problems, if not solved, may create crises whose destructive forces will then be irreversible (Commoner, 1963). Thus, the most important generic problem faced by all contemporary societies is the inadequacy of their social policy decision making. The reasons for this seem to be twofold: (1) the method of finding solutions appears inadequate when juxtaposed against the problems at hand, and (2) even when solutions are discovered, societal institutions seem to resist their implementation.

Facing these two problems—a poor decision-making process and institutional stagnation—what resources can science bring to bear? By nature and training, scientists have typically adopted inactive social roles that do not place them in the centers of action where decision making and resistance to change actually occur. They have been less than enthusiastic about becoming involved in survival problems at the work-a-day level. But the destructive potential represented by such problems as environmental degradation, population growth, and unjust human relations makes it absolutely mandatory that scientists aid their society in whatever way they can in order to ameliorate these problems. The chapters in this book are devoted to a procedure that will bring the techniques of science out of the laboratory and classroom and into the public policy arena where they can help decision-makers in the choices that will determine the quality of life for the next several generations. In that sense this book is more than a presentation of field research methodology—it represents a new social philosophy for science.

These proposed changes in the scientist's social role should gain acceptance if the relationship between adequate decision making and scientifically sound decision processes is clearly understood. The *need* for a change in the scientist's role from one of reflective thought to one of social program development, evaluation, and implementation can only be seen in its true light when an understanding of the inadequacy of the contemporary social decision-making processes is comprehended. The burden of this chapter is to inform scientists and laymen of this deficit and present the parameters of new, more enlightened decision-making techniques. Subsequent chapters of the book present the details of this decision process as it goes from the creative idea to social products. But first let us explore what the actual barriers are to adequate decision making in contemporary American society.

BARRIERS TO ENLIGHTENED SOCIAL POLICY DECISION MAKING

The Search for Political and Economic Power

While perhaps only differing in degree from other western industrialized societies, it is clear that most social organizations in contemporary America are locked into a "power" conflict with one another. Whether this is an extension of frontier psychology or a manifestation of capitalist economics is unclear. What is clear is that in one way or another many individuals, groups, and organizations within the American society are consumed by attempts to garner economic and political power so that they or their constituents can gain higher social positions or maintain themselves in the social positions they have already assumed or achieved. This is often, if not always, done at the expense of others. How the search for political and economic power affects survival decision making can readily be seen in some recent historical events and social scientists' writings.

The sociologists Mills (1956) and Rose (1967) have both suggested in their writings that political decisions are made in American society by a trade-off among powerful special interest groups that influence decision making in one way or another. While Mills identifies this as one group—an economic élite—and Rose believes that there are several special interest groups (such as the military, the industrial, and others), *both* agree that societal decision making is strongly affected by these groups, whose principal goal is to accrue more power. Those living in the 1970s have witnessed an unending struggle among organized special interest groups—industry, labor, and recently even minority groups—for control of the human and physical resource pool. While a self-interest competition for power is not new in human affairs, in contemporary America it has nearly become institutionalized.

Of course, this in itself is not bad. What is bad is the increasing striving for power for its own sake, and a displacement of original goals and purpose. Decisions in the society are often based upon political trade-offs and pressure from various groups without regard to whether the solutions that they propose will *actually* solve the problems that confront the nation, such as those of environmental degradation, overpopulation, and unjust human relations. Many of the proposed decisions may not improve the social or physical environment at all and can even add to their destruction. A recent article by the scientist Eipper (1970) illustrates this principle quite well in the arena of environmental planning. In discussing the creation of a nuclear energy plant on a lake in upper New York State, he comments:

> The special interest groups promoting such developments may be industries that wish to use the water or other resources in a way that will yield them maximum profit, or they may be persons whose welfare or sympathies are more indirectly tied to an industry's success. The latter category includes groups of citizenry primarily concerned with immediate industrial benefits to the local economy, and persons in state or federal agencies who are much concerned with promoting the develop-

ment of industrial technology. (Unfortunately, many of these agencies are assigned the dual role of promoting *and* regulating an industry.) Technological interest groups often make irrational assertions (based on questionable assumptions) to support programs that will exploit public natural resources. These assertions—or implications—include the following:

The program—as proposed—*has* to be enacted *now*.
The program will be enacted in any event. You can't stop progress.
The program is needed to fill the demand that will be created by the program.
No one opposes the program. It will benefit the majority, and harm no one.
Data used to estimate effects of the program are the only valid, pertinent data available.
Since there is not proof that the development will damage the environment, we can safely assume it will not.
All effects of the program have been considered.
The program, as presented, represents the sum total of the development contemplated for this particular resource.
All applicable alternatives have been considered.

Not only should such assumptions be questioned when they appear in discussions of pollution issues, but other questions should be asked, such as the following:

Who participated in formulating the assumptions and conclusions about this program's desirability?
What lasting social benefits—and costs—will this program produce? Who will derive these benefits?
What environmental problems will, or may, be created?
What alternatives exist? Has the relative desirability of not enacting the program been evaluated?

The problem that we have been attempting to describe is the seemingly unending struggle for social and economic power by contemporary groups and institutions, often without apparent regard for long-term effects upon the social and physical environments. While Galbraith (1971), in the heyday of optimistic liberalism, heralded the era of countervailing power, the manifestation of that policy has been a mindless search for control of the system.

The Myth of Legislating and Funding Away Problems

Too often the American way to deal with crises has been to pass laws against them, develop a bureaucracy to deal with them, or create a pool of money to buy a solution for them. The obstacle to effective social policy decision making emanating from this approach is the magical belief in the "knowhow" inherent in money and governmental action. Some examples from the recent past are instructive. During the Johnson era, a number of community action programs were designed and implemented that attempted to improve the social positions of persons who participated in them, particularly minority group members. The central and often single idea behind these programs was to involve poor people in planning for improving their own fate. Based on some not too clearly articulated theoretical notions about group participation, the programs were implemented on a broad scale with heavy funding. The less than desirable outcome of this approach to social problem solving has been documented elsewhere (Marris & Rein, 1967).

A specific example from this approach is the Job Corps. It was designed to place large numbers of minority persons into the mainstream of employment after participation in a program for upgrading their skills. Unfortunately, the program was rapidly conceived and heavily publicized; it never actually dealt with one of the principal problems of minority group employment—that of racial discrimination. No adequate evaluation of that program was ever carried out in a well-designed comparative experiment. Even today the results of the program are unclear.

There are a number of other examples of lack of problem solutions that could be sighted. From them, it appears clear that governmental action as represented in legislation and funding does not in and of itself solve societal problems. Laws can create programs and fund them, but they cannot determine to what degree programmatic efforts are successful in ameliorating the problem. This can be done only through systematically planned scientific evaluation. Simply giving a snappy title to a program is not the same as alleviating a social problem. It is equally true that money expended on programs is not a clear predictor of satisfactory output (Coleman *et al.*, 1966; Fairweather, Sanders, & Tornatzky, 1974). The entire literature on social innovation shows that any new social process—regardless of how it originates —may or may not be successful depending upon many factors (Barnett, 1953; LaPiere, 1965). The inadequacy of problem solutions through the creation of legislated new social programs is further reflected in the scientific literature. The outcome of any social innovation will remain unknown without adequate planning and clear evaluation. However, since many legislators, bureaucrats, and voters believe in the magic of money and programs, this belief itself operates as a barrier to creating a more adequate decision-making process.

The Propensity for Organizations to Perpetuate Themselves

A somewhat cynical associate of ours made the following observation about contemporary American institutions: "The educational establishment's goal is to get everybody educated through the Ph.D.; the correctional system's goal is to get everybody in jail; the automobile business' goal is to have every man, woman, and child in the United States own a new car every year." Though somewhat absurd, there is a bit of insight here that points to a current phenomenon of some importance. Institutions within the American society tend to perpetuate themselves at all costs. It is probably their primary function (LaPiere, 1965). An implicit rule of organizational functioning is to strive for the survival of the organization. Unfortunately, this may have serious implications for hindering an effective social policy decision-making process. An adequate social policy decision-making apparatus must not only have the capability to create innovation but also to eliminate outmoded programs and institutions. For example, higher educational institutions tend to perpetuate outmoded norms of intellectual reflection resulting in "ivory tower" solutions to problems and in the belief that solutions found in laboratories and published in learned journals will somehow lead to a better world. Similarly, the current organization of medical services with its adherence to a fee for service system is singularly outmoded when juxtaposed against unmet needs of the poor in contemporary America.

The point to be made here is not that this perpetuation of the *status quo* and organizational insularity are necessarily evil. They may or may not be. More often than not, however, it is an inherent characteristic of modern complex organizations to be structured in such a way as to make change difficult. The intent of the modern bureaucratic system is to rationalize and make predictable the task environment in which it is involved. As such, it is particularly unresponsive to pressure for change, with the uncertainty that change always brings. Few contemporary bureaucratic systems have built-in subcomponents to deal with the problem of change or to prepare the organization for change. While some authors have heralded the creation of a new type of organization (Bennis, 1966) in which reliance is placed in "temporary systems," this more responsive type of organizational form has not been adopted to any significant degree. Even if it were, there is this further question: To what extent is organizational rigidity also a function of personal needs and characteristics? It has often been observed that individuals tend to avoid and resist situations of uncertainty. One way of doing this in an organizational context is to manifest particular resistance to innovation and change.

The fact that most contemporary bureaucratic organizations are not geared for change has significant implications for a national investment in innovation. Contrary to some opinion, there *are* considerable monies, both public and private, available for fostering innovation through research and development. However, most of these monies are often funneled into existing organizations, with traditional ways of functioning, with no acknowledgment of a need for new and innovative approaches to problem solving. More often than not money allocated for pilot programs in innovation goes to organizations whose basic premises for functioning are themselves unchallenged by the money givers. The manner in which the perpetuation of the *status quo* is brought about may be reflected in the current use of family planning as an answer to population problems. This process has been described by one of the authors in the following manner (Fairweather, 1972):

A great deal of money is being invested in establishing family planning centers. The family planning unit has been *uncritically* accepted by governmental planners as a means through which population can be regulated. Unfortunately, family planning has not yet demonstrated by comparative experiments that its application will result in reducing birth rates. Nonetheless, if the created family planning centers follow the usual bureaucratic procedures for acceptance as a societal institution the following events are likely to occur. First, the units will be established as a national policy with a large investment of federal money. Second, there will eventually be some inquiry by the Congress about whether or not these units are, in fact, reducing the birth rates. At that point, research money will become available (notice, it will not be available until after the governmentally sponsored units are almost unchangeable institutions). Voluminous data will show interested members of Congress that, indeed, these units are being dramatically effective in reducing fertility rates. However, a close scientific scrutiny of that data would probably reveal that *no* definitive scientific information validating family planning in direct experimental contrast with other forms of population regulation will be presented. Since the researchers evaluating the family planning program will usually be hired by the agency itself, their continued employment may depend on a positive evaluation of it. It is highly unlikely under these circumstances that any negative information will get to the congressmen. Current research is often aimed at supporting existing governmental programs whatever they might be. Comparative experiments that question the program or the social policy from which it emanates are typically not funded.

Thus a cycle of action is established that results in the creation of information which corroborates the initial social decision. The generic process goes something like this: An agency establishes a program designed to implement a particular social policy. Once having established the program there is some question by the Congress or the administration about whether or not it has accomplished the purpose for which it was established. The program is then *evaluated* by researchers who usually collect *selected* kinds of information. This information often supports the notion that the program is accomplishing its goal. Because of these reassurances, more money is appropriated to the program and more evaluations positive to the program are forthcoming. Thus, a vicious circle is created in which a particular governmental policy is supported by "*scientific*" evidence which results in the creation of a bigger and bigger bureaucratic organization with more and more funds at its disposal. *The basic question about whether the governmental program is better or worse than other programs the government might have adopted to solve the problem is never raised.* In the example just given, no one has raised the issue as to whether or not the family planning model itself is valid.

The important point to grasp is that powerful organizations have emerged in American society and that they maintain traditional practices even when they are not aimed at solving pressing social problems. By perpetuating such traditions, they prevent change. This is, therefore, another element linked to the decision-making process which prevents adequate solution of contemporary human problems.

The Belief in Compromised Verbal Solutions

This obstacle to effective policy decision making is related to the difference between the language of science and the language of politics. An implicit assumption of political practice inherent in the democratic process is that problems can be *solved* through extensive debate and compromise. Most legislative and administrative policy decisions are compromises among differing solutions to a problem. This is the essence of democratic decision-making practice in day-to-day politics. The high verbal skill and legal background found in most state and federal legislatures is no accident. Their skills are totally congruent with this verbal decision-making process.

The "solutions" reached in various problem areas during the past several years have been of this type. Most of the civil rights acts have been a combination of solutions as a result of the compromise process in which they were generated. Analogous to the whole computer science anecdote "garbage in, garbage out", the results of programs implemented under these laws has been ineffective to say the least. This continued reliance on compromise solutions developed and validated *only* by verbal debate will be particularly acute in the environmental area in the forthcoming years. Thus, many decisions being reached now in this area on the basis of very limited scientific data will have far-reaching effects for generations to come. Compare this compromise verbal-debate solution against both the language and the basic methodology of science. Here problem solutions are posed in clear operational terms in such a way that other scientists in other locales could replicate the proposed solutions if necessary. Ultimate solutions are not reached by combining alternatives whose individual or combined results are unknown but by comparing alternatives one against the other. In this sense the solutions that are found have empirical validity. All this simply shows that decisions based solely upon debate and group agreements are not necessarily valid decisions to the solution of a problem *until* they have been tried and evaluated empirically.

THE UNDERLYING PARAMETERS OF AN ENLIGHTENED SOCIAL DECISION-MAKING PROCESS

It appears that the current decision-making processes—strongly influenced as they are by special interest groups, common sense solutions to complex social problems, institutional stagnation, and dependence upon verbally debated compromises—are probably not adequate to the task of providing a meaningful quality of life on this planet in the late 20th and 21st centuries. It therefore seems necessary that societies' members, and particularly scientists, help develop decision-making processes which will both preserve the democratic principles of the American society and at the same time yield empirically valid solutions to society's problems. In order to accomplish this, two primary conditions must exist: (1) scientific methods must be integrated into the decision-making process and (2) a new generation of scientists who perceive the solution to these problems as one of their primary responsibilities must be trained. The necessary conditions for such training are discussed in Chapter 14.

Social support will be necessary if science is to be adequately integrated into the decision-making processes of the nation. As a necessary first step, society's decision-makers and the public will have to lose their fear of science, which has often resulted from a misunderstanding of what science really is. A justifiable fear has developed among the population because of *some* of the behaviors that *some* scientists have shown in the past. For example, recently there has been the revelation that some black persons were denied treatment for syphilis even after penicillin was discovered simply because they were considered a control group in a research program; and, of course, the hideous and inhumane experiments conducted in Germany on humans during World War II will always serve as a reminder of science allied with horror. Unfortunately, much of the public believes that this inhumaneness is the predictable result of science grown too powerful. Actually it is the result of its unjust use. About this matter one of the authors has recently written the following (Fairweather, 1972):

> Unfortunately, other roadblocks appear in a scientific approach to human problem solution. Among them is the commonly held idea that experimentation is bad. It seems immediately to conjure up ideas of another Nazi Buchenwald or Auschwitz. Experimentation with human beings has thus been judged as being bad. Persons whose children participate in new school programs, for example, are often reported to say that "my child is not going to be a guinea pig for any experimenter." And very often, persons who have been subjected to medical procedures regard themselves as paying the price for someone else's curiosity without any voice in the matter. The fact is, however, that human beings have always been the subjects of experimentation because they have been alive when certain events have taken place that have changed their environment. What their position would have been had the events not happened will never be known. For example, the development of atomic fission happened and no person, other than a few scientists and politicians, had a voice in its discovery and its use. Thus no one asked the public whether or not they wanted the atomic and hydrogen bombs. The bombs were manufactured and the people of the world were therefore participating in one of the most potentially dangerous experiments of all times. Who decided that the public would be the guinea pigs for the automobile with its internal combustion engine? In fact, the public is only recently becoming aware that automobile manufacturers are daily experimenting with "their atmosphere" by continuing to produce the internal combustion engine.
>
> And is the same not true of new laws? Aren't they all social experiments? Are legislators better predictors than anyone else? Do they know what the final and total outcome of a law will be before it is placed in action? Who would have guessed that the Eighteenth Amendment, rather than controlling alcoholic indulgence, would actually create a

generation of lawbreakers who flaunted their contempt for that social experiment by drinking at the speakeasy. Thus man is forever being subjected to experimentation. His life, however momentarily secure, is a risk-taking adventure in which there is never absolute—only relative— certainty. The industrialists who manufacture detergent soaps, cars, and drugs and the legislators who are continuously passing new laws are establishing experiments under which the people live as experimental subjects. Would it not be more humane if a group of humanistically oriented scientists tried, in collaboration with the elected officials and the public, to find better ways in which man could live—particularly if the scientists had been educated to place the highest value on improving the quality of man's life? After all, the industrialists are motivated by the search for short-term profits and the politicians by political power. Surely with our current survival problems someone should be attempting to improve the general quality of man's life. Since experimentation occurs as a process of living, it cannot be escaped. The real question now, as it has always been, is: toward what ends will experimentation be carried out? And who will decide to what uses knowledge will be put? What legacy will be left to our children as a result of such experimentation?

Thus, if science is to be used in the decision process for the solution to human problems, scientific activity must emanate from a humanitarian perspective. And there are certain other key characteristics which must be embodied in what science must become. It involves a change from what historically has been the role characteristics ascribed to scientists by those whose role model was mainly that of the natural or physical scientist. Some of the key characteristics of the new role beyond its value orientation are its active nature, its social use of experiments, its problem focus, research constancy, and its social utility. Let us now examine each of these in turn.

A Humanitarian Value Orientation

In 1961, the sociologist Gouldner wrote an article entitled "Anti-minotaur: The myth of a value-free sociology." Gouldner pointed out that sociology was value-free by political necessity and not by any inherent characteristic of the scientific discipline. He made this point by tracing the history of a social science—sociology—and showing that the origin of the "noninvolved and value-free" orientation to sociology was basically a maneuver in response to political pressure rather than a logical premise of what the science of sociology ought to be. Essentially, at the time Max Weber proposed his value-free approach, the German authorities frowned on the involvement of scientists in the political activities of their time. Extensive political involvement could bring about sanctions by those in political power. Thus, political pressure was an important factor (in addition to Max Weber's own personality characteristics) in determining a basic philosophical position of sociology which has permeated much of American thought in this discipline; in fact, in different forms, it has permeated most of the social science disciplines.

When considered in the light of contemporary events, it becomes apparent that there is no *necessary* scientific payoff to be achieved by abstaining from involvement in social or political problems as a necessary prerequisite to science itself. In fact, other scientists are increasingly warning about the need for scientists to become less preoccupied with methodological niceties and more involved in the human problems of their time. Sanford (1965) pointed to the lack of concern that psychologists have demonstrated for the humaneness of their endeavors when he said:

> We have produced a whole generation of research psychologists who never had occasion to look closely at any one person, let alone themselves; who have never imagined what it might be like to be a subject in one of their experiments, who, indeed, have long since lost sight of the fact that their experimental subjects are, after all, people. (Let us leave the rats out of it for the moment.) They can define variables, state hypotheses, design experiments, manipulate data statistically, get publishable results—and miss the whole point of the thing. Reading their papers you get a strange sense of the unreality of it all; the author's conceptions of variables and processes seem a bit off; and then you realize that the authors have never looked at human experience, they went straight from the textbook or journal to the laboratory, and thence into print—and thence into the business of getting research grants.

Another psychologist, Kenneth Clark (Harrington, 1968), has also stated this position quite clearly in the following manner:

> I am more compassionate than I once was toward my colleagues who address themselves to attitude testing, toward developing highly effective and impressive systems of trivia and irrelevance. I see this now as an understandably protective attitude. It protects psychologists from the awesome and often intolerable sense of futility that seems to be the lot of those of us who try to use our academic training to effect social change.

Natural scientists have demonstrated an equal concern. The late physicist Oppenheimer (1954) showed considerable concern about how the atomic bomb would affect man's future, when he described in the context of the Congressional hearings his reactions to the early successes of the nuclear research program:

> There was, however, at Los Alamos a change in the feel of people . . . This was partly a war measure, but it was also something that was here to stay. There was a great sense of uncertainty and anxiety about what should be done about it.

Recently, biologists and ecologists have shown an even greater concern. Perhaps the two leading spokesmen of the need for scientists to become directly involved in the solution to contemporary human problems have been Barry Commoner (1963) and Paul Ehrlich (1968). Commoner, in discussing the problems of pollution and perceiving that a solution for them is necessary if man is to have a meaningful quality of life, discusses the threat in the following way:

> As a biologist, I have reached this conclusion: we have come to a turning point in the human habitation of the earth. The environment is a complex, subtly balanced system, and it is this integrated whole which receives the impact of all the separate insults inflicted by pollutants. Never before in the history of this planet has its thin life-supporting surface been subjected to such diverse, novel, and potent agents. I believe that the cumulative effects of these pollutants, their interactions and amplification, can be fatal to the complex fabric of the biosphere. And, because man is, after all, a dependent part of this system, I believe that continued pollution of the earth, if unchecked, will eventually destroy the fitness of this planet as a place for human life.

He also indicates that it is the *responsibility* of the scientists—especially because they have an awareness of what might happen to the planet earth if remedial action to restore clean air and water is not accomplished—to at least inform all citizens of their knowledge.

Ehrlich (1968) goes even further. In addition to having engaged in a campaign himself to attempt to stir remedial action about overpopulation and to call it to people's attention, he has written widely about the devastation that eventually will accrue if man does not control his population. In his popularized book, *The Population Bomb*, he suggests several courses of action, including political confrontation and lobbying. He gives examples of letters that citizens might write "urging actions related to the population problem". While the change tactics that Ehrlich suggests may not produce his desired results, he speaks and argues forcefully for the morally committed scientists.

All of these examples have inherent in them the philosophical position that the scientist can no longer stand away from the survival issues of our time. It is very clear that each of the individuals just mentioned has an humanitarian value system serving as a basis for his use of scientific information. It is also quite clear that each, in turn, has adopted the basic philosophical position that the quality of man's life on this planet must not be diminished and that there are definite and clear values that can serve as a basis for scientists' actions. About such a value system, Fromm (1968, pp. 88–89) has said:

> The value system corresponding to the point of view presented in this book is based on the concept of what Albert Schweitzer called "reverence for life". Valuable or good is all that which contributes to the greater unfolding of man's specific faculties and furthers life. Negative or bad is everything that strangles life and paralyzes man's activeness. All norms of the great humanist religions like Buddhism, Judaism, Christianity, or Islam or the great humanist philosophers from the pre-Socratics to contemporary thinkers are the specific elaboration of these general principles of values. Overcoming of one's greed, love for one's neighbor, knowledge of the truth (different from the uncritical knowledge of facts) are the goals common to all humanist philosophical and religious systems of the West and the East. Man could discover these values only when he had reached a certain social and economic development which left him enough time and energy to enable him to think exclusively beyond the aims of mere physical survival. But since this point has been reached, these values have been upheld and, to some extent, practiced within the most disparate societies—from thinkers in the Hebrew tribes to the philosophers of the Greek city-states and the Roman Empire, theologians in the medieval feudal society, thinkers in the Renaissance, the philosophers of the Enlightenment, down to such thinkers of the industrial society as Goethe, Marx, and, in our age, Einstein and Schweitzer. There is no doubt that in this phase of industrial society, the practice of these values becomes more and more difficult, precisely because the reified man experiences little of life and instead follows principles that have been programmed for him by the machine.
>
> Any real hope for victory over the dehumanization society of the megamachine and for the building up of a humanist industrial society

rests upon the condition that the values of the tradition are brought to life, and that a society emerges in which love and integrity are possible.

What seems inescapable here is that a humanitarian value system needs to be adopted by scientists as the forcing bed for their scientific inquiry. This simply means that scientists can no longer be unconcerned in their scientific inquiry about the future of human beings or the biosphere on which they live. The biological and social consequences of the scientist's acts must be rooted in a deep and continuing concern about the value of human life.

An Active Social Role for the Scientist

Historically, scientists have perceived their social *role* as that of inactive observers of social and physical nature. It is a role that emphasizes detachment, an objective search for "truth," and an explicit disdain for applied areas of human knowledge. This role is epitomized in the stereotyped white-coat traditions of the laboratory scientist. While new ideas upon which future action can be based are indeed an important aspect of science, it is not the only role available to scientists and should not have historically been construed as such. What has been lost in the debate between the pure and applied science adherents is that the core of science is *method*, not content. The inactive role is clearly seen in many universalities today. It may have been handed down from the early monasteries where it was perceived as essential that man divorce himself from worldly concerns.

Such reflective traditional role behaviors have been reinforced and will probably continue to be rewarded by the scientific community. However, ironically, scientific research itself may force a reconsideration of this inactive role, particularly for social scientists. There has been a rapidly accumulating body of information showing the lack of relationship between words and deeds (Deutscher, 1966; Mischel, 1968). This implies that institutional change cannot be assumed to occur automatically from the mere creation of social science facts—thus, the need for placing scientific research in action settings rather than *only* in the laboratory or in contained environments. A recent article (Fairweather, 1972) presents this relationship and the need to emphasize action in the following manner:

> The reason that this concern must be behavioral is easily seen when we realize the lack of relationship that exists between words and deeds. The studies just mentioned question whether an expressed verbal or written concern about a particular human problem has any relationship whatever to actual problem-solving behavior (Wicker, 1969). There is

serious question, therefore, whether persons who talk about social change will actually carry it out. Black people have learned, often to their dismay, that the white liberal who espouses their cause and decries discrimination against people because of the color of their skin is not always happy to have a black family move next door to him in his middle-class, suburban, all-white neighborhood. This classic example highlights the lack of relationship between verbal behavior and behavior required to place in action a social change at the level of daily living experience. For this reason the emphasis in a new approach to solving man's contemporary dilemmas must be upon direct action—the behavioral expression of a continuing concern about man's well being, not what a person says his values are. Of course, there is the continuous hope that eventually man's behavior will directly reflect the values that he verbally espouses—a situation that has not been true historically and must today remain a utopian hope.

What is explicitly being questioned here is the "trickle-down" theory of science and its effect on societal functioning. The detached scientist has *assumed* that change will somehow emanate from pure knowledge when the applied technologists get hold of it. Research in the adoption of innovative practices (Havelock, 1969) suggests that this usually does not occur easily, if at all. Recent experiments (Fairweather, Sanders, & Tornatzky, 1974) emphasize the need for an active social role for scientists if their evidence is to be used for corrective social change.

Innovation

In order to address new and emerging social problems, a society is often in need of new and innovative solutions. When problems such as population overgrowth, mental illness, environmental degradation, and the like become overwhelming to a society, it is readily apparent that the manner in which society has been meeting these problems is no longer valid. When the obvious failures occur, it becomes necessary to create new social programs that do meet a society's needs. Invention and innovation are essential characteristics of any valid decision process. The literature on innovation, particularly the works of Barnett (1953) and LaPiere (1965), indicate that *innovations* are basic to meeting cultural needs and creating corrective change in all societies.

The technological innovations of the electric light and the wheel, and the social innovations of the large bureaucracy and the public school are examples of historically adopted innovations that have created extensive changes in societies where they have been accepted as a solution to a particular problem. Thus, it appears that corrective social action stems from the creation of new processes and their implementation throughout a society. Simply put, in order to do something better, we will have to start doing something new.

Democratic Participation

Another aspect of the decision-making process that is central to its functioning in this and other democratic societies is that it must involve participation by all concerned groups. We take this position on philosophical, strategic, and tactical grounds. The philosophical adherence to a democratic society stems directly from a humanitarian value orientation and is, to that extent, related to altruism. Since innovation always requires *social change*, it should be obvious that such change must be incorporated into the society through the appropriate democratic processes.

It seems clear from our history that only in the context of a free and open society can the full propensity for individual growth and maturity be realized. For this reason, it is important that we do not adopt a decision-making apparatus that inhibits the continued growth of a full and free society. There are however, other considerations in opting for democratic participation in any decision-making process. On a very gross strategic level, the democratic processes are compatible with an experimental approach. The flexibility in which new institutions and new programs can be created, particularly in the context of the federal system, is particularly compatible with an experimental approach to problem solving. It would be foolhardy to opt for more restrictive alternatives.

At a more tactical level, it is becoming a fairly common finding in the social change literature that democratic participation in decision making is highly related to the widespread adoption of innovations (Fairweather, Sanders, & Tornatzky, 1974; Havelock & Havelock, 1973). To attain democratic participation, it is essential that the innovation of new social models and their evaluation be accomplished through the use of planning and action groups that include the members of society most directly affected. Thus, the scientist must work cooperatively with the elected officials or their appointed administrators who are responsible for program development and, in addition, with a representative group of persons who are suffering from the problem and who will have their own perceptions about how such problems might be solved. In this society, groups representing these three diverse participants of the decision-making process—scientists, elected officials or their administrators, and the problem population—all should have an input into the decision-making process about new social programs; unless they do, it is unlikely that any social innovation discovered to be beneficial could actually be implemented. Thus, it is important that the governing body and the problem population as well as the scientists have a personal stake in the solutions found. Such a consideration is most important in implanting innovative models in society, evaluating them properly, and in trying to implement throughout the society those new models that are found to be beneficial. In a democratic society there are many examples of failure to implement or even to accept a needed innovation simply because persons most directly affected had no voice in its discovery or use.

Scientific Evaluation

Before accurate decisions can be made about the effectiveness of any social program, it is quite obvious that there must be a complete scientific evaluation of it. Since the program might eventually be adopted nationwide or even internationally, it is important that it "does what it says it intends to do." As pointed out in the last section, many social programs in the past have been adopted as compromises among special interest groups and have not been adequately evaluated. When such is the case, it may never be known if the actual program yields the results spelled out in the theory or proposed by the politician An adequate scientific evaluation would show the results of such programs; it would show their benefits or deficiencies.

Because the costs of large-scale programs are so vast, particularly when adopted on a national scale, it is important that small-scale models first be established so that they can be evaluated *prior* to a regional, national, or international diffusion of such programs. It is further important that the evaluation be very sound from a scientific point of view. This essentially means that the evaluation must be an actual *experimental* one. The new social program must be compared to the traditional way in which society handles the problem in order that accurate outcome statements can be made.

While social scientists have come up with many methods of evaluation (which will be elaborated in the next chapter), there is only one true experimental method. It involves not only the comparative aspects mentioned above but also random assignment of persons or units to the various experimental conditions, keeping the conditions constant over time, continuous evaluation over an extended period of time, accurate development of measuring instruments, and so on. If time and thought is given to such techniques and to the problem involved, it is usually possible to create an experiment for almost any social problem. Most techniques that are currently used in social program evaluation are *not* used in actual experiments. These techniques have often been developed by social scientists because they do not have sufficient administrative control in the organization charged with problem solution to create and implement new social models. But there is little question that such nonexperimental techniques, meaningful and appropriate as they are when used in their proper context, do not yield the definitive results that are essential in making decisions about whether or not a new program has sufficient beneficial effects so that it should be used by a subgroup of the society or the entire society. It is for this reason that in the final analysis an accurate, scientific evaluation means an experimental evaluation.

Problem-oriented Focus

It is exceedingly important that the new application of science to problem solution be one that is problem-oriented and not discipline-oriented. Thus, the research should be conceived as one that focuses on problems such as racism, mental health, drug addiction, and education. In the past most service programs have been problem-focused, while most research programs have been discipline-focused. This is often attributed to the relative lack of communication between service and research people. Without a problem focus, field researchers often find that the research becomes vague and general (or trivial), and very often a great deal of time and treasure is wasted.

America has several examples of problem-focused research in the nation's recent history. Perhaps the most obvious has been the space research effort. Here, a number of scientists and individuals from all walks of life committed themselves to placing a man on the moon. Doctors became astronauts, astronauts became publicity men, and so on. The roles that were taken by individuals were roles that needed to be fulfilled in order to place a man on the moon. In such cases the group focused its attention on the *problem* of getting a man on the moon. *Our current social problems require no less commitment.* Whatever new roles need to be developed for problem solution will require that someone on the research team play them. A commitment to the total social problem is one way through which this can be accomplished.

In addition to improving the cooperation among persons from different disciplines, the problem-oriented focus also brings information from any discipline having something to contribute to the problem. This is important since it should be quite clear by now that most of our contemporary social problems are cross-disciplinary in subject matter areas. The problem of over-population may serve as one example. Here, the problem is agricultural, biological, religious, sociological, political, economic, psychological, legal, and medical, to name several involved disciplines. Information from all of these academic fields must be used and integrated if an adequate solution to the ever-pressing problem of over-population throughout this country and the world is to be found. It cannot be discovered by taking a narrow disciplinary approach. A problem-oriented focus permits each discipline to contribute whatever variables are necessary to the solution of the problem, since the focus is on the problem and not upon a single discipline or a person's professional status.

Beyond the value of integrating the various disciplines which comes about by focusing their derivative upon a particular problem, there is the additional value that comes from transcending the separateness of subject matter usually emphasized in the traditional training of scientists. Since the scientific community trains persons in individual course work and grants academic degrees in such fields as psychology, sociology, law, medicine, and the like, it typically does not prepare scientists to work together on the solution to a particular problem. However, it is just such mutual teamwork that is required for the solution to contemporary problems. It is this mutual cooperation and shared responsibility focusing upon problem solution that helps break down the barriers of the independent and separate nature of subject matter so ingrained through the educative process.

Inferential

While this might be considered a part of the evaluation procedure, it is such an important aspect of the use of science in social decision making that it has been reserved for a separate discussion. What is most important about the use of science in decision making is that it creates knowledge about the inferences that can legitimately be made about the future course of events by using the experimental information collected by the scientist. From scientific experiments, the social policy decision makers, when they are making a decision about a new social program, should know what the probabilities are that it will yield a particular outcome. The degree to which certainly can be obtained in the decision-making process through the participation of scientists is one of their essential contributions to problem solution.

Two conditions must be met in order to obtain adequate inferences from a proper evaluation. Science must explore the selected alternatives in their *natural setting* because it is well known among social scientists that the social situation within which an innovation is examined can determine its outcome. Since one wishes to make the most valid inferences that can be made, the alternatives should be evaluated in an environment as close as possible to the social environment in which they will eventually operate.

For this reason, it is necessary that the social innovations that are created be *implanted* in naturalistic settings and that they be evaluated over a long period of time. The *longitudinal* nature of the evaluation is important for accurate inferences, since the solution eventually adopted by the society will probably be "in place" for a considerable period time. Various forces of the society can impinge upon the outcomes at different moments in time; thus, for adequate inference, it is important that the study be longitudinal in nature and not simply a "look-see" at alternative solutions.

It is also desirable that the sample drawn to participate in the social innovation is a *representative* sample from the problem population itself. This is extremely important because inferences that are made about the value of the innovation in solving a particular social problem usually refer to the population that is suffering from that problem. To take an obvious example, it would be very difficult to make accurate inferences from an educational program that included only middle-class white students and faculty if the program had as its eventual goal the improvement of the educational position of poor non-whites. In addition to concern for the representativeness of the social situation, it is also important that a problem population be appropriately represented in the sample.

Continuous Monitoring of Solutions

In any adequate decision-making process within a society, any particular social problem becomes changed over a period of time. What may have been a social problem or its solution in the 1800s may not be a social problem or its solution in the 21st century. Even if the problem does remain over extended periods of time, those variables that enter into problem solution at one time may very well change with changes in social conditions. It is for this reason that a *problem should never be considered solved, only ameliorated for a particular moment in history.* Since the problem may not be a problem at a second moment in history or since it may have different ingredients, it is essential that continuous innovative alternatives be created and explored for their effect upon any given problem at a given time. It is this continuous evaluation that gives scientists and decision makers an understanding of when a particular problem is no longer important to the society and/or when the solution that has been adopted is no longer valid. It is essential that a continuous mechanism for problem definition, innovation, and evaluation be carried forward.

Usable Solutions

No innovation can be considered at any given moment as a help in solving a particular problem if that innovation cannot be used by the society. There are probably solutions to all problems which are so expensive or otherwise socially unacceptable that their implementation would be prohibitive. For example, it might be possible to create fresh water from salt water, but the cost may be so expensive that most of the resources of the society would have to be spent in that manner in order that fresh water could be created. Such an investment of the society's resources usually makes extremely expensive innovations difficult for the society to adopt. It is quite clear, therefore, that cost is an important element in the degree to which a society can use a given innovation.

Other aspects of an innovation enter into its usability by a society. One is the basic violation of the norms of a society so that the society considers the innovation unusable. For example, a solution to the high divorce rate might simply be the disbanding of all families. Yet such a solution would not now be accepted by the society, so it is unlikely. Many examples are clearly at hand. Perhaps the most outstanding was the 18th Amendment to the Constitution which simply meant that persons could not drink alcoholic beverages. Of course, the 18th Amendment could never be rigidly enforced since many people continued to drink alcoholic beverages at the local speakeasy or purchased them illegally. The social innovation of making the sale of alcoholic beverages illegal was not usable to this society, at least at that moment in its history.

Also related to the usability of an innovation is its ease of dissemination. Thus, not only must we be concerned about the content of an innovation and the extent to which a new solution violates widely held societal norms, but we should also be concerned about the extent to which problem solutions can be "packaged" since the type of packaging affects the dissemination of an innovation. The variables affecting them will be dealt with in some detail in later chapters, however let it suffice to point out now that unless an innovation is of such a nature that it can be utilized beyond the small-scale pilot stage, it will not be a viable problem solution.

In this chapter we have tried to show that contemporary decision making is not adequate to the tasks facing society in the late 20th and 21st centuries. Based as they are upon strategies among different power groups, verbal rather than action solutions, institutional rigidity, and political compromise, it seems extremely clear that new and more enlightened decision-making processes must be adopted if man is to preserve the "space ship earth." The basic parameters for a more adequate decision-making mechanism must be based upon humanitarian values and they must also be politically and socially active, innovative, democratic, and scientific. The manner in which these characteristics can be combined into an adequate decision-making mechanism is spelled out in detail in the next chapter.

CHAPTER 2

Integrating Science into Social Policy Decisions: Experimental Social Innovation

Conceptualizing an adequate social policy for the late 20th and 21st centuries is one thing; showing how it can be accomplished is quite another. Chapter 1 was devoted to the former; this chapter is devoted to the latter.

Scientific methods typically used by social scientists do not, taken separately, meet the basic requirements for an adequate decision-making process spelled out in Chapter 1. However, when taken together and given an interdisciplinary, problem-oriented, and humane focus, they can. Before attempting to show how they can be integrated into the democratic decision process espoused in Chapter 1, it is important to understand what these methods are and how they have historically been used.

Research methods for investigating social problems are, of course, not new to the social sciences. These methods have been developed by the pioneering efforts of individuals interested in the social issues of their society. Collectively, their work contains methods that need to be combined and focused on a specific problem in order to complete social innovative experiments. We will review the most commonly used research methods so that their contribution to experimental methods for social innovation can be perceived. For clarity, we will categorize approaches to the investigation of social problems into six commonly used methodologies.

A REVIEW OF SOCIAL SCIENCE METHODS OF INQUIRY

Description and Theory

First, there are the *descriptive-theoretical* discussions of important social science issues and social problems. These serve as the basis for the formulation of hypotheses and they generate interest which can result in social innovative experiments. Descriptive-theoretical treatises summarize empirical facts to illustrate theoretical positions about selected problems. Often problem solutions are proposed. No new empirical evidence is presented. Their impact upon the subsequent course of social change is frequently great since quite often these summaries and deductions from them arouse interest in the selected social problems and are sometimes used as a basis for legislation. Most often the writings define and describe social problems by synthesizing current knowledge. *An American Dilemma*, Myrdal's (1944) provocative work about the social and economic position of black persons in America, is one example of such a descriptive-theoretical discourse. Another contemporary social problem—the effects upon people of mental hospitals and other total institutions—was summarized and discussed by the sociologist Goffman (1962) in his book, *Asylums*. In his work, *The Affluent Society*, Galbraith (1958), an economist, identified and discussed the social problems that accrue to a society possessing extraordinary wealth. Harrington (1962) presented the problems created by poverty in such a society in his book, *The Other America*. These four selected works illustrate descriptive-theoretical writings that analyze and describe specific social problems.

The Survey

A second category of methods used in exploring social problems is the *survey*. Surveys are most frequently utilized to define clearly the variables operative in social problems, particularly in describing the demographic characteristics of populations. Demographic studies such as the census, public opinion polls, and attitude questionnaires about consumer products are all examples. In the arena of social problems, *The Academic Market Place* (Caplow & McGee, 1958) presents a survey concerning the mores and folkways of the academic institution. Other illustrations of the survey technique as applied to the social problems of mental illness and of drug addiction are Hollingshead & Redlich's (1958) *Social Class and Mental Illness* and Chein's (1963) *The Road to H*.

The survey yields defining data which measure some of the important parameters of the social problem. The survey method, like the descriptive-theoretical method, gives the researcher some information about the social problem. However, unlike the descriptive-theoretical method, it usually quantifies selected aspects of the problem.

Laboratory Research

A third category of research methods for social problems are those used in *laboratory* settings. Here, important social problems are explored by creating artificial microcosms of the relevant variables and manipulating them. Studies with biracial work groups (Katz & Benjamin, 1960, Katz & Cohen, 1962), under artificially created and controlled conditions, are excellent examples of this method. Experiments with democratic, *laissez-faire*, and authoritarian social climates are classic examples of the approach (Lewin, Lippit, & White, 1939). Work with game theoretical approaches to studying conflict resolution is another example. Laboratory research defines a significant social problem, isolates a few significant variables to be explored under artificial laboratory conditions, and designs experiments to evaluate selected aspects. Beyond classifying and evaluating those selected variables, the experimental methods designed for laboratory research can sometimes be modified for use in naturalistic settings.

Participant Observation

A fourth category of methods utilizes the *participant-observer*. An example can be found in the research done by Stanton & Schwartz (1954) as presented in *The Mental Hospital*, and by Caudill (1958) in *The Psychiatric Hospital as a Small Society*. Such researchers supplement data gathered by the formal methods of interviews, testing, and questionnaires, and by informal methods of taking notes in situations such as lunch hours, spontaneous or arranged meetings, and so forth. Other examples of such research are to be found in the Sherif & Sherif (1964) publication, *Reference Groups*, and in Whyte's (1955) book, *Street Corner Society*. The participant-observer allows for direct experience and observation while the processes are in action. Studies using participant observation are valuable methods for social innovations because they are done in a naturalistic setting and provide real-life observational information so necessary in understanding the complexities of social problems.

Pilot-demonstration Studies

A fifth method establishes new social service delivery systems and studies them in a noncomparative, case study manner. The Synanon House for drug addicts, as described by Yablonsky (1964), is an example of one such service program study. Descriptions of Alcoholics Anonymous (1955) and sheltered workshops (Olshanky, 1960) are examples of others. In the field of treating mental illness, Maxwell Jones's (1953) *The Therapeutic Community* is a classic representative work. It describes the establishment of a new social model in a mental hospital. The Job Corps of the antipoverty program is another. It established a new learning and living social subsystem for the socially deprived. Demonstration projects provide services that create *one* innovated solution to a social problem. Information from data collected in service functions can be used as background information for a more extensive comparative experiment which the creation of the new single service model does not provide.

Quasi-experimental Techniques

A sixth method has been called *quasi-experimental techniques* (Campbell & Stanley, 1966). Quasi-experimental techniques have some of the features of an experiment, such as comparing social programs, but are used when random assignment and the experimental control demanded for a "true" experiment cannot be obtained. They have the advantage of permitting some degree of comparative evaluation of different programmatic solutions under these conditions. They also permit making some limited statements about causal relationships between variables. Included in this general methodology are such techniques as interrupted time series, cross-lagged panel correlations, and other deviations from a "true" experimental design. Their importance is that they provide a basis for comparative inference when the conditions for an actual experiment are not present. They have several drawbacks when compared with experimental methods such as those described by Snedecor (1956) and Lindquist (1953). Quasi-experimental techniques have the advantage that the experimenter can enter the social system without having to manipulate it or require that it change. The trade-off is that the experimenter sacrifices the confidence he can have in the inferences made from the results. This is in contrast to an experiment where conditions are created and controlled and where random assignment of participants is obtained. Under these latter conditions, more confident causal inferences can be made. An example of the use of quasi-experimental techniques is an analysis of the effect that a "crackdown on speeding" had upon traffic fatalities in Connecticut (Campbell & Ross, 1969).

It should be quite clear from this cursory review of methods used by social scientists that in order to meet the goals for an adequate decision-making process an integration of them with a focus on social problem solution from a humanitarian perspective needs to be accomplished. A modest beginning on such an integration was made in 1967 with the publication of the book *Methods for Experimental Social Innovation* (Fairweather, 1967). A subsequent publication, *Social Change: The Challenge to Survival* (Fairweather, 1972), spelled out in considerable detail the manner in which science and social processes could humanely proceed. This book attempts to complete that integration.

Before we further address the issue of integrating methodology, we should impress upon the reader that historically the methodologies described here have often been used in isolation from one another. Thus, those who have been survey researchers have often done *only* survey research. Researchers who use participant observation techniques often use them to the *exclusion* of other techniques, and rarely do laboratory experimentalists use participant observation techniques and quasi-experiments. Thus, accompanying the disciplinary chauvinism described in Chapter 1, the history of social science has involved a methodological parochialism. In this context we will attempt to provide a comprehensive, integrative view of these available techniques. An operational definition of the details of this multidisciplinary problem-solving perspective will be discussed in Chapters 3 through 13.

TOWARD AN INTEGRATIVE MODEL: EXPERIMENTAL SOCIAL INNOVATION

To accomplish the humane use of scientific methodology in the social decision-making process, we have adopted an approach described as "Experimental Social Innovation" (Fairweather, 1967, 1972). We might characterize this as a gestalt of scientific methodology blended with many philosophical and ethical considerations. Encompassing all the characteristics of an adequate social policy decision-making apparatus described in Chapter 1, it also provides methodological coherence to the array of social science techniques just described.

When a society is unable to solve a particularly pressing social problem, it becomes necessary for someone in that society to innovate new social programs that might alleviate the problem. The new social models that are created to solve the problem represent the *innovative* aspect of experimental social innovation. Thus, when a society has a problem that current programs fail to resolve, it is axiomatic that new programs must be created to replace them. It is this process of innovating new social programs for comparative purposes that represents the first process in experimental social innovation. Some examples have been presented in the following manner (Fairweather, 1972):

> In the social sphere one thinks of educational models, health delivery models, models for the treatment of drug addiction, mental illness, criminality, the problems of the aging, and the like. All of these require social models aimed at making life biologically and interpersonally more satisfying. They typically require experimentation in social organization and interpersonal relationships.

Take contemporary schooling, for example. All Western and Eastern societies are in the process of questioning the entire structure of education within their respective countries. Students all over the world are questioning the goals of an educational program. They are concerned with such issues as: should societies develop educational programs aimed at meeting the full spectrum of contemporary social needs? should admission policies be arranged so that the goals of schools are the education of all persons to the limit of their capacities? or should we continue, as we have in the past, to isolate educational institutions from society and to limit entry to those students who can economically afford to attend them? To discover answers to these questions, one might set up two model schools. One could have an open admissions policy and the other the more typical closed admissions policy. The outcomes of open and closed admission policies could thus be evaluated . . .

There are, of course, many other different human problem areas where contemporary practices need changing. Examples of such areas and models that could be tried come quickly to mind. Current medical practices are one area. Contemporary health delivery systems are daily showing that traditional medical practices cannot cope with the complex problems of a highly industrialized, overpopulated society (Daniels, 1969). The high cost of medical service has placed first-class medical treatment beyond the reach of the average citizen. To correct this situation, it appears that new medical delivery systems should be established. Some of the characteristics of such new models appear to involve as a basic issue the redefinition of the physician's role. It is estimated that a high percentage of the work that physicians do could be done by less well-trained personnel. The resulting freedom of time would permit the physician to work more directly with the actual medical aspects of his practice. Such a program might not only improve patient care but might do so at a marked reduction in cost. To discover the advantages and disadvantages of such new medical roles, a model could be created where paramedical persons could assume many of the functions previously carried out by physicians. Historical interviews, certain physical tests, and other routine aspects of medical practice could be delegated to persons who have been specifically trained for carrying out these delegated behaviors . . .

The creation of social models does not have to be limited to those requiring a new social subsystem or even the reorganization of social roles. It would be possible, for example, to evaluate the negative income tax or prepaid medical care insurance through experimental designs comparing them with how society usually solves these problems. For example, the negative income tax might be thought of as improving the social posture of people on welfare. It could be compared with the welfare program currently practiced on such issues as the degree to which those who received the negative income tax feel their social roles are enhanced, their economic well-being, the cost to society, the degree to which other persons see it as a valuable program, and so on. A similar evaluation could be carried on for those receiving prepaid medical insurance: the social innovation could be compared with typical medical financing for contemporary medical services on such outcomes as satisfaction of patients and medical personnel, cost, and so on.

But how do the social science research techniques briefly reviewed in the first section of this chapter merge into this model-building stage of experimental social innovation? Needless to say, before any plausible innovative solutions can be tried a great deal of knowledge about several different problems must be gained. Often actual data is unavailable for a given social problem so that methods of gathering information need to be utilized. Participant observation can be used to accomplish this. For example, considerable light has been shed on the social structure of mental hospitals through participant observation studies such as the landmark works of Goffman (1957) and Stanton & Schwartz (1954) mentioned earlier. One of the foremost examples of the use of participant observation in defining a social problem can be found in the work of Whyte (1955). His carefully recorded observations while "hanging around" with the youthful members of street gangs have shed much light on their social dynamics. Other participant observation work in the area of drugs and prisons, for example, has been done.

During the planning of new models, it may also be worthwhile to make use of survey techniques. It may be particularly helpful when the "problem population" is comprised of normal people. For example, in the area of family planning and birth regulation, considerable utilization has been made of survey research to gain further insight into the processes related to family planning choices.

Another technique that can be of value in defining the parameters of a new social model is laboratory experimentation. Clearly, while laboratory experimentation is extremely limited in its naturalistic aspects, it often can be used to answer questions of a conceptual nature related to the social problem at hand. For example, considerable light has been shed on some of the basic parameters of small group dynamics over the past years through well-planned laboratory experiments.

A fairly innovative use of this technique stands out in the work of Zimbardo and his associates (1975). He created a simulated prison setting and had students live in the setting as either guards or inmates for extended periods of time. Many of the social role behaviors seen in the real prison setting began to manifest themselves rather rapidly. Here is an example of a participant observation technique used in a contrived "laboratory" setting that yielded information useful in the problem area. Although not directly transferable to real-life situations, the output of some laboratory research can help define the questions and some of the social parameters that social models *must* be created to answer.

It is also important to note here that information about the variables that enter into the construction of any model should come from any discipline that might contribute to the problem solution. Thus, personal satisfaction, community acceptance, legal implications, and medical outcomes, to name a few, may be as important in problem solution as the cost per individual. This *multidisciplinary* approach to problem solution means that the background information coming from surveys and participant observation must include all pertinent variables regardless of their disciplinary (psychological, sociological, economic, etc.) origins.

This process of model development in experimental social innovation must be *humanitarian* in many aspects. To accomplish this, members of the research team will *not* consider any social model as a candidate for problem solution that will not, in their best judgment, be beneficial to the problem population for which it is proposed. Thus, what develops is tantamount to a process of consensual agreement about problem solution by representatives of the problem population, societal administrators, and the involved scientists about which problem solutions are potentially palatable to all parties. The combined moral and ethical forces of these three groups enter into the judgment about which models will be selected for experiment trial. Potential models for experimental comparison must be approved by all three groups.

While this clearly restricts the number and type of social models that can be created, it more importantly prevents the creation of social programs that are unwanted or are perceived as potentially harmful to the persons who will later participate in them. Thus, no programs that might be considered physically harmful or emotionally disturbing are permitted in the pool of potential programs. By adopting this procedure, not only are the models selected for comparison humane, they are also desired by the problem population and social administrations. For this reason, they are potentially *useful* to both groups.

New models that are agreed upon are created on a *small* scale and are implanted in the *naturalistic* setting for experimental comparison. Smallness is essential for two reasons: economics and ease of abandonment. A considerable investment in time and resources is essential to start pilot programs. In the state of ignorance that exists when an experiment begins, it is better to test it on a small scale than a large one. This prevents excessive investment in models that may not yield beneficial results. Additionally, if data indicate that the pilot program does not work, there are fewer people who have become ego-involved in the new program so that it can be abandoned with more ease than if it had been initiated on a large scale. Furthermore, it is essential that these pilot programs be evaluated in a naturalistic setting. There is considerable research information that has been accumulated during the past few years indicating the situational specificity of behavior (Mischell, 1968). From this information, it becomes obvious that the social situation in which a concept is tested is particularly important in determining the outcomes achieved. This is one reason why there is often limited direct transfer of behavior between laboratory experimentation and the field testing of pilot solutions. Situational similarities are also important in replicating the original models so that they will yield the same beneficial results as the prototype model. For these reasons, the model-building experiment should be carried out in the same naturalistic setting where it will eventually be used.

It is necessary to emphasize that the process of comparing these new social models should be conducted in the context of a *longitudinal experiment*. The longitudinal aspect is essential because of the profound implications of any "false positive" successful outcomes. For example, if a model is put into operation and a "successful" outcome is achieved only for a single 90-day follow-up period and then only on one dependent measure, inferences should be conservative. If this "success" were used as the basis for a massive national implementation effort, the results are likely to be extremely unfortunate. Quite simply, success in social models is so variable and will-of-the-wisp that what is needed is a set of temporal replications which define the outcomes in longitudinal terms. If success is achieved in 90 days and again in 180 days and in one year and once more in two years, the experimenter can say with considerable confidence that the social model is a true long-term success. A researcher should be aware—as a citizen may not be—that hasty *ad hoc* solutions implemented nationwide on the basis of limited data are no assurance of social achievements. Also we argue for controlled experiments where social models with randomly assigned participants representative of the problem population are *compared* because this is the way of making the most accurate inferences possible from the model evaluation process. Only with true longitudinal experiments can direct causal inferences be made from the data derived.

We believe that the experimenting process should be *continuous* and never ending. A programmatic effort at experimentation must be involved, with one experiment building on another and so on. Often, a problem solution found empirically successful at a given time will lose its effectiveness as the cultural milieu changes or as the outcome criteria change. For example, in periods of high employment the most important outcome criterion might be job satisfaction rather than employment, while in periods of low employment the outcome criterion might be reversed.

Even though the process of creating and comparing social models as solutions to human problems must be continuously ongoing, it should not be overlooked that a second process in the experimental chain of events takes place *after* a beneficial model has been discovered through experimentation. This is the process of disseminating the model throughout a particular geographic area—city, county, state, or nation. A social model cannot be beneficial to the problem population unless it can be *used* by them. Dissemination is accomplished by developing a series of *experiments* through which information about valid dissemination techniques for the particular model under consideration is discovered and fed back to the experimenters. In keeping with the *humanitarian* goals of experimental social innovation, new helpful social processes must be promoted so that they can be made available to the public. The humane use of science requires nothing less. The *socially active* role of the scientist becomes defined through implanting the original models to be evaluated in the natural community settings and through attempts to disseminate its use more widely.

In order to give the readers a clear example of the entire approach *in vivo*, we shall present an example of programmatic research in which the senior author has been involved for most of the past two decades. What the readers should bear in mind as they follow through the chain of research studies is the extent to which the aspects of the social policy decision-making process outlined in Chapter 1, and the various social science methodologies outlined in the first section of this chapter, are intertwined inextricably into a comprehensive social problem-solving approach.

A WORKING EXAMPLE

An example of how different research techniques were actually used to solve a particular problem is illustrated in the mental health research that was completed by Fairweather and his colleagues. These studies were undertaken in an attempt to discover what could be done about the *problem* of increasing chronic hospitalization that has constantly plagued the mental hospitals of this and other countries. An initial *survey* by Giedt and Schlosser

(1955) showed that "61% of admitted patients left the hospital during the first 90 days of hospitalization, 25% during the next 15 months, and only 2% during the remaining 24 months." What seemed apparent from this survey was the likelihood of rather permanent residence for those patients who remained for more than 90 days.

A *quasi-experiment* was then created to compare patients who stayed less than 90 days (61%) with those who remained for more than 90 days (39%). This study was completed in an attempt to discover if there were variables that differentiated the less-than-90-day-stay group from those who remained for more than 90 days. The *literature* on the length of stay was reviewed and 29 variables that had been found to be associated with length of stay in the past comprised the variables compared. In anticipation of some sort of social intervention in the system producing chronic hospitalization, it was hoped that an index that would be used upon admission to predict length of stay could be created from this comparative information. This would permit any new program to be focused upon the problem group at the outset of their hospital tenure. Through this quasi-experiment, the researchers found that five of the 21 variables significantly differentiated the short (under 90 days) and long stay (over 90 days) groups. Persons who tended to remain in the hospital were more often single, diagnosed as psychotic, adjudged to be severely incapacitated upon entry, considered legally incompetent, and did not indulge in the use of alcoholic beverages. These five characteristics were used to predict length of stay with considerable accuracy (Lindeman *et al.*, 1959). This study also showed that individuals who did not leave the hospital by the end of the first year were very likely to be there at the end of the second year, the third year, and so on.

Having used the survey and a quasi-experiment to isolate some of the characteristics of those who remained chronically hospitalized, it then became important to develop program alternatives that might aid such patients in returning to and remaining in the community. From the two studies just mentioned, perusal of the literature, and observations, the researchers became convinced that progress toward remedial action was contingent upon the answer to three major questions. They were: (1) Are any of the current treatment methods, available to patients who resided in neuro-psychiatric institutions, helpful in bringing about their discharge and adjustment in a community setting after leaving the hospital? (2) Did patients who had become chronic respond differently to the treatment programs than those who were less chronic or who were neurotic? (3) Were there any significant relationships among the various adjustmental criteria that had been historically used to evaluate patients—i.e., self-concept, paper and pencil diagnostic tests, adaptive behaviors, and so on.

To answer these particular questions, it was necessary to carry out an *experiment* that was designed so that questions could be answered. Since it was now clear that a *major problem* had been defined—that of the chronicity of the mental patient—it was now necessary to field an initial experiment to find out what could be done about it, specifically to answer the three questions listed above (Fairweather & Simon 1963, Fairweather *et al.*, 1960; Forsyth & Fairweather 1961).

This experiment *compared* four treatment programs that were used quite commonly in mental hospitals at that time. It was essential to find out whether any of these methods would yield more beneficial results when compared with one another. The four treatment methods that were contrasted were: (1) individual psychotherapy, (2) group psychotherapy, (3) group living, and (4) a work-only program. In order to evaluate whether or not people who were neurotics responded differently from acute and chronic psychotics, three different patient groups were assigned to participate in these four treatments in order to assess the treatment effects upon them. Specifically, the three groups were neurotics, psychotic patients hospitalized less than one year, and psychotic patients hospitalized more than one year. It is important to note here that as a condition for an actual experiment patients were *matched* on background characteristics within these diagnostic categories in groups of four, and each of the four patients were then *randomly assigned* to one of the four treatments. Thus, each treatment was carried out with an unbiased sample of persons who were socially disabled to a similar degree.

All of the necessary *administrative agreements* were completed so that the experimental conditions could be held constant throughout the experimental period. Thus, a ward was set aside solely for the purpose of carrying out the experiment; staff were provided, patients were screened, and data processing procedures were arranged. The results of this study showed that though there was an initial significant difference in community adjustment in favor of those who participated in the three therapy groups contrasted with the work-alone control, these differences disappeared by the end of 18 months. Highly significant differences obtained between the diagnostic groups; regardless of treatment, those who were most chronic showed the poorest community adjustment.

The relationships among outcome criteria were equally interesting. There appeared to be limited relationships between any measures taken within the hospital setting (behavioral or perceptual) and community adjustment. Thus, such commonly used evaluative tools as the MMPI, ward behavior, self-concept, projective devices, and the like not only did not correlate with each other, but they also were generally unrelated to community adjustmental indices such as employment, desirable family relationships, and so on.

The results of this study showed very clearly that the current treatment programs available in the hospital setting yielded few if any more beneficial results than simply assigning an individual to preferred in-hospital work. Furthermore, persons who had a history of mental illness and were considered "chronic patients" failed completely regardless of the type of treatment they had had in the hospital so that 72.4% had returned to a hospital setting by the end of 18 months; those who were diagnosed as neurotic failed at a 55.6% rate by 18 months; and acute psychotics, termed short-term psychotics in this study (less than one year of previous hospitalization), showed only a 29% return rate for the same 18-month period.

The following conclusions seemed warranted at that time: (1) Chronic psychotic patients, followed by the neurotic, were the most prone to failure of individuals for whom rehabilitation programs needed to be created, while acute psychotic persons created only a minor chronic hospitalization problem. (2) New types of treatment programs would have to be innovated since current treatment programs were not very helpful in reducing the chronicity problem. (3) Outcome criteria would need to measure appropriate community adjustment as the key defining variables. It would also have to include several areas of adjustment-behaviors, attitudes, and other categories of measurement rather than one single measure as was typically the case because of the lack of relationship among these measures.

From this study, it seemed clear that a *new* type of program needed to be *innovated* which would lead to a more adaptive community adjustment for long-term hospitalized patients on a new multivariate outcome criteria. In an attempt to accomplish this, the researchers began to explore one possibility that seemed appropriate to the problem—small groups in treatment programs. The ideas followed from the notion that return rates among the chronic psychotic and long-term neurotic patients often occurred very quickly—after only a few days in the community—and that during this time many had no social support. The idea had taken shape among the researchers that if small cohesive groups of mental patients could be developed in the hospital they might function to maintain each other in the community and thus lead to a reduction in recidivism and an improved adjustment in the community. Accordingly, a series of studies were begun to find the answer to another three questions: (1) Could small groups of patients be organized so that they could function autonomously? (2) Could these groups serve as a vehicle to bridge the gap between the hospital and community? (3) If questions (1) and (2) were answered positively, could they be used to maintain the ex-patients in a community setting?

The first study in the series was accomplished by Lerner and Fairweather

(1963). The main interest in the study was to discover the degree of autonomy that chronic mental patients were able to assume in their own work situations. For purposes of this *experiment*, two group work situations were *innovated for comparison*: one with minimal supervision in which there was no formal staff leader present and one with maximum supervision where a mental health professional supervised the work of the group. The necessary *administrative agreements* were completed and they provided the sample of patients, a research ward, staffs, and data processing procedures. *Random assignment* of persons *matched* on background experiences was made to each of the supervisory conditions of work. The results of this experiment showed that even though the unsupervised groups took longer to perform a given task than the staff-supervised groups, the unsupervised groups in addition to task accomplishment were at the same time becoming a cohesive group unit. The staff-supervised group, even though it showed more rapid improvement in job performance, did not show behaviors indicating that the participating persons were becoming a cohesive unit. Thus, unsupervised groups developed group cohesiveness; supervised groups did not. It seemed quite obvious from this beginning experiment that organizing groups of patients into autonomous problem-solving groups could be accomplished and that such groups might be a valuable means of moving and maintaining their members in community settings. Even though group cohesiveness seemed at least partially dependent upon group autonomy, some questions still remained: How could such groups quickly be formed? What were their basic parameters?

A subsequent five-year *experiment* was undertaken in an attempt to answer these questions (Fairweather, 1964). Again, *administrative agreements* were completed in order to obtain a sample, to obtain wards (one for each new social subsystem), to get staff, and to arrange for data collection and processing. Persons were *matched* in pairs on background experiences and *randomly* assigned to the two experimental conditions. Since patients participating in the condition of work-alone had, after 18 months of follow-up, done as well as any of the more costly programs—typical psychotherapeutic techniques—and it was much less expensive, the work condition was considered as the social model *control* in the new study. A new *social model* was *innovated* to be compared with this control condition.

The innovative program consisted of a ward organized along small-group principles in which the patients made the major decisions about their lives in the hospital and for the future. Rather than supervising such patients in a traditional way, the staff's role was to give information to the groups about problems that needed solution. The patient groups could then use their own decision-making processes in an attempt to solve them. Group responses that were realistic and helpful to the group as a whole were rewarded; unrealistic and foolish responses were given negative staff feedback. By contrast, the traditional program assigned persons to individual work assignments and one-to-one relationships with the staff. It was specifically not, however, organized around activities that would improve or enhance the small-group processes.

The results of this study showed that the small-group social model enhanced all aspects of within-hospital adjustment *contrasted with* the traditional program. Staff and patient expectations and satisfactions with the program were enhanced, improved social interactions occurred, time in the hospital was reduced, and almost all other aspects of within-hospital adjustment were improved by the small-group program contrasted with the work-alone situation. It was very clear in this *longitudinal* five-year study that small cohesive groups of chronic mental patients were created that did solve their members' problems and take care of one another. However, these *comparative* differences disappeared when the patients lost their groups by returning to the community individually. It was found that the former group members returned to the hospital as quickly as those in the work-only control condition. Follow-up *survey information* and *observation* showed that the reason for the high return rate was that they had lost the support of their reference group so assiduously developed in the hospital setting. This was most clearly shown by a correlation of .86 that existed between the supportiveness of the community situation where the ex-patient resided and whether or not the person was able to make an adequate adjustment there. This correlation, along with other observational and statistical evidence, led to the *inference* that groups of patients created in the hospital and trained to solve their own problems could be moved into the community as maintenance units if the conditions for community living permitted democratic decision processes and patient autonomy. The evidence further suggested that unless new and supportive community conditions were created, the high return rate to the hospital would continue.

Throughout the preceding experiments, continuous feedback of information from the ex-mental patients in follow-up interviews brought to the awareness of the researchers this need for a community supportive system. The preceding studies had also laid the groundwork for what appeared to be the necessary *next experiment*. One social model would link the within-hospital small-group program with traditional community mental health agencies, which was the experimental condition in the experiment just discussed. A second social model was *innovated*. It linked the within-hospital small-group program with a newly created small society run by ex-patients (The Community Lodge), so that the hospital training would permit the continuation of cohesive small-group membership in the community. The group would be moved out of the hospital as a unit under this condition. In the traditional social model (within-hospital small-group linked to traditional community service), the patients were moved out individually (Fairweather *et al.*, 1969).

This experiment permitted the comparison of two social models—one at first innovative and now traditional (small group and traditional community mental health programs) with a newly innovated one (small group and community lodge). Again, all necessary *administrative agreements* were made with the community agencies involved, the hospital itself, and a large university so that the transition to the community could be made and residences and work equipment purchased for members who would participate in the innovation, and the forming of a research team to evaluate the models could be accomplished. In addition, agreements about *random assignments* of patients, hospital and community residences, data collection and analyses were completed. This *longitudinal* experiment took place over five years with the experimenters bearing the responsibility for the welfare of the persons who were entering the community setting.

Even though the small group had been well trained in the hospital to care for its members and made reasonable and adequate decisions, the immediate move to the community as a group was chaotic. The group decision process and organizational structure broke down, partly because it had been so closely linked to the hospital social structure itself. New training procedures were then introduced and the lodge society developed its own rules, its own work situation (gardening and janitorial service), and gradually progressed through periods of staff-structured activities to the development of a cohesive, totally autonomous small society.

The primary outcome measures showed the employment rate to be significantly greater in the lodge society *contrasted* with those who went to traditional community mental health settings; the return rate to the hospital was significantly reduced through the use of the lodge; and patient cost went initially to one-third the cost of hospitalization and finally to a totally self-supporting and self-managed cooperative society. The *matched* and *randomly assigned* patients who went to the lodge showed very clearly, in the outcome results, that it was the supportive and democratic social situation which resulted in the more adequate adjustment than those who participated in the traditional mental health community programs. Furthermore, this was accomplished at a great decrease in cost simply because the ex-mental patients were placed in a situation where they were able to take more responsibility for their own behavior and where they became responsible citizens operating their own society. In fact, the society eventually became self-supporting.

The major variable manipulated in this study, of course, was the social role and status structure that historically exists in mental health organizations between patients and mental health workers. Rather than mental health professionals supervising patients' behaviors, they helped them attain and sharpen their own decision-making processes and thus participated in liberating rather than controlling them.

Following the creation and evaluation of the beneficial prototype society, two *replicates* were established and compared with *quasi-experimental* techniques. Both *replicates* yielded positive results similar to those found for the original social model (Fairweather, Sanders & Tornatzky, 1974). These additional beneficial findings made the experimenters more confident in the *inferences* they had drawn about the social value of the lodge model. But, alas, further replicates were not forthcoming. It might be assumed by those unfamiliar with social decision making and the actual dissemination process that such new social models, particularly when accompanied by replications verifying the positive results of the initial study and the reduced cost rate, would immediately result in implementation elsewhere. Unfortunately, dissemination on a national scale is a slow process about which little is known from an experimental point of view. Because of this lack of meaningful data, and a desire to make the new beneficial social model available to other mental patients, the researchers felt it incumbent upon them to launch a national experiment in an attempt to discover how newly found innovations can be introduced into existing social practice. A national dissemination experiment was therefore begun (Fairweather, Sanders & Tornatsky, 1974).

Administrative agreements providing experimental staff, traveling expenses for them to serve as change agents with hospitals throughout the nation, space for the staff to work, and arrangements for data collection and processing were successfully completed. An experimental design was created to compare the effectiveness of alternative approaches to inducing hospitals to adopt the lodge program. To accomplish this, 255 mental hospitals (all but eight mental hospitals in the nation) were randomly assigned to different conditions of persuasion and supportive assistance.

The experiment in which the hospitals were involved compared written brochures, face-to-face workshops, and social change agents in order to assess their effectiveness in persuasion; it compared written and action approaches to activating the lodge program; and assessed the effectiveness of other variables including the geographic location of the hospital, the amount and type of bureaucracy, and the effect of approaching persons with different social status in the hospital hierarchy. Other factors of importance that were assessed were the communication processes, whether there was unilateral or hospital-wide decision-making, the financial condition of the hospital, its size and location, and many other pertinent variables.

From this experiment, several principles of approaching, persuading, and activating social models were discovered and used as feedback to create *another experiment* with those hospitals that did not accept the lodge model during the course of the first experiment. Thus, it was found that active approaches lead to more adoption than the verbal or written approaches; change agents are indispensable to persuasion and adoption; small groups of persons interested in change within organizations are essential to the creation of change; organizations with democratic leadership that encourage participation by others more readily create conditions for change; and active attempts at communicating the value of social innovations must be carried out. It was further discovered that all of the processes should act in concert to create the needed change—no one condition alone can accomplish it.

Since only a small percentage of the hospitals throughout the nation actually implemented the lodge in the first experiment, it was decided to compile the relatively uncommitted residual hospitals (those who did not adopt the first time) which would be matched on experimental background and *randomly assigned* to new conditions of persuasion-adoption that were the outgrowth of the first implementation experiment. This study is currently underway. The experiment is designed to answer the following questions: What is the most effective combination of persons in a decision-adopting group? What social status positions should be included? How does an organization become change-oriented?

These several studies have taken over 20 years to complete and have resulted in the creation of a new social innovation that has often become an alternative to hospitalization itself. Future experiments will have to determine whether an entire program of social participation and decision-making processes can change the role of marginal persons and help them become an integral part of society. If such is the case, the end result of these innovative experiments would be the creation of an entirely new social complex that would enhance the lives and welfare of those who are today marginal citizens of their society.

The primary burden of this chapter, however, has been to demonstrate that contemporary *scientific methods* can be combined into a unitary problem-solving approach that can be integrated into democratic decision processes. Both by description and a working example, we have attempted to show the reader how descriptive theory, survey techniques, laboratory-like controls, participant observation, pilot-demonstration studies, quasi-experiments, and actual experiments can be integrated to accomplish selected tasks in longitudinal problem-oriented experiments that can be used as a basis for social decisions and actions.

In addition to the integration of scientific methods, the working example just presented also shows how the basic ingredients described in Chapter 1 can be operationally defined in the day-to-day work of scientists interested in an adequate social policy. An integration of this 20 years of research into an adequate problem-solving technique such as that proposed in Chapter 1 can now, summarily, be accomplished by reviewing the nine necessary basic ingredients. The first component in the nine-point scheme stressed a humanitarian value orientation. Throughout the 20-year course of the researches presented, the model was oriented toward the *patient's* needs. Patient feedback showed that stressing first-class citizenship roles, new social positions which provide employment, and adequate living conditions were essential to community adjustment. These were agreed upon by the administrators, the scientists, and the patients themselves.

A more active *social role* for the scientists was accomplished through the hospital and community experiments. All researches were carried out in the naturalistic setting and were created by a group effort where active roles in both establishment and evaluation were carried out by the concerned scientists.

The approach, of course, was *innovative.* Beginning with the unsupervised work situation created by Lerner and Fairweather and continuing through the small group ward to the community lodge, new social programs were created.

It was *democratic.* In addition to establishing the work situation on the ward, the small-group program and the lodge by the patients, administrators, and scientists mutually, all agreements to create these programs were done on the basis of contractual arrangements with the involved groups. In addition, attempts to implement the lodge society on a national scale were done in an experiment which stressed the techniques of persuasion and autonomous group decision-making of the involved organizations—an essential element in any democratic society.

The *scientific evaluation* should be clear enough from the previous section. Here, as shown in the discussion, the different social science methods (including descriptive theory, survey techniques, laboratory-like controls, participant observation, service to a particular social group, and quasi-experiments along with "true" experiments) were incorporated into a programmatic effort aimed at solving a particular problem.

The *problem focus* was maintained by continuing to explore the problem of chronic hospitalization for mental patients. There is little question that the results of this study have implications for a wide variety of social problems which should result in further experimentation.

In this way additional experiments will be done both in model creation and implementation research which makes the experimental effort *continuous.* For example, a new society for marginal individuals is now being planned as an experiment using many of the features established in the prototype lodge society. In addition, a further implementation experiment in exploring additional variables about implementing the lodge society itself is currently underway as described in the previous pages.

The final lodge model, of course, is very *usable* in this and other societies. As pointed out earlier, its cost was negligible in comparison with alternative treatments and eventually its members became self-supporting; thus, its results in terms of socially meaningful criteria such as cost, employment, and reduction of chronic hospitalization, were not only significant but dramatic.

Finally, the results led to *inferences* both in terms of new programs, new diffusion efforts, and the social and experimental processes themselves. Replicates of the original lodge yielded much the same results as the prototype lodge.

From a methodological point of view, it should be easy for the reader to see that a longitudinal series of problem-oriented researches, when beneficial results are implemented through a continuous action research effort, eventually lead to problem solution and social change. This longitudinal example shows that the value of the innovative model building and comparative experiments is not only to find new and more beneficial programs but also to provide the basis for rational decisions about social change itself. Furthermore, they show that social experiments are most valuable to a society when incorporated into the decision processes of that society, particularly when they are used by the agents of that society to enhance the quality of life for its members.

Generally, then, the processes of experimental social innovation can aid the society in meeting the challenges of the future. They begin with problem definition, go through the processes of innovating and trying new social models as solutions, result in an actual comparative experiment to discover the benefits or lack of them when the innovative model is contrasted with the usual social practice, and are completed with the use of information derived from experiments to disseminate the social models found to be beneficial. This beneficial problem-solving change process assumes the following form: Innovating social models→evaluating those created→replicating those found to be beneficial→evaluating the replicates to discover if the same results obtain→innovating approaches to diffusion of the beneficial model→evaluating the diffusion approaches to discover the most productive ones→using those approaches found most productive in a national diffusion effort. The process may be viewed as a paradigm; it is presented along with its associated research techniques in Table 2.1.

The remainder of this book, except for Chapter 14, will present the details

TABLE 2.1
The Use of Different Social Science Research Techniques in
Experimental Social Innovation*

Problem definition →	Development and trial → of a new social model	Actual social experiment → with comparison programs, random assignment of participants, etc.	Experimental implementation
All of the following can be used to help to define the problem: 1. Descriptive theoretical 2. Survey 3. Participant-observation 4. Quasi-experimental information	1. Demonstration program (set up first program to get it operational) 2. Quasi-experiment (optional to compare with existing social practice)	1. Laboratory (methods developed in the laboratory may help control excessive sources of variance here: the use of control conditions preciseness of measurement, etc.) 2. Information for comparison comes from surveys, participant-observation, and other selected techniques	1. Uses an experiment to compare different processes of approach, etc. (uses decision theory, survey, laboratory controls, participant-observation to gain initial comparative information) 2. Uses quasi-experiments to evaluate social model replicates

* There can be one or more innovative social models, each designed to ameliorate the social problem at hand.

of these processes as they go from problem definition to experimental implementation efforts. Chapter 14 is reserved for a discussion of an organization designed to carry out social experiments and train experimentalists.

CHAPTER 3

The Parameters of Social Models and Dissemination

New techniques for handling the problems with which a society is confronted are essential when old techniques fail. In American society new programs are established through legislative action, thus affecting all individuals within a state, a region, or the nation. These programs are often aimed at groups of individuals (the poor, those suffering from disease, the elderly, and so on). Sometimes they take the form of providing new services such as health care, while at other times they are mainly concerned with changing the economic balance, such as efforts to create new tax programs. The goal of all such programs is stated to be the improvement of the general welfare. Regardless of the social variables manipulated in any particular social intervention, the program affects individuals, groups, organizations, and often state, national, and international governments.

Unfortunately, when new programs are established by law and when they apply to a state, region, or the nation *there is no way of knowing beforehand through the usual legislative process what their eventual outcomes will be.* Thus, programs that are aimed at improving the health, education, or welfare of the citizenry are *assumed* to improve those aspects of living for which they were designed. But new social programs are social innovations and the literature on social change and innovation is clear on this point: The effects of any innovations are unknown at the time they are first established (Barnett, 1953; LaPiere, 1965). This is why evaluation of new social programs is so essential.

The degree of uncertainty (muddling through), relative to new social programs need not always be the case. Procedures described in this book provide early warning for success and failure in new social programs. The vehicle that we advocate is the use of small, scale-model version rigidly evaluated prior to any national legislative plans of broad-scale adoption.

SOCIAL MODELS

These prototype social models may vary in complexity because of the problem involved, but it is desirable for experimental purposes that they are first established as *small scale models*. This is important for several reasons. First, the creation of a new social model is expensive and the cost of creating even a small scale model for field trial may be great. If the expense is too great, the probability of being able to create it even for evaluative purposes is diminished. Another reason for small scale models concerns the need for outcome knowledge prior to diffusing the model as a state, federal, or international program. This evaluative knowledge must be gained *prior to* implanting the model on a broad scale if excessive failure is to be avoided. This is the price any society must pay for ignorance.

One goal of the social innovative experimentalist is to create and compare the effectiveness of new social models in solving a selected social problem. The created social model is the basic social condition to be evaluated in experimental social innovation. In the language of research design, the presence of the social model is the independent variable of the experimental design. However, since a social model is also a highly complex social event, it is also important to evaluate *which aspects* of the social model are producing the desired effects. Thus, for example, a researcher may be doing an experimental evaluation of a new delinquency treatment program and the salient and crucial aspects of such a program could go undetected without a fine-grained analysis. This analysis can be most clearly defined in terms of the functional relationship between the social model and its outcome. For this reason, when a research team attempts to establish a social model as an alternative solution to a given social problem, it is primarily interested in the outcomes of that model. And the outcome of a social model, whether it is large or small is dependent upon the individuals who participate in it and the social context, in which it is operative. It is this functional relationship between outcome, participants, and social situation that operationally defines a social model. This generic relationship may be stated in the following manner: *The outcome of any social model is a function of its participants and its social situation.*

Thus, the experimenters may conceptualize the social situation and the participants as the dimensions of a social model. These are most often the variables that are manipulated to bring about changes in outcomes. The *outcomes* of models are specific to the kind of social problem for which one is seeking a solution. For example, if the social problem is education, the social change outcome criterion may be academic achievement; if the social problem is post-prison adjustment, the social change outcome criterion might be reduction of recidivism.

Participant variables are those that describe the attributes of the sample of participants, such as age, education, medical history, attitudes, and expectancies.

The *social situational* variables may be classified as those that are internal and those that are external to the social organization. Internal social processes are those intrinsic to the social model, such as group morale, type of work, and fiscal processes. The external processes are those that impinge upon the model and result from the model's interaction with the larger environment. These involve variables such as the state of the economy and the social model's interaction with other institutions.

Social models are placed in operation in a dynamic society; for this reason, the behaviors, perceptions, or social organizational variables cannot be rigidly assigned to particular categories that transcend time. Thus, the behaviors, perceptions, or social organizational variables that are categorized as outcomes in one study may not be categorized in the same class in subsequent studies. For example, employment, the use of leisure time, or self-satisfaction may be more important to a society in some years than in others. Thus in the 1930s employment might be society's outcome criterion for its educational system, whereas in the 1990s it might be the use of leisure time. The experimenters' categorization of measures as outcome is contingent upon the condition of the society and its needs at the time the experiment is done. Although for the purpose of clarity, outcome, participant, and social situation variables are presented independently in Tables 3.1, 3.2, and 3.3, it cannot be overemphasized that such a classification is arbitrary and that the variables listed as outcomes can change with changing social conditions and different experimental needs.

Outcomes

The multivariate nature, situation specificity,
and temporal instability of social outcomes

At the outset, it must be understood that an adequate evaluation of contemporary social programs can only be accomplished if the outcomes for any social model are perceived as multivariate and changing. Unfortunately many social programs are evaluated on only one criterion. For example, it is often the case that social programs are evaluated solely on the basis of their cost per individual without considering the complexity of outcomes and effects that one outcome can have upon others. Even when cost-benefit analyses are made, the benefits are often not operationally defined in human behavioral forms (happiness, morale, human dignity); thus, their relationship to cost is often unattainable. Simplistic views of outcomes give a totally inaccurate picture of what the outcomes of social models might and ought to be.

Outcomes are usually multivariate in nature and consist of several dimensions which are often independent. To give a very simple example, several researches have shown that cost, attitudes, expectancies, morale, and so on are essentially unrelated to behavioral aspects of outcome (Fairweather, 1964; Fairweather, Sanders & Tornatzky, 1974). Several simple examples quite clearly point out this discrepancy. It is often *assumed* that because students have positive feelings toward their teachers they will also be well-adjusted behaviorally with their fellows in social contacts and with their families; or that people will be more receptive to change if paid more; or that persons who are productive are also happy. Unfortunately, these different aspects of human activity (affect, behavior, attitudes) have often been found to be unrelated. These findings therefore mean that a proper evaluation of outcome must contain well-defined measures of all of these dimensions and a determination must be made of their interrelationships before a meaningful and accurate evaluation of a social model can be made.

There is also the empirical fact that the relationships among the variables change over time. *What is an appropriate outcome at one time may not be an appropriate outcome at another.* Changes are rapid and it must be recognized that outcome criteria change over time. It might be important to a society at one time to be concerned about the employment of criminals who are discharged from a prison but at another time this might not be nearly as important to the society as their future education. Or, if society should change dramatically, it is possible that the society will become more interested in their use of leisure time.

In addition to the temporal instability of outcomes, there is clear evidence accumulating that much of human behavior is situationally specific (Mischel, 1968). Thus, certain kinds of outcomes will manifest themselves in one social situation, while other types of outcomes will manifest themselves in another. The net result often is a very limited cross-situational generality of behavior and outcome.

Since these outcomes may be unrelated, it is important to evaluate the social model on all of them simultaneously. Such an evaluation can also provide information about the interrelationships among different outcome criteria so that the evaluation information can still be logically used at a later date when and if social needs change. For example, suppose all possible outcomes were measured and interrelated. If the outcome criteria changed in a few years, it would be possible to examine earlier studies to discover what relationships were established between these two criteria at that time.

An examination of this information might make further evaluation unnecessary. At least it would make it easier to accomplish and its generalizability over time could be ascertained. These examples simply illustrate that not only are outcome criteria multivariate but they also change with time. For these reasons, it is necessary to consider a large number of criteria and discover their interrelationships at particular times and in selected social settings when attempting to determine the outcomes of social models.

The social change outcome criterion

While pointing out the need for considering the multivariate nature of outcomes, it does not follow that all potential outcomes should be considered of equal importance. At particular times, some outcome variables are more important than others. Their importance derives directly from the nature of the problem at the time it is being studied. Some of the planning preparatory to fielding researches such as those described in the previous chapter can be used to explain how outcome criteria are developed. As researchers, lay people, and members of the dysfunctional social system all share their ideas about the nature of "the problem," some clear definitions usually are derived. Often, however, the diverse groups involved in planning the research will be interested in outcome criteria that are quite different. Thus, in the aforementioned example, one group may be interested in employment as an outcome criterion for treating mental illness while another group may be interested in changes in self-esteem.

Although many groups may be involved in this give-and-take in planning, the experimenters are attempting to solve a social problem so they must first be concerned with those outcomes that have a certain face validity relationship to the social problem as defined. To give a fairly mundane example, if the problem is unemployment and the social model being evaluated is an employment counseling program, it makes very little sense to focus attention on self-actualization rather than employment itself as the outcome criterion. Thus, in the very nature of defining the social problem of study the principal outcome variables can often be determined by deduction. But one variable can usually be designated as the most important by those members of society charged with the responsibility for solving the problem. *The criterion that is reserved by society's agents as a solution to the new problem is considered of primary importance and therefore is designated as a social change outcome criterion.* Table 3.1 presents some general and specific outcomes. A discussion of their measurement may be found in Chapter 9.

TABLE 3.1
Some General and Specific Outcome Criteria in Experimental Social Innovation

General criteria	Criteria specific to problems of:		
	Mental health, criminality, delinquency, drug addiction	Education	Poverty, race, urban development
Satisfaction	Recidivism	Academic achievements	Employment
Self-regard	Behavior control	Social adjustment	Living standards
Morale	Employment		Family development
Cost of maintaining model			Integration
			Housing and living conditions
			Criminal behavior

Since the experimenters and those members of the problem population who are involved in the planning will undoubtedly have many other criteria in which they are interested, this information can be documented and correlated with the social change outcome criterion. But the information about what society's agents consider the necessary outcome—the social change outcome criterion—should be measured in every experiment along with the other criteria considered to be important by the research team.

An example can be found in the recidivism of criminals. If the representatives of a society who are responsible for the rehabilitative programs for prisoners agree that the criterion for successful rehabilitation is a reduction of recidivism, then the social change outcome criterion becomes just that—reduction of recidivism. The social change outcome criterion is, therefore, determined by the representatives of a society. The experimenters simply determine, define, and describe it. The experimenters and the problem population representatives, of course, can and should be interested in the effects of the model upon a wide variety of other behaviors and perceptions.

What it is important to recognize here is that the experimenters should make certain that socially important outcomes are *included* as measures in the experiment. There have been too many social program evaluations in which the "outcome" variables have nothing to do with socially obvious outcomes. Thus, for example, an evaluation of a police patrol program that does not include some measure of crime or crime reduction seems patently foolish.

There are certain other reasons why the social change outcome criteria should represent an agreed-upon criterion by the society's representatives. Since upon completion of a social innovative experiment the experimentalists will attempt to implement the social model found to be most beneficial, it is necessary that the findings of a research project be of such a nature that they will be attended to by potential users of the research. This will aid in the dissemination of the created social model in the future by providing the basis for communication between the research team and the persons who will be responsible for adopting it later—society's agents. Often researchers err in attempting to be too sophisticated in their outcomes. This may be because they are concerned most about communicating with other scientists. However, in social policy research, lay administrators and citizens comprise the primary audience. Thus, complicated indices that are unintelligible to them have negative implications for the dissemination of the research. Finally, of course, another positive aspect of providing a consensually agreed-upon social change criterion is that it may provide the basis for expanding and broadening the criterion itself as the results are disseminated to potential users. Thus, a feedback process may be set in motion that will eventually result in a more usable definition of the outcome.

Because the social change outcome criterion reflects a limited consensus of a society's representatives, it can usually be stated in terms of real-life behavior. For the experimentalists, this has important consequences because of the research studies just mentioned that question the relationship between real-life behavior and perceptions about it.

The possibility of a loss in the social value of an innovative experiment when the results are not clearly defined in behavioral terms can be seen in the following example. If the researchers choose expectancies about employment as the criterion and if the recent studies just mentioned are valid (a zero relationship between expectancies and behavior exists), this choice would yield little information concerning job performance—the outcome criterion society's agents would most likely be interested in. So it is most important that information about the outcome criterion (job performance in this case) be obtained as a primary focus of the research rather than attempting to infer about performance from attitudes or expectancies that might readily be the only aspects of unemployment assessed in the experiment.

As successive experiments are completed, the social change outcome criterion can become empirically elaborated because successive correlational analyses will show the interrelationships of the various measures. To elaborate the criterion, those measures not related to it can be excluded while those with high relationships can become an integral part of it. In this way, experiments can generate information that may be used to shape a new social change outcome criterion. One aspect of social innovation research is to provide new information derived from experiments which can be used by a society's representatives to help formulate a somewhat more scientific consensus. Their responsibilities as scientists and as citizens merge at this point.

When research information indicates that the criterion in use needs redefinition, it is the experimenters' obligation, in their role as educators, to help shape a new consensus. Of course, these responsibilities are an inherent part of the concerned citizen's role in any democratic society.

Participants

Not only are outcome variables highly complex and multivariate, so are the two other dimensions of social models—the participants and the social situation. Since the outcomes of social models are determined by the participants and the social situation, it is important to elaborate their attributes. In this section, therefore, we will delineate those aspects of participants which very often influence the outcomes of social experiments.

The experimenters must clearly define the attributes of the participating sample so that their effects upon the outcomes can be ascertained. For a complete description of the participants, it is necessary to accumulate information about their many characteristics. Certain demographic features (such as age, religion, education, family, employment, and social status) should be obtained. It may also be important to describe the sample on selected test scores. The experimenter may wish to have information on tests of achievement, interests, occupational preferences, and personality. And there is also the need for rather specific items of information, such as minority group membership, residential area, and languages spoken.

The following are a list of selected key participant variables that have been found to be related to outcomes in social research. A brief discussion of each variable gives some indication of why the experimentalists need to consider the contribution that each *might* make in a particular experiment. It should be obvious to the reader that the list is not exhaustive and that other participant variables might need to be considered in a particular experiment. It should also be pointed out that this particular list of participant variables assumes that the participants in the experiment are *persons*. In some cases, however, the unit of analysis may be groups, organizations, and so on.

Age

Age is a variable that must be accounted for in its determination of what individuals do behaviorally and what social role expectations are. The types of behaviors and perceptions of a child going through the socialization process are obviously quite different from those of the elderly, whose main concern at that point in life sometimes is simply to survive from week to week and to gain some measure of enjoyment from the aesthetic qualities of their environment. Age has been considered such an important variable that entire segments of psychology and sociology have been devoted to age differences. There has been the psychology and sociology of child development, of adolescence, of early adulthood, the middle years, and the declining years. Thus, it is important to incorporate the variable of age in accounting for the results of any social experiment.

Education

The achievement of a particular level of education not only changes individuals' lifestyles and life chances but it also changes the perception of others toward them and thus often influences what they are able to do. Education is highly correlated with many other important elements in a person's life—income, level of employment achieved, and so on. Because of the differences that exist within the society by persons who have achieved different levels of education, it is an exceedingly important variable to be considered in any research design.

Employment history

The type of employment that persons achieve is also an important aspect of their definition as persons, particularly in the American culture. Employment history refers not only to the occupational level achieved but also to the degree of lateral and vertical job mobility.

Economic status

This is related to education and occupation but is considered here as a separate category since very often in American society a person's social status is interrelated with income. As with education and occupation, the amount of money an individual makes permits him or her various freedoms in a society which determines the lifestyle alternatives one has. In this sense economic status is important because it can affect social roles.

Social class

Although employment, educational achievement, and the like can be considered independently, they can also be combined into an index of social class. Students of social stratification going back at least to Warner (1960), have proposed that the main ingredients of social class are: (1) a person's *economic status* (described above), (2) a person's *occupation* (described above), and (3) *dwelling*. The last category, *dwelling*, is the third classification in Warner's social class index. It has to do with the size and location of a person's house. Where a person dwells, and the size and type of house is related to personal satisfaction, aesthetic interests, as well as the degree to which the individual is perceived as desirable by neighbors and friends. While these three indices (economic status, occupation, and dwelling) can be considered independently, they can be combined into a single score—using all of them as an index of a person's social class and social position in a society.

Marital status

Aside from the difference in lifestyle that married and single, widowed and divorced relationships give a person in general adjustment to life, there are specific indicators that this variable is related to other aspects of adjustment and would be a determinant in how an individual adjusted to a particular social system. For example, it has been shown (Lindemann *et al.*, 1958) that very few married persons or those who have been married are found among the chronically hospitalized for mental illness. Married and single status are also related to other social role aspects of life. Hence, this is an important variable to be accounted for in determining the outcome of an individual in any social system.

Medical history

The state of an individual's health will affect his or her participation in a social model. To take an extreme case, an individual who has had a history of tuberculosis or emphysema might find certain kinds of physical labor difficult to accomplish and therefore would be unable to participate in activities requiring physical exertion. On the other hand, a person may be in excellent health and thus physically be able to participate in most human activities. It is important to know the medical history of persons in order to gain some understanding of their past, present, and future life chances.

History of institutionalization

It is frequently important to know if individuals have had a history of institutionalization because such a history tends to influence the person's behavior in new social situations. For example, persons who have spent long periods of their life in mental hospitals or prisons very often do not adjust well in traditional community settings. This background information must be taken into account when evaluating the effectiveness of social models in which such persons participate. This is particularly true when the model is developed to improve the adjustment of marginal people. Since every individual who participates in a social model can affect its outcome, it is important to account for each participant's history of institutionalization.

Military history

If an individual has been in a military setting, it may be important to know about his or her adjustment to it. Some persons leave the military early for various reasons, others adjust well to it. Such information may be important in understanding how a person might adjust to a new social model, particularly if the model has any similarities to a rather rigidly designed social system that is similar to the military.

Family history

According to some psychological and sociological theorists, a person's family history has a great deal to do with the eventual shape of his or her personality, which again affects his or her role in society. Persons who have experienced early childhood traumas such as parental separation and loss or lack of affection often have difficulty in later life adjustment. Such experiences may affect behaviors, attitudes, and expectancies of others. For this reason, it is exceedingly important to know a person's family history and it should be taken into account when measures of the participants are gathered.

Race

Many recent books and articles have attested to the effect that racism has upon individuals in our society. Persons with dark skin color have historically had difficulty in being accepted by the majority white American society and have often been actively discriminated against. The effects of racial prejudice are well known to most persons by now. The Presidential commission's report on race relations in the society has now become a central source showing the effect of discrimination upon individual development (1968). The historic desegregation case of *Brown* vs *the Board of Education* at Topeka, Kansas in 1954 brought to light information documenting the effects of discrimination on the opportunities an individual has as a citizen and its effect upon his or her personal growth. Certainly this variable must be recognized and its effects carefully documented in social research.

Sex

The current movement to obtain equal rights for women in the American society makes clear that sexual differences in employment opportunities and other avenues to social position have been denied women in this and other societies. It should therefore be apparent that sex is an important aspect of an individual's characteristics and that one's life chances are directly affected by it. Thus, the sex of an individual, like race, must be considered an important determinant in one's participation in a social system.

National origin

Although this variable is of questionable importance as an important participant variable, it has been accepted in a large number of studies in the past and probably should be documented for comparison. Whether one's parents are from a Western or Eastern European country is an important historical fact because different cultural backgrounds may affect a person's perceptions and behaviors. Persons from different cultures also often have different racial characteristics, so that in some cases (third world) national origin is also related to racial characteristics; even here there are subgroups within each group whose information may be relevant to participant description in later social model analyses.

Membership in organizations

This variable is related to social class mentioned earlier but also gives some indication of one's social definition and relationship to others in the society. Self-perception—whether one perceives oneself as a liberal or conservative, a social or intellectual person, to mention a few characteristics—is often revealed in the number and type of organizations an individual belongs to. Organizational memberships sometimes give an indication of how an individual perceives others.

Personality characteristics

Personality characteristics are known to psychologists through several different avenues, including behavioral descriptions, scores on personality tests, ratings by peers or friends, and so on. It is clear that considerable variability exists among persons in their affective response to situations, their social activity, their interaction with others, etc. However, the past several decades have seen a plethora of personality trait measures and scales developed to assess an equally baffling array of personality attributes. For the person involved in social model-building experiments, it is all too tempting to "shot gun" a battery of personality tests and attempt to determine their relationship to social outcomes. This is to be avoided if possible. If there is reason to believe that some personality attributes will affect outcomes, it is much more worthwhile to use selected personality tests in which the attribute measured has some *conceptual relationship* to the behavior under study. Particular attention should be given to those personality attributes which might be significantly related to outcome behavior.

Intelligence and skill aptitude

This category of variables encompasses both scores on standardized intelligence tests and/or indicators of specialized problem-solving ability. There are a number of ways this might be measured—formal testing clearly being one. In certain cases it might be important to know the participants' achievement test scores or intelligence test scores. It is well known that people who score high on intelligence tests also do well in reading and other specific skill areas. It is also fairly well established by now that creativity is not necessarily related to test score intelligence (Holland, 1961). In a particular case it might be important to assess the participants' creativity rather than their test intelligence. In other cases it may be important to discover their aptitudes—for example, a mechanical aptitude if the task in which the individual is involved is one of a mechanical nature. Other aptitudes might also be important in a given situation. All of these areas—intelligence, creativity, and aptitudes— can be measured and can be helpful in determining the characteristics of persons in a particular social role. It is also of *extreme* importance that the population upon whom the test is being used be appropriate for the test itself. For example, it has now been well documented that black persons do not score as high on standardized intelligence tests that were mainly designed for middle-class white persons (Knowles & Prewitt, 1969).

Religion

Like all other participant characteristics, this variable may or may not be important depending upon the particular human problem under investigation. Historically, sociologists have shown correlations between different religious beliefs and certain attitudes and behaviors—for example, the concern expressed by the Catholic church against the use of abortions and contraceptive devices. It should be obvious, therefore, that when problems of population regulation are being investigated, the person's religious background may have a great deal to do with his or her attitudes and behaviors about sexual matters. Because of the relationships that exist between some religous beliefs and social attitudes and behaviors, it is important to document each person's religion so that any effect it might have upon the outcomes of the particular social programs can be ascertained.

A number of key participant variables that can affect the outcomes of social models have been discussed. A summary list of the common participant variables is presented in Table 3.2. The procedure that needs to be used in sampling and planning for these experimental variables can be found in Chapters 7 and 8. Methods for ascertaining and measuring the attributes of any sample can be found in Chapter 9.

TABLE 3.2
Participant Variables

Demographic
    Age
    Economic status
    Education
    Employment history
    Family history
    History of institutionalization (prison, mental hospital, etc.)
    Marital status
    Medical history
    Membership in organizations
    Military history
    National origin
    Race
    Religion
    Sex
    Social class
Personality Characteristics
    Behavior description
    Ratings
    Test scores
Intelligence
    Educational achievement (grades and awards)
    Test scores

Social Situational Variables

The second category of variables that can affect outcomes of social models are social situational variables. The logic is, of course, congruent with the previous section where the attributes of the participants in the models under evaluation were explored. The rationale behind taking a close look at these variables is to attempt to impute causation to those social situation variables that influence outcomes. Thus, if we compare program A against program B on outcomes x, y, and z, our evaluation will only be useful to the extent that we can define the *social situational parameters* of programs A and B and determine their separate and interaction effects. A comprehensive consideration of social situational variables not only enables us to identify those crucial parameters related to outcome but also provides the detailed information necessary to replicate it. Since any social model is a complex phenomenon, in order for it to be adopted in other settings the crucial variables responsible for the success of the social models must be identified empirically.

The social situation within which the innovative social models are operative can best be understood by describing and defining its internal and external processes. The internal processes include the model's internal economics, its social structure, and its group dynamics. The external processes include the manner in which it is related to the community through function, position in the social and economic structure, and interaction with its social surroundings. The following selected social situational variables are those that have been found to influence the outcomes of social models. It is necessary for the experimentalist to take account of them in any social experiment as outlined in subsequent chapters. This list is not exhaustive but does present many of those variables that have been found to have an important influence in a wide variety of social experiments.

Internal social process variables

Every social model is implicitly or explicitly some type of organization. Thus, we can look at any of the social model-building experiments that we have alluded to thus far and point out how each of them had different types of decision making, statuses, roles, etc. For example, the Fairweather (1969) community lodge program can in many ways be considered as having some mixture of informal and bureaucratic organizational components. It should be obvious that *any* programmatic social model typically has a social milieu or organizational context in which it operates. Even a program of face-to-face therapy carried out by individual therapists has organizational components. The individual therapist has a certain role relationship with intake and referral, the client, and so on.

It is important for the model-building experimenters to measure all of these internal social process variables. By doing so, they accomplish two tasks: (1) they are able to provide an operational description of the social model as it is tested in the experiment so that exact replicates of the model can later be created; (2) they can determine, at least correlatively, which of these variables is particularly related to outcome. Thus, when a social model is being evaluated against a control model in which internal social processes are different, it is important to determine which aspects of the experimental social model are the most crucial. This may enable the experimenters to perfect and expand the social model in subsequent experiments. For example, in the social models being tested Fairweather (1964) found that a critical aspect that related to the outcome of recidivism was employment opportunities. This led directly to the creation of employment possibilities in the subsequent community lodge experiment (Fairweather *et al.*, 1969).

What follows, then, is a list of brief descriptions of some variables that ought to be measured and evaluated either as experimental conditions or correlates of outcomes in the context of a model-building experiment. The list is likely not exhaustive, but will provide the reader with a springboard for further thought in experimental planning.

Organizational components

Hierarchical structure. Hierarchical structure is one of the principal variables defining the bureaucratic nature of organizations. Hierarchy can be conceptualized as the degree to which power authority is organized in a vertical ascending manner or is diffused horizontally throughout an organization—in other words, to what extent an organization is "tall" rather than "flat." Some types of organizational structure combine both horizontal and vertical organization so that communications flow both up and down and across the organization. Such organizations are frequently created along small group discussion lines where informal groups participate in decision-making. The hierarchical structure of organizations is one of the important variables to consider when social models are created within organizations or related to them. Some indices of hierarchy are the following: number of levels in the organizational chart, degree to which decisions are shared or accomplished unilaterally, and number of units involved in the decision process.

Size. Size of an organization is important because size may be related to outcomes in a number of plausible ways. Indices of size include the number of personnel, the amount of budget, the number of clients the organization has, and the like. This is an important attribute of an organization and should be measured and described in any social innovative experiment.

Complexity. Recent literature (Hage & Aiken, 1970) indicates that organizational complexity may have some predictive value concerning change and innovation. Indices of complexity include the number of subunits within the organization, the number and different types of jobs, and the use of professional persons.

Formality/informality. Another aspect of an organization that must be considered important is the type of *communication* utilized within the organization itself. This is another separate but important indicator of the bureaucratic or nonbureaucratic nature of the social unit. Of particular importance is the informality or formality of communication patterns. Thus, social organizations in which communication is face-to-face are usually different organizations than those in which communication is accomplished via formal methods such as memo, letter, etc. Another index worth looking at is the gross amount of communication within an organization. This concept is somewhat related to that of hierarchy but is more germane to communication considerations.

Group dynamics. In considering group process variables it is important to appreciate their longitudinal dynamic nature. Each group dynamic property can be treated as a variable, because it can change rapidly with time and with changes in other dynamic properties. Usually dynamics, when contrasted with structure, must be measured longitudinally because of their changing qualities. This is particularly true in real-life groups where membership is frequently transitory. Take the dynamics of leadership as an example. In a group there is a high probability of new informal leadership with the departure and arrival of members. As new members arrive and old ones depart, the informal leadership of any group usually changes. Whether this is reflected in the formal structure is dependent upon the degree to which the formal structure reflects the informal structure. Nonetheless, it is necessary in describing the dynamics of the group's internal processes for the experimenters to be able to trace longitudinally the emergence of the new leaders and the departure of the old. Leadership, of course, can and does change within groups having the same membership, but the likelihood of such changes increases with increased group turnover. Many other variables which should be measured can change with the turnover of members. They are described below.

Group cohesiveness. A large number of studies have shown the importance of the individual's acceptance by and desire to belong to a group. Individuals participate in quite a different manner when they have a common goal. Athletic teams, military groups, social clubs, and the like have had this as a premise since organized groups were first systematically studied. Many social psychologists have discussed the importance of the cohesiveness of the group. Jackson & Saltzstein (1956) in their discussion of group membership propose that persons who want to belong to a group and are wanted by the group are much more concerned with the goals of that group.

Norms. Groups establish norms of behavior which guide the activities of their members. General studies have shown this to be the case in many diverse situations. Early studies by Asch (1956) showed that some persons were affected by the judgment of their peers even when they believed them to be wrong. Coleman, Katz & Menzel (1966), in a study of the diffusion of a new drug, showed that one of the most important factors in determining who would use the drug was the judgment of the individual doctor's peer group members. Norms of each group need to be known and measured in order that an understanding of the individual and group action itself can be assessed.

Leadership. A number of studies have shown the effect that leadership has upon the performance and attitudes of the group. For example, Fairweather (1964) showed that leadership was extremely important in the functioning of autonomous groups, while groups without strong leadership very often showed poor performance. Fiedler (1967) has developed a theoretical rationale and a large set of data supporting a contingent theory of leadership depending upon task demands. Thus, a relatively authoritarian leader was more effective when the "task environment" was either extremely good or extremely bad, while a democratic leader was more effective in the mid-range of task demands. Lerner & Fairweather (1963) showed that directive leadership resulted in much more rapid improvement in performance but at the expense of group cohesiveness.

In measuring leadership variables it is most appropriate that the evaluator of a social model look at specific leader behaviors and leader-follower inter-actions, rather than searching only for traits of leadership. Not only is there theoretical and empirical support for this position but such an approach is congruent with trying to create social models that are replicable. Leadership behaviors which can be operationally defined can be replicated.

Composition. The types of individuals that comprise a group have been shown to affect the performance of that group. Katz & Cohen (1962) have shown that biracial groups can give quite different responses than groups that are comprised of only one race. Studies of the elderly show the effects upon the elderly that children and adolescent groups have. And Sanders, MacDonald, & Maynard (1964) showed that groups performed better when they were comprised of individuals who were heterogeneous with regard to social activity—groups comprised of all individuals who were socially active or inactive did not perform as well as a mix of the two types of persons. Numerous other studies have shown that the composition of a group is an important determinant of group processes.

Morale. Morale is another attribute of group process that needs to be considered when defining and describing the characteristics of a group. Fairweather *et al.* (1969) found morale to be an important group dimension that was not directly related to performance—i.e., it was independent of performance so that groups could perform well or poorly whether or not they had high or low morale. The morale of a group refers to the group members' satisfaction with the group, its leadership, and their membership in it at any given moment in time. When all individuals are satisfied and happy with their group membership, morale is high. The converse is also true—morale is low when dissatisfaction of all or most of the members occurs. This is an important group process and should be considered as a parameter of group functioning relative to but more global and effective than cohesiveness.

Reinforcement system. Every group must have a system of reinforcement so that its members can be rewarded for good performance or the group itself may not continue to function. Thus, for example, good leadership and good group membership need to be rewarded so that people will strive to belong to the group and to perform its functions well. Very often the reinforcement system is money. This is most prevalent in production organizations. On the other hand, there are rewards in belonging to certain organizations quite beyond any monetary returns. For example, some groups bring about considerable prestige to the individual and are therefore sought after by certain people. Whether the rewards are intrinsic or extrinsic, it is essential that a continuing group establish a reward system through which it can reinforce the roles of the individual members.

Fiscal processes

Another of a social model's internal functions is its own fiscal processes —the way in which it handles monetary matters within its organization.

These are the statuses and operations which are purely internal to the subsystem and which do not directly involve the wider social environment. They constitute the financial management of the social model. Some members of the lodge model described in Chapter 2 (including staff, consultants, or members) had certain fiscal responsibilities as a part of their statuses. For example, the executive committee could grant loans to members out of a fund accumulated from part of the job revenue. Similarly, the member in charge of the kitchen and diningroom was delegated the responsibility for buying food and kitchen supplies, whereas certain consultants decided on other expenditures.

These statuses generate certain operations of budgeting and accounting which are necessary to make the financial decisions and dispositions within certain social models. Budgeting usually allocates certain money to purchasing food, buying equipment, and leasing property. Accounting operations are simply means of ensuring that the budget is followed by the persons responsible. All these operations are carried out by members of most social models who have those duties as part of their statuses. To continue with the example of the community lodge, a differential wage scale was established (or budgeted) for the three grades of members—supervisors, assitsant supervisors, and workers. One member held the position of business manager and did the bookkeeping. Consultants were responsible for checking the bookkeeping and auditing the lodge books.

The defining characteristic of these internal fiscal processes is that they all deal with monies after they are in the model and before they leave it. Monetary transactions between the model and its social environment (including income from work and from supporting institutions as well as output into the economy of the wider society by spending) form the external economic processes which will be discussed later.

Income. Income is the total amount of income available to the social model from whatever source it comes. If it is an industrial organization, income can come from production as well as from investments and the like. On the other hand, a social organization may be a nonprofit corporation and only have income from donors or incomes from investments of the organization. This is an exceedingly important parameter of social models, particularly in a capitalistic society.

Costs. Costs are the expenditure per unit within the organization. The cost might be related to the cost of production of an item or personnel costs in a service organization, or whatever. In the case of the latter the costs might be the costs per client, which is often a central issue when one is computing the costs of mental health care, rehabilitation, or education.

Rate of pay. Rate of pay is the rate of payment per person within the organization. It is often desirable to know how the rate of pay is determined since it may be determined simply by management fiat, by collective bargaining, by agreement among the workers in the case where they are also owners, and so on. Rate of pay is an important variable in a social model.

Bookkeeping procedures. This is a general term for the deriving of profit and loss statements and the keeping of books. It includes accounting systems in large organizations, auditors, and various other personnel. It is the manner in which the records of the fiscal matters of the organization are maintained.

Membership

Voluntary-involuntary. All persons have membership in one group or another. The manner in which this exists may have an important effect on outcome. This concept concerns the degree to which membership in the organization is voluntary. For example, in grade school students are involuntary members of the organization. This is also true of prisoners and some persons in mental hospitals or rehabilitation centers. On the other hand, membership in a social organization or in an industrial organization is usually voluntary. The difference between voluntary and involuntary participation is an important variable even though as social programs move further and further into the community settings they depend more and more upon persons to participate voluntarily in them. There still will probably remain, however, involuntary assignments such as assignment to rehabilitation houses by the courts.

Turnover. Turnover in membership is a relatively important parameter of a group. It is important to know whether the membership of a group is permanent or temporary. The members of a family usually participate in a group with relatively stable membership but rapid turnover in membership is clearly demonstrated by a student in grade school. Thus, some memberships are relatively permanent and others last only for brief periods in life. Turnover in membership is an important matter because it helps define the role and status structure of an organization.

External social process variables

Aside from the internal social processes germane to a new social model, it is axiomatic that any new model will be interacting in a larger social milieu. Thus, any new implant will typically have some relation and interaction with the larger society of which it is a part. This interaction may in turn be related to the particular outcome variables of interest in the social model. Just as the internal social process variables may change over time, the social milieu's external social process variable will likely change during the course of a longitudinal experiment. Therefore, it is important that external social processes also be measured and evaluated over the entire course of the experiment.

The exact type of external social process variables to be considered often depend upon the nature of the social model being evaluated. For example, a social model designed to improve the employment opportunities for disadvantaged persons may be particularly sensitive to changes in gross economic climate. On the other hand, a new innovative educational program may be more sensitive to changes in educational policy and legislation in the state or locale in which it is located. The principal point here is the interactive phenomenon; the new social model may affect its social surroundings and in turn the external social processes may affect the social model and affect outcomes.

What follows is a selected list of potential external social process variables to be monitored in the context of a longitudinal experiment. This is particularly important when one considers the replicability of a particular social model.

Social climate of the society

It is abundantly clear that the social mood of a nation, state, or community can fluctuate over a period of time. A number of dimensions are involved here such as liberalism-conservatism, optimism-pessimism, etc. Social models which are particularly sensitive to fluctuations in public mood may display changes in outcome success. Thus, during the course of an experiment, some indicators of social climate broadly construed should be measured. For example, the conservatism-liberalism of electoral results in a given locale, state, or region is often a good index of something akin to social climate. Systematic data gathering from media sources is also a possibility.

General socio-economic indicators

Some social models are particularly sensitive to fluctuations in the state of the economy. This may be particularly true of those programs that involve finding employment for certain clientele. Since these variables are often fluctuating over the course of a longitudinal experiment, they should be monitored and evaluated with respect to social system outcomes. Sources for such data often include the United States Department of Labor and other regional economic data-gathering organizations. A plethora of possible indicators would include some obvious ones such as: rate of unemployment, consumer optimism, interest rates, etc., In times of depression very few new programs are permitted, whereas in times of affluence it is much more likely that new social models will be underwritten provided the social climate is supportive. Outcomes can be greatly affected by economic conditions of affluence or depression. An outcome measure of employment, for example, would clearly be different in good times and in bad.

Specific socioeconomic indicators

Some social models may be particularly influenced by the immediate socioeconomic surroundings of their location. This can be particularly true about programs of a residential nature. Thus, if the social model is implanted in a certain neighborhood, it is extremely important to describe the social and economic aspects of that neighborhood and to determine their effect upon the social model itself. An excellent example of this is the difficulties that have been encountered in the creation of halfway houses for mental patients. Often when they have been implanted in middle-class and upper middle-class neighborhoods there is a very high probability of rejection, whereas when they are implanted in lower class neighborhoods there is a high probability that they will not be excised from the community. This simple example indicates that the social and economic conditions existing in the area of implant have a great deal to do with the success or failure of the social model.

Measurement obtrusiveness

No social model can be evaluated without the systematic gathering of data. Often this implies some involvement or intrusion into the ongoing social processes of the social model. Assessment techniques must be considered as an impingement upon the normal functioning of the social program since once the initial research is completed it is highly doubtful that all the assessment devices used during the evaluation of the prototype model will be used in future replications. Accordingly, the use of assessment techniques must be clearly documented and attempts must be made to measure their impact upon the social program.

Geographical location

This may or may not be an important factor in the implementation of a social model. In some cases it could have a significant effect upon it. For example, social models requiring racial integration might have different outcomes if implanted in geographic areas where racial strife is minimal contrasted with areas where racial strife is widespread. Geographic location can have other effects. For example, an urban or rural area may be better or worse for the location of a social model depending upon its function and use.

Folkways and mores of the institution or community

These will affect any social model that is implanted in an institution or in a local community. If the social model is perceived as violating the norms of the institution or of the community, there is a high probability that it will be expelled. For this reason, the mores and folkways of the locale in which the implant is made must be clearly understood and planned for in the social model-building process.

Publicity and media exposure

One everpresent component of contemporary life is the information transmitted to us by media sources such as TV, newspapers, or radio. If not affecting our norms and values, such information at least has some temporary effect on certain attitudes or perceptions. This may have particular relevance to the success or failure of a social model. Thus, for example, when there is media publicity about a social model this may affect the public's receptivity of the program. More often neglected is the fact that such publicity may affect the clients and staffs of the social model. There is a relatively reliable phenomenon which might easily be described as the "pilot program" syndrome. This refers to the often found fact that new programs that are accompanied by considerable publicity and acclaim often succeed, while unpublicized replicates do not. The social model evaluators should be particularly aware of the dangers and possible implications of media exposure. During a longitudinal experiment, the researchers should record either systematically or observationally media references to the social model being evaluated or to the raising of consciousness about the problem in general. An attempt to determine the effect of this information transmittal should be carried out.

Relationship to other community organizations

Another important aspect of external social processes is the relationship of the social model to other community organizations. In a world of scarce resources the relationship between too many programs is one of partial dependency. Thus, even an experimental social model will be involved in some transactions with other social agencies. In turn, the nature of this relationship may change over the course of the research. To the extent possible, this should be documented and data gathered to analyze its effect on social model outcomes. For example, most social programs are dependent to some extent on referrals external to the system. This may include referrals from other agencies, self-referrals, etc. To the extent that interorganizational relations are jeopardized, the mixture of clientele may change.

Part of the general problem of interorganizational relations resides in the possibility that there may be contact among persons participating in different experimental social models when there is more than one social model being evaluated at a given time. This interaction should be recorded and evaluated in the context of the design.

Legal constraints

This is to some degree a subspecies of the geographic location variable. One should be cognizant of legal constraints that impinge on the establishment and continuous operation of a social model. Thus, over time and between locations, differences may emerge between zoning practices, bonding regulations, contractual agreements, etc. To the extent that these can be feasibly related to social model outcome they should be evaluated empirically.

Time

Since all social phenomena vary with time, this is an important major variable that interacts with all other social process variables. Differences of many types—socioeconomic level, size of population, political power, and the like—are different at different moments in time. For this reason, time itself must be accounted for in any social experiment.

The last few pages have presented a discussion of a number of social situational variables that can affect outcomes. Table 3.3 provides a summary description of the different categories of social situational variables which have been presented in this section. At the beginning of this chapter, the basic proposition was made that the outcomes of the created social models will be affected by the characteristics of the persons who participate in them and the internal and external social processes operative in and outside the model itself. Therefore, the three attributes of any social model which should be clearly defined, described, and measured are those of its participants, the social situation in which the social model operates, and the outcome criterion on which it is evaluated. The degree to which any social model can be replicated depends upon the degree to which these dimensions are clearly defined and measured. In addition, the value to society of any social model depends upon the degree to which the outcome criterion upon which it is evaluated represents a consensual solution to a pressing social problem. Procedures for making social models comparable on the social situation dimension can be found in Chapter 7. Measurement of the internal and external processes is presented in Chapter 9.

TABLE 3.3
Social Situational Variables

Internal	External
Organizational Components	Social climate
Hierarchical structure	Socioeconomic indicators (general and specific)
Size	Measurement objectiveness
Complexity	
Formality/Informality	Geographical location
Group Dynamics	Folkways and mores
Cohesiveness	Publicity and media exposure
Norms	Relationship to other organizations
Leadership	Legal constraints
Composition	Time
Morale	
Reinforcement	
Fiscal Processes	
Income	
Costs	
Rate of pay	
Bookkeeping	
Membership	
Voluntary/Involuntary	
Turnover	

DISSEMINATION

Anyone who is involved in social program research and development, and who has an active fantasy life, has likely imagined the following scenario: You develop a social model that theoretically solves the selected problems; your data from an empirical model-building experiment yield outcomes in favor of the model at a probability level of .001, which indicates that it is a very beneficial program; agencies from all over the country begin to besiege you with requests for help in establishing replicates in their own setting; in a brief period of time the program that you have developed has ameliorated to a significant degree the social problem it was designed to address. This fantasy, of course, is without any basis in reality whatsoever simply because the process of change does not proceed in such a rational, spontaneous way. For this reason, the special problems relating to the dynamics of the dissemination of innovations become the foremost concern of the social innovative experimentalist who is interested in the social utility of a beneficial innovation.

The Failure of Dissemination

The best analogue to the process of social innovation in this country is that of a very expensive series of shops all inventing the same wagon-wheel over and over again. Many "new" social innovations are not new. A number of imaginative programs that one hears about have been tried before, found worthwhile in many cases, yet eventually faded from the scene because of a failure to disseminate them. Some examples are instructive. During the 1800s, one of the most significant programs in treating the mentally ill was known as moral treatment. This involved a treatment of patients that focused on tangible tasks, cooperation with the family, participation of the patient in real-life activities, and the like. Needless to say, many of the features of moral treatment are quite similar to aspects of the focus on community treatment in mental health during the past decade. It is also interesting to point out that the results of this early program were highly encouraging. Yet this type of treatment failed to become fully implemented on a nationwide scale, and was eventually replaced by a medically dominated system of incarceration and questionable somatic or physical treatments. In another context, it is interesting to note that the recent growth of methadone maintenance programs for drug treatment is not without precedent. From 1919 to 1921, clinics were established in this country in which maintenance dosages of morphine were given to registered opium addicts. While no data are available, some descriptive reports are at least partially favorable (Ives, 1974). Needless to say, this type of innovative treatment was not continued, although it has eventually reemerged in another form in the English drug-treatment system, and it was the precursor of the methadone maintenance programs in this country. A similar situation is observed with the halfway house movement. This type of residential facility was initiated during the late 19th and early 20th century but it did not obtain a high degree of utilization until the past ten or 15 years (Keller & Alper, 1970). Once again, the dissemination of a social innovation was not particularly contingent upon either its effectiveness or its promise.

The lack of systematic adoption of new innovations is not exclusively the province of the public sector. For example, in the American automobile industry one major innovation, the V-8 engine, was initially adopted by

Chevrolet in 1919, discarded one year later, eventually picked up by the Ford Motor Company some 13 years later, but not fully adopted by the industry at large until 20 to 30 years following that. Another example that has clear relevance to the present environmental situation is an early version of the stratified charge automobile engine which was reasonably pollution free. Needless to say, this early low pollution engine has yet to be adopted by the major automobile manufacturers (Gunn, 1973). In order to obtain an appreciation of the extent to which most innovations regardless of their outcomes remain unavailable to the public, one need only note the following quote from a report by NASA—an agency which was involved in its own major dissemination effort developed in the context of the space program:

> Of the 21,000 companies which NASA thought could use the inventions, 30 companies or 0.15% had adopted or seemed to have a good prognosis for adoption. Of the 3,100 companies from the preceding 21,000 which had agreed with NASA that the invention did sound relevant, 1% were in this adopted or likely to adopt group of 30, and of those 550 companies which on further investigation with NASA did not drop out of contact or say 'No', only 5.5% ended in the final favorable group of 30 who had adopted or seemed to have a good prognosis for adoption. (Wright, 1966)

It is experiences such as these that support the notion that a plan for an intentional and experimental progam of dissemination is a necessary second phase to social model comparison experiments. *Many, if not most, social innovations will never reach a widespread degree of adoption, regardless of demonstrated success, and often disappear after their initial piloting and development.* One of the basic arguments for an intentional dissemination research program stems from the simple fact that most social innovations never become adopted. From the above discussion, it can be seen that there is an incredible potential for wasted motion in the program development area. There are too many lonely "innovators" reinventing the wheel.

Toward an Understanding of the Dissemination Process

Aside from making sure that dissemination occurs, there is another problem that is relevant: "quality control." An intentional effort must be made to insure that the most effective innovations receive priority in any dissemination effort. For at least two reasons, dissemination activity should be tied directly to a program of experimental innovation development.

First, program development efforts must have a dissemination component tied directly to them in order to achieve continuity in the selection of the innovation to be disseminated. Since the experimentalists who have developed and evaluated the innovation have a stake in seeing to it that *only programs that are evaluated as beneficial are used in the dissemination process*, the social model experimenters themselves should be directly linked to a process of program implementation so that a degree of control over total social programming can be insured. This will enable a selectivity in terms of which innovations are disseminated.

A second aspect of control is relevant here. If different groups do the dissemination and the initial program development, the *replicates* of the program may fail to reach the initial outcomes shown by the prototype model. This is particularly true with complex social innovations which include many parameters—all the parameters must be specified, in many cases new roles must be established, and all this information must be included in a total knowledge package in order for replication to occur. For example, recent experience in compensatory education has indicated that replications are difficult to develop, and most successful programs in terms of their replicability are those in which all procedures, processes, and practices are cogently specified (Hawkridge *et al.*, 1968). The researchers who painstakingly developed the social innovation in the first instance are the only persons with sufficient knowledge from their own experiences to adequately describe and activate the new social model. Therefore, it is clearly incumbent upon the initial program development researchers to spend whatever time is required in either direct dissemination activities or in the packaging of the innovation in such a manner that adequate dissemination can proceed.

A Research Tradition in Dissemination

Space does not permit a complete review of the literature of the dissemination process. But it seems important to acquaint the reader with what appears to be the two most complete sources in this area, and to present a short summary of what each of these reference works contributes to our initial understanding of the process. Before doing so we will attempt to describe the general nature of the existing literature. While on the one hand the province of dissemination literature encompasses all social science (since it is argued that anything dealing with changing someone in order to do something different is applicable), the directly relevant literature is more limited. Looking at this literature, one is immediately made aware of the general dearth of *experimental* data in the field. Most of the concepts and generalizations from them that have been developed to describe dissemination activity have, at best, only marginal empirical support. The usual research techniques used in dissemination are the case study and survey. The deficiencies of these approaches for making inferences with confidence have been outlined in Chapter 2. In a sense the dissemination literature itself is a good argument for the need to conduct dissemination experiments. Since little is known, we must develop experimental programs to identify and evaluate the relevant parameters. With an understanding of this lack of experimental data in mind, we present the following categorizations.

The communication model of Rogers

(Rogers, 1962; Rogers & Shoemaker, 1971). Rogers is clearly one of the most prolific and encyclopedic writers in the diffusion of innovation area. The tradition from which he emerges is the agricultural extension model, with much of his own research, and research that he reviews emanating from problems dealing with the dissemination of farm practices. Generally the research within this tradition has focused on the *post hoc* tracing of the process of how new products have become adopted. There is a great deal of emphasis on communication patterns—who talks to whom, what modes of communication are used, what communication practices are relevant at a given stage in the diffusion process, etc. Reflecting the background in international agricultural diffusion, there is a strong concern for such issues as disparity in cultural background, cosmopoliteness, and disparity in norms and values between the change agent and the target of change. One of the most significant aspects of this research literature is that it does place an explicit focus on *change* and the role of the change agent. One of the difficulties is that Rogers develops well over one hundred "generalizations" which range in utility from the mundane to the abstract and have a corresponding degree of empirical support ranging from none to some.

Some of the do's and don'ts emanating from the works of Rogers and Shoemaker are instructive. They argue that the dissemination process proceeds through stages of knowledge, persuasion, decision about adoption, confirmation, and ultimate adoption. They present evidence to indicate that highly educated cosmopolitan individuals are more likely to be early adopters than late adopters and to point out the necessity for involving subordinates in the decision to adopt when the target of change is an organization.

One of the major difficulties of these "generalizations" is simply their large number. The process of distilling what Rogers and Shoemaker have presented is not complete since there is no relative weighting of the generalizations. Thus, their work does not translate immediately into specific dissemination tactics.

The dissemination review by Ronald Havelock

Havelock (1969) has provided what is perhaps the most comprehensive review of the dissemination process. Beginning with a basic systems approach to the problem, and a labeling of the principal actors in the process, Havelock reviews relevant aspects of individual psychology, interpersonal relations, and organizational parameters related to dissemination. He further delves into different conceptualizations of the change agents, or their equivalent, and discusses the utilization of different communication modalities and processes. As a way of summing up the vast amount of literature that he reviews, Havelock presents two major contributions to the literature. First, he categorizes what has been done in dissemination into three perspectives on the process. Secondly, he describes seven factors which he believes account for most dissemination utilization phenomena.

Regarding the three perspectives on change dissemination phenomena, one of the "perspectives" is that of "Social Interaction." This is essentially a category applied to the work of Rogers & Shoemaker (1971) just described. A second perspective Havelock calls the "RD&D" approach. This model is essentially a descriptive, and prescriptive, model of how science should proceed from basic research through applied research to diffusion and adoption. As a body of literature, it is most descriptive, and the processes that it describes assume rational behavior by the participants. Thus, it is assumed that each useful product at each stage in the process from basic research through applied product development will result in nearly automatic acceptance by the participants or the actors in the next stage, so that making people aware of research findings and new products is assumed to be sufficient to produce further utilization. Havelock's third perspective is the "problem-solver perspective," which is roughly equivalent to the planned change school expressed by Lippet, Watson, & Westley (1958), Bennis, Benne, & Chin (1969), and others. This approach to the change process emanated from work in the late 1930s and early 1940s at the National Training Laboratories, and is basically a method focused on change in an organizational context. There is emphasis on interpersonal interaction with a resultant use of T-group techniques, interpersonal confrontation, and related tactics. The change agent's role in this scheme is construed to be considerably less active in terms of promoting specific innovations than the change agent's role in the RD&D perspective. For example, the problem-solver perspective depends on client initiative in the change process with the assumption being that the target of change must seek out alternative programs and not be provided them by a change agent.

In addition to the perspectives just described (RD&D, Social Interactions, and Problem Solver), Havelock also points to several factors that need to be accounted for in any dissemination effort. They are: Linkage, Structure,

Openness, Capacity, Reward, Proximity, and Synergy. *Linkage* is seen as a factor signifying the degree of interconnectedness between participants and the dissemination process. The greater this degree of interconnectedness, the more likely there is to be a successful dissemination. Thus, users of innovations must be linked to resources for innovations. In turn the innovation disseminator must have a *Structure*, and a logical sequence of steps for implementation, and the user must similarly be structured to receive the dissemination knowledge. A message must be coherent and understandable and a structured program for getting messages across must be present. *Openness* is a motivational component ascribed to different units and elements within the total dissemination scheme. Thus, there must be a readiness to give and receive information, to help, to teach, and to transmit knowledge. Since the transmission and receipt of knowledge and the general activity related to dissemination involves the use of resources, the term *Capacity* describes the possession of resources. Thus, the more people, power, and money that both resource and user systems have, the greater the likelihood that dissemination will occur. Havelock developed the notion of *Reward* to highlight the fact that dissemination activities tend to be reinforcing events for user and resource systems. The sixth factor is *Proximity*. The point he makes here is that physical and psychological adjacencies seem to be predictive of greater dissemination success. Factor seven is *Synergy*. Synergy is in many ways a conceptual catchall to convey the fact that combinations of the above factors, or redundancy, seem to produce greater results than each factor taken separately.

The Necessity for Experimental
Evaluation of Dissemination Approaches

The sense of incompleteness conveyed by the above brief review of the literature is probably accurate. As mentioned in our introductory comments, the dissemination literature is widespread, but is essentially not developed into a systematic and clear set of precise variables related to specific tactics for change. Although some efforts have been made in this direction—specifically Havelock's (1973) guidelines for innovation—much remains to be done. From our vantage point, *what particularly needs to be done is a systematic comparative experimental evaluation of alternative approaches that occur during the various stages of the dissemination process.* Thus, one must not only have a valid product to disseminate, one must also create and carry out an experiment about the dissemination effort. This is necessary not only to find the factors that affect the dissemination but also to advance the art and science of dissemination.

Basically it seems clear that the change process should be conceptualized in stages or phases. We have found it useful to categorize the adoption process into four action phases. They are (1) approaching, (2) persuading, (3) activating, and (4) diffusing. Each of these four phases may be thought of as relatively independent subexperiments of a general implementation experiment. Each may be affected by some combination of the concepts of linkage, openness, etc., just mentioned. And these concepts can, in turn, be operationally defined in terms of the participant and social situational variables presented in Tables 3.2 and 3.3. Considering openness, the readiness to transmit knowledge in an organization is affected by the persons who are contacted by the change agent (whether they are persons with open or closed minds), the group dynamics of the organization (highly cohesive groups may deny the agent entry or may band together to promote admittance), the hierarchical structure of the organization (face-to-face decision making or bureaucratic hand-downs), and the social climate of the society (a state of change may or may not exist). These may be only some of the participant and internal and external social processes that affect organizational openness. But this example should make it clear that the functional relationship that holds for social model-building outcomes also is applicable to the implementation effort.

The generic paradigm that expresses this relationship is the following: *The outcome of any implementation effort is a function of the participant and social situational variables operative in the approaching, persuading, activating, and diffusing phases.* Thus participant and social situational variables presented in Tables 3.2 and 3.3 also need to be considered in each of the four phases of the implementation process. Figure 3.1 elaborates this paradigm.

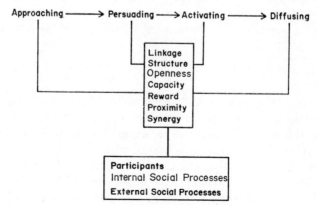

Fig. 3.1. The implementation paradigm

Outcome

As in social model-building experiments, there are many outcomes of a dissemination experiment. But the *social change outcome criterion* of any dissemination effort is the number of beneficial social models that have been adopted by different individuals or organizations from the population of individuals or organizations that might adopt the innovation. As with the social change outcome criterion for social models, the implementation outcome is a simple behavioral measure.

Approaching

Much dissemination activity stops before it even begins. One glaring deficit in the dissemination literature is answers to the basic question of how to make initial contacts with target organizations, people, or units. Thus, such basic questions as modality of approach, who to approach, intensity of approach, and their interrelations all need to be systematically explored through experiments.

Persuading

There seems to be a consensus in the literature that before the target unit can make a verbal decision to adopt an innovation, there must occur a process of cajolery, "unfreezing," coercion, accompanied by reinforcement. Some process must occur which bring the clients or users from the point of initial awareness of an innovation to the point where they have decided, at least verbally, to integrate it into their own system. To these processes, we have given the term "persuading." The general research here involves comparing experimentally different persuasion techniques. For example, at a *strategic* level one can compare different approaches to change—i.e., a strategy of economic reinforcement versus a strategy of interpersonal discussion.

Activating

At some point, the unit being changed will make a commitment to proceed from a symbolic level of change activity to a "real" area of activity. Once persuaded, the user must proceed to action. To this process of translating verbal acceptance into the actual physical adoption, we have given the term "activating." This opens the door to an area of research directed toward the following basic question: What are the important variables related to activating? Similar to the previous section, we could compare alternative strategies of affecting adoption. In addition to the comparative evaluation of process variables the researchers also should consider the comparative manipulation of resource variables of other kinds. For example, how could one systematically change staffing patterns or user organizations to facilitate the adoption process? Could the creation of innovation adoption units in large bureaucracies facilitate adoptions of specific innovations? If one were in a position to do so, the amount of financial resources which units had could be varied to see if this had any effect on innovation adoption activity.

Diffusing

It is generally conceded in the dissemination literature that at some time during the change process further adoption of an innovation becomes essentially independent of explicit intentional change agent activity. Thus, when a critical mass of adopters has been attained, subsequent adoption by others will proceed without appreciable change agent activity. In short, a "fad" effect will manifest itself. To this process of unplanned dissemination, we have given the term "diffusing." A fascinating approach to this fad problem might be the attempt to experimentally manipulate and enhance its occurrence. The question becomes: What variables could potentially be manipulated to enhance these spontaneous effects?

While it is important to recognize that each social model found to be beneficial through evaluative research should be disseminated through a separate research effort, it is equally important to recognize that even the most successful dissemination experiment will leave a large number of nonadopting units. For this reason, the dissemination effort may involve further experimentation with these "residuals." Thus, the experimental disseminators may wish to "recycle" those persons or organizations that did not adopt in the first dissemination experiment because they did not participate in the most effective experimental conditions. This "recycling" process will undoubtedly still leave a residual group of nonadopters. This group of hardcore nonadopters can itself be subjected to a second full-scale dissemination experiment using as yet untried conditions of approaching, persuading, activating, and diffusing so that the effects of these new conditions upon the laggards can be assessed. This process of experiment-recycling, and so on, can continue until the beneficial innovation is generally adopted or the experimenters decide further cost is not commensurate with the adoption payoff.

It should also be recognized that while dissemination experiments have a twofold purpose—to find the conditions for implementing a particular model and to expand knowledge about implementation—it is extremely unlikely that the time will come when such experiments will not be needed. Certainly, increasing knowledge will aid the experimenters in selecting the participant and social situational variables that may be most productive in implementing a particular model. But changing times may change the factors that affect outcomes in implementation research the same as they do outcomes in social model-building experiments. The variables that are important in implementing today may not be as important tomorrow. Furthermore, each social model has some unique characteristics that make its implementation somewhat different than every other model (mental health contrasted with educational models). For these reasons, implementation experiments may be as continuously necessary as are social model-building experiments.

In this chapter we have attempted to present a general schema of the parameters for social model and dissemination experiments. We have emphasized in both processes that behaviorally specific outcomes can be identified and measured and that they are a function of the participants and internal and external social process variables operative at that particular moment in time. We have also proposed that while the parameters of a social model may be perceived as a one-stage operation, the same is not true of implementation experiments. Here the process of implementation encompasses four interrelated but almost separate processes, which we have chosen to call approaching, persuading, activating, and diffusing. These four processes must be subject to experimentation during the course of a major effort at implementing the social models found to be beneficial. With an understanding of these basic parameters and research paradigms, we now turn to the first requirement for the experimental process—the identification of a significant social problem.

CHAPTER 4

Defining the Social Problem and Planning its Solution

At any moment there exists in every society a population of significant social problems whose solution is essential to the survival of that society. The greater the number of changing conditions within the society, the greater the number and severity of such problems. In 20th-century America there has been a recent and rapid expansion of unsolved social problems arising from continuously changing social conditions. Researchers concerned with social innovation relative to these problems must be particularly astute in defining them, since this is the first step in planning a solution.

In contemporary American society there is no lack of awareness about social problems. In fact the popular media for the past several years has deluged the public with elaborate scenarios about social problems. A good argument can be made that contemporary America is more aware of the complexities of its social problems than any nation in recorded history. However, from a scientific point of view, particularistic knowledge about them is lacking. The type of problem definition and understanding that is necessary for experimental social innovation involves knowledge about the many variables that could cause specific outcomes that are central to the social problem. From these variables, a few that seem to affect the problem directly will be chosen for experimental manipulation and evaluation. The major problem of the prisons and correctional system can serve as one example. While it is worthwhile and notable to understand all the intricacies of correctional systems, what might be most important to experimentalists at the present time is an appreciation that recidivism is a major problem that may be sharply reduced when post-release jobs are available to parolees. Thus, problem definition and understanding is a process in which a multitude of possible variables associated with a social problem are sifted through by the scientists and narrowed down to those few that are deemed most important and that can be tested comparatively in the context of a naturalistic experiment.

81

THE PROCESS OF PROBLEM DEFINITION

The scientist is popularly perceived as a person isolated in a laboratory wearing a white coat and working with animals, instruments, and gadgets. As an introduction to this section on problem definition, we would like to explore that perception, particularly as it applies to problem definition related to experimental social innovation. The role of social innovative scientists, as we envision it, involves a considerable return to earlier more naturalistic methods of gathering background information. In addition, the gathering of background information relative to problem definition should be one that is explicitly multidisciplinary. Social problems are simply too broad to be contained in disciplinary boxes.

Thus, experimental social innovators must use many sources of information in defining the problem under investigation. There is another reason why this must be done. Eventually researchers will have to formulate alternative solutions to the social problem under study. These alternative solutions must at least be acceptable to society at large and the problem population in particular. If researchers cannot attract sufficient social interest to establish even a modicum of social support, the problem usually cannot be experimentally investigated. Thus, experimental social innovators are often constrained by the limitations of maintaining what is tantamount to a "working majority" in support of possible solutions for social problems.

At some point, then, from the social problems that are important to society, the researchers select the one problem which seems most interesting and which at the same time appears amenable to experimental test. It is then incumbent upon the researchers to define and understand the problem from a scientific perspective. To accomplish this, knowledge of the social problem is sought primarily from four sources—(1) observations and experiences with problems in the social context in which they occur, (2) historical development of the problem as revealed in the theoretical and technical literature, (3) exposure to the direct experiences and ideas of peers involved in the problem area, and (4) the researchers' own past experiments when they are pertinent to problem solution.

Observation of social processes in naturalistic social settings where one experiences their effect is probably the single most important factor in accumulating the information that is essential for problem selection. It is also the one source of information most frequently lacking in the experimenters' training. Little time in formal education is usually devoted to simply observing social processes as they actually occur in the society. Youthful experimenters typically come to the social innovative research setting with an extensive background in the theoretical propositions of their major discipline, knowledge of experimental design, and common statistical methods. They usually have little, if any, day-to-day living experience with a social problem that might be under consideration. Our society's policy of involving its children, from infancy to young adulthood, in formal educational activities divorced from real-world contact no doubt contributes to this problem. Nonetheless, observational experience is an especially important ingredient in selecting problems for experiments in social innovation. Social problems are by their nature multidisciplinary and therefore no single academic discipline can adequately provide its students with a thorough understanding of them. For this reason, there are no well-developed multidisciplinary theoretical models. More often than not at this early stage of the development of cross-disciplinary theory, social problem definition and the subsequent experiments are, by default, mainly empirical in nature.

This embryonic state of theoretical thought makes it exceedingly important to accumulate a body of knowledge through accurate observations and descriptions of the relevant social phenomena. For example, researchers who wish to become involved in the educational problems of delinquent children should spend a good deal of time observing the behavior of such children in their homes, at school, and at play; they should become acquainted with these children, their parents, their siblings, their goals, their socioeconomic status, their health problems, the area in which they reside, the role society has prescribed for them, and other related information. It is necessary to understand and have some insight into these children's perceptions of themselves, others, and their environment before meaningful hypotheses which will result in practical changes for improving their general education can be formulated.

As another example, researchers concerned about the problems of black persons should spend a great deal of time living in their situation before formulating theories about them. Life in black communities is frequently unknown through daily experience to many of those who propose programs to alleviate the conditions of individuals residing in these segregated areas. Many proposals emanating from these nonparticipant observers fail to meet the perceived needs of the residents of these areas and therefore their cooperation is usually not forthcoming.

No program, whatever its merits, can be a realistic solution to such social problems without the cooperation of those for whom the solution is designed. Not only must the residents of such areas participate in and be an integral part of the research from the outset, but the researchers must share their perceptions and, at the very least, have an empathic awareness of their problems. It is only by direct observation and experience that an accurate picture of the individuals and the social variables affecting them can be adequately ascertained. This is equally true in understanding prisoners, the mentally ill, the physically handicapped, delinquents, or racial and ethnic groups.

Although emphasizing the need for naturalistic observations and experiences, the value that an exhaustive review of the technical literature can have in selecting the social problem for investigation should not be minimized. The review should include literature from every discipline that might contribute to an understanding of the problem. The technical literature can provide meaningful background information. It can be divided into two generic categories: the *problem-focused* literature and that devoted to the discussion of *theory*. These two categories of literature must be incorporated into a single approach aimed at identifying the variables that need to be considered in problem solution. An example from family planning may serve to clarify this amalgamation. The problem-oriented literature generally emanates from the publications of the medical demographers, religious organizations, law books and journals, and other persons and groups having an interest in the problem itself. Examples of this type of literature would include information about contraceptive devices, available health services, the concern of religious groups, and so on.

In addition, there are the various theoretical articles that usually are written for scientific journals. Most of this information can be found in journals of the involved academic disciplines, written by various theoretically inclined authors. Recognizing that the theoretical literature is traditionally written from a *single* disciplinary perspective, the experimental social innovator tries to abstract from the review those variables that are believed to be related to the particular problem at hand. Since there are at the current time few if any meaningful multidisciplinary theories, this integrative job falls by default into the hands of the experimental problem solver. Carrying forward the example about family planning, the pertinent literature might include such disparate areas as decision theory, operant conditioning, social stratification, dissonance theory, and so on.

This task of surveying existing literature may seem monumental, but in recent years several aids in these services have developed to make the process of a literature search considerably easier. For example, a number of federal agencies have established computerized clearing houses on topics related to certain problem areas. Thus, the ERIC system in education catalogs program information in research relative to the educational area. Similar clearing house services are offered by the National Institute of Mental Health, in which computerized literature searches can be obtained for a variety of areas even when they are only tangentially related to mental health, and by the

American Psychological Association. The experimental social innovative researcher has a wide variety of source aids to develop a fairly comprehensive literature review relative to a particular social problem.

Beyond the literature review and direct observations innovative scientists should search out professional persons who have had a lifetime of experience in dealing with the particular problem. Considering juvenile delinquency as an example, interested researchers might discuss the problem with police officers, parole officers, court officials, psychologists, and criminologists who work with delinquents. These persons have accumulated a wealth of information, often of an unrefined nature, that may have particular relevance in the planning of a solution to that social problem. The same is true with other social problems. This source of information is often untapped in classical research, but the ideas and thoughts of persons with extensive experience can contribute a great deal to problem solution.

In addition to obtaining information from "applied" professionals, researchers should try to get feedback on their germinating ideas from scientific colleagues. As the problem definition and solution become more articulated, it is mandatory that the researchers obtain a critical review from professionals in the field and from other researchers.

The fourth source of background information in designing a social innovative experiment is preparatory research done by the experimentalists. Often, as a result of exploring the information sources described above, researchers may have narrowed down the variables to a relative few. But before embarking on a fairly expensive and laborious longitudinal experiment, they might want to gain further information about which of these variables seems to be the most important for resolution of the problem under consideration. What may be involved at this point is some preliminary survey research, or an organized field situation might be designed to address itself to very specific issues relative to the design of the longitudinal experiment. An example can be drawn from the earlier work of Fairweather and his associates in their initial and growing conviction that autonomous functioning of groups of mental patients was an important social condition for group problem solving. They were also aware that such autonomy would have to be tied to recognized acceptable rewards if it were to have meaning to the patient groups. Prior to establishing the final design of what was to become an experiment in patient-led group decision making, the experimenters established a short-term program on a hospital ward where patient groups took care of their members under conditions of increasing monetary reward for improved group responsibility as shown in performance. This short-term controlled observational situation led the researchers to the conclusion that these two variables, when properly related (increased reward tied to increased group responsibility as shown in behavioral performance), were important variables that needed to be incorporated into any social system designed to achieve autonomous group functioning.

These four sources of information—field observations and experiences, review of the literature, discussion of the problem with scientists and others with relevant experience, and personal research—serve as background material for the selection of a research problem. Not only does such information aid the experimenters in problem selection, it also illuminates the whole of the problem. It is a truism that individuals must distill from their experiences, observations, readings, and discussions those variables that are most important in contributing to particular problems. The insight into the role of these key variables in solving the problems results in the formulation of meaningful hypotheses which can be subjected to experimental test through the creation of new social models.

But the identification of the problem's important variables is not the only use for the knowledge gained in the problem-selection period, for inferences from the results of any subsequent experiment will be only as valid as the experimenters' knowledge of the problem. The information gained in exploring the problem will serve, in the future, as the background material for making inferences from any experiment conducted.

This problem-selection process will probably reveal several important social problems that need to be subjected to experimentation. In selecting the one problem to be investigated, researchers are strongly influenced by their own interests. For despite the global nature of social problems and their general interest to every researcher concerned about the society, the selection of a particular problem requires such an investment in time and energy—usually of several years' span—that a great deal of consideration must be given to the long-term interest the problem has for the investigators. Thus, the experimentalists' interest must be one of the most important factors in finally determining the choice of a problem.

Observations, experiences, readings, and discussions appropriately precede every experiment in social innovation, but they are most valuable as an aid in selecting the first problem to be investigated. Once the first research has been completed, the choice of a new investigable hypothesis usually emerges as a direct result of the information gained from it. The longitudinal nature of social innovative research and the mass of data collected present the researchers with information not available from any other source. Accordingly, the completion of the first research is usually the clue to the second, the second to the third, and so forth.

Integrating all the aforementioned sources of information and considering their personal interests, the researchers tentatively select a problem and attempt to conceptualize different social models that might have a high probability of solving it. Each conceptualized model is thought of as a total social organization, clearly defining the rights and obligations of its members, able to be meshed into society without instigating such social upheaval that society automatically rejects it.

In order to provide the most adequate test of new models, it is necessary to utilize existing social practice as a baseline comparison program. This is not only logically necessary because institutionalized practices should not be changed if they cannot be improved, but it also increases the probability of gradualness in change—a situation most socially desirable. In the examples to follow, therefore, the first social model in each paradigm is that currently established as the usual social practice.

THE CONCEPTUAL PROCESS OF
CREATING PROBLEM SOLVING MODELS

Once the background information concerning a social problem has been obtained, it then becomes necessary to synthesize from it the key variables that need to be manipulated and to generate from this residual pool the ingredients of a social model designed to solve the problem. In this section we will present some selected examples of the logical process through which the research team must go in order to conceptually create models that can then be actually developed and implanted in the naturalistic setting for comparison. Models can, of course, be simple or complex, depending to a large extent upon the number of variables with which they are concerned. Thus, a simple model might be one in which a single variable is comparatively evaluated in a longitudinal experiment in contrast to a complex model in which several variables would be compared.

Simple Models

As an example of an important social problem where controlled experiments are clearly needed, let us turn to the field of education. Many pressing problems are amenable to experimental social innovation, such as the following: (1) What are the most appropriate teaching methods for different student groups? (2) How can racial integration best be accomplished? (3) How can adult illiteracy be reduced? (4) What is the most appropriate high school curriculum to educate the future citizen? (5) Do independent study programs, such as honor programs, help or hinder the social, personal, and intellectual development of students? (6) What are the effects of various kinds of technical and liberal arts training upon the personality, achievement, and humanitarian values of the student? (7) What are the effects of such traditional programs as school guidance upon the personality, achievement, and humanitarian values of the student? (8) What are the results of introducing schooling before six years of age upon the individual and the society? Let us take an example where controversy is continuous—the advantages and disadvantages of grouping children in classes according to their ability. Leading authorities do not agree on the merits of such a division (Conant, 1959; Katz, 1964). Logically this breaks down into an evaluation of the effect of a single, simply operationalized variable: homogeneity-heterogeneity of classrooms. Example 1 presents a simple comparison of two different compositions of student groups that might yield some direct empirical evidence useful for the resolution of this disagreement.

Example 1. Social models comparing the effect of group composition upon the academic achievement and social adjustment of students.
   Model 1. Heterogeneous groupings of students.
   Model 2. Homogeneous groupings of students.

Another example of a simple one-variable social model comparison may be illustrated in the field of drug addiction. Here many maintain that one of the major problems contributing to drug abuse is widespread socialization of children by the media into early habits of drug usage. Many different educational schemes have been proposed to counteract this influence, virtually all without being empirically tested. This, too, yields to a simple experimental test. Thus, a particular drug education program could be introduced in selected classes (third and fourth grades, for example) while students in other classes (also third and fourth grades) would not receive the drug education program. If appropriate sampling and experimental procedures were followed, the value of such educational procedures upon drug consumption could be ascertained. This example presents another simple one-variable experiment.

Example 2. Models comparing the effectiveness of drug education programs.
   Model 1. Drug education of grade school children.
   Model 2. No drug education of grade school children.

Complex Models

Let us first take an example from the prisons. Recent studies show that two of the most important problems are those of chronic institutional residence and recidivism (Fairweather, 1964, p. 3; State of California, 1965, pp. 90–94). These studies reveal that the highest rate of recidivism with prisoners occurs among those individuals who have been institutionalized for the longest time or those who have had the most releases. The researcher now conceptualizes different models that might alleviate the high rate of return to those total institutions. Arbitrarily selecting prison recidivism as the example, and without a detailed exploration of the variables which must be controlled and of other experimental necessities which are presented in subsequent chapters, the models presented in Example 3 might be suggested for comparison. Each of these six models attempts to explore the effects upon recidivism of *two* variables—namely, time in prison and the nature of the extramural situation. Thus, the two variables manipulated in Example 3 are the amount of time in prison and the community situation to which the ex-prisoner returns.

Example 3. Social models for reducing institutional recidivism for criminals.
Model 1.   Usual time in a selected prison program and return to the
(Control)   community through the usual methods—parole officer, etc.
Model 2.   Usual time in a selected prison program and return to a work situation where meaningful jobs have been established for the ex-prisoner in an industrial setting.
Model 3.   Usual time in a selected prison program and return to a peer group subsociety of ex-prisoners where a living situation combined with the operation of a business is provided.
Model 4.   Minimum time in a selected prison program and return to the community through the usual methods—parole officer, etc.
Model 5.   Minimum time in a selected prison program and return to a work situation where meaningful jobs have been established for the ex-prisoner in an industrial setting.
Model 6.   Minimum time in a selected prison program and return to a peer group subsociety of ex-prisoners where a living situation combined with the operation of a business is provided.

The plight of children who are unable to cope with the usual social demands of their age group can be taken as another example of a pressing social problem. Some of these children can be classified as neurotic or psychotic, others as delinquent, some as socially disadvantaged, and still others as mentally retarded. Parents and schools are frequently unable to establish a consistently meaningful program resulting in socially acceptable behavior and academic achievement for such children. Assuming appropriate sampling, design, and statistical techniques, Example 4 presents different social models which could be compared for their effects upon changing behaviors and perceptions. One should recognize that these programs are initially broad in order to maximize the possibility for differences to appear. When such differences do appear, further studies can define more precisely those variables contributing the most to the differences discovered in the broader studies. It should also be noticed that the three variables manipulated here which might affect social adjustment and education are the living situation, peer-group identification, and professional guidance.

Example 4. Social models for improving the academic achievement and social adjustment of problem children.

Model 1. Living at home and attending public school.
(Control)

Model 2. Living at home and attending special school.

Model 3. Living at home, attending special school, and receiving special professional help.

Model 4. Living at home only on weekends, with school group on week nights, and attending public school.

Model 5. Living at home only on weekends, with school group on week nights, and attending special school.

Model 6. Living at home only on weekends, with school group on week nights, attending special school, and receiving special professional help.

Model 7. Visiting home monthly, living the remainder of time with school peer group, and attending public school.

Model 8. Visiting home monthly, living the remainder of time with school peer group, and attending special school.

Model 9. Visiting home monthly, living the remainder of time with school peer group, attending special school, and receiving special professional help.

As another example of the use of controlled experiments in contributing to the solution of social problems, one might explore the possibility of training high school drop-outs to achieve their maximum social adjustment. Assuming appropriate experimental techniques, Example 5 presents eight different models for comparison. The social models involve different conditions of training and community living and working arrangements as the key variables to be manipulated.

Example 5. Social models for the training of school drop-outs to their highest level of achievement.

Model 1. No training and residing in the community.
(Control)

Model 2. Training in a center followed by release to the community with no special planning.

Model 3. Training in a center followed by placement in industrial jobs.

Model 4. Training in a center followed by a peer-group living situation and industrial job.

Model 5. Training in a center followed by a living situation where participants also operate a business.

Model 6. No training, with placement in industrial jobs.

Model 7. No training, but living in peer-group situation with industrial jobs.

Model 8. No training, but living situation where participants also operate a business.

It is possible, of course, to initiate more global experiments in real-life settings. Suppose, for example, that experimenters wished to take selected blocks in black communities and establish different social models as proposed solutions to problems. The most productive solutions as determined experimentally could then be carried out on a larger scale. Or, again, there is the possibility of sampling small communities in poverty-stricken areas and instituting different self-help social practices as community projects. Their effects could be compared before committing society to a course of social action. Some recent experiments have reached this level of magnitude. In a study of police operations, Kansas City (Kelling *et al.*, 1974) was divided into geographical sections which were assigned to various experimental conditions involving different types of police patrol. Similarly, a recent study of decentralized police operations in a large mid-western city (Green *et al.*, 1976) involved 24 census tracts which included over 75,000 people.

THE MODEL-BUILDING PROCESS

The two previous sections have shown the logic and conceptual processes involved in defining a social problem, gathering background information about it, and planning a social model solution. They do not, however, describe the actual processes that occur as the researcher moves through these stages and arranges the final models to be compared. It is now important to go through these processes at the work-a-day level of the researcher. Several examples are now presented.

The Health Users and Providers Experiment

One of the chronic problems of our society has been the unevenness of health care provided its citizens. As a partial answer to this problem, recent federal efforts have been made to provide comprehensive health planning at a community level. One feature of these programs has been their mandated requirement of majority involvement by health users.

In research by Beck (1973), her own observations, a detailed review of the literature, and discussions with health providers and users, suggested to her that the 51% participation of users in planning their own health programs as required by federal standards was not reality but fantasy. She arranged to "sit in on" monthly health planning sessions in order to ascertain the actual participation of users in health planning. She tape recorded the meetings and interviewed the participants (providers and users) in order to assess their relative involvement and participation in the planning. After one year of meticulously collecting data, Beck (1972) analyzed all of her information and completed tests of significance on the most important information collected in the study. She concluded on the issue of participation:

> The most basic feature of effective input into the decision-making process is participation in those meetings where binding decisions are made. Even if a structure is created to give recipients of such decisions 51 percent of the voting power in determining the decision, the right to vote must be exercised for the potential to become reality. Unfortunately the results revealed that such participation by consumers has been sadly lacking, leaving the voting as well as persuasion opportunities in meetings in the hands of the professionals.

And on power:

> The results on powerlessness were expected. They demonstrate a very acute power imbalance in the agency. This is most vividly demonstrated by the fact that there was general agreement between consumers and providers on the significant differences between their influence.

Her general conclusion was:

> Consumers began with some basic features of marginal status and even after formal and majority inclusion in the decision-making process of the agency still occupied a marginal status, which was operationally defined in terms of attendance and features of powerlessness, normlessness, and social isolation. Thus it may well be the responsibility of those seeking meaningful participation for these recipients of the decision-making process to stop these processes of non-involvement and reverse them if possible so that meaningful participation in a democratic society can occur and a position of power, task assignment, and social inclusion can be accorded to the consumers.

Because of these findings defining the problem, Beck set out upon a plan to establish a new social model in which the users of health services would be educated in health matters and trained as a group to support one another in matters of debate, attendance at meetings, and the like. Her intent here was to form a cohesive group of users which would provide mutual support in carrying out the goals of participation in health planning. She therefore set forth a research design in which as an experimental treatment she would create a cohesive group and compare its participation with a group that participated without benefit of an especially created peer support group. The principal outcomes, or dependent variables, would be measured in the actual meetings themselves where behavioral indices of participation could be obtained. The design of her problem solution, therefore, took the following form:

Model 1.   Autonomously trained consumer support group
Model 2.   Traditional participant group

The traditional participant model would have no systematic intervention into the health planning group's activities. They would continue whatever degree and style of participation they had become accustomed to in whatever activities were available to consumers in the agency. This usually consisted of one committee or Board of Trustees meeting monthly. They were usually notified of these in advance by mail with an RSVP card enclosed. No special measures were taken to insure their attendance. The only information they usually received was the standard packet of materials relating to matters on the next meeting agenda. These were generally copies of proposals to be acted upon but without any analytic explanation. They received no systematic help to encourage the quantity or legitimacy of their participation, either in the meeting conversation itself or in extra-meeting activities. Those who attended agency meetings generally arrived immediately before meetings, left immediately after, and did not meet or talk with other consumers or providers between meetings.

The autonomously trained consumer support model would be established in three major phases. In Phase I the staff coordinator would actively lead the group, transmitting health planning information and promoting the legitimacy of consumer participation in comprehensive health planning. The coordinator would also actively promote the development of an autonomous group by using a number of specific tactics. Meetings would be temporally spaced to allow for the group experience acquired in one meeting to be practiced between meetings and subsequently reinforced. The emphasis of the first two meetings would be on initiation of the program and group formation rather than health information. Group development was still important in the last two meetings of Phase I, but increased emphasis was given to task-related information. Throughout all Phase I meetings, the co-ordinator actively promoted the legitimacy of consumer participation where possible and reinforced conversation and behavior related to consumer legitimacy.

Phase II would generally follow a "developing autonomy" format in which the staff coordinator would assume the role of reactor rather than initiator. During this period, the members themselves would assume leader-ship of the group, develop their own mechanisms of group functioning, begin making contacts with relevant people outside of the group, generate informa-tion for themselves, and promote the legitimacy of their own participation as consumers and that of all the consumers in the agency.

Phase III would follow an "attained autonomy" format. The staff co-ordinator would withdraw completely from the group and the members would now operate as a self-sustaining autonomous group. In addition to functioning independently of project staff, the group also should display a strong cohesiveness, group identity, and awareness of the role of the group itself.

The generic hypothesis developed by Beck was that the autonomously trained consumer groups would show greater participation in the health planning meetings, greater cohesiveness and assertiveness contrasted with the traditional program, and would in large measure lose their concerns about social inequality fostered earlier by the providers of health services.

The Student Housing Problem

Another problem of considerable significance in university settings has been the changes of housing arrangements that have occurred over the past several years. Jacokes (1975), who had considerable experience in institu-tions of higher education, became interested in coeducational housing arrangements because of the controversial nature of this emerging practice. In reviewing the literature, Jacokes found many studies drawing different inferences about the effects of coeducational housing upon the activities of students. Through discussions with students, he found that they too had many different opinions about the value of housing arrangements. Most importantly, Jacokes found virtually *no* experiments in which the effects of different housing arrangements were comparatively evaluated. He therefore decided to establish different models of coeducational living arrangements and to compare their outcomes. He worked with a major university in estab-lishing three different models of living arrangements so that they could be systematically compared. They were:

Model 1.   The "traditional" segregated dormitories in which all males are in one dormitory and all females are in another dormitory with no sharing of facilities.

Model 2.   A wing-by-wing arrangement in which the males are housed in one wing and the females in another wing, sharing common eating and recreational facilities.

Model 3.   An arrangement of a floor of males on the same level and a floor of females, connected by a common entrance way.

His purpose was to evaluate experimentally the effects that coeducational living had on a wide variety of perceptions and behaviors by establishing these three social models which could then be compared on outcomes.

Architectural Planning Teams

Another exceedingly important study has been outlined and proposed by Goldsteen (1974). Drawing upon a technical background in architecture and social sciences, and his own professional work with planning agencies, he became concerned about creating a better social and physical environment in which people could raise their children. An extensive review of the literature from both an architectural, social, and personal perspective resulted in his arriving at the following conclusion:

> People are receiving too few choices in their physical environments. According to personality theories, there is a great impact of the immediate physical setting upon human behavior; and its importance is not adequately considered. Planners are acting to provide impetus to current entrepreneurial marketing decisions which are based upon past economic successes, rather than fully investigating the social implications of these physical patterns . . . In many local planning agencies the neighborhood planning team is being adopted—often quite unrelated to the structure of government and those cities which are governed as "federations of neighborhoods." This operational method may, indeed, have serious impact on residents of an area quite beyond the outcome of the quality of plans and their acceptance. As a means of continued resident interaction, planning team situations may do much to advance a longitudinal commitment to living by giving people chances to improve their physical environments. By using the tools of social science (a relatively unknown repertoire to the planner), the urban planner may be able to improve his decision-making and improve existing physical and social conditions, with benefits to both the structure of the planning process and to the well-being of the neighborhood (and city) residents.

In an attempt to discover the quality of neighorhood planning that would result from different mixes of planners and citizen participation in the planning of neighborhoods, he designed an experiment to compare the effects upon residents of "well-designed" and "poorly designed" neighborhoods. The type of planning team became the social model for the experiment. Six types were to be compared. They were:

Model 1.   Residential team, with no experts, from well-designed neighborhoods.

Model 2.   Residential team, with no experts, from poorly designed neighborhoods.

Model 3.   Mixed residential and expert team from well-designed neighborhoods.

Model 4.   Mixed residential and expert team from poorly designed neighborhoods.

Model 5.   Technical experts only on team from well-designed neighborhoods.

Model 6.   Technical experts only on team from poorly designed neighborhoods.

The purpose of this section has been to give the interested reader some idea of the use of information from observations, discussions, surveys, research, and the literature that goes into the creative plan of a new social model or models for problem solution. It is also important to reemphasize the creative and comprehensive nature of the problem definition and solution formulation process. We have proposed that many sources of information should be used in problem definition. Such a thorough search is essential in a scientific endeavor where many sources of information can contribute to an understanding of a social problem. To consider all available sources of information is both desirable and, in the case of experimental social innovation, essential for the planning of a problem solution formulation process. It is now important to move from planning the model to planning for the diffusion of social models that have been found to be beneficial to the problem population.

PROBLEM DEFINITION AND SOLUTION
FORMULATION IN DISSEMINATION RESEARCH

It is equally important in dissemination research to conduct a wide-ranging information search process to define the problems of the longitudinal research effort. In a sense all dissemination research involves the same *generic* problem: how to get organizations or individuals to adopt new innovative practices. However, the actual variables that affect adoption in one type of organization (mental hospitals, for example) might be radically different from those that affect innovation adoption in others (schools and industries, for example).

Many of the variables that need to be considered in dissemination research have been outlined in Chapter 3. We also pointed out some entrees into the existing literature. It is important to realize that, as with social models, information about the important variables in a dissemination effort will come from the same sources: personal observation, the theoretical and technical literature, concerned scientists, and personal research. This procedure is used to define and understand the variables that might be important in a given dissemination effort. Two aspects of the effort require description and understanding so that the experimentalists can determine the effective variables that need to be studied. These two aspects are (1) the definition of the target population and (2) an identification of the techniques that might move the process of dissemination to adoption through the sequential phases of approaching, persuading, activating, and diffusing which were described in Chapter 3.

The first task in the sequence—that of target identification—is a rather simple straightforward matter. It is dependent upon the social model being diffused and the population for whom it is intended. Some examples of how the social problem solution determines the target population can be seen in different diffusion experiments. With the community lodge experiment mentioned earlier, the experimenters needed to get the large mental hospitals to adopt this new model since the prototype model had been designed for this population. Thus, the target was the *mental health organization*. Fergus (1973) completed a study in which the innovative model that required diffusion was a *nursing home program* which provided for greater participation in its management by the aged residents themselves. The researcher found that she needed a sample of two organizations: *private nursing homes* and *state hospitals*. They became the target population. On the other hand, Lounsbury (1973) recently completed an experiment dealing with attempts to change the habits of *persons* so that their behavior would be more helpful in conserving energy. It seems clear from these examples that the target population for the diffusion of a particular innovation can be either *persons* or *organizations*. Although both may be involved, one is usually primary. Which it is depends upon the model one is attempting to implement. The importance of determining the target population lies in the fact that defining it will determine which variables most need to be explored for their contribution to a dissemination effort. For example, when the target population is persons, as was the case with the Lounsbury experiment, organizational variables can largely be ignored in dissemination planning. On the other hand, when the dissemination target is organizations, it should be obvious that the social situational variables related to organizational functioning as mentioned in Chapter 3 should receive special consideration. A thorough discussion of the sampling procedures that should be used in dissemination experiments is presented in Chapter 8.

With a knowledge of the search procedures and target population in mind, let us explore the cognitive processes involved in determining which variables might most productively become the experimental variables in a particular dissemination effort. To accomplish this most important aspect of planning implementation solutions, we turn now to some specific examples.

Dissemination of a Nursing Home Model

Fergus (1973) became interested in improving the treatment given aged persons in nursing homes. She discovered an innovative program for nursing homes that increased the aged's participation in decisions about their daily living, resulting in improved behavior and morale. Her search of the dissemination literature led her to conclude that the number of persons contacted in an organization might influence an organization's decision to adopt a new program. She also discovered that private nursing homes might be more receptive to change than hospital wards used for treating the aged. She therefore devised a dissemination experiment to discover the degree to which these two conditions (number of staff persons contacted and private or public nursing homes) affected the adoption of the new program. Her diffusion conditions were:

1. No staff contacted in private nursing homes.
2. No staff contacted in state hospitals.
3. One staff contacted in private nursing homes.
4. One staff contacted in state hospitals.
5. Three staff contacted in private nursing homes.
6. Three staff contacted in state hospitals.

Birth Regulation

Taylor (1975) became interested in the problem of birth regulation in American society. A perusal of the literature, a survey conducted with his colleagues (Tornatzky, Taylor, & Hedrick, 1972), and discussions with professionals in the field, indicated to him that several variables might be important in persuading persons to use contraceptive devices. One variable concerned the degree to which different modes of presentation of information were helpful in persuading people to act. Of primary concern here was the use of face-to-face small-group contacts or face-to-face contacts with individuals. Taylor also decided that it was most important to find out whether birth control information presented to individuals or small groups was more persuasive. Beyond the media itself, his search for important variables suggested that the content of the presentation might be equally important. It became a question of whether information about contraceptive devices should be given alone or with other educational information. The final shape of Taylor's design, therefore, involved an exploration of these two dimensions (message and audience) and their effect upon the adoption of the use of contraceptive devices. The diffusion conditions he decided to explore were:

1. Information only about birth control devices presented to group.
2. Information only about birth control devices presented to individuals.
3. Information about the conception and birth processes presented *along with* birth control devices to a group.
4. Information about the conception and birth processes presented *along with* birth control devices to individuals.

These planning examples should have shown clearly that the first process in creating a solution to a social problem or in disseminating a valid model is an understanding of the important variables or dimensions that might contribute to problem solution. This is essentially an information-collecting and cognitive-sorting process which involves a knowledge that comes from four basic sources. These sources have been described in detail as those of personal experience and field observation, a review of the technical and theoretical literature, sharing of information with other professionals, and one's own research. Used with good judgment and foresight, these sources of information can provide interested experimentalists with information from which the crucial variables can be culled. After the social problem has been defined and the general characteristics of a planned solution clarified, no field research can get underway until a research team is formed. It is toward this crucial aspect of experimental social innovation that our attention now turns.

CHAPTER 5

Forming the Research Team

The process of identifying a problem and creating some general solutions as presented in Chapter 4 provides the outline of a social innovation experiment. This initial planning can usually be completed by one or more interested persons. However, the specific details of the experiment now need to be developed. Proceeding beyond this preliminary planning stage requires a *group effort*. Therefore, the next action that is necessary in conducting a major experimental effort in social model creation or dissemination is to assemble a research team. In order to establish and maintain longitudinal research, a great many people must coordinate their activities over extended periods of time. The research program itself constitutes a social model whose purpose is to establish, preserve, and investigate the innovated models. In organizational characteristics and devotion to task, the research team has many of the same requirements for its members that any highly motivated team has for its members. The team effort requires the integration of different professional and nonprofessional persons into a research effort where each member makes his own particular contribution to the team's goal, which in turn demands a complete and total ego-involvement in the task.

Establishing and maintaining a research team is contingent upon the successful completion of four essential activities—(1) integrating research and service roles, (2) maintaining a multidisciplinary effort, (3) developing role clarity, (4) building cohesiveness and commitment.

INTEGRATING RESEARCH AND SERVICE

It should be clear to the reader by now that a major characteristic of the research methodology proposed in this book is an expanded role for researchers in the service program that is being investigated. Rather than being relatively passive observers and data gatherers in relation to the social model under study, we have consistently advocated that the researchers manage the program that they are evaluating. When considering that most major researches of this type will be accomplished by *teams* of researchers, the problem of integrating the research and service components becomes crucial. Since the world of research and the world of service are often perceived differently—in time frame, ideology, attention to detail, and so on—accomplishing this integration can be a difficult task. To the extent that one team provides both research and service, conflicts that must be resolved will almost always occur. Thus, for the research team there is a recurrent need to address problems of intraorganizational cooperation.

One of the ways to integrate the research and service activities of these two components is to have *every member* of the team perform both service and research tasks. Thus, in organizational parlance, every team member will be functioning as a liaison or "link pin." This should insure that neither the research nor the service component is slighted at the expense of the other. The manner in which this can be accomplished is illustrated in two experiments.

In a hospital rehabilitation program nurses on the research team completed research forms for medication and, along with the nursing assistants and the social worker, rated the performance of the patient task groups and their leaders. Later they wrote a chapter in the research publication (Fairweather, 1964). This involvement in the research aspect of the program, even when these personnel were mainly concerned with the service function, contributed invaluable research data and, in addition, created a personal identification with the program.

It is equally true that the research project staff should participate in the service phase of the program, although such participation may be quite minor. This may be illustrated by describing the role of one researcher who participated in the community lodge experiment previously mentioned (Fairweather *et al.*, 1969). In order to permit observations of the work and living situation of the janitorial and gardening service (operated mainly by discharged chronic mental patients), a research team member—a psychologist by training—was initially appointed coordinator of the community program. He spent from 2 to 12 hours each day, depending on his duties, in the community working and living situation. In this role, he had to learn all the statuses, roles, and procedures involved in the operation of a janitorial and gardening service. He periodically had to review the bookkeeping done by the member business manager, drive some of the work crews to their jobs in a truck, consult about a job training program for new members, establish and enforce procedures to make certain that each member was taking his prescribed medication, and generally perform the managerial duties of the organization.

This was the service aspect of his job. The research side of his job involved the daily rating of the job performance of each work crew, keeping a log of daily observations that were pertinent to the research, periodically administering written tests, scheduling interviews for the members, and pursuing other activities concerned with data collection and daily observations. After eight months in this position, as required in the research design, he returned to the hospital setting where the institutional part of the research was being carried out. Here, his role, established in the research design, required that he lead a ward service team comprised of a social worker, nurses, and nursing assistants. In this role he led group discussions to evaluate patients, collected research information, rated patients and groups along with other service personnel, scheduled patients for interviewing, entrance and exit testing, and the like. After eight months in this role, the action phase of the project was completed and he returned to the administrative and data processing center of the project. Here he aided in the scoring and computer processing of the data. Finally, he wrote, along with other researchers who shared his experiences, a report in which observations and analyzed data were presented.

Another example comes from Whitney's study (1974). Whitney was a research team leader who established an automobile cooperative repair program which he compared with a traditional program for juvenile delinquents (assigning them to individual jobs in separate and disparate organizations). It was necessary for Whitney to complete the following events in sequential order. After having done a thorough study of the literature and making observations and discussing the problem with service personnel, scientists, and delinquents, he decided upon the need for the automobile co-op. He became an advocate for the project with Model Cities and an interested youth program. He was permitted, at this point, to make an application for grant funds to establish the new co-op under Model Cities jurisdiction. This he did. Once it became clear that the funds would be received, he began preparing himself for the new service role required by the automobile cooperative. To do this, he entered school in order to understand how to tune automobile motors and do the other automobile repairs that this organization's members would have to be trained to do. Once the money was received and he was able to get an old warehouse where the program could operate, he helped the young juveniles learn how to repair the automobiles by direct personal supervision. In addition, he began implementing the social processes that would result in a cohesive group where his role would eventually become only a part-time consultant. Thus, his role changed from complete involvement to partial involvement as the organization's members demonstrated more and more ability to handle their own affairs. Eventually the program became autonomous and ran without him. As this process was going on, he helped collect research data on a daily basis about the internal social processes of the organization, the response of the neighborhood and other individuals to it (external processes), and the outcomes (recidivism rates and so on) of the participants themselves in the two programs. It will be noted in this example that Whitney was intimately involved in all phases of the research and service aspects of the innovated social model.

Not only must the research and service components be integrated and on an equal footing, but an optimal degree of organizational *distance* should be maintained. It has been pointed out (and will be discussed further in Chapter 6) that research and service components are inherently different types of activities. In this regard, then, and in order to facilitate team members moving from one activity to another, some distance should be maintained between the two areas. There are a number of ways in which this can be accomplished. For example, actual physical distance is one way of monitoring some degree of separation. Thus the service activities may be in one building, with the research activities in another. Another way to maintain some degree of distance is through time. As cited in the examples above, members of a team may participate in service activities during one time period and research activities during another. Different members of the team may be rotated with each other through these different roles.

Although different locations and times may facilitate an easier accommodation to the research and service activities, it is absolutely essential that all persons involved in the project continue to perceive themselves as a team. To facilitate this perception, the maintaining of optimal distance between the research and service components should be done by interpersonal contact and not through memorandums or other bureaucratic devices. There is considerable data in the organizational literature (Litwak, 1961) to indicate that the greater the magnitude of the coordinating task, the more necessity there is for face-to-face and personal involvement in maintaining coordination and group identification. The use of people in multiple role assignments accomplishes this task quite well.

MAINTAINING A MULTIDISCIPLINARY EFFORT

It should be apparent by now that the nature of social innovative research is inherently multidisciplinary and multivariate. In fact the problem selected for investigation will in large measure determine the composition of the research team. For example, if the newly created models concern educational institutions, several educators should be on the team. As mentioned in Chapter 3, every experiment, regardless of its subject matter, involves a study of the *internal processes* of the social model, the effect of the social models on the surrounding community (*external processes*), and the perceptual and behavioral processes of the individual members who are *participants* in the social model. To accomplish this at the present time, several social science disciplines must be represented on the research team. Logically, each researcher should be a multidisciplinary individual. The ideal situation would be one in which every member of the team would have sufficient breadth of training to be able to contribute insight from a number of disciplinary perspectives. Unfortunately, the narrowness of most current graduate and professional training programs usually precludes this. For this reason, several disciplines will need to be represented on the team. Although the composition of each team is specific to the problem selected, several general considerations seem to be warranted regarding such teams. The most important of these is that the total spectrum of knowledge about the social problem must be represented on the team. The determination of whether an area needs to be represented on a full-time or consulting basis depends upon the nature of the social problem. Since the social models and the dissemination processes that are being studied with this type of research are by their nature inherently complex problems, the researcher must learn to think in multidisciplinary, social systems terms. These experimentalists must view themselves as social system scientists who attempt to understand and identify all of the variables that may be important in a particular human problem that must be manipulated, measured, and evaluated during the course of an experiment. Thus, for example, if one is establishing a new social model in the third grade in a particular city for evaluation, it is important to recognize that it will have an effect not only upon the students and teachers but also on the school in which it is implanted for research purposes and on the educational system in that city. Indeed, if dynamic enough, it could create an impact upon regional educational and national systems as well. This broad view of social experimentation means that several academic fields (depending upon the problem at hand) must be represented on the research planning team.

Following is a list of professional persons who may need to be involved as either consultants or on a permanent basis in the planning of an experiment.

Anthropologists

Anthropologists can make a considerable contribution, particularly to the impact of cultural and subcultural variables upon the outcomes of a social model. Thus, the entire culture of a region, state, county, city, or area within a city may affect the implant of a social model there.

Biologists

Even though certain medical variables may be involved, in some experiments the need for biological scientists is clearly evident. Biological variables involved in water pollution, environmental degradation, and so on require the advice and consultation of an *ecologist* who, in fact, may be a whole systems biologist. Other advice and consultation from biologists about other variables that might be important in a particular problem—such as that in population regulation—can be very helpful to the experimentalists.

Computer Scientists

Almost all data collected in longitudinal field experiments will need to be prepared for computer processing. This aspect of experimental social innovation is discussed further in Chapter 8. It is necessary in the planning phase of the experiment to set up procedures for the receipt of the data to enable proper categorization for analysis when the study is completed. It is sometimes necessary to get on-line feedback about data analysis so that it can be used in the experiment proper. For example, some projects involving work by groups need information from observations made during the work itself as feedback to the individuals or groups for their own information. Such information can be obtained by adequate computer programming. The data collected during an entire research project can be subjected to computer analysis at the various points throughout the research when the information is essential. When the researchers themselves are unfamiliar with the appropriate computer techniques, they can receive aid from computer programmers and other computer experts who may be available.

Economists

Very often it is important to discuss the economic variables involved in a model with an economist, particularly one who may have a background in business and labor economics. This is extremely important for advice concerning the operation of economic variables in the models. Often, administrators responsible for the human problem under consideration will view cost as the most important outcome. Not only can economists help isolate these costs but they can also theoretically relate the economics of the model to the general society as well. Consultation with an economist and others he or she may recommend (such as accountants, bookkeepers, and the like) could have an important impact on what is considered relevant and what can be measured in a particular experiment.

Geographers

Geographers have an excellent knowledge of spatial conditions in neighborhoods, states, regions, and on the national level. Many are involved in their own research, which very often concerns the spatial relationships of various areas of a geographical location in relation to services. For example, the lack of medical facilities in certain regions of the city (such as in areas where the poor often live) has been of continuing concern to some geographers.

Lawyers

Unless the research is done in a well-circumscribed organization that has its own legal counsel and where part of the administrative commitments involve legal coverage for the research team and the participants in the social model, it is often necessary to get the advice of legal counsel about matters that may effect the research staff or its innovative models. If the research project involves a problem such as social or psychiatric rehabilitation of children, the experimenters may need legal counsel about the extent to which they as responsible persons can be sued by distraught participants or their relatives. There is also a host of legal entanglements that may need to be clarified in the maze of administrative agreements (to be mentioned in Chapter 6). Often several organizations along with their personnel are involved in the experiment and legal arrangements need to be made with them. Usually the lawyer can advise the researcher about other related professional groups they should see, such as insurance agents and so on.

Physicians

In many instances the persons participating in the model will need medical advice and counsel. This may be constant over a period of time (as in a halfway house for alcoholics, drug addicts, and the like). It may be less frequent in social programs for school systems, where typically people will not need direct and constant medical attention. Nonetheless, the degree to which the model must meet the medical needs of the persons it serves should be determined and consultation about meeting these medical needs should come from a qualified medical person.

Political Scientists

Of course many of the problems facing persons in naturalistic settings involve political power in one form or another. A political scientist who is familiar with the local area's politics can be an invaluable source of information. Such a person will also know about various political science variables such as personal power and prestige, the practical politics of the city, county, or state, and other sources of information about variables that could be important in influencing the outcome of implanted social models. Thus, the political scientist can advise the research team about specific areas needing to be measured and evaluated.

Psychologists

Psychologists are very diverse by their training and can themselves make considerable contributions to the identification of important variables and their potential interactions. An understanding of the psychological variables and their early identification is an important aspect of the planning for social model evaluation.

Social Workers

Skills accumulated by social workers are important in many experiments. Well-versed social workers not only have a thorough knowledge of agencies and organizations that deal with many of the human problems in our society, but they also have interviewing and other skills that are learned through both their education and real-life experience.

Sociologists

Sociological variables are very often an extremely important aspect of a social model's operation. It is often necessary in the creation of social models to get the advice and consultation of sociologists who may be familiar with the particular problem or otherwise have expertise that may be invaluable. For example, from the sociology of the criminal process (criminology), mental health, education, and so on come critical variables that need to be considered in establishing social models and in measuring the appropriate aspects of the models and their relationships with the broader society.

Statisticians

As will be mentioned in Chapter 9, it is often important to seek statistical consultation for the experimental design and evaluation of the various measures taken in the study. Very often new evaluative statistical techniques are required because of the diverse nature of the data involved. It is most important that this consultation be obtained during the planning phase of the experiment so that it can be incorporated in the experimental plan.

This list of scientific personnel to be involved in social model-building and dissemination experiments is, of course, selected and limited. Nonetheless, the groups represented here are those that will most often be involved in social innovative research either directly as researchers or in a consultant's capacity. Others, not mentioned here (natural scientists, other social scientists, and particular fields of specialization such as architects, educators, and the like), will need to be involved whenever the problem concerns their fields. Research team members should not hesitate to seek their advice and counsel.

The above list of disciplinary and professional specializations will clearly add a multidisciplinary coherence to the research effort. It will also be a source of difficulty in the operation of the team. As anyone who has worked with members of other disciplines knows, it is often extremely difficult for people from different backgrounds to either communicate or work together. Thus, just as in the problem of integrating service and research, the researchers have an additional problem of intrateam cooperation that is of serious proportions.

There are a number of ways that conflict about this problem can be minimized. In the recruiting of team members, an intentional effort should be made to recruit people whose commitment is primarily to problem solving rather than to the advancement of their own disciplinary based expertise. The ideal team members are persons who are not "disciplinary chauvinists," but rather are willing and interested in involving themselves in other areas of knowledge. Conflict resulting from disciplinary rivalry among the research team can also be reduced or avoided by the judicious use of research task assignments. Research team members should be involved in the collection of *all* the data, not just the data that reflects their own disciplinary outlook. To have a psychologist collect only psychological information and a geographer only geographic data, is to invite rivalry and dissension among the team. It is the team leader's responsibility to insure that research tasks are not based on narrow disciplines.

In the previous two sections we have indicated that every team member should be involved in service and research, and in different disciplinary aspects of the research. In addition, each person's *specific* duties must be clearly established and spelled out.

MAINTAINING ROLE CLARITY AND FLEXIBILITY

One of the most crucial roles on the research team is that of team leader. As the various phases of the research program—recruiting team members, designing the research, becoming involved with numerous community organizations, and the like—take place, it becomes very obvious that the team leader needs certain personality characteristics to manage successfully such a plethora of organizational and interpersonal relations. The leader must be willing to advocate the use of the new social model to disparate groups by speaking their language and helping them to perceive some "payoff" for themselves should they participate in the research program. This advocacy role of the leader must be coupled with insight into the needs of the various team members; the leader must have a genuine concern about their future. At the same time, the team leader must be knowledgeable about the particular social problem—whether it is drugs, delinquency, higher education, or whatever—so that he or she has legitimacy within the community of persons with whom the researchers must inevitably interact. Beyond these achievements, it is important that the team leader's research skills be sufficiently well-developed so that the basic research design and the experimental plan are well carried out. Whether the results are positive or negative is not important. What is important is that the voluminous man hours expended do not result in an inaccurate evaluation. Finally, it is extremely important that the leader has the welfare of the problem population at heart because this humanitarian motivation will have to provide sustenance through numerous "doors slammed in his or her face," eruptions of team tensions regardless of how well meaning the team member may be, changes in personnel that usually occur, and a myriad of other detours, disruptions, and entanglements. This leads social innovative experimentalists to cherish the remark that Harry Truman is reported to have made: "If you can't stand the heat, get out of the kitchen." Since community intervention research is also a political act, it should not be surprising that a statement so apropos of the politician's role is also applicable to the role of the experimental social innovator.

The above comments outline the general parameters of the team leader's role. For complete team functioning, however, it is also important to clearly define each team member's roles as much as possible. A distinct role can usually be established by assigning a particular aspect of the total research effort to each person. This can be done either by assigning an individual a subject area (the interpersonal processes) or by assigning the researcher a specific task (budget, interviewing, etc.)

Another vehicle that can be used to maintain role clarity during the longitudinal research effort is the staff research conference, which should be held on a regularly scheduled basis. At such meetings, every team member's activities during the preceding week can be reported by the member and reviewed by other staff personnel. Not only does this provide peer feedback, it also enables the members of the research team to learn the boundaries of activities of other team members. Used appropriately, these discussions can contribute to role clarity. In either case the assigned task should be one in which the researcher has a specific interest.

Generally, complete role clarity, although desirable, cannot be fully achieved because the needs of a project at any one moment may require a change in role. Researchers initially very interested in work on a particular project eventually may find it incompatible with other interests and may terminate their association with the project. If this should occur, another person in the research organization may need to be shifted to this position which, of course, will require a complete change in role. Because of unpredictable developments such as these, the researchers' commitment must be to the total project rather than to any one aspect of it.

BUILDING COHESIVENESS AND COMMITMENT

It is now important to consider some of the pressures that a longitudinal research of the type we have been discussing puts on maintaining the coherence of a research team. There is a heavy degree of personal and group commitment that must be nurtured in team members in order to sustain activity over what is often months and sometimes several years. In addition to the technical skills which the members of the research team bring to the human problem, it is important to recognize that the team itself can serve as a support base for individuals who are attempting to create something new. Pear support is an extremely important aspect of longitudinal innovative research because the experiences that persons have in this activity can only be appreciated by others sharing the endeavor. Very often persons engaged in new and innovative projects will be belittled by those who are staunch traditional defenders of the *status quo*. It is therefore extremely important that the individual members of the research team feel the personal support of their research collaborators and that they are accepted members of this reference group.

It should therefore be quite obvious that for membership on such a team particular personality characteristics are helpful. Members of the team, in addition to their professional and technical qualifications, must be personally compatible with each other. The attitude of the researcher is as important as his or her cognitive qualifications. There is no room for unbridled individualism here. Those people who find working with others difficult, those who wish to do their own research quite independent of what others do, those who are preoccupied with the importance of their own ideas, those who are prestige seekers, and those who have a stereotyped perception of the role of the researcher and are therefore unwilling to perform such mundane activities as scoring instruments when it is essential to completion of the project should not become involved in longitudinal naturalistic experiments. The experimenters must make a total personal commitment to the goal of the research. This is important mainly because at any time during the course of the experiment an emergency may require that they play research roles quite different from their major roles. Researchers must be able and willing to accept such an obligation from the outset.

Also, team members should have a high degree of motivation and interest in the social problem to be investigated because they must be willing to devote several years of their lives, if necessary, to finding a solution for it. The possession of positive attitudes and the willingness to make such a commitment usually eliminates from consideration those individuals who have a temporary curiosity about the problem or those who are attempting to use a research project solely for personal gain.

Another important attitude that research personnel should have is a healthy skepticism about the outcomes of any social model. Inseparable from a commitment to finding solutions to the selected social problem is a skepticism about any and all proposed solutions. Such an attitude is best summarized in the statement, "I don't know." It is exceedingly important, since social innovative research is multidisciplinary and essentially empirical in nature, that those individuals *who are committed* to a single approach or theoretical position do *not* become involved in these experiments. Problem-solving experiments incorporate variables from many disciplines. As the basis for formulating hypotheses, experiments use theoretical and integrative knowledge from all those disciplines involved.

What must be emphasized is the investment that each member of the team must have in seeing to it that all experimental conditions get carried out as fully and completely as possible under the naturalistic conditions of the field experiment. This means essentially that each person on the team is committed to carrying out the different experimental conditions from the beginning to the end of the experiment with a constant eye toward preventing a breakdown of the system which would make a comparison impossible. Ives's study (1974) is exemplary of what happens when no such commitment exists on the part of the other members of the research team. Ives attempted to compare a drug program that emphasized drug addict participative decision making and voice in community matters with a traditionally run autocratic program, where all of the addicts' activities were supervised by professional personnel. It turned out, however, that the persons administratively responsible for the innovative program emphasizing drug user participation were unsympathetic to the program and hence did not permit the participation required for its adequate establishment and evaluation once it was started. Furthermore, their anger about the program was so great that they tried to prevent random assignment to conditions because the administrators themselves were convinced that the more traditional, authoritarian, social program was by far superior. What seemed to have happened was that the administrators had indicated they would cooperate when the experiment initially was discussed. However, once these initial pressures were removed and the programs were actually begun, they found themselves unwilling or unable to help Ives establish it. Accordingly, the program could not be evaluated as an experiment and many previous hours for a large number of people were lost in the ensuing problems that arose. This chain of events is common when social model-building experiments are *not* done by *volunteers* who have an investment in seeing that *all* social models to be evaluated are implanted, activated, and operated as outlined in the research proposal. Deviations from the experimental design on the basis of personal whim or antagonism cannot be permitted if the experiment is to be properly carried out. Individuals who are unwilling for whatever reason to establish and participate in the innovative problem-solving models should not become involved in such experiments.

Jamison's study (1974) gives another example of a situation where personnel not committed to the successful completion of the research program contributed to the loss of research material that was of paramount importance to the project. Jamison evaluated nutritional counseling for a four-county area. After counseling had been accomplished, it was absolutely essential that continuous follow-up be done with the persons who participated in the study in order to assess whether or not they were following the counselors' instruction so that the amelioration of health conditions such as anemia, high blood pressure, and the like could be evaluated. Unfortunately, some of the persons charged with the follow-up did not work for the researcher and hence did not feel a strong commitment to obtain the required follow-up information. Accordingly, much valuable information was lost. Jamison might have avoided this problem if he had insisted from the outset that only involved individuals who had volunteered would participate in the follow-up. In this way he could have identified persons who were not interested and replaced them at the outset with individuals who would have been more committed to the collection of the necessary data. This would, in turn, have required a degree of control over the program not available to Jamison since he did not have the appropriate administrative agreements (discussed in Chapter 6) to control the study.

The problems described above in the Ives and Jamison studies are by no means peculiar to researches involving either volunteers or demanding the cooperation of nonresearch personnel. The generic difficulty here is trying to nurture a sense of *group goal attainment versus individual goal attainment.* To accomplish this, each person's rewards should be at one with the success or failure of the group research effort. Obviously this demands a considerable personal investment in and identification with the research project. In order to foster this identification and commitment there are a number of things that can be done by the team director in the context of the research.

First of all, it is essential, if at all possible, that members of the research team be involved in the project *from the beginning of the planning stage.* There is a certain amount of identification with the project that develops when a person feels that some of his or her ideas are being tested by the research effort. In contrast, of a person is "hired on" after a research has already been designed, the sense of ego-involvement is considerably decreased, if it can be developed at all. This sense of ego-involvement can be maintained during the course of the research if as much use as possible is made of *group participative decision making.* Thus, whenever possible, research policy decisions should be put to the group at large in the context of regular staff meetings. The team director should endeavor to avoid a continuous pattern of authoritarian decisions regarding the direction of the research. Of course, strictly operational or simple administrative decisions such as scheduling should remain exclusively in the hands of the team director to foster the meeting of research deadlines and role clarity just discussed. But beyond those obvious administrative decisions, all others, whenever possible, should be made by the group as a whole. There is too much data on the positive effects of group participation (Coch & French, 1948; Fairweather, Sanders, & Tornatzky, 1974) to ignore it in the context of a team research effort.

One other pressing issue, particularly to professional researchers, is that of publications. For a person whose life's career is that of an experimentalist, research publications in the form of articles and books are a payoff of considerable value. They are also instrumental in furthering the researcher's career. To the extent possible and appropriate, authorship of publications should be shared among all members of the research team. Thus, credit and authorship should not consistently and exclusively accrue to the team leader. If possible, publication agreements should be made prior to the actual onset of the research and should be put in written form and signed by all members of the research team. This will avoid possible disagreement and bad feelings during the weeks and months of the research effort. A similar policy should be employed regarding other benefits accruing from the research. For example, during the research itself it may be possible for team members to deliver papers, attend meetings away from the research site, and participate in other professional activities. Such opportunities should be shared equally among all team members. It should be recognized that the intent of these policies is to foster a sense of group cohesiveness, making rewards contingent upon group performance.

A WORKING EXAMPLE

In order to get a better appreciation of some of the concepts just mentioned, it may be informative to explore the composition of a research team in an actual field situation—the research involved the community lodge program mentioned as an example in Chapter 2. Table 5.1 presents a list of the personnel and the institutions with which these research team members had their primary affiliation. The table shows that the chief social innovative experimenter was the only individual listed under more than one institution. He had primary affiliations with both the hospital and the university.

TABLE 5.1
Personnel Participating in the Hospital-Community Study with Their
Primary Institutional Affiliation

Hospital		University		Nonprofit rehabilitation corporation
Service	Research	Consultants	Research	Service
One psychiatrist One social worker Two nurses Four nursing assistants	One chief social innovative experimenter (principal investigator) One experimental assistant	Legal Accounting Insurance Statistical Computer Medical Janitorial	One chief social innovative experimenter (principal investigator) Two social innovative experimenters Three experimental assistants	Board of Directors

The chief social innovative experimenter presented in Table 5.1 is the team leader. It cannot be overemphasized that the team leader must be a trained social innovative experimenter, thoroughly familiar with the administrative, training, and experimental needs of the team. This is particularly important since the team members will repeatedly come to him or her over the course of the experiment for guidance and decisions about all research aspects. Individuals without experience in such experiments, regardless of their other professional qualifications, are typically not sufficiently grounded in the day-to-day operations of experimental models in action to manage successfully an innovative social research program.

In the community lodge experiment the team leader selected the problem for investigation and made arrangements for management commitments. He was responsible for the total research effort and had both administrative and research duties. His research duties, in addition to selecting the problem, included selecting the final design, supervising the creation or selection of the measuring instruments, establishing appropriate sampling procedures, choosing the appropriate statistics, supervising the computer analysis of the data, and so on. As previously mentioned, all of these decisions were made by thorough discussion with the team members.

Hiring of the research team was his first official act after obtaining administrative and budgetary commitments. Other administrative duties included making arrangements for office space, computer time, supplies, and, most important, keeping the experimental conditions constant during the action phase. The team leader delegated most of the aforementioned obligations, but whether he did or not, he was finally responsible for all administrative and research activities. Among his administrative duties, one of the most important was that of maintaining the research group itself. He attempted to provide each person with as unique a role as possible (a morale factor mentioned earlier) and, upon occasion, was the arbitrator of disputes within the staff. Most importantly, he established lines of communication among staff members so that interpersonal problems could be solved before they grossly affected the research effort. The role of the two other social innovative researchers for the community lodge experiment was also quite varied. The actual social role of one of them was discussed in the first section of this chapter, under the heading "Integrating Research and Service." In addition to the team leader and these two social innovative researchers, the research team which carried out that experiment included several other persons. Two experimental assistants (one from the hospital and one from the university) had many duties, mainly concerned with the daily operation of the research program. They prepared correspondence for other researchers and for relatives of the former mental patients who now operated the janitorial service. They mimeographed testing forms; administered tests; interviewed staff, hospitalized patients, and former patients; and prepared budget requests. In all these duties they followed the research schedule, making certain that the many programmed procedures occurred on time. Here again each assistant had a set of duties that were his or her individual responsibility.

Two other assistants were hired after the project had begun. They were trained by the researchers to coordinate the service activities of the janitorial and gardening service. The introduction of these individuals was planned at the outset of the research. They replaced the experimenters in administering the janitorial and gardening service. Interviewing, testing, and other more technical matters were still performed by the experimenters, but the collection of certain research data, such as keeping a log of selected events and rating the work crews, was done by these assistants.

The service personnel—psychiatrist, social worker, nurses, nursing assistants—were employees of the hospital, who, along with one of the researchers, established and implemented on a daily basis the hospital aspect of the research effort. In addition to their primary service duties, each played a role in the research effort. The psychiatrist met periodically with the team leader to discuss patient sampling requirements, medication, and other research matters. The social worker, nurses, and nursing assistants served as members of an evaluation team which rated patient task groups on the ward. In this capacity, they worked closely with the researcher who was assigned to the ward. This team also contributed other research data without which the experiment could not have been completed.

Consultants also had an exceedingly important role in the overall project. They served in this capacity because their duties, although essential, did not require full-time assignment to the project. Thus, the accounting consultant periodically audited the books of the janitorial service. The legal consultant was contacted when problems of a legal nature arose. On one occasion, the janitorial service was sued by a dissatisfied customer, and this was handled through the legal department. The lawyer recommended the appropriate malpractice and personal liability insurance for the research staff and the former patients who operated the janitorial service; he drew up the management agreement between the university and the nonprofit corporation under whose auspices the former patients worked; he also arranged for the lease of the dormitory in which the former patients lived. His duties, broadly conceived, included the legal representation of the research staff and the former patient members. The insurance consultants followed the recommendations of the legal consultant in obtaining appropriate coverage for these two groups. Certain carriers, for example, will not insure former mental patients, whereas others will; his specialized knowledge made him aware of this. The medical consultant served as the house physician for the members of the former-patient group. He prescribed medication, was on emergency call, gave physical examinations, and generally met the medical needs of the ex-patients residing in the community dormitory who operated the janitorial and gardening business. The janitorial consultant recommended supplies for the work teams of the dormitory, proposed new work procedures, demonstrated new products and advised the workers about all the janitorial aspects of the work situation.

These consultants were involved in the service aspect of the community dormitory where the janitorial and gardening services were located. The statistical and computer consultants, however, were needed for the research aspect of the experiment. From the onset of the study, the statistical consultant had been actively involved in all research planning. He advised about design, appropriate instruments, and correct analytic procedures. Although it is the final responsibility of the principal investigator to select and implement the statistical procedures, it is frequently necessary, because of the complex nature of the design and data involved in social innovative experiments, to seek the knowledge of a theoretical mathematical statistician. The computer programmer, on the other hand, worked directly with the principal investigator and was responsible for punching computer cards, carrying out the analyses on the established programs, and presenting the data to the principal investigator upon final analysis. It is important to note here that all of the consultants whose positions have been described worked full-time elsewhere, and consulting ordinarily required only a few hours of their time each month.

The nonprofit corporation, appearing in Table 5.1 as the Rehabilitation Corporation, provided the janitorial service with corporate membership. Since this corporation already had obtained agreements with local industries and unions because its primary function was the rehabilitation of mental patients, a management agreement between the university and the corporation provided the appropriate relationship with community businesses and unions. In addition, the corporation provided an organization through which workmen's compensation and other needed insurance could be obtained. In the daily operation of the research project, whether in the hospital or the community, no individual associated with the nonprofit corporation had a service or research role, but its Board of Directors were kept fully informed of the business activities of the janitorial and gardening service. Annual audits and other business information were provided to it as necessary to fulfill its legal obligations as a nonprofit corporation. Simply stated, the nonprofit corporation provided the janitorial and gardening service with a corporate affiliation that integrated it into the work community.

The institutional affiliation of the research personnel presented in Table 5.1 again reveals the need for cooperative relationships among the many institutions that are often involved in social innovative experiments. The university and the hospital, as shown in Table 5.1, needed to have the closest relationship because personnel involved in the research, whether their primary institutional affiliation was with the university or the hospital, had to have a strong identification with the research program. Each institution had to recognize the need for this identification and promote it, for the primary identification of each member of the social innovative research team, whether predominantly service or research personnel and regardless of institutional affiliation, was with the research effort and not with departments within the institutions or with the institution itself. The research transcended the institution.

An identification with such a research project is most difficult when an institution or department within the institution is predominantly a service organization. The hospital service personnel, shown in Table 5.1, were permitted by their department heads to perform some research duties as long as such duties did not interfere with their service function. The nurses, for example, not only dispensed medication and performed the other usual service functions required by their status, but they also completed research forms and carried out other research functions. However, they were administratively responsible to the supervisor of the nursing service and not to the research team leader. It is therefore clear that conflicts might have developed between the nursing supervisor and the research team leader had there been no appropriate prior agreements with department heads. Such agreements (discussed in Chapter 6) are obviously essential to the successful conduct of social innovative experiments.

Another important consideration regarding the selection and assignment of service personnel when such research is conducted within an institution is that the department heads are aware of the cooperation and dedication required of researchers in such projects. Occasionally the department head of a service organization may agree to allow service personnel to be involved in such a research project and then assign to the research program personnel who do not wish the assignment or who have had difficulty in adjusting to their previous service position. Individuals so assigned rarely become identified with the research effort and frequently oppose it. Therefore, it is exceedingly important that service personnel volunteer to participate in the research. Also, a trial period during which they can request a release from the project or during which the team leader can request their transfer should be provided. The practice of arbitrarily assigning service personnel to a research program on a nonvoluntary basis may only insure the program's failure.

A team research effort also requires that no one individual be indispensable to the total effort. Thus, team members should be able to substitute for others on the team in the event of an emergency. It is also important that social innovative research be a full-time pursuit for those researchers primarily involved in establishing and carrying out the experiments. Except for consultations, whose positions are defined as part-time employees, all other researchers should have full-time positions with the research team. Such positions help obtain identification with the project and clearly define the reciprocal obligations.

A NOTE ON DISSEMINATION RESEARCH

Virtually all the comments developed so far apply equally to longitudinal dissemination research such as the Fairweather, Sanders, & Tornatzky (1974) study briefly described in Chapter 2. However, it is most important to recognize that those persons who have completed the social model-building experiments are the ones who bear primary responsibility either to conduct the dissemination experimental effort themselves or to help organize a team that can conduct it. This is the experimental team's obligation because they alone know through their own experiences and analyses of the research data how beneficial the social model is and how it can be described and activated. It is imperative, therefore, that they either carry out the dissemination experiment themselves or train others to do it so that the dissemination experimental team has the knowledge to replicate the model to be disseminated. In addition there are some peculiar features of dissemination that bear further elaboration.

In any dissemination effort that is targeted at other than strictly a local audience there is likely to be a considerable amount of traveling on the part of the research team. Thus, for example, in the national mental hospital change study just mentioned at least one or two members of the research team were on the road at all times; this frequency of travel lasted for two and one-half years. Such extensive travel schedules have considerable implications for the functioning of a research team. It offers many problems for the administration of the research effort. The demand of scheduling visits and work activities are considerable. More important, perhaps, such an effort puts considerable strain on maintaining the group cohesiveness necessary for the research effort. When team members are unable to interact and work together as a coherent group for some appreciable time, feelings of group commitment may be reduced. The research team leader must be aware of this problem and double the efforts to remedy it.

Another unique characteristic of dissemination research is that it sometimes involves some type of persuasion activity. These persuasion efforts are often on a person-to-person basis—such as those used in lectures, workshops, consultations, and so on. In recruiting for a research team involved in this type of activity, the team leader should be particularly aware of whether or not the potential researchers can carry out this type of activity. Team members must be willing to function in a manner akin to salesmen in the context of a dissemination project. If this type of activity is incongruent with the potential team members' self-perceptions or values they would likely do considerable harm to the research effort. Thus, in recruiting for dissemination efforts, particular attention should be made in clarifying to the potential team member what the actual demands of the research role are. Related to this problem is the fact that in dissemination efforts the "change agent" often is perceived in a negative light by institutions which he or she is attempting to change. Thus, the research team member in this type of research should have a "thick skin" to ward off the negative reactions of the defenders of the *status quo*.

In this chapter the authors have attempted to explore some of the major attributes of research teams capable of carrying out longitudinal problem-solving experiments—the need to integrate service and research roles, to maintain a multidisciplinary problem-oriented focus, to create cohesiveness and a group orientation, to provide the team members with role clarity while simultaneously expecting that research jobs may have to be changed to enhance the research effort. A discussion of some of the similarities and differences between social model-building and dissemination research team activities was also presented. The next procedure in a programmatic research effort is to obtain the administrative agreements necessary to further experimental planning and action.

CHAPTER 6

Obtaining Administrative Agreements

Whenever longitudinal field research is undertaken, whether it is for social model-building or implementation purposes, there is the necessity of providing the research team with the social conditions under which such experiments can be carried out. This usually requires the negotiation of essential "contracts" with those who will be involved in one way or another in the experiment itself. The term "administrative agreements" has been given to these contractual negotiations. For purposes of clarity, those agreements essential to model-building are presented in a separate section from those used in dissemination experiments.

THE DISTINCTIVE FEATURES OF
ADMINISTRATIVE AGREEMENTS

Their Necessity

Many potentially good social experiments never make a contribution to the solution of a social problem because of shoddy administrative agreements; in fact, more experiments are nonproductive for this reason than as a result of poor experimental design. It is a mistake to think of a social experiment as merely a neutral application of scientific method to a field problem setting because the launching of a field experiment is a political act. Experiments in social innovation are typically long-term, longitudinal studies which require the maintenance of experimental conditions for extended periods of time. This necessitates the cooperation of a representative sample of the problem population, continuous administrative support from the agencies involved in the research program, and the maintenance of the research staff's morale so that their personal commitment to the research goals is maintained from the beginning to the end of the experiment. Because of these features, such experiments require administrative agreements that are of considerable complexity. In this chapter we will explore some of the recurrent problems pertinent to obtaining such agreements.

Norms Regarding Service and Research

One difficulty in social experimentation stems from the fact that it involves an integration of both service and research into a single programmatic effort. In juxtaposition to this is the fact that in the typical service and rehabilitative agencies which often must become involved with the experiment, norms of procedure have been established that define research and service as separate entities. Often research and service persons never interact because the physical location of the research is generally in a separate building or on different floors from the location where treatment or rehabilitative programs take place. As a rather classic example, it is a rare school district in which the research and development division is located in a place other than a central administrative building separated from teachers and students. There are usually separate research and service budgets. Frequently, there are separate research and service professional positions; even within a given discipline, such as psychology, two individuals with equivalent backgrounds, including academic degrees, may be labeled differently—one as a service person and one as a researcher. Because of these institutional traditions, administrators tend to perceive professional personnel as either research or service personnel, rarely as both. Researchers themselves have often contributed to this problem. Institutional researchers frequently isolate themselves from organizational problems. In prisons and mental hospitals, for example, they often define their role as "pure" researchers and carry out their activities independent of the rehabilitative programs which are the primary responsibility of such institutions. Because of these traditional institutional practices, it is difficult for administrative personnel to understand that a social experiment must involve research-in-service.

The World of Administration and the World of Experimentation

Aside from the specific norms regarding research just outlined, there are some very basic differences in orientation separating the administrators of cooperating agencies from the social experimenters. There are time perception differences between the typical program administrator and the researcher. As Lindhold (1964) has pointed out, administration is usually "the science of muddling through." The day-to-day response to emergent crises is the usual *time frame* within which the administrator operates. This is especially true in the human service area which is unlikely ever to become fully rationalized in the bureaucratic sense. In contrast, while social experimenters are also involved in the day-to-day problems of administrating an action program, they must at the same time retain a longitudinal, scientific perspective. It is this long-term perspective that administrators often do not grasp, and they therefore often do not appreciate the need for making agreements with the experimenter that encompass months or sometimes years.

A similar disparity exists between the administrators and the experimenters' respective ideas about "truth" and program effectiveness. To program administrators, truth is in the eye of the beholder. An effective program is one which "feels good" and generates good public reactions. In contrast the experimenters' assessment of a good program is based on the outcome data of longitudinal experiments. While administrators protect programs, they often see the role of experimenters as that of snoops. Needless to say, this generates a social atmosphere fraught with difficulty, forcing the administrative agreements necessary to establish and maintain the conditions needed for a social experiment.

The Issue of Control: Constancy and Sampling

In many ways the essence of administrative agreements lies in the social experimenters' need for a degree of *control* over activities that are usually managed by service personnel in human service programs. To give a geometric analogy, the experimenters are trying to negotiate an area of untouchable social space within which the pertinent variables are substantially within their control. Thus, not only is normal control of an experimental program being requested, but control of a duration and magnitude that is likely to be seen as excessive by participating agencies. Although several areas of control are important, two particular areas are crucial: (1) creating the experimental conditions and maintaining them, and (2) establishing scientifically valid sampling procedures.

In creating and maintaining the constancy of the experimental conditions, care must be exercised in clearly communicating to management the importance of insulating the service units to be used for research from any institutional practices that would destroy the experiment. Thus, management should be told that it is imperative to label officially one or two areas as research units and to isolate them from the remainder of the institution. In a mental hospital these may be wards; in a prison they may be cell blocks; and in a home for delinquents they may be cottages. Since experiments in social innovations are well controlled and often involve small numbers of matched persons, it is typically necessary to isolate only one or two such units from the major institution. These units will be used to house the experimental programs which may be quite different from those in the remainder of the institution. Management must also be informed that once the experimental procedures have been initiated and the research has begun, the innovative procedures cannot be changed until the research has terminated without destroying the project itself. This requires the continued protection of these research units from administrative practices that would necessitate such changes in the research program. This protection, in turn, always requires effective management support.

Clearly, the above agreements go against the grain of usual management practices. It is rare that a new program is either isolated or maintained in its original form in the typical service setting. Usually, either by administrative fiat or by "professional judgment," a new program will be changed dramatically over a period of time. Such judgments are typically made on the basis of subjective, global assessments in an atmosphere separated from data feedback.

The second major issue related to experimental control is probably *the* major bugaboo in obtaining administrative agreements for social experimentation. Random sampling procedures (described in Chapter 8) that are so essential to experimentation, are often viewed by program administrators as an unnecessary intrusion of their administrative domain. There is no procedure—so ostensibly simple—which is so difficult to explain to nonscientifically trained persons. And even when administrators of cooperating organizations understand the procedure, they will have at best a limited grasp of the conceptual rationale behind it.

Problems of sampling, particularly randomization, are compounded when an experimental design establishes an existing program as a control condition. This puts the social experimenter in the position of assigning randomly selected participants to the administrators' own programs and thus magnifies the problems of securing adequate control by their agreement. Few administrators believe that a random number table is fair, since many administrative decisions are determined by economic or political power factors. For this reason, it is incumbent upon the experimenter to impress upon the administrators of cooperating agencies the necessity for using randomization and systematic sampling procedures to obtain scientifically valid information. To do this, the experimenters must embark on a concentrated educational effort to impart the scientific rationale behind random sampling procedures. The experimenters can give real-life examples of how random sampling procedures will give all programs equally "fair" samples of persons that are necessary for accurate, objective evaluation. For this reason, the procedures involving random assignment to the experimental conditions must be carried out. To attain them, the experimenters must spell out specific administrative agreements about the necessary sampling procedures with all involved organizations. In no other subcomponent of a social experiment is the need for a written agreement more necessary than in the area of sampling.

Exploitation of the Experiment

Not only must agreements be reached that pertain to the scientific validity of an experiment (such as those of maintaining the constancy of experimental conditions and of adequate sampling procedures), but certain potential problem areas that might arise during the course of the experiment should be dealt with beforehand. The problem of exploiting the experiment by sponsoring agencies is of particular significance. Like many other aspects of personal and group greed, this source of corruption originates in the money and potential fame that surround a successful social experiment.

The problem created by research money develops from the fact that social experiments often bring a considerable influx of contractual money into a community or an institution. Misunderstandings arise with institutional management because of the frequently held preconception that the research staffs' principal aim is to bring additional services to the institution without cost to the organization itself. This is sometimes believed possible by administrators when large research grants can be obtained for exploring a given problem. In such a case management often views the research budget as a supplement to the institutional budget which they can use to pay for the existing service programs rather than as funds for meeting new research needs. When this is the perception of management, conflict will almost inevitably arise in the course of the experiment because the expected increase, usually in service personnel, does not occur. When this happens, initial research agreements are often not honored. To prevent such misunderstandings, the experimenters should clearly describe the use of the research budget to management.

A second problem is related to the fact that social experiments often involve new service programs that are innovative, interesting, and, unfortunately, newsworthy. The typical program administrator lives, at least in part, by the approbation of his colleagues and the general public. For this reason, the stage is often set for a conflict with the social experimenters. It is usually important to management that much publicity be given these research projects. Since the experimenters are attempting to generalize to future situations where publicity will probably not be an important variable, it is sometimes necessary for research purposes that the project be protected from such publicity until the data collection phase has been completed. Not only can publicity put generalizability in jeopardy, it can also set in motion dynamics which can destroy the integrity of the evaluation itself. Rossi & Williams (1972) discuss how the New Jersey negative taxation experiments were jeopardized by a premature disclosure of the project and an ill-considered release of results. Similarly, in a case known to the authors, a social experiment in the area of juvenile corrections was compromised. A small experimental subgroup of released offenders was being assigned to a pilot parole program, while the rest of the client population was being released to the normal aftercare facilities. Shortly after the experiment began, the state director began a publicity drive focusing attention on the new program. This advertising campaign generated pressure from within and without the organization to extend the program to the entire client population. This was done, and the experimenters found themselves without a comparison group and, of course, without an experiment. Here again the needs of the researchers can be at variance with the institution. For this reason, it becomes imperative that agreements concerning publicity should be made prior to the onset of the experiment.

There is another problem frequently faced when the research is carried out in an institution. It involves publication rights. Quite often administrators, particularly if they are professional people interested in the research being conducted, expect to have their names appear on the publication without any material aid in the research except for making the necessary administrative arrangements. This can be devastating to researchers, and it has brought about the demise of more than one project. The role of administrators in scientific publication should be clearly agreed upon prior to the research effort. One of the most forthright statements on this matter was made in the American Psychological Association's publication, *Ethical Standards of Psychologists* (1953, p. 126). "Administrators are expected to take or be given credit for authorship of professional reports only when they have made significant contributions to the conduct of the research or to the writing of the report." Thus, the commitment to research is sometimes misunderstood by both the researcher and management. In these cases it seems that management has a general interest in the prestige and money that research may bring to the institution without an understanding of the reciprocal responsibility of managerial personnel themselves for support of the research. For this reason, when discussing research proposals with institutional management, the researcher should ask concrete, meaningful questions stated in terms of money, space, and other needs with which administrators are familiar.

Economic Considerations

It is, of course, always necessary to find support for a social innovative experiment since the new models have to be first established before they can be evaluated. The search for financial support often constitutes a central issue in obtaining the necessary administrative agreements.

Sometimes it is possible to develop an innovative model within an organization or agency with its support. In such cases the organization typically supports the development and evaluation of the new model. The comparison of psychotherapy programs and the development and evaluation of the small-group autonomous treatment program are examples of this type of monetary support (Fairweather *et al.*, 1960, Fairweather, 1964). Both of these researches were conducted in Veterans Administration mental hospitals where the needed wards, research personnel, data analyses, and the like were provided by the organization as part of their ongoing research effort. This is an example of *one* sort of funding. Clearly, here the researchers seek an interested organization and attempt to gain financial support from it. This approach is most often possible when the organization has accepted research as a part of its daily operation. A word of caution, however, is in order here. It is often necessary for the researchers to establish their legitimacy in the organization prior to requesting funds or organizational aid in a research program. This sometimes requires that the experimental social innovators establish their commitment to the organization through some service for it so that others can perceive their willingness to participate in the daily problems that the organization employees usually confront. In the two hospitals just mentioned, for example, the researchers *first* carried out routine treatment procedures (all were trained psychotherapists) in order to gain the support of the staff who then knew that the researchers themselves were fully qualified mental health professionals. This work for the organization also established that the researchers were willing to help the organization meet its goals—a distinctly different role than that often assumed by researchers who are not acquainted with the daily problems of the staff and who show little concern for those persons working in the organization. The need to establish good interpersonal relationships and acceptance is a paramount issue in successful negotiations for organizational support in this sort of setting.

An interesting example of this search for legitimacy is commented upon by Fergus (1973) in discussing the social climate she needed to create in order to gain organizational support for her research project. About this necessity, she states:

One of the initial steps before the implementation of any design before a field study can proceed is the need to build legitimacy within the organization. In this case it involved the Institute of Gerontology and specifically with the milieu therapy training staff. To develop legitimacy, I made myself available for discussions and attended their training sessions. It was very important to them that I show a commitment to the problems of aging. My offering of services was very influential in getting the administrative agreements to work with the training team.

A second approach to the problem of financing a social innovation for research purposes is to gain agency support through close interpersonal contact and work with them while, at the same time, applying for outside funding. The community lodge described in Chapter 2, was an example of this approach. Here both a major university, a private nonprofit corporation, and a mental hospital all cooperated in the establishment of the community lodge but did not provide funds for that purpose. They provided other support such as legal aid, medical help for the ex-patients, and the like. The actual monetary support was provided through a National Institute of Mental Health grant applied for through the university by the researchers. It is most important to understand in this context that the researchers had held positions in the various organizations for extended periods of time and *had legitimacy within those organizations* as a precondition to an agreement on the part of the three organizations.

Another example can be given in Whitney's study of juvenile delinquents (1974). He worked in a Model Cities program for several months in order to establish his interest in the youth program that was under its direct supervision. Finally he applied with Model Cities sanction for the funding of a juvenile delinquency research program. It was through the combined mechanism of agency support and outside funding that the juvenile-operated automobile co-op was established as an experiment with provisions made for its evaluation. Another example can be found in the experiment of Beck and her colleagues (1973). They needed to get the support of a health planning agency before they could explore the communication processes and the roles established for the user and providers of health services. In order to accomplish this, the researchers participated as observers for almost one year in the health planning meetings of the agency. In addition, they held many other meetings with the health planning agency in order to discuss how their research might help the agency more creatively accomplish its mission. Finally, they were able to obtain outside funding from a governmental source in order to carry out their research. In all three of these examples it was the coordinated effort of an agency, the researchers, and outside funding to support the research that permitted the research conditions to be established and evaluated. The need to establish one's legitimacy in the organization and not to be perceived as a disinterested and unconcerned outsider is obvious.

Another way in which funds can be found is shown in the research done by Jamison (1974). Jamison's interest was in exploring the value of nutritional counseling which has become a common practice in agencies charged with providing health care for the poor. He was mainly concerned about the nutritional problems of poor women who were pregnant, particularly those who had physical disabilities such as anemia, high blood pressure, and other such debilitating illnesses. He was able to get the support of four county agencies which themselves were concerned about whether or not their clientele were following their prescribed diets and whether or not their physical conditions were improving as a result of the nutritional counseling they were receiving. The county health services therefore provided the clients and the research funds for a major evaluation of this effort. Another example of this same process was that completed by Tillman (1976). She was interested in the degree to which the effectiveness of health care for low-income mothers was affected by the differing perceptions that doctors and patients had about their own needs. She was able to work closely with an agency handling the problems of low-income medical care for expectant mothers. The agency provided most of the research funds and the persons to participate in a new social model she constructed with agency assistance. Here again, as with the Jamison study, the financial burden was borne by the organization itself.

On some occasions, however, the innovative scientists will be unable to find support from agencies or interested groups that can aid in the funding. In such cases the researchers must seek funds from other sources. This search can follow a three-way scheme. First, the researchers can apply for a grant from county, state, and federal government agencies or private foundations along with the interested social administrators in the hopes that the entire project will be funded by one group. If they are unsuccessful in this endeavor, which they very often will be, they then can propose a much smaller scale research by modifying the initial study through selecting one or two of the principal parameters from the major social innovation for specific investigation. Upon occasion, such an experiment can be accomplished with relatively little money and the help of some small organization. Lounsbury's research was of this nature (1973). He applied for a large grant and was turned down. Eventually he reduced the size of the project while retaining his interest in two of the important variables; he was able to secure some small funding, $500, and carried out the research by himself with a few interested colleagues. This is sometimes necessary when only a few hundred dollars of funding can be found. On the other hand, it sometimes is to the researchers' advantage to move to another location or join another organization which does have an interest in the research being proposed.

METHODS FOR OBTAINING ADMINISTRATIVE AGREEMENTS

Considered in light of the above problems, the development of appropriate administrative agreements in support of a social experiment is indeed a complex problem. From the perspective of organizational sociology (Litwak, 1961; Litwak & Hylton, 1962), the problem can be seen as a special instance of interorganizational and intraorganizational *linkages*. As Litwak points out, the effort needed to foster and monitor linkages is directly proportional to the potential conflict between the participating organizations, their differences in structure and process, and the degree of awareness and acceptance of the need for coordination. The above-mentioned problem areas also clearly point toward the necessity of a strong linkage system of administrative agreements.

Not only does the creation of a social experiment demand the existence of a network of agreements, it should also be clear by now that the establishment of these linkages is a *social change process* in itself. In view of the many areas of possible conflict in goals between the experimenters and participating organizations, the obtaining of administrative agreements clearly involves persistent persuasion and, sometimes, cajoling. It is only partly a rational process, and then perhaps only a small part. The social experimenters should assume that the administrators that they approach for research agreements are very likely to be either ignorant, hostile, or indifferent about social experiments. Most likely they will be right.

Presentation of the Proposal

During the initial negotiations of administrative agreements, it is essential that the experimenters meet face-to-face with all parties that form the network of persons that need to be involved in the agreements. If the experimenters expect to forge agreements after merely sharing a written proposal with them, they will be sadly mistaken. Most program administrators will neither read nor understand the research or its implications for their organization. There is considerable organizational literature to support such an interpersonal tactic. Litwak (1961) and Litwak & Hylton (1962) again point out that it is essential to have primary group face-to-face interaction in order to achieve linkages in areas of complexity or conflict. Fairweather, Sanders, & Tornatzky (1974) report experimental results indicating that face-to-face workshops or consultations were much more effective than written materials in persuading organizations to establish a social change relationship with a research team. One watchword pertinent to the initial approach to administrators: use the format of face-to-face meetings.

A second point to bear in mind during initial discussions is that the experimenters should have a fully developed research plan as described in Chapter 10, and, more important, they should know how their experiment will potentially affect other organizations. It is also exceedingly important that the researchers have sufficient experience with field experimentation to have a detailed knowledge of the needs of the research team. Without such knowledge, they cannot meaningfully bargain with administrators for the requirements to carry out the actual research itself. In this regard, the researchers need to know how much space their research team will need, the supplies and equipment they will need, the access they will have to have to computers, and the places and space for the storage of data and the housing of the team. Thus, beyond the knowledge of organizational structure and an understanding of how the experiment might affect them, the researchers need to have a detailed knowledge of the financial, spacial, and other needs of their research organization.

The experimenters should develop a complete, written research proposal detailing their research needs. Administrative agreements that are stated in generalities are worthless. Unless the experimenters know a great deal about the practices of the organizations with which they must cooperate they will be unable to articulate the specifics of the agreements that are needed. For example, experimenters might be planning an educational experiment in which lay persons assume teacher roles and responsibilities. Unless they are completely familiar with current administrative practice in this area they might not know when a state law requires board action granting such lay teachers a special civil service rating. The action phase of such a research would be jeopardized unless a prior agreement had been worked out with the appropriate organizational entities. A second guideline to follow during initial discussions of administrative agreements, then, is to become an expert about those organizations with whom one needs to launch a cooperative effort.

But the researchers would be remiss in planning if they thought that the aforementioned agreements could be accomplished without a basic sensitivity to the personal needs of those with whom they will discuss the need for the research itself. Each administrator finds himself or herself in the unique position of being constantly at the mercy of pulls, pushes, and tugs from many quarters during each work day. The constant stress of being administratively responsible for an organization should be foremost in the thinking of the experimenters when discussing matters with administrators. Even though the administrators' fears about the impact of the research upon the host organization are often based upon a lack of knowledge of the research itself, the experimenters must be aware of these fears and attempt to alleviate the accompanying anxiety as much as possible. One of the most important techniques in accomplishing this is to assure administrators that information about the research program will be continuously communicated to them throughout the course of the research and that any unforeseen problems will be brought to their attention for discussion and mutual decision making. Further, it should be pointed out to them that the new social programs are small-scale models that need only a few participants, and that only *minimal changes* in the organization are therefore required. Thus, a true sensitivity to the individual or individuals involved and the particular pressures they face in the responsible positions they hold requires a combination of continuous education about experiments and feedback from the research and about any problems the research creates for them. Since the negative perceptions of the administrators can scuttle any research project at its inception or while it is in process, continued attention to these interpersonal processes is of paramount importance to the success of the research endeavor.

Finally, it should be apparent that the involvement of cooperating agencies is both intensive *and* extensive. It is better to explore areas of possible conflict and cooperation with all remotely potential adversaries than to be surprised later on. To accomplish this, it is important to bring together leaders of relevant local industry, unions, representatives of the legal profession, medicine, insurance, the press, and others to present clearly the need for the research and to elucidate its goals. Thus, representatives of the community institutions can become, if they wish, an integral part of the research effort. In this regard they may serve as members of a community research committee. It is better to spread the net of participation wide and secure stronger agreements with cooperating agencies, than to have the research itself threatened during the action phase.

Agreements with the potential participants in an experiment must not be overlooked. Unlike traditional laboratory experiments, social experiments involve people who are willing to participate in them. For this reason, it is essential that each person understand clearly and fully the reason for the experiment and the range of alternative results that might come from it. No experiment under the humanitarian guidelines of experimental social innovation is possible without the consent and help of the problem population, so it must be clearly understood that such individuals should be brought into the planning of the experiment from the beginning. Thus, it is important that a detailed description of the experiment and its possible outcomes, so far as anyone can guess, be presented to each potential participant so that he or she can decide whether to actively engage in it. This matter is more fully discussed in Chapter 8.

Development of the Formal Agreement

At some point during discussions, it will become apparent that the moment for consummating an agreement is at hand. There are no guidelines for discerning when this occurs, since experience is the best guide. We can, however, outline the types of agreement that can be reached and the specific content areas which an agreement should cover.

First, it should be emphasized that a *verbal agreement is usually not perceived as a binding agreement*. Often, during the presentation-discussion phase, apparent agreements are verbalized between the experimenters and heads of cooperating organizations. It is at their own peril that researchers accept these for anything more than what they are: talk. The experimenters should have something in writing which can be invoked months or years later when the integrity of the experiment may become threatened. It is too easy for administrators to claim that they did not understand the research requirements when pressed about a prior verbal arrangement. For this reason, agreements should be written and as formal (and, in fact, legally binding), as possible.

The minimal acceptable form of an administrative agreement is a letter, or letters, between the participants. While this is not very formal, and usually not legally binding, it is still something tangible which could be invoked during subsequent disagreements. Procedurally, the experimenters could, for example, verbally ask for a series of specific agreements, outlining the reciprocal responsibilities and request that letters about these responsibilities be exchanged. An alternative form might involve the experimenters sending a letter to the responsible organizational officials specifying *both* sides of the agreement and requesting a written reply confirming the contents of the letter.

In addition to organizational agreements, an understanding must also be reached with persons who will volunteer to participate in the experiment. The experimenters should carefully avoid any activity that might later be perceived by the potential volunteers as a coercive act. For this reason, considerable time should be spent with the prospective participants in answering questions and discussing any concerns they might have about their involvement. If the experimenters should detect any marked difficulty on the part of any potential participant, they would be well advised to drop such individuals from the research prior to the experiment itself. It is usually the case, however, that where the experiment is clearly perceived as a positive one by the problem population which, if successful, would enhance the social welfare and social position of the participants, it will not be difficult to find volunteers. The experimenters, in fact, probably will be deluged by many more persons than can be accommodated in the experiment itself. The manner in which extra volunteers may be used to gain additional information about the value of the study is outlined in Chapter 7.

The next most desirable form of agreement might be called a *memo of agreement*. In format and style it resembles a legal contract. It, of course, may ultimately have no legal status whatsoever. By using contractual language and format, it is hoped that the appearance will become a reality. If it *looks* like a binding contract to administrators perhaps they will act as if it is. This is the most desirable form of agreement to be obtained when legal arrangements are impossible.

The ultimate form of a negotiated administrative agreement is, of course, a *contract*. Here all parties to the arrangements specify the exact nature of the agreements and are bound by law to follow them. Unfortunately, many, if not most, human service organizations with which the social experimenters will deal are not able, by statute, to enter into these kinds of agreements. Similarly, it is an inappropriate vehicle to use when negotiating intra-organizational agreements such as those between departments or units of a single institution.

The aforementioned do not exhaust the types of written administrative agreements that are possible. They are merely the ones that are particularly applicable to organizations which will be actively involved in fielding the experiment. Now let us briefly consider the potential *content* of these administrative agreements.

Content of the Agreement

While not exhaustive, the following is a list of potential areas of agreement that the experimenters might request:

(1) An understanding that the research budget is to be expended in the manner, and for the purposes, intended in the research proposal;

(2) An understanding giving the researchers authority to select and randomly assign persons to the conditions presented in the experimental plan;

(3) An agreement to support the experiment when it receives complaints about special treatment, funding, or staffing;

(4) Agreements concerning the sharing and/or assignment of personnel, funds, and/or space;

(5) An understanding not to interfere with the model in the proposed experimental plan;

(6) An agreement not to violate the integrity of the research design nor to participate in procedures designed to curtail a full-time research effort;

(7) An agreement not to seek either inflammatory or self-serving publicity.

In turn, the experimenters could agree to:

(1) Not exceed the dimensions of the agreed-upon experimental program in size, type, or duration;

(2) Not violate any of the existing institutional norms except those agreed upon by all parties as an inherent part of the research;

(3) Provide those services proposed in the research proposal;

(4) Give periodic progress reports, as appropriate, to all cooperating parties;

(5) Not change any of the agreed-upon procedures without specific permission from cooperating units; upon the emergence of any unforeseen difficulties involving other cooperating units, the experimenters will request a meeting to discuss these problems.

The establishment of these reciprocities between administrators and the research team is essential not only to clarify the obligations of each but also to provide a mechanism for continuing communication between the participating parties, each of whom should be interested in finding solutions to the social problems which are their joint responsibility.

EXAMPLES OF ADMINISTRATIVE AGREEMENTS

In order to give the reader a better flavor of the nature of administrative agreements, several examples of agreements reached for a variety of projects are presented in this section. Before proceeding, one additional bit of nomenclature is needed. We have found it useful to distinguish between *intraorganizational* and *interorganizational* agreements. The former refers to the situation in which administrative agreements are typically negotiated with, and within, one organization. Often this is the case when a social experiment is being conducted within an institution such as a hospital, prison, or school. An extension of the one-institution case is the interorganizational agreement, which involves the experimenter and a number of cooperating organizations. This is often the case when an experiment is being conducted in a community context. One of the operational differences between intraorganizational and interorganizational agreements is that the former is considerably simpler and typically involves ascending the hierarchy within a given organization. The interorganizational case is more complex. It involves considerable political juggling and takes more effort to maintain. It is also of extreme importance that all agreements should be made between the researchers and the top management official of the institutions. In the hospital setting, this would be the manager, superintendent, or director; in a prison, the warden; in an educational institution, the principal, president, and so on. Active support of top management is essential for social experiments. The person with the highest status in an institution may not necessarily feel bound to the commitments made by subordinates. Recently, failure to secure such agreements with the superintendent of a home for delinquent girls brought an abrupt termination to a research program agreed upon by an assistant superintendent. Such a failure could readily have been prevented had the initial agreements been made with the superintendent himself or with an individual or body appointed by him. Here then are the examples.

Intraorganizational Agreement: The Junior College

This research was concerned with an experimental comparison of three modes of teaching introductory psychology in a junior college setting (McKenzie, 1976). After developing the initial experimental plan, the principal investigator, who was at the time an instructor at the college, had a series of informal discussions with all potential parties to the research. This included fellow teachers, the department chairman, librarians, and so on. These initial discussions dealt with the general conceptual framework of the proposed innovation and with the types of administrative support that would be needed to mount a full-fledged experiment. Following this, the experimenter prepared a complete formal research proposal. Although all specifics of the necessary agreements were enclosed in the proposal, a separate memorandum of agreement was prepared covering sampling, assignment of space, explicit permission to begin and carry out the teaching programs required by the experiment. One objection that the departmental chairman had to this agreement was that the experimenter would be playing both a research and teaching role. To meet this objection, an agreement was added that the experimenter would not teach in the experimental program, but would use his salary to hire adjunct teaching personnel. While the chairman refused to sign the memorandum of agreement (since "his word was his bond"), both he and the experimenter mutually agreed to file the agreement. The experimenter prepared memoranda of the agreements with the teachers outlining their specific responsibilities *vis-à-vis* the service and research aspects of the project. All parties signed the agreement. An agreement was also reached verbally with each of the students who participated in the experiment. To accomplish this, the experimenter stationed himself at the registration table and informed each potential student for the course that he or she was being asked to enroll in a demonstration class and that certain time constraints would be imposed for experimental purposes. Each person who volunteered agreed to these stipulations. This, then, was the final "agreement" in the planning phase of the experiment.

Intraorganizational Agreement: The Health Planning Agency

This particular research (Beck, 1973) was unusual in that the people with whom administrative agreements were obtained were also the participants in the experiment. Focusing on a community health planning agency, the research concept was designed to test experimentally the feasibility of providing skills of participation to lay citizen health consumers. The agency itself consisted of a small staff which channeled the planning activities of a large group of volunteers, consisting of both health professionals and health consumers. The planning agency was divided into various committees and subcommittees to facilitate the planning process.

The experimental team developed a fairly comprehensive proposal which called for the establishment of an experimental consumer self-education group. Working with the experimenters, the self-education group would hypothetically develop into active participants in the agency planning process. Persons participating in the control condition were those not exposed to the training program.

The proposal was initially shared with a chairman of one of the main committees at an informal face-to-face meeting. He happened to be a health professional who endorsed the concept verbally. At the next meeting of the full committee, the experimenters were asked to make a formal presentation of their proposal. The committee approved the proposal "in concept," and referred it to a subcommittee for further study and development. Several meetings were held between the subcommittee and the experimenters, and every research and service aspect of the project was examined and re-examined. Eventually, the subcommittee approved the proposal "in concept and form" and recommended its approval by the full committee. This was quickly obtained, and the proposal was sent to the executive committee of the agency (essentially a subcommittee of the board of directors). They recommended approval "in concept and form" and sent it to the full board of directors. The board of directors approved the proposal *in toto* and the research was implemented.

Intraorganizational Agreement: The University Residence Hall

Jacokes (1975) became concerned about the effect that coeducational dormitory living had upon the social perceptions and behaviors as well as the academic accomplishments of individuals and groups. In order to carry out the experiment, it was necessary for Jacokes to receive permission to gather information from students living in residence halls at a major university. In addition to the agreements made with the students who would participate in the sample protecting their rights (as described in Chapter 8), Jacokes had to negotiate with university personnel the possibility of having students in select dormitories participate in the program. This required negotiations with university administrators of the residence halls and agreements with the managers of each residence hall. In both the aforementioned cases the role of the experimenter had to be clearly spelled out. Figure 6.1 shows in a succinct form the agreement that was signed among these three parties: the coordinator of the residence halls, the manager of the residence halls, and the researcher.

ON THE PART OF THE MANAGER OF RESIDENCE HALLS

1. Allow Mr. Lee E. Jacokes to conduct a study of Residence Hall Environments as outlined in the attached document entitled, "A Study of Residence Hall Environments," from Jnauary 1973 through June 1974.
2. Agree to follow the method of randomly assigning entering first-time freshmen of September 1973 as outlined in the attached document.
3. Agree to provide a list of 1973 freshmen students assigned to each of these Residence Halls by May 1973.
4. Allow Mr. Jacokes accessibility to student housing files as appropriate to the information needed for the study.

ON THE PART OF LEE E. JACOKES

1. Agree to assume full responsibility for the design, implementation, analysis, and publication of the study as outlined in the attached document.
2. Agree to follow University procedures for insuring the confidentiality of information from participants in the study.
3. Agree to make available all reports on research as they become available.
4. Agree to use the information collected from this research to meet doctoral dissertation requirements.

Coordinator

Manager

Lee. E. Jacokes

Fig. 6.1. Administrative Agreements with Student Residence Halls

Interorganizational Agreement: The Delinquency Project

The experimenter in this research (Whitney, 1974) was an employee of an innercity federally funded youth rehabilitation agency. After some time working in the agency, initially as a volunteer and then as a paid staff member, the experimenter developed the notion of creating a peer-run community-based automotive shop. The shop would serve as a training center for innercity youth and would hopefully contribute to the general economic well-being of the community. This was the proposed experimental social model. At this point, a formal proposal was developed and discussed with agency administrators.

Initial discussions with the agency director and assistant director were encouraging. Figure 6.2 shows the internal memorandum-of-agreement which was drawn up and signed by the experimenter and the administrators of the youth agency. The agreement stipulated that the youth agency would act as the "umbrella" support for the project; would supply volunteer innercity youth as participants and permit their random assignment to the experimental condition; and would supply capital for the business, staff salaries, insurance, and space. In turn the experimenter agreed to establish a non-profit agency to be the operating unit, to establish a program as outlined in the proposal, and to inform agency administration of results of the program.

Following these agreements, the experimenter made a number of additional agreements which are not presented in sequential order. Since the young trainees needed an initial formal training experience, negotiations were held with a local junior college to provide a shortened course. This agreement was consummated by a letter from the experimenter to the junior college. Forms were filed with the state taxation division to achieve tax-exempt status. Forms were also filed to achieve nonprofit status and to obtain the authority to withhold taxes. Workmen's compensation for the trainees was obtained by filing forms with the state department of labor.

Immediately prior to the opening of the automotive shop a number of other agreements were made. An adjacent repair business agreed to send its overflow tire business there. A reciprocal towing service located in a nearby service station agreed to provide this service when needed. Finally, each of the experimental trainees was informed verbally of the pilot nature of the project and its overall intent. The agreement stated:

The following agreement has been drawn up between all interested parties with regard to the automotive cooperative research project being conducted by Young Peoples' Rehabilitative Agency (Y.P.R.A.). This project is being carried out in an effort to determine the effect of delinquents working in group employment (automotive co-op) and individual employment (work-interns) on their rehabilitation and ability to become effective organizers in their community. In order that the responsibilities of all individuals involved in the project are not misunderstood, the following responsibilities of each are hereby agreed to:

ON THE PART OF THE ADMINISTRATION OF Y.P.R.A.

1. Finance the project according to the specified budget and provide stipends for the project participants according to the work-intern criteria.
2. The utilization of Y.P.R.A. clients as participants of the project.
3. The random assignment of project participants either to the automative cooperative or to work-intern positions.
4. That all data concerning the project participants shall be made available to the project director.
5. That the outreach staff of Y.P.R.A. will participate by referring prospective project participants and assist the project director in collecting follow-up data on the project participants.
6. That the project director administer questionnaires and interviews to the participants of the project upon their approval.
7. Individuals not selected to participate in the co-op will be given employment commensurate with their education and ability. If employment is not obtained in 30 days, the project director will then be notified.

ON THE PART OF THE RESEARCH PROJECT DIRECTOR

1. Assume complete responsibility for the daily operation of the automotive cooperative project.
2. Keep the confidentiality of all data concerning the project participants.
3. Make available all reports on research evaluation and monitoring of project to Y.P.R.A.
4. Control project expenditures as specified in the budget.
5. Assign the project participants into small groups for community organizational purposes.
6. Be responsible for assigning the duties and responsibilities to members participating in the operation of the cooperative.

These agreements shall be in effect during the eleven months the project is expected to run, beginning the week of October 30, 1972 and ending the week of October 1, 1973, subject to any changes or extensions by the granting agency. Young Peoples' Rehabilitation Agency Administration.

_____

_____

Project Research Director

_____

_____

Date

Fig. 6.2. Administrative Agreements with the Juvenile Rehabilitative Agency

Interorganizational Agreement: The Community Lodge

As a final, fairly comprehensive example, we will consider the community lodge research of Fairweather *et. al.* (1969). It may be helpful to take this research as a model and to explore its administrative agreements in great detail. In an earlier study (Fairweather, 1964), it had been established that chronic mental patients organized into groups according to certain principles could and did solve problems in much the same manner as other groups. It was proposed, therefore, that groups of these chronic mental patients could be moved as units into the community where they would work and live in their reference group. An experiment was proposed to explore the proposition that membership in these community groups would reduce recidivism and chronicity as well as improve the former patients' perceptions of themselves. Adequate arrangements were made for controlling important variables, acquiring a representative volunteer sample, creating the measuring instruments, and preparing a social innovative design. After the research had been carefully planned in all phases, appropriate commitments to implement it were sought.

The first step was to discuss fully the research proposal with the hospital psychiatrist on whose ward the research would be initiated. It is important to note here that the psychiatrist had been intimately involved in the original hospital research project establishing the feasibility of creating problem-solving patient groups. Because of his own research experience and interest in the proposal, he agreed to support the research effort on his ward. The proposal was then submitted to the hospital research committee whose members agreed that it was a desirable experiment and further agreed to commit the hospital to engage in it. The director of the hospital was a member of the research committee and became an investigator of the research project with a clearly defined status. The principal investigator, who was jointly a member of the hospital staff and of a local university, applied for a grant through the university. The granting agency sent a site visit committee to the hospital, where the entire research proposal was reviewed and the hospital director affirmed the hospital's commitment to the research. The agency approved the grant.

Since the experimental social model involved the establishment of a discharged patient-managed business in the community, it was necessary to secure a residence and a place of business and to make all legal arrangements for the upkeep of both. To accomplish the establishment of the business, the university contracted for the management of the proposed business with a local nonprofit corporation which had been engaged in rehabilitative efforts with mental patients for the past several years. The corporation had agreements with labor unions and other local organizations which made the formation of a gardening and janitorial business relatively easy to accomplish. The university then leased a dormitory in the community to house the discharged patients. A research staff was hired by the university. Equipment to perform the gardening and janitorial work, such as trucks and power equipment, were purchased or leased by the university.

The nonprofit corporation which had signed the management agreement with the university insured the discharged patients, who were now its employees, for liability and workmen's compensation as well as bonding them. They formed a subcorporation for the discharged patients' business. The ex-patients were then able to conduct business under their own name. As part of their new business, they contracted for jobs, kept their own business records, advertised in the local papers. established their own bank accounts, purchased new equipment and supplies, kept their work equipment in repair, and generally, operated a rather extensive business. For their living arrangements, they purchased and prepared their own food, kept the dormitory in repair, scheduled appointments for their members to visit the doctor, and, in the main, contracted with representatives of food handling, medical, and other community organizations to meet the needs of their members. The extensive contractual arrangements and the agents necessary to establish the innovative model so that it would be studied in the community setting are presented in Fig. 6.3.

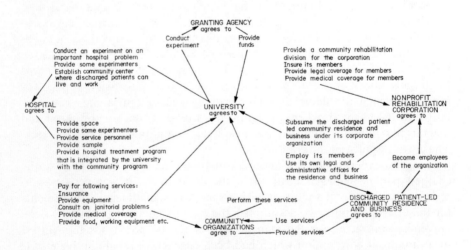

Fig. 6.3. Contractual arrangements among the cooperating institutions

DISSEMINATION EXPERIMENTS

Obtaining administrative agreements for dissemination research is in some aspects similar and in others quite dissimilar to obtaining such commitments for the creation and evaluation of social models. One resemblance is that both require financial support. For dissemination experiments, one must usually obtain agreements from private foundations or the federal government because these experiments are concerned with the spread of useful models or techniques. The financial arrangements are often difficult to obtain since implementing beneficial models has not historically been perceived as an experimental endeavor. It is also difficult to obtain funds for dissemination research because this is often not seen as an important part of a funding agency's experimental effort whether it is county, state, federal, or private. This is why it is exceedingly important that dissemination research be linked from the outset with social model-building evaluative research so that it is perceived by the research team and the funding agency alike as a unitary process. When this is the case, the funding should be obtained through administrative agreements made at the outset of the research program which involves funding both the social model building and dissemination research efforts as a package. When a single agreement cannot be made, it then becomes necessary for the members of the research team to attempt to obtain funds for implementing the beneficial model. In this case efforts to secure financial support will be similar to those presented in the preceding section.

Although achieving funding is difficult, let us assume for the moment that funding has been obtained and that the researchers may now proceed to obtain the other administrative agreements that are necessary in a dissemination research. Further, let us assume that the research team that initially implemented and evaluated the social model has contracted to do the dissemination experiment as well. What is left, of course, are the agreements that have to be made with persons and organizations in the society who may become involved in the diffusion attempt either as individuals or agents of organizations.

While the agreements necessary for financing the project are similar to the agreements reached for social model-building experiments, there are often differences with regard to establishing the conditions for carrying out the experiments. Quite often these agreements require a *behavioral* commitment to carry out a particular experimental procedure for a given period of time. For example, Lounsbury (1973), created a dissemination experiment in which he attempted to evaluate the effectiveness of the written word (newspapers) in getting people to change their habits about the use of energy. He therefore made an agreement through a letter with those individuals who were to participate in the experimental condition that contracted for the reading of the newspaper. The letter said in part, "The purpose of this project is simply to show the private citizen how he or she can help preserve environmental quality through his or her individual actions. Thus, over the course of the next few months you will receive a regular eco-action newsletter which outlines various environmental problems and specific things you can do to help solve these problems. There is no charge or obligation on your part. *We ask only that you (and other members of your family) read the newsletter and try out some of the tips and suggestions.*" It can be seen from this agreement that the experimenter was dependent upon the participants to establish and carry out the experimental condition of reading a particular newspaper. Of course, he continuously *monitored* those who agreed to read the newspaper to see that they were actually carrying out this agreement. The difference here between social model-building research and dissemination research that often occurs should be clear by now. One essential difference is that very often in dissemination research, because of the large number of people or organizations involved and because the experiment takes place in many different homes or organizations, the carrying out of the research conditions (in this case reading newspapers) is "handed over" to the participants. The reader can readily see why agreements must be clearly made and *monitored* under such field conditions.

Sometimes dissemination research requires *behavioral* commitments as well as the commitments of space and staff mentioned in the last section. For example, one phase of the dissemination experiment of the lodge program (Fairweather, Sanders, & Tornatzky, 1974) required that different techniques of persuasion be compared. To accomplish this comparison, it was necessary to establish three different experimental conditions: a written brochure, a verbal workshop, and an action demonstration. These were established in several hospitals throughout the United States so that their effectiveness in persuading hospital personnel to adopt the lodge could be ascertained. To establish these conditions, the hospital had to agree to disseminate brochures, hold workshops, or establish the demonstration unit depending upon their experimental condition.

An example of how the agreements were made to establish the conditions can be seen in the negotiations required to create the demonstration units. To establish the demonstration units, the hospital had to commit a ward and a service staff as well as a sample of patients in order that the demonstration program could be established for comparison with workshops and brochures. A letter showing this agreement and sent by the researcher to one participating hospital said in part: "I am writing to acknowledge your acceptance of a three-day consultation to establish a demonstration ward at your hospital.

It is our understanding that you have agreed to commit, for a two-month period of time, a ward staff typical for your hospital; a group of patients ranging in size from twenty-five to one hundred; and a ward for the purpose of this demonstration." What is important to recognize here is that sometimes the establishment of the actual experimental condition is dependent upon an agreement to carry out certain behaviors as shown in the energy and lodge implementation experiments just discussed.

The agreements in implementation research, therefore, not only require that the research teams secure funds to carry out the research, but also require special arrangements with the target persons or organizations. These agreements are primarily concerned with establishing the experimental conditions for evaluation. Continuously monitoring them to insure that they are being carried out according to the agreements is an experimental necessity that is more fully discussed in Chapters 7 and 10.

IN CASE OF FAILURE

What happens to the experiment when, despite all attempts to secure the necessary agreements the experimenters are unable to do so? At this point, the experimenters are faced with a very serious decision which involves their own philosophy of science and the use of their time. If they have become convinced that the necessary agreements for an actual experiment cannot be obtained, they must either change the physical location of the research by moving to another setting where administrative agreements to their liking can be obtained or they may, if they wish to continue to work in the same geographical area, decide to use quasi-experimental techniques or associative techniques such as those described in Chapter 12 that do not require the stringent conditions of random assignment and experimental control essential for a "true" experiment.

Before the experimenters move to another geographical location, they should obtain assurances through the processes of negotiation just discussed that the experiment can be performed in the new setting. Under these circumstances, the experimenters continue to view an actual experiment as essential to problem solution and accept nothing less. The experimenters thus place the highest priority on information that can give them the highest level of generalizability and the greatest knowledge about causation. Experimenters who find themselves relegated to one geographic area often are not aware that similar organizations in other geographic areas may not be as unreceptive to the research ideas as those with which they are currently working. For example, if the experimenters are working in a state prison in one area of the country it may be possible by shifting their location to a federal prison or to a state prison in another geographical area to find administrators and prisoners who are interested in what the experimenters wish to do and who will help them begin an experiment in their area.

On the other hand, the experimenters may wish to remain in the same geographic area and work with the organization that will not permit a "true" experiment. In this case they will have to pitch the level of their investigation at one which is acceptable to the organizational management. Under these conditions, the experimenters may find it necessary to sacrifice scientific information for practical matters such as the familiarity of living and working surroundings. Whether this type of trade-off is desirable or not is a philosophical question of personal values that each experimenter must answer.

MAINTAINING ADMINISTRATIVE AGREEMENTS

Viewed retrospectively, the administrative agreements just presented indeed represent a complex organizational morass. Unfortunately, this is not the last to be heard regarding the problem of administrative agreements. Each of the problems of sampling, control, publicity, budgets, and the like, that have ostensibly been "solved" by developing a pre-experimental agreement is likely to emerge again when the research action begins. Thus, to avoid a feeling of overconfidence, we encourage you to remember that the organizational glue holding these agreements together is thin, and that actually carrying out a social experiment can do much to disrupt them. But then, that's another story, which is discussed at length in Chapters 7, 8, and 9.

CHAPTER 7

Selecting the Research Conditions and Making Them Comparable

Making research conditions comparable is achieved by designing experiments where those conditions that the experimenters wish to evaluate are created and held constant throughout the course of the experiment or by systematically equating each condition for those that can be controlled and assuming that they affect each condition equally. These two processes—selecting the experimental variables (conditions) to be evaluated and those to be held constant through equating the conditions for them—need to be considered both in the experimental design and during the course of the experiment. This chapter is concerned with the initial design of the experiment. The problems inherent in keeping the experimental conditions constant over the longitudinal experiment are discussed in Chapter 10. The final shape of the comparative and correlative aspects of the design are discussed in Chapters 11 and 12. The planning of a well thought through design—so that the experimental conditions are operating in such a manner that they can clearly be evaluated and the extraneous variables can be eliminated from consideration through adequate control—is essential to both social model building and dissemination research.

SOCIAL MODELS

Any social system can be made comparable with any other system by controlling the effects of selected variables. However, unlike laboratory research, variables in field experiments cannot be eliminated from consideration simply by deleting them from the research situation, because researches must occur in a natural social setting. Social innovative experiments therefore have, as the usual mechanism to control extraneous variables, the equating of the created subsystems on those variables the experimenters do not wish to evaluate at the moment. As a first step in making models comparable, the experimenters must draw upon their own knowledge of the social problem to identify and define those variables that may affect the participants or social processes of the relevant models.

The experimenters are typically interested in the effect upon the social model's outcomes of a limited number of important variables. The researchers may, for example, be concerned about the effect of different groupings of people, such as homogeneous and heterogeneous ability groupings of elementary students, upon their perception of others, and upon their academic performance; or about the effects of guaranteed post-prison employment upon prisoner recidivism; or the effects of other social models with different sample groups or social situations on a variety of outcome criteria. In order to ascertain the effects of the selected participant and social situation variables on the outcomes of a model, it is necessary to isolate their effects from the whole of the social organization. Tables 3.2 and 3.3 contain a number of participant and social situational variables, any one of which could affect the outcomes of a social model. Since the experimenters are usually interested only in evaluating the effects that a few of these variables have upon the social change outcome criterion, it is necessary to control all other identifiable variables that might affect the outcome. Logically and ideally, this can be accomplished by equating each model for every variable except those whose effects the researchers wish to evaluate. Suppose, for example, the researchers are interested in the effects of guaranteed post-prison employment upon criminal recidivism. Two matched groups of prisoners could receive the same conditions of incarceration, such as living in the same cell block, working in the same place, and being imprisoned for the same length of time. Upon release, those participating in the experimental group could be placed in employment while those participating in the comparison group could be continued under the traditional parole practices of the prison, provided that guaranteed employment was not its usual practice. For even more information about the effects of guaranteed employment upon criminal recidivism, post-prison employment could be varied in a graded series so that different experimental groups would have equivalent prison programs but different conditions of post-prison employment, such as different places and types of work.

Making models identical on all variables except those one wishes to evaluate enables one to distill the effects of the experimental variable or variables of the model. To make models comparable, so that the effects of the selected experimental variable or variables can be readily ascertained, the experimenters equate the comparative models on important variables whose effects they are not interested in evaluating at the time. It is here that the experimenters' knowledge of the social problem, usually accumulated through extensive personal observation, is so important. The research team must decide which are the important variables that must be evaluated or equated for control. For example, the experimenters may wish to discover the effects of different methods of teaching upon the achievement of the participants. Since current studies indicate that residence based on socio-economic factors may affect intellectual performance (Katz, 1964), the experimenters would wish to have areas of equivalent socioeconomic status in which to activate the programs. On the other hand, the experimenters might decide to evaluate the effect of such areas upon the performance of students, in which case they would offer the same educational program in different socioeconomic areas. In these two examples the participants (criminals, students) or social situation variables (educational programs, socioeconomic areas) can be either independent variables (experimental), dependent variables (outcome), or one of the variables equated (controlled) so that their effects are constant in each model. Equating social models for important variables so that they are constant in each model results in controlling sources of extraneous variance.

It is also important to recognize that the variables of the first experiments involved in a particular social problem are more crude than they will be when knowledge has been accumulated. Thus, in the prison example just given, the post-prison employment situation is considered a variable that differentiates one model from the other. If an experiment shows that post-prison employment does significantly affect the recidivism rate (outcome), the experimentalists may then wish to utilize different employment situations as variables in subsequent studies so that the type of work situation that contributes most to reduction in recidivism can be ascertained. The experimenters may, for example, compare group with individual work situations, money with peer-group acceptance as rewards, and others more refined variables. The variables are also more crude in the initial researches because they are carried out in order to ascertain the effects of gross differences between models. Again, referring to the prison study just mentioned, from a logical point of view it is first essential to determine whether post-prison guaranteed employment significantly reduces recidivism. If it does, then more finite comparisons concerned with type, amount, and other more refined attributes of particular employment situations can be explored. If it does not, other promising broad variables which might reduce recidivism can be explored. This essentially follows the decision-making paradigm of successive approximations to problem solution as suggested in decision theory (Luce & Raiffa, 1957).

There are, of course, certain variables, unique to specific situations, which the experimenters may not wish to control but would rather observe and measure so that their relationships through statistical associative techniques

can later be determined. One example would be the use of drugs in treating the mentally ill or drug addicts. The amount and type of these biochemical agents are determined by the prescription of physicians. Thus, individuals participating in the experimental models may receive different dosages depending upon their particular needs. If the drug or drug dosage is not varied systematically by the physician as an integral part of the research program, accurate records must be kept. An analysis of these records would reveal whether drug or drug dosage has had an impact upon the population of the model. If the effects of such variables appear exceedingly important, systematic studies under appropriate supervision can later be accomplished. Upon occasion, however, there are events that occur only once and for this reason escape reliable quantitative measurement. In such instances the experimentalists must rely upon observation rather than precisely controlled conditions for information. With adequate planning, however, such instances can be relatively rare.

While the variables that are to be manipulated, controlled, or only observed in any experiment must be determined by the nature of the social problem under investigation, there are general classes of variables that are relevant to all social innovative experiments. These variables have been defined in Chapter 3 as those describing the sample participating in the social model, those internal to the social model, and those external to the social model. Tables 3.2 and 3.3 present lists of common variables in these categories. A detailed discussion of these variables appears in Chapter 3 and techniques for measuring them can be found in Chapter 9.

A careful examination of Tables 3.2 and 3.3 shows that any one of the listed variables could affect the outcomes of the models. Any variable, molar or molecular, that might affect the performance of a model must be treated either as an independent (experimental), dependent (outcome), or equated (controlled) variable in the social innovative experiment. That is why it is useful here to examine closely how the three classes of variables can affect the social models and how these effects can be controlled.

A clearer perception of this logical process can be gained by reviewing some of the social model examples presented in Chapter 5 in terms of the generic paradigm: outcome is some function of participant and social situation variables. Table 7.1 presents these social models in this functional relationship. Paradigm 1 shows that time in prison and the community situation are the experimental conditions, while the participants are equated. Paradigms 2 and 4 also vary the social situation and hold the participants constant through the equating mechanism. Paradigm 5 varies the participants (group composition) and equates the social situation. Paradigm 3 varies both the social situation and participant relationships.

TABLE 7.1

The Relations of the Variables in the Paradigms Presented in Chapter 5

Outcome . . . is a function of . . . social situation . . . and . . . participants		
Paradigm 1 Reducing criminal recidivism	(a) Time in prison (b) Community situation	Equivalent
Paradigm 2 Reducing chronic mental hospitalization	(a) Time in hospital and (b) Community situation	Equivalent
Paradigm 3 (a) Improvement in academic achievement and (b) Social adjustment	(a) Living situation and (b) Professional help	With or without peer group
Paradigm 4 Highest level of personal achievement	(a) Conditions of training (b) Community living and (c) Working arrangements	Equivalent
Paradigm 5 (a) Improvement in academic achievement and (b) Social adjustment	Equivalent	Heterogeneous and homogeneous group compositions

Now let us turn our attention to the detailed cognitive process that goes into planning an experimental design.

Participant Variables

The first important category of variables which affects the outcome of social models is the sample of people who participate in it. This includes all individuals—whether professional staff, service personnel, or the participating members themselves. Because experimental social innovation occurs in institutions or community settings where a research staff establishes the models, the staff has roles and statuses in the models, at least during their developmental phases. Therefore, the experimentalists need to be cognizant of the population characteristics of the staff as well as those of members participating in the social model.

It is also important in this connection to examine some of the methods that can be used to equate models for participating members. As shown in Table 7.1, the experimenters often wish to vary internal or external social process variables to find how they affect the outcome. In such cases the models may need to have equivalent member populations. Table 3.2 presents demographic, personality, and intelligence characteristics which can be measured. Then a score can be assigned to each member of the sample. After such scores are ascertained, *individuals can be matched on the appropriate characteristics* and then they can be randomly assigned to the different models. Each population experiencing a particular social problem usually has a few defining attributes which, when equated, make the sample of the models comparable.

For example, Whitney (1974), in order to make his two experimental groups of delinquents comparable, matched them on a number of important variables but he paid special attention to matching them on their past history of antisocial behavior since he knew this variable was of extreme importance in predicting future antisocial behaviors which would be an important outcome measure of his experiment. A detailed discussion of matching procedures for samples is presented in Chapter 8.

Determining the nature of an individual's membership in the social model is also exceedingly important, particularly whether such membership is voluntary or involuntary. Prisoners, elementary and high school students, and some of the mentally ill, for example, are involuntary members of social models. For experimental purposes, it is important that *membership in the different models be equivalent*. Thus, one cannot logically compare two models, one with voluntary and the other with involuntary members, on outcome and processes because the two conditions of membership might differentially affect both the outcome and process measures. The conditions of membership in an experimental sample are an increasingly important problem with the advent of the new social programs whose members are usually voluntary. In such cases, it is possible to generalize only to other voluntary populations, a matter discussed more fully in Chapter 8.

Each model usually has a staff of professionals who participate in planning and creating the prototype model. They serve as leaders, consultants, and in other statuses. Because of this, it is necessary to *equate staffs* for each model. Even though individual staff members are matched on variables such as age, education, socioeconomic level, and so on, they are likely to behave differently as groups. The experimenters must be cognizant of this difference in group behavior because staffs usually play a dominant role in experimental social innovation, particularly where total institutions (such as prisons and hospitals) are the research setting. When the experimenters wish to compare models with established statuses and roles, it is essential that the individual demographic characteristics and team styles of the staffs be equated for each model.

Another way in which staffs can be equated is by having the same staff function in both social systems simultaneously but playing the different roles required by the social organization of the two social models. Thus, Tucker (1947) completed a social innovative experiment where he created the same classroom learning situation but varied the learning material—one class was taught to read by using only standard English material where another matched group of students spent an equivalent amount of time learning the same material in a bilingual setting by reading the material first in black dialect and then in standard English. The same teacher was trained to teach in both situations by playing the role appropriate for it. In this way the impact—if there was to be any—of the reading materials themselves could be found.

When there are several staffs, they may be rotated through the models in a prearranged order, spending equivalent time in each, so that the effect of the staffs and the order in which they serve in the models is equated. This methodological technique is called counterbalancing and is fully discussed by Lindquist (1953, pp. 162–163). It is frequently the case, however, that time and money will not permit the large number of staffs necessary to achieve adequate counterbalancing. In such instances, each research staff should spend an equivalent amount of time in every model even though the order in which the staffs participate in the models, first in one and then the other, cannot be varied to eliminate the order effects of such a rotation. However, the effect of the order in which the staffs serve can be somewhat minimized by having each staff spend a rather lengthy and equivalent period of time in each program.

The result of switching staffs in order to equate the staff's impact on the model is presented in a 1964 publication (Fairweather, p. 33). There, only two staffs were available for the two experimental conditions. Obviously, one staff had to appear in one of the experimental conditions first so that the order in which the staffs participated in the models could not be absolutely equated. However, the two staffs were switched from one program to the other in order to provide equal time in each. It was found that the change in staff morale accompanying the switch was more pronounced when one model was valued more than the other. Nonetheless, the immediate effects of the change were largely dissipated in about three months. From this information, therefore, it appears that staffs serving in the same experimental condition for periods of six months to a year, provided they spent equal time in each model, would greatly reduce the order effects. Also, it is possible to analyze the experimental measures in small time increments, such as months, and then to compare the different months for the effects of the switch, giving particular attention to those months immediately prior and subsequent to the switch.

This example illustrates that experiments in social innovation must, upon occasion, rely upon careful observation rather than the more desirable controls, because time and money do not permit experimental procedures that could readily be accomplished in the laboratory. It is questionable whether most research budgets could afford the number and varying compositions of staffs that are necessary to meet counterbalancing procedures. regardless of how desirable this procedure might be. Extensive observation and measurement are substituted for experimental control in these instances. An example of this technique is discussed by Vitale (1964, pp. 218–230).

Social Situational Variables

Internal processes

The second category of variables that can affect the outcomes of the models is the social situation. One class of its processes are those that are internal to the model; some describe its structure and function and others define its dynamic properties. A list of these internal social processes, found in Table 3.3, can constitute the independent variable or variables of the social model. Thus, the effects of vertical or horizontal social organization, of different reinforcement systems, and of different status and role relationships can define differences between the internal processes of the created models and are often independent variables in the social innovative experiment. These internal processes, however, are not independent of one another. As far as group organizations are concerned, for example, a recent study reveals that three common dimensions explain the structure of group dynamics. They are morale, leadership, and performance (Fairweather *et al.*, 1969). In any naturalistic social setting, certain of these process variables are the result of social organization and cannot be independently varied; among these are performance, cohesiveness, attitudes, and morale. To elaborate, let us take morale as one example. It is the product of the social model and it is difficult to conceive of a naturalistic social situation where the researcher could create beforehand a precise experimentally required amount of morale so that it could function as an independent or equated variable. Those variables that can be experimentally manipulated and, therefore, can be independent or equated variables are those that can be varied *prior* to the onset of the experiment.

Table 7.2 presents the internal process variables classified into those that can be experimentally manipulated (independent or equated variables) and those that are the products of the system (dependent variables). If the experimenter desires to make internal social processes equivalent-constant for each experimental population—in order to vary the population or external process variables, then *all manipulatable variables must be equated* for the experimental models. On the other hand, when the experimentalists desire to explore differences between the internal social organizations of the models they must clearly identify those internal process variables they are equating and those they are experimentally varying. For example, in the hospital study (Fairweather, 1964), the member and staff roles were varied for the two models while keeping other internal variables constant.

... In the traditional program, all problems regarding the patient are taken up with him as an individual matter. His role is very clearly a

TABLE 7.2
Experimentally Manipulatable and Nonmanipulatable Internal Social
Process Variables in a Naturalistic Social Setting

Manipulatable—Varied (independent or equated variables)	Nonmanipulatable—Resultant (dependent variables)
Hierarchical structure	Performance
Size	Cohesiveness
Complexity	Attitudes
Formality/Informality	Morale
Composition	
Type of work (social, productive, etc.)	
Work organization (team or individual)	
Norms	
Reinforcement	
Communication	
Leadership	
Statuses and roles	
Degree of autonomy	
Voluntary or involuntary membership	
Fiscal processes	
Program (time spent in activities)	

subordinate one in which he relies upon the staff for their final decisions without any voice about possible courses of action. On the other hand, the social system of the small-group treatment program clearly delineates the patient's role as that of participant in group discussion and recommendations. . . .

The different roles for the patients, in turn, required different roles for the staff. . . .

On the traditional ward, the psychologist was responsible for scheduling the patients' daily activities, discussing problems with them. . . . In this program, the role of the social worker usually involved contacts with relatives and discharge plans for selected patients. . . . The nurse dispensed medication, kept accurate accounts of patients' behaviors, assigned beds to new patients. . . and, in general, carried out the nursing function with the help of the nursing assistants.

On the other hand, the roles were quite different on the small-group ward. . . . Once a week, each of the four task groups of patients met with staff and presented their recommendations to them. The staff, then, adjourned to a room where the recommendations were discussed and either accepted, rejected or amended. Usually the psychologist led the discussion but had no vote. . . . The nurse, social worker, and nursing assistants voted upon each recommendation of the patients' task groups. When discharge plans for their members were completed by the task groups, an appointment was arranged for the potential dischargee with the social worker. During this meeting the plans were discussed and were approved, disapproved, or changes were recommended. The decision reached was presented in writing to the task group. The psychologist received notes from the various task groups which concerned task group recommendations about their members, requests for appointments, and requests for consultation during the task group meeting hour. In addition to the usual medical responsibilities and membership in the staff evaluation team, the nurse and nursing assistants frequently placed notes in the task groups' boxes informing each of the task groups about problem behavior of task group members. . . . (pp. 31–32).

Social models are also typically *equated for programs*—time spent in the prescribed activities—except for those differences required to evaluate the independent variables. An example of equating models for programming in order to make them comparable may also be found in the hospital experiment just cited. The two models in the hospital experiment (traditional and small group) were equated for their programs except for those aspects of the models that constituted the independent variable. Table 7.3 presents these two programs.

TABLE 7.3
Program for the Two Social Models

		Small group ward	Traditional ward
A.M.	6:00–6:30	Lights on in dormitory	Lights on in dormitory
	6:30–7:30	Bedmaking, shaving, bathing	Bedmaking, shaving, bathing
	7:30–7:55	Breakfast	Breakfast
	7:55–8:00	Medication	Medication
	8:00–9:00	Task group ward housekeeping	Individual work assignments
	9:00–10:00	Ward meeting hour	Individual work assignments
	10:00–11:00	Recreation hour	Ward meeting hour
	11:00–12:00	Autonomous meetings of task groups	Recreation hour
P.M.	12:00–12:05	Medication	Medication
	12:05–12:30	Free time	Free time
	12:30–1:00	Lunch	Lunch
	1:00–4:00	Individual work assignments	Individual work assignments
	4:00–5:30	Ward activity—patients' choice (recreation, shower, socialize, etc.)	Ward activity—patients' choice (recreation, shower, socialize, etc.)
	5:30–6:10	Dinner	Dinner
	6:10–9:00	Off-ward recreation, i.e., library, dance, etc.	Off-ward recreation, i.e., library, dance, etc.
	9:00–9:05	Medication	Medication
	9:05–10:00	Free time	Free time
	10:00	Bedtime	Bedtime

This table shows that the only differences between each day in the treatment programs, with regard to patient assignments, are the hours from 8:00 to 9:00 and from 11:00 to 12:00 on the small-group ward. From 8:00 to 9:00 they engaged in a ward housekeeping task, and from 11:00 to 12:00 they held task group meetings during which decisions and recommendations about group members were discussed. To provide a control for these two hours, patients participating in the traditional program had work assignments. The differential use of these two hours in the treatment programs provided the time and the social atmosphere for the development of problem-solving task groups, which is the major experimental variable in this study. (Fairweather, 1964, pp. 28–29).

External processes

The third category of variables that must be controlled or varied are those external to the model that can influence the outcomes. Table 3.3 lists them as social climate, state of the economy, socioeconomic area in which the model is implanted, geographical location (urban, suburbs, rural), social location (institution or community), the measuring techniques used in the experiment, publicity, legal constraints, time when the experiment is conducted, and relationships to other community institutions.

The social climate concerns the degree of acceptance of the model by those in whose area it is implanted. If the experimenter wishes to evaluate the effect of social climates, he may vary them and measure their effect on some selected outcome criterion. To achieve this, he might compare the same social model implanted in an institution or community hostile to it and in another institution or community friendly to it. Repeated measurements over a period of time might reveal how the social climate in which they are implanted affected the models and how the models, in turn, affect it. Usually, however, the experimenters wish to equate the social climate in which different models are placed so that the effect of participant or internal social process variables can be measured. Accordingly, the experimenters attempt to locate the two models in the same institution (school, prison, hospital) and the same community locations. Thus, models would be implanted in the same area—particularly if different areas of the institution or community have different social definitions such as closed contrasted with open wards in a mental hospital, or industrial contrasted with residential areas in a community.

Closely associated with social climate, and sometimes indistinguishable from it, is the variable of geographical location. This variable, like social climate, may be varied or equated. Here, the experimenter needs to consider the state, county, and city similarities or differences, the urban or rural nature of the setting, and, if urban, the socioeconomic area of the city in which the social model is to be located. Suppose, for example, that two elementary school models were created and placed in two schools where the social change outcome criterion was academic achievement. It would be of great importance that both schools be located in the same city and in the same socioeconomic neighborhoods if the experimenters were attempting to control socioeconomic environment and geographical location by equating them.

This presents another important place for control in social innovative experiments. It also points up a difficulty. In making social models comparable, it is often necessary to locate them in as similar an environment as possible while, at the same time, preventing the social interaction of the different models' participants so that the effects of one model do not contaminate the others. Particular care, then, must be given the location of the models. If located in the same environment, there must be sufficient geographical or social distance among the models to prevent the contaminating interactions. One method of accomplishing this is to place the models within the same socioeconomic area but separated by sufficient geographical distance so that the people living in the models use different community facilities—stores, and so on. Thus, the probability of their interaction is very small indeed. On the other hand, if the geographical area where one model is located is too small to accommodate more than the one model, others can be located in geographically separate areas where the same socioeconomic conditions exist. Krech, Crutchfield, & Ballachey (1962) present a socioeconomic index developed by Tryon which can be used for this purpose. It is especially valuable because scores for different geographical locations can be directly obtained from census data.

One variable external to the models impinges upon them as one attempts to investigate them: this variable is the measuring procedures employed. Tests, interviews, ratings, and other assessment devices are the measuring tools of the experimenter. Equivalent procedures should be applied to all experimental models, since the assessment techniques are not usually independent or dependent variables. To accomplish this, the same individual should do the testing, rating, or interviewing for all participants in every model. The room where the testing and interviewing takes place should be the same for people participating in all the models. The instructions should be the same. The hospital study just mentioned also gives an example of this.

> ... the recreation hour was a rather *laissez-faire* situation. Patients were informed that they could do anything within the confines of the ward that they wished to do, and with whomever they desired during this hour. To describe the patients' behavior during the recreation hour,

the Location Activity Inventory . . . developed at FDR Veterans Administration Hospital in Montrose, New York, was selected and extensively
modified to accomplish the desired comparisons. The same trained rater
recorded patients' behavior for both wards. . . . (Goldman, 1964, p. 49).

Time is another important variable that may substantially affect most
social innovative research. For this reason, it is important that all models
are activated and terminated on the same date. Fluctuations in economic and
political climates, as well as attitude changes among the citizens, will influence the conditions present at any given moment. Information gained in one
time period may not be comparable to that gained in another. To take
but one example, community models that use employment as an outcome
criterion measure would yield quite different results if some models, activated
during a general depression were compared with models that operated during
a period of prosperity. It is, therefore, necessary to compare models during
the same periods of time. In this regard, experimenters who do not establish
comparative models but, rather, attempt to use a single model as its own
control by measuring the outcome criterion at different moments of time,
cannot logically attribute any changes found solely to the variables operating
in the model, because processes that occur between measurements can affect
some conditions that might, in turn, change outcomes. About this matter,
Cochran & Cox (1957, p. 14) have said:

> If a control is required, it must be an integral part of the experiment
> so that results for the control are directly comparable with those for the
> other treatments. This point tends to be overlooked in experiments with
> human subjects when it is difficult or troublesome to assemble the
> desired number of subjects. For example, if a new drug is to be tested in
> some ward of a hospital the recovery rate in the ward before the drug
> was introduced is not a satisfactory control, nor is the recovery rate in
> a different ward where patients happen to be receiving the standard
> drug. An observed difference between the effects of the new and the
> standard drug might be due to differences in the severity of the disease
> or in the type of patient or in other aspects of the medical care in the
> two time-periods or the two wards. . . .

The use of comparative models opening and closing on the same dates is the
only manner in which the outcomes of experimental models can be logically
compared.

There are also the traditions of the institution or community where
the models are operative. Different institutions or different units within an

institution frequently have quite divergent mores and folkways. Thus, for example, one prison may parole inmates as quickly as possible while another, with a norm of maximum custody, may rarely parole prisoners at all. In mental hospitals, the ward social climate is established by the staff on that ward. Thus, one ward's social climate may be authoritarian, another democratic, and yet another *laissez-faire* so that two wards within the same mental hospital may have drastically different social climates. In order that the experimental programs are operated under the same conditions, the different models should be activated in the same institutions and in the same living and working areas. The two models of the hospitals study (Goldman, 1964) can again be used as an example of attaining an equivalence in physical setting.

> The two wards were located in opposite ends of the building, and, consequently, their floor plans proved to be almost mirror images of each other. These plans included a porch, dayrooms, a number of ward and staff offices, two large dormitory areas, and their adjacent lavatories.
> ... by the time the program was under way, the wards were equally well equipped with books, magazines, playing cards, dominoes, checkers, and other recreational items. A 21-inch television set and regulation pool and ping-pong tables had long been established features on both wards. The wards were, however, physically separated by a locked hallway of approximately 100 feet (Goldman, pp. 45–46).

It is also necessary to control the publicity given the experimental program, especially that publicity which might unduly affect the models. This is particularly important when new models are started, because inferences from the experimental results will be made to future situations where, usually, little or no publicity will occur. Furthermore, such publicity may affect the participants in one model and not those in another. This is most likely to happen when a society has an immediate interest in the new model but not in the old model that is the control condition. Publicity also frequently arouses the interest of lay people who may wish to visit the experimental residences and talk with the participants and, in this and other ways, interfere with the experimental procedures. For these reasons, it is important that the experimenters limit publicity about the experimental program until after the study has been completed.

Since the nonmanipulated variables of a social innovative experiment can be from any of the three classes of experimental variables (participants, internal, and external social processes), the experimenters assume that constancy of manipulatable internal social process variables will yield similar results in performance, cohesiveness, attitudes, and morale (the nonmanipulatable variables) for all experimental models. Despite this assumption by the experimenters, it is imperative that all of these variables, whether manipulatable or nonmanipulatable, be measured throughout the course of the experiment, so that the model can later be compared on any chosen variable at any given time and its relationships with all other measured variables can be determined.

The control and manipulation of these three classes of variables—participants, internal, and external social processes—constitute the means through which social models are made comparable. It is this aspect of the research planning that requires great attention to detail and it is also the aspect of planning that clearly reveals the experimentalists' knowledge of their subject matter. It cannot be overemphasized that the variables discussed in this chapter are those usually present in natural social situations but it is not an exhaustive list and there are many variables, not mentioned here, that are operative in specific situations. The procedures of identifying, controlling, or evaluating them as independent, dependent, or equated variables is the task of the experimentalists and should be directed to the specific social problems with which the experiment is concerned.

Making the models comparable is frequently the phase of experimental social innovation that is most discouraging to the researchers, for it is here that the complexity of social problems comes clearly into focus. The large number of variables which can affect outcomes and processes and which, therefore, must be taken into consideration in the research planning, comes forcibly to the experimenters' attention. This awareness can be extremely discouraging and it may very well be that the complexity of social phenomena has prevented the growth of experimental methods for social innovation. The experimenters cannot ignore these variables if they value the results of their research efforts. However, the complexity of such planning should not serve as an excuse for failing to conduct such experiments. With considerable effort, the important variables can usually be managed in a way that permits a test of the experimental hypotheses. And even though complete control of experimental variables is probably never attained in practice, it is the logical model upon which inferences rest. Thus, all models in each experiment must be made as comparable as possible on those variables that need to be controlled. This close attention to constructing an adequate design in the planning phase of the experiment will be rewarded at its conclusion, because such attention to detail will eventually lead to the most accurate inferences possible under the natural field conditions of a social innovative experiment.

DISSEMINATION RESEARCH

Planning a dissemination experiment so that inferences can be attributed to the experimental conditions themselves is as difficult a process (if not more difficult) than designing an experiment to compare different social models. It should be obvious that the outcome of an implementation experiment—the adoption of a new innovation—is itself affected by the same variables (participants, internal and external social processes) as those extant in social model experiments. The same logical attempts to control for extraneous sources of variance by matching procedures with samples and equating those variables one wishes to control across conditions once the variables to be manipulated have been identified is followed in dissemination researches.

In planning the design these can be handled in various ways. Let us look at each of the possible sources of variance in turn and attempt to logically decide and review how the participant, internal and external social processes have been accounted for in different experimental situations.

Participants

As with social model-building experiments, making the experimental conditions constant for participants when they are not to be varied is an extremely important procedure. Thus, Lounsbury (1973), who was concerned about the adoption by individuals of more ecologically sound behaviors, chose to have only middle class socioeconomic persons participate in the experimental condition. In this way, he equated the different conditions of persuasion for the participants by limiting the sample to a particular socioeconomic class which constituted the sample under each experimental condition.

Taylor (1975), on the other hand, designed an experiment to account for possible differences in socioeconomic class by stratifying his sample in terms of upper, middle, and lower socioeconomic groups. He therefore planned to vary the participants by stratifying his sample into different socioeconomic levels from which he would be able to account for the variance due to socioeconomic position. In the Fairweather, Sanders & Tornatzky (1974) study a key participant variable based upon other experiments was that of the social status of the individuals contacted within the mental hospital. Since several studies showed that persons at the top level in management might readily destroy an innovation if they were not concerned with it, this study divided the participants into various social status groups within the mental hospitals in order to account for that important participant variable. In that study one of the experimental conditions, therefore, was the social status of the person —called the contact—who was to promote the adoption of the mental health model in the hospital. Thus, the social power of the advocate (superintendent, psychiatrist, psychologist, social worker, nurse) became an experimental condition, so that the effect that the contact's social status had upon adoption of the lodge society by each hospital could readily be ascertained. The effect of the superintendent's characteristics (education, professional experience, etc.) upon adoption was also explored.

These examples show that in implementation experiments, like social model-building experiments, the various participant variables are either controlled through matching or varied as experimental conditions. It is also important to note here that in every experiment participant variables—such as age, health, and the like—should be measured and correlated with the outcome measures. For, as mentioned earlier, it sometimes happens in field research, particularly in complex social processes such as dissemination, that variables cannot be controlled. They should, however, be measured and their results assessed as accurately as possible through correlative techniques such as those described in Chapter 12.

Internal Social Processes

A glance at Table 3.3 shows that the internal social processes are most relevant when the target of the implementation experiment is a social organization rather than individuals. While it is clear that the type of social organization, group processes, fiscal processes, and the like need to be accounted for throughout the course of any social model comparative experiment, it is also true that some additional internal processes gain considerable importance in the design of implementation experiments. Fairweather, Sanders, & Tornatzky (1974) list these as the decision-making, communication, and organizational receptivity processes. It is especially important, therefore, in implementation research that those variables related to decision making (communication and the like) be considered in planning the experimental design. The communication process relates to not only the task of communication but the degree to which the communication is clear and whether it reaches its audience or is blocked by the organizational structure. A related process of receptivity concerns whether or not the organization is responsive to intervention attempts from the outside.

While some of the internal social process variables need to be considered when the audience is persons, they are fewer in number and much less complex than when the sampling unit is the organization. Examples of this can readily be seen when two recent experiments, one whose target population is people and another whose target population is organizations, are contrasted. Two of the important variables in Lounsbury's (1973) study concerned the processes of persuasion and communication. These were handled by varying the two variables as experimental conditions. In the persuasion condition (prod) he repeatedly called individuals requesting that they adopt ecologically sound practices, where in the control "no prod" condition no calls were made. He varied the communications variable by creating two conditions of reading about ecological matters—in one an ecological newspaper went to the participants and in the other it was also sent to the residents and their neighbors. In the Lounsbury experiment the adoption target was persons and there were only two central variables. By contrast, the Fairweather, Sanders, & Tornatzky (1974) experiment involved 255 organizations. In it different types of communication (brochure, workshop, action demonstrations) were created as experimental conditions. Many other social process variables were measured but not controlled. An example of some are: the degree to which participative decision making was accomplished, the financial condition of the hospital, and development of new programs internally.

The simple increase in number and type of internal social process variables that need to be controlled, equated, or varied increases dramatically when the target audience is organizations rather than people. Such complexity clearly means that organizational dissemination experiments require extensive experimental planning to account for internal processes.

External Social Processes

External social processes also have to be considered in dissemination experiments. They may be handled in a number of ways which vary with the complexity of the research and the target population. For example, Taylor (1975) was concerned that his family planning research might not get local community acceptance. Since the target population was people, he was able to reduce external pressure against his research by holding his group meetings for the discussion of the use of contraceptives in a local church. Fergus (1973), in attempting to implement her nursing home program, was also concerned about particular external factors. She stratified her sample into those nursing homes that were publicly and privately operated because she believed that the organizational environment generated by outside funding (public contrasted with private) might grossly affect the adoption forces. The Fairweather, Sanders, & Tornatzky (1974) study also had to account for external factors. Being a national study, the urban or rural nature of the mental hospital and its federal or state affiliation was stratified in the design so that information about the hospitals' locations and administrative affiliations could be ascertained directly from the experiment. It was also possible to look at other external factors such as the region of the country that might affect adoption.

It should be clear that in the design of a social model or implementation experiment it is exceedingly important to plan from the outset for those participants, internal and social external variables that can affect outcomes. Where the variables are important enough to constitute an experimental condition, they should be incorporated into the design through stratification or as a central feature of the social model so that their contribution to the outcome can be evaluated directly. Whenever they cannot be incorporated into the social model or dissemination evaluation, they should be matched (if participant variables) as experimental condition variables or equated across the experimental conditions (if social process variables) so that the effects of each variable will be equally felt in all experimental conditions. If important variables cannot be varied as experimental conditions, arranged as strata, equated, or matched across conditions, they should be measured so that at the very least a correlative study can be made of any relationships that might exist among them and between them and the outcome criteria. Experimentalists can take an initial step towards making their experimental conditions comparable by showing how each participant and social process variable (listed in Table 3.2 and 3.3) will be accounted for (matched, equated, varied, or measured as an uncontrolled variable) in each social model or dissemination condition.

CHAPTER 8

Defining the Population and Obtaining the Sample

One of the most crucial dimensions affecting the outcomes of innovative social models is the characteristics of the persons and social organizations which participate in them. Also affected is the dissemination of beneficial social models since this process too involves sampling considerations. It is exceedingly important, therefore, that the researchers have a clear understanding of adequate sampling procedures and how they are used in both social model innovation and dissemination experiments. This will be the burden of this chapter.

SOCIAL MODELS

Randomness and Representativeness

At any given moment a certain number of people experience a particular social problem in a society. The total number of individuals in the society who are victimized by a given problem represents the *population* for that social problem. Thus, for example, there are a certain number of people who are chronically mentally ill, socially deprived, school drop-outs and other marginal persons in the entire country who are participants in its many social problems at any one particular time. These populations overlap and change from moment to moment as the result of several variables, such as population increases, economic conditions, and changing attitudes. Because the social innovative experimenters wish to establish social models that have *general* applicability, they attempt to select from the total problem population a sample that is representative of it.

A sample that is to be representative of those individuals experiencing a given social problem—one that yields valid information about the effects of a social model in solving the social problem for the population—*must be selected at random*. To attain randomness, the experimenters must exercise

169

no choice about the selection of individuals within the framework of the sampling procedures chosen. Exercising such a choice makes useless the probability tables from which inferences about the effectiveness of the social models will later be made. It is easy for social innovative experimentalists to ignore the principle of random selection because random samples are often difficult to attain. Such difficulties are particularly pronounced when the research is completed in institutional settings, since appropriate sampling procedures require institutional commitments to new solutions for their problems. Experimental necessities for innovative solutions are quite often in conflict with existing institutional norms. Nonetheless, the experimentalists must strive for random selection although even with perfect cooperation —a condition rarely achieved—it is doubtful that randomness ever occurs in naturalistic settings.

Concerning random selection under field conditions, Snedecor (1956, pp. 7–8) states:

> Randomness in sampling is perhaps never quite attained in practice. It is nevertheless the mathematical model on which most statistical theory rests, and since the theory must be used in drawing conclusions from work-a-day samplings, it is to the interest of the investigator to approximate, as closely as feasible, the ideal conditions. The better the approximation, the more nearly correct will be the inferences drawn.

The selection of the problem is the first step in determining the population with which the experimenters are concerned. For example, if the experimenters choose to study the effects of heterogeneous and homogeneous (track system) groupings of students upon academic achievement, by this choice they have limited their population to students. They then may decide that they are interested in the effects of these different group compositions on the performance of elementary school students. And then later they may be concerned only with elementary students in suburbs around large urban communities where middle-class and upper middle-class families reside, because their information might show that homogeneous and hetereogeneous groupings occur most frequently in these settings and they are a continuous source of difficulty there. The problem therefore has immediately limited and defined the population with which the experimenters must be concerned. In turn the researchers have also limited the inferences drawn from the results to this selected population, a matter discussed more fully in Chapter 13.

In order to select a sample which meets the conditions of randomness, it is necessary after problem selection to define the characteristics of the population which will provide the participant sample. The experimenters define the population by describing its attributes. They need to know the distribution of age, socioeconomic status, health, educational level, and other demographic information of the problem group along with their behavioral and biological characteristics. These attributes define the problem population. Such information comes from three main sources. They are personal experience, surveys, and historical records.

Becoming acquainted with individuals who are experiencing the social problem the researchers wish to investigate is an important first step in gaining information about the attributes of the experimental population. For example, several weeks of observation and discussion with those in a mental hospital make the experimenters keenly aware that people living in closed wards behave differently than those in open wards, despite other similarities in case histories. This then, is a key attribute differentiating the two groups that cannot usually be obtained from surveys but must be taken into account in sampling procedures.

As another example, the experimenters interested in school problems should spend time observing the students in different schools. They may find gross differences in teaching methods, teacher and pupil behavior, health, and values among schools located in different socioeconomic areas. Accordingly, the experimenters may use this information to establish stratified sampling procedures for children from the different socioeconomic areas. On the other hand, they may use this information to define more clearly the population they are interested in. They may, for example, perceive the problem as more acute for pupils in one socioeconomic class than for those in another. Thus they may become concerned about lower socioeconomic groups, and if they then had interpersonal contact with them, these direct experiences might enable them to describe more adequately the lower socioeconomic population so that procedures could be initiated to sample this group appropriately.

The results of a lack of direct experience with problem groups can be seen in the recent controversy about the I.Q. scores of non-white students. For many years, black psychologists have been informing their white counterparts that their own experiences have led them to conclude that the scores black students obtain on these tests are more indicative of cultural biases inherent in the test and the test setting than of intellectual ability. It is only recently that any credence has been given to this argument despite the *lack of* direct observation and personal information on the part of the white psychologists. Errors can be made in interpreting information when the interpreters are unfamiliar with the population about which they are trying to predict.

Other examples of observations in schools, prisons, rehabilitation centers, and neighborhoods could be made. They all illustrate that it is imperative for the experimenters to have immediate experience growing out of empirical observation to acquaint themselves directly with the defining attributes of the research population. Direct experience is thus a necessary but frequently ignored source of knowledge that should be used in defining the problem population.

An additional but not substitute source of information that may be used to determine the characteristics of the population under consideration is the survey. Questionnaires may be given through interview or the mails to determine many of the demographic characteristics of the population under consideration. The data from these questionnaires may be utilized to define further the attributes of the problem population. Information from the problem population, family, friends, employers, associates, etc., can yield valuable defining information. Other sources of information—such as school records, census data, and hospital files—may be used to supplement the descriptive information collected from observations and questionnaires.

In addition to personal experiences, surveys, and other records, it is important that the social innovative experimentalists discuss the nature of the population characteristics with individuals who have extensive experience in day-to-day contacts with them. The experimenters who wish to establish models for the blind should discuss their behaviors, perceptions, and living situations not only with the blind but also with those who daily live and work with them. The defining attributes of the problem population result from a collation of all these sources. A list of the most common descriptive information obtained from them that is most useful in describing research populations can be found under participant characteristics in Table 3.2.

An example of how the techniques of observation, survey information, and discussions with problem population can be combined is shown in one of the author's researches with tubercular patients (Moran, Fairweather, & Morton, 1956). The problem of irregular, ill-advised, self-discharge from treatment by some tubercular patients came to light in the late 1950s. A research team spent considerable time in a tubercular hospital observing and talking to the patients and staffs, studying ward designs, and talking with relatives in an attempt to gain a comprehensive picture of the tubercular patients' situation and of their particular characteristics so that an attempt could be undertaken to discover what differentiated those patients who remained for cure and those who left early still infected. Interviews were taken from all important persons. A description of regular and irregular discharges showed:

Differences between the regular and irregular discharge groups in past life adjustment are striking. In grade school the irregular discharge group was significantly more truant, had more difficulty with peers and teachers. In adolescence they had fewer friends, fewer social interests, and quit attending church earlier. In the military, they were more frequently disciplined, they more often disliked officers and they more frequently failed to gain in rank. Occupationally, they changed jobs more frequently because they were "tired of the job" or were dismissed; they held more menial jobs, were less well-paid, and were more frequently unemployed. In most of the prehospital behavior areas measured the mean of the irregular group is in the direction of maladjustment, and in over half of the areas significantly so.

This maladjustive pattern, as reflected in the gross examination of past behavior, is magnified by the direct observation of behavior in the hospital. Here the behavior of this group, as independently rated by four observers long before voluntary discharge against medical advice, was in the direction of maladjustment on every variable measured. The maladaptive nature of their behavior in the hospital was most evident in their disregard of regulations designed to protect their own health and the health of others, and in their friction with hospital personnel.

In a second illustrative study by a research group (Lindemann *et al.*, 1959), the experimenters were interested in the characteristics of the population of persons who seemed to remain indefinitely in mental hospitals. Essentially the question became: Are those persons who remain indefinitely in the mental institution different types of people than those who leave quickly? Here again extensive observations of and discussion with the population, relatives, and staffs were involved. A survey of a sample of patients was conducted and an index was constructed with which the length of hospital stay could be predicted. A brief description of this index was reported as follows:

> The potential value for research in chronic mental illness of an instrument for the early prediction of length of hospital stay was indicated. Data on 21 demographic variables, available within three weeks of hospitalization, were gathered from clinical record folders. Five variables were found to predict significantly for the initial and cross-validation samples. Based on the combined samples (N=457), an index was devised which predicted Short Stay (under 90 days) and Long Stay (91 days or more). The validity of the index depends on the cutting point selected. Prediction can be made for the entire sample with 77% accuracy, or for approximately one-half the sample with 91% accuracy.

After the population is defined, it is then necessary to select a *representative* sample from it to participate in the experimental models. Representative samples are needed because, if differences are found when comparing the outcomes of the models, the experimenters will want to generalize the observed results to the problem population from which the samples were drawn. Many and varied sampling procedures have been established to accomplish this. A complete discussion of them is outside the scope of this book, but the essential characteristics of sampling techniques as applied to experimental social innovation will be presented. For a more detailed discussion of the complex problem of sampling, surveys, and experimental design, the reader is referred to Yates (1949) and Cochran (1963).

Matching

The sampling techniques utilized by the experimenters must be those that yield the most information from a relatively small sample. This is necessary because the social models that the experimentalists must create are expensive and difficult to establish. Usually the experimenters have a limited budget that they use to establish these social models in either institutions, the community, or both. If these new social models require living arrangements, a frequent occurrence with marginal groups, there typically will be very limited space. Size of sample thus becomes extremely important. Therefore, the experimenters must often utilize the most efficient sampling procedures possible consistent with an adequate research design. To receive the most accurate information for the research investment, the experimenters, whenever possible, use matched samples as participants in the created models. Matched samples contrasted with unmatched samples of equal number, increase the probability that accurate inferences about the outcomes of the models can be made from the research results by minimizing the differential effects that participants can have upon the outcomes of the social models. Reducing differences between participating samples is particularly important when the experimenters are attempting to establish the effect of social situational variables upon outcomes.

To control for the effect that different participants might have on the models outcomes, then, it is most efficient to *match* individuals who will participate in the models and then to assign each of them *randomly* to one of the experimental models. The gain in efficiency and information brought about by using matched samples compared with unmatched samples is discussed by McNemar (1962, pp. 82–86), and the techniques of random assignment to the different models (conditions) can be found in Snedecor (1956, pp. 9–14) and Dixon & Massey (1957, pp. 33–35). It is especially important that this technique of *matching and then randomly assigning* the matched persons to each experimental condition is *not* confused with *post-hoc* matching, where individuals are matched for comparative purposes *after* the experiment is completed. Such non-random sampling procedures create problems of inference that have recently been elaborated by Campbell & Stanley (1963). *Post-hoc* matching, however, can sometimes be used to yield information not available elsewhere as discussed in the volunteer section of this chapter.

Before matching procedures can be initiated, it is necessary to *define the key variables* on which the participants should be matched. However, if the experimenters have been living and working with such individuals, have conducted surveys, explored records, and discussed the problems of this selected population with people who have experience in the field as just mentioned, they should be able to identify the key defining characteristics of the population. They can then collect items of information that describe these characteristics. To do this, they obtain descriptive statistics (usually means and standard deviations) about these population items. Since the geographical area from which the sample is drawn may limit its representativeness, the collected descriptive statistic can be compared with national figures, if they are available. Comparisons of the sample with national statistics on key defining variables gives the experimenters information about the representativeness of the sample.

It is important, however, to caution the experimenters about the use of national statistics collected by others. The experimenters should meticulously investigate the manner in which the national data were collected and how the statistics were computed before using them for comparative purposes. Data may be distorted because of collection procedures and the computation of the statistic itself. An example of the latter was found in the tubercular patient example (Moran, Fairweather, & Morton, 1956) as shown by the authors' conclusions:

> One further point about the nature of the irregular discharge problem should be mentioned. A small group of individuals, probably no more than 10 or 15 per cent of all people hospitalized for tuberculosis, appear to constitute the entire irregular discharge problem. This small group, through repeated irregular discharges, builds up the reported annual "irregular discharge rate" to almost 50 per cent. For example, the nineteen patients in the present sample have already contributed an average of four irregular discharges. Thus, a relatively small group of maladjusted individuals seems to provide the source for the technically accurate but somewhat misleading statement that almost half of all hospitalized

tuberculous patients leave the hospital against medical advice.

It is most important that complete demographic information is obtained for the sample population and is presented in any publication of the research results. This is necessary because future researchers may wish to replicate the study or compare the sample with other samples.

Since the experimenters wish to generalize from a finite sample to the problem population, it would of course be desirable if the sample could be drawn from the national population. Suppose the experimenters are establishing different models for a national program. Let us further suppose that the researchers are interested in males between the ages of 18 and 21 who are in lower to lower-lower socioeconomic positions. Any number of indices of socioeconomic status could be used here. A classification that ranks a person according to scores on occupation, income, and housing—such as Warner's (1960) index of socioeconomic status—could be used. Another example of a classification scheme is Tryon's index of census data, which provides a means of scoring geographic areas on the basis of socioeconomic variables (Krech, Crutchfield, & Ballachey, 1962, pp. 318–326). Those falling into lower and lower-lower socioeconomic levels in any census tract in the United States can thus be identified. Then, appropriate sampling methods can be applied to the national geographical areas involved, using procedures such as those developed by organizations (such as the Bureau of the Census) doing national surveys. In this way individuals from different geographical areas can be matched on key variables and each of the matched participants can then be randomly assigned to the created social models. This desirable national sampling procedure, however, is usually not available to the social innovative experimenters. Often they must obtain the samples under far less than ideal conditions. They may, for example, have access to the population of only one institution or, at best, several institutions within one geographical area. Although the experimentalists always attempt to compare the descriptive information of their sample with national figures and continuously advocate replications in order to discover the generality of their findings, the researchers still must establish the sampling procedures within the framework of the practical limitations imposed upon them by the social situation.

Because the social innovative experimenters are often interested in marginal populations, their sampling procedures are typically less complex because key defining matching characteristics of these populations are often limited in number. Simplification of matching procedures occurs because most marginal groups have a few well-defined attributes that clearly differentiate them from other social groups and, in addition, are slow to change over time. For example, most chronically hospitalized mental patients receive high dosages of tranquilizing medication, without which they become grossly disorganized—hallucinated or deluded—and they have long hospital residence; culturally and socially disadvantaged persons have low educational achievement, have high rates of school drop-outs among adolescents, are frequently minorities, and have high rates of unemployment; the blind and the physically handicapped also have obvious differentiating features. Because of the high probability that these attributes will appear in particular marginal groups, it is frequently possible to generalize quite widely from a small sample of participants who are carefully matched on these key features.

In one experiment, for example, the effectiveness of four psychotherapeutic treatment programs was compared for three different groups of mental patients (Fairweather *et al.*, 1960). Previous experience and research information indicated that different patient groups (neurotics, acute and chronic psychotics) might respond differently to the four treatment regimens. Research information further suggested that patients of different ages might also respond differently to the treatment conditions. Accordingly, patients in groups of four were matched on age, diagnosis, and length of hospitalization (the three key variables) and each member of the group was then randomly assigned to one of four treatment situations. By matching on the three key variables, the participants in each treatment were also matched on other important characteristics, such as education, level of employment, and occupational status. The degree of similarity that was achieved by matching on these three defining variables is shown in Table 8.1.

Further examples may be found in other areas for social innovative research. Katz's article (1964) suggests that to be comparable, students should be matched on educational background with special reference to socioeconomic level, and a summary article by Holland & Richards (1965) indicates the need to consider past academic achievement (grades) in any matching procedures applied to students. Thus, grades and socioeconomic level are two key variables that need to be considered when creating relatively equivalent groups that might participate in different school social models. Another example may be found in the relationship between recidivism and chronicity in a criminal population (State of California, 1965, pp. 90–94). The number of previous incarcerations is one key variable that must be considered when matching such populations in order to explore the effect of innovated rehabilitative programs.

These illustrations all indicate that when knowledge is accumulated about a particular problem, it is often found that samples can be equated by matching the participants on a few important key variables. It is the experimenters' knowledge of the variables that noticeably identifies a particular population which aids them in creating the matched samples.

TABLE 8.1

Comparison of the Four Treatment Groups on Demographic Characteristics

	GG[a]	G[a]	I[a]	C[a]	Test of significance
Matching variables					
Diagnoses					
% character disorders	12.5	12.5	12.5	12.5	
% neurotics	20.8	20.8	20.8	20.8	$\chi^2 = 0$
% psychotics	66.7	66.7	66.7	66.7	
Mean age	36.25	33.17	34.21	34.92	$F = ...$ [b]
Mean weeks of prior NP hospitalization[c]	51.6	49.2	53.8	54.8	$F = ...$
Concurrent variable					
% receiving tranquilizing drugs	54	58	58	42	$\chi^2 = 1.58$
Demographic variables					
Education					
Mean grade completed	10.5	10.6	11.0	11.2	$F = ...$
Race					
% White	79	75	75	75	
% Negro	21	25	25	25	$\chi^2 ... 0.17$
% pensioned for NP illness	67	50	67	58	$\chi^2 = 1.52$
Mean age of first NP hospitalization	28.5	27	29	31	$F = ...$
Employment					
Mean % time employed in past 10 years	71.5	75	68	71	$F = ...$
Mean weekly salary of last job	74.3	63.2	68.5	62.7	$F = ...$
Occupational status					
% professional-managerial	12.5	20.8	25	16.7	
% skilled trades, sales clerical	33.3	20.8	20.8	20.8	$\chi^2 = 2.48$
% unskilled workers	54.2	58.4	54.2	62.5	
Marital status					
% currently married	25	33	25	25	
% single or divorced	75	67	75	75	$\chi^2 = 0.53$

[a] GG—group living; G—group psychotherapy; I—individual psychotherapy; C—work.
[b] The F-ratio value ... indicates that the within-group variance was greater than the between-group variance.
[c] NP—neuropsychiatric.

Multistage Sampling

These procedures are sufficient if the models within which the individuals are to participate are closed social systems without input or output of members. However, such is rarely the case in naturalistic settings. In these settings the experimentalists usually draw their matched pairs, triads, etc., at the beginning of the study in order to achieve equivalently matched participants at the outset. Matching procedures and random assignments are thus only the first stage in a *multistage sampling process* that continues over time. After the initial matched sample is obtained and the models become operative, the major sampling problem becomes one of securing additional matched participants while, at the same time, preserving the dynamic naturalistic properties of the social models.

There are, of course, many multistage sampling procedures which can be adopted to assure randomness and adequate matching that will increase the possibility of attaining representative, matched samples to participate in the created models. If the research is carried out in an institution, arrangements for a sampling pool can be made. After the initial matching procedures have been completed and assignments to the models have been made, the models can then be put in operation. At the same time, a building to house incoming participants can be located at a considerable distance from the building where the research is being conducted. New participants can live in this unit for an equivalent and prearranged time during which demographic and other information is obtained from them. The new residents can then be matched in pairs or groups of individuals, depending on the number of models, and randomly assigned to one of them. The advantage of this procedure is that it guarantees a matched sample while also controlling for the influence of the time variable. The disadvantage of the pool system is that it requires considerable administrative commitment and the establishment of a separate unit in which the new members of the sample can reside prior to their assignment. However, these multistage sampling procedures are most important when the research is done in an institutional setting.

An example of the use of a sampling pool for matching purposes can be found in the Sanders, MacDonald, & Maynard experiment (1964, pp. 197–198). The purpose of this experiment was to compare the effects on group performance that group homogeneity-heterogeneity would make. Four groups were formed. Each represented a different composition of low and high socially active participants. Sanders *et al.*, describe the sampling process as follows:

> For two weeks prior to the assignment of patients to their respective task groups, social activity measurements were taken daily. By the use of these scores, each patient was assigned a mean social activity number. The total distribution of these numbers was then divided at the median and four experimental groups were composed as follows:
>
> Homogeneous-high: All social activity scores above the median.
> Heterogeneous-high: Two-thirds of the scores above the median and one-third below.
> Heterogeneous-low: One-third above the median and two-thirds below.
> Homogeneous-low: All scores below the median social activity score.

It should be noted that patients were selected at random from the above- and below-median groups in order to comprise the four task groups. A fifth group, entitled the "Orientation Group" was established. Its function was to orient all new admissions to the ward program and procedures. Each new patient remained in the Orientation Group for a minimum of one week, while daily social activity scores were obtained. The mean of these scores determined whether the new patient was above or below the social activity median established for the initial sample. This was done so that when any task group member left the ward, his replacement would *maintain the predetermined composition of the group at the desired level of social activity.*

A second and somewhat less desirable multistage procedure may be employed when management cannot or will not support the establishment of a separate residence where matching procedures can take place. The first stage consists of the matching and random assignment procedures just described. It is followed by a second stage, consisting of simple random assignment to the experimental models. The procedure merely requires that after initial matching and random assignments each new candidate for participation in the created models is assigned to any of the models in the study on admission, without bias. This procedure is less precise than the two-stage matched procedure used when an actual sampling pool is available, because it depends upon chance phenomena to continue the equivalence of the matched samples achieved in the first stage. Nonetheless, this less efficient technique is sometimes necessary in institutional research where research procedures are frequently perceived as interfering with ongoing service programs and where permitting the initial matches is distressing enough to institutional management. A detailed discussion of management commitments required to establish appropriate sampling procedures was presented in Chapter 6.

Multistage sampling procedures are also used in community settings where assignment is accomplished by making agreements with the appropriate institutions for a random selection of matched participants prior to their leaving the participating institution. Here the experimenter may be concerned with mental hospitals, prisons, and other total institutions or with schools, industries, and other organizations that are integrated into the social complex of a society. Several institutions of either or both types may cooperate in the overall sampling by each contributing a specified number of matched participants to the study. After matching, these participants are then randomly assigned to the different community models upon release from the institution. Thus, a continuing flow of matched participants can be provided, as with the organization just discussed. However, with this type of sampling, it is necessary to establish a sampling pool by close cooperation with the involved institutions.

Sometimes the sampling procedures involve an existing organization and a newly created social model. The sampling problem concerns providing a constant number of persons to the innovated social model and other comparative models from a sampling pool located within the *one* cooperative organization. The recent lodge society study exemplifies this type of sampling problem. Two community social models—the traditional mental health facilities that exist for any person returning to the community (the naturalistic condition) and the newly created community lodge—were contrasted. The process of arriving at an adequate sample for each social model is described in the following manner:

> The ward in which patients were assigned to each of the experimental programs was an open ward in a large 2123-bed general hospital comprised of two divisions. The division where the experimental ward was located contained 1123 beds, all for neuropsychiatric patients. Patients were assigned to the experimental ward without bias from open wards within the hospital when bed space became available. All patients participated in the small-group program just mentioned. When an individual arrived in step 4 of the small-group program, hospital departure plans had to be made (Fairweather, 1964). At this point in each patient's hospital stay, the lodge program was described to him and he was asked whether he wished to volunteer to participate in it. If he did, he became one of the volunteers in the study and was matched on age, diagnosis, and length of hospitalization with another volunteer. Each one of the matched pairs was then randomly assigned to either the traditional or lodge community programs. This same random assignment procedure was followed for all individuals who subsequently entered the sample. However, since each individual entered the ward at a different time, every person entering the sample after the initial matches was singly assigned to the two community conditions. Thus, initial sampling was done on a matched-pair basis and subsequent sampling by simple random assignment (Fairweather *et al.*, 1969).

Volunteering

Research in community settings often has an additional sampling problem that does not exist when the research is one in more restrictive institutions. Total institutions—mental hospitals, prisons, and so on—assign their residents to the programs established by the institution, and usually such assignments are involuntary. Schools, particularly elementary and high schools, frequently assign students or require certain courses so that there is little or limited choice by the student concerning his or her courses or the method of teaching. On the other hand, participation in community social models, particularly those that involve living and working situations, requires that the participants *volunteer* to live and work in the created programs. The experimenters therefore often have the variable of voluntary or involuntary participation as a differentiating feature of community research compared with institutional research.

The problem of volunteering for scientific studies has been a rapidly changing one over the past several years. There has been a tendency for the American public to become increasingly concerned about the welfare of those who participate in social experiments. If it had not been for the unfortunate experimentation of some individuals who were not as concerned about the welfare of the participants as they should have been, this problem may not have arisen. The prototype of the unethical experiment is the Birmingham study in which persons who had contracted syphilis were placed in a no-treatment condition in which they were deprived of antibiotics for years *after* the discovery that penicillin was an adequate treatment for that disease. Events such as these have made the public and the concerned members of the scientific community more keenly aware of what can happen to persons who participate in experiments when the researchers are not totally committed to advancing the welfare of the participants.

There has also been an increasing concern among civil rights leaders and others who have raised the issue about who should participate in experiments and for what reasons. In response, the federal government has in recent years demanded more and more assurance that those individuals who participate in experiments are aware of their rights in such circumstances. Ethical guidelines for research, such as those presented in the American Psychological Association's report *Ethical Principles in the Conduct of Research with Human Participation* (1973), have blossomed. These recent events have increased the awareness of socially responsible researchers and have made it imperative that those individuals who are not under court order to participate in a program or who are not minors be informed of the experiment itself and of their rights and obligations. If there are several different programs those who volunteer need to be told that they may be assigned to any one of the different models all of which, if the principles outlined in Chapter 2 are followed, *must* have the purpose of benefiting the participants.

It is important here for the experimenters to realize that *today* there is no such social program as a *no-treatment* control condition. The responsible agents of a society must provide *some* program for those who need it. All such programs must of necessity be designed to help the individuals involved. The theory upon which the programs are based may be incorrect and benefit may not accrue to the participants, but the underlying motivation to aid others is there just the same. It is for this reason, as mentioned in Chapter 2, that the control condition for experimental social innovation is *the* existing program; it is *not* a no-treatment program. It is thus much easier to explain to the prospective volunteers that they will receive some treatment considered to be beneficial but the comparative value of each one is unknown at the time of random assignment.

In these times and with the increasing enlightenment of the public, social researchers, administrators, and others there is today less concern about the effects of volunteering as an experimental variable than there has been in the past. In the vast majority of studies *all* those who participate *must* be volunteers. Since any individual who enters a social program usually does so voluntarily, the act of volunteering is nowadays part of the entire naturalistic process to which one would wish to generalize in most cases and so it often is a standard condition for participation in any social model.

Nonetheless, there are still some instances when volunteering is not necessary. Those who are committed by courts or are otherwise in the hands of various agencies of the government (criminals, certain mental patients, those unable to care for themselves, and the like) may be *assigned* to participate in a particular program by the official of the society (judges, etc.). In such cases the responsibility, as mentioned in Chapter 2, for not providing any treatments—which could be considered inhumane—must be borne by the experimenters and society's officials. If simple humanitarian rules are followed, even when individuals do participate in programs through court order or through societal decree, such programs should in no way do harm or an injustice to the individual.

There is also a volunteering problem with minors. Consider here new educational programs that might be designed for pre-school children. If the teachers who are responsible for the program through society's delegation, the parents, and the researchers all are involved in an effort to improve the quality of education so that new programs are believed to have the potential of improving the education of the individual, then the participation of persons in the researches will, in the long run, be enhanced. But most significant here is the need to emphasize the responsibility that concerned researchers have under such instances of participant assignment. It increases their responsibility since those whose rights have been denied (children and court cases) do not have the authority to refuse to participate in prescribed programs.

When conditions of volunteering exist and in cases where there are also nonvolunteers, it is often informative to compare volunteers and nonvolunteers in an attempt to discover if the volunteers differ from the nonvolunteers in any way. There are several ways in which conditions for this type of comparison can be established. A random sample of the nonvolunteers, for example, can be compared with the volunteers on a variety of information

TABLE 8.2

Comparison of Volunteers and Nonvolunteers on Demographic Characteristics

Variable	Volunteers	Non-volunteers	df	χ^2
Median age	43	42	1	1.26
Race, %:				
White	80	80	1	0.00
Other	20	20		
Military service, %				
Service-connected pension	55	60	1	0.31
No service-connected pension	45	40		
Military service, 0–122 weeks	49	47	1	0.80
Military service, 123 weeks and over	51	53		
Military rank, buck private	29	22		
Military rank, PFC or higher	71	78	1	1.66
Neuropsychiatric hospitalization				
Median age at first hospitalization	29	31	1	0.07
Median number prior hospitalizations	2	2	1	0.60
Median weeks prior hospitalizations	239	120	1	7.78[b]
Type of hospital admission, %:				
Voluntary	45	39	1	0.70
Commitment	55	61		
Parents' marital status, %:				
Married and living	18	21	1	0.45
Other	82	79		
Brought up by, %:				
Both parents	54	54	1	0.00
Other	46	46		
Days since last contact with relatives, %:				
0–89 days	64	74	1	2.45
90 days and over	36	26		
Employment:				
Social classification of last job, %:				
Lower middle class and upper lower class	29	49	1	8.07[b]
Lower lower class	71	51		
Median number of jobs held in last 10 years	2	3	1	3.87[a]
Median highest grade completed	12.0	11.7	1	1.93
Drinking behavior, %:				
Heavy drinkers	33	27		
Social drinkers	41	53	2	3.86
Non drinkers	26	20		
Police arrests, %:				
One or more	57	57	1	0.00
None	43	43		
Marital status, %:				
Single and never married	54	43	1	0.00
Other	46	57		
Current monthly income while hospitalized, %:				
0–$101	47	38	1	1.96
$102 and over	53	62		

[a] Significant at 0.05 level.
[b] Significant at 0.01 level.

that may be pertinent to the subject under investigation. For example, Beck (1973) used volunteers to participate in a health planning experiment. Some health consumers volunteered and some did not. In comparing volunteers with nonvolunteers on demographic information, Beck found several significant differences. The volunteers had larger families and lower incomes. It sometimes happens that the volunteers who serve as a control—the naturalistic treatment—can be contrasted with the nonvolunteers to extract the effect of volunteering when both groups receive the same experimental treatment. The lodge society study (Fairweather, *et al.*, 1969) provides an example of this sample comparison. The conclusion from this comparison, as shown in Table 8.2, was: "the volunteers compared with those who did not volunteer for the community lodge have been hospitalized for a significantly longer period of time, have more frequently held lower lower-class employment positions, and have held fewer jobs. It seems apparent that the volunteers have made a poorer psychological and social adjustment in their past histories."

Volunteers were matched and randomly assigned to the lodge society or to the usual community program, which consisted of rehabilitative counseling, needed medication, and the like based upon individual prescription. The nonvolunteer controls, by virtue of not having volunteered, also participated in the usual community program just described. Thus, these groups of volunteers (usual community treatment) and nonvolunteers (usual community treatment) differed only with respect to volunteering, because both of them received the traditional community treatment.

Since significant differences did exist between the volunteer and nonvolunteer groups upon entry into the program, as shown in Table 8.2 and as just described, additional post-experimental matching was needed before the volunteers could be equivalently compared with the nonvolunteers on treatment outcomes. The procedure to accomplish this was described in the following way (Fairweather *et al.*, 1969):

> The volunteer- and nonvolunteer-nonlodge groups were significantly different on three variables. The nonvolunteers had spent significantly less time in mental hospitals; they more often held lower middle-class and upper lower-class employment, that is, employment of a higher social class level; and they had held more jobs during the past ten years. In order to compare for the effects of volunteering alone, both groups must be equated on these historial adjustmental variables so that sample differences do not affect comparisons designed to assess the effect of the act of volunteering itself. This can be accomplished by a matching process whereby 75 participants in the nonlodge-nonvolunteer group are

TABLE 8.3
Comparison of Volunteers and Nonvolunteers on Demographic
Characteristics after Matching

Variable	Volunteers (N = 75)	Non-volunteers (N = 75)	df	χ^2
Median age	43	43	1	0.00
Race, %:				
White	80	79	1	0.00
Other	20	21		
Military service, %:				
Service-connected pension	53	60	1	0.43
No service-connected pension	47	40		
Military service, 0–131 weeks	51	49	1	0.01
Military service, 132 weeks and over	49	51		
Military rank, buck private or PFC	57	53		
Military rank, higher than PFC	43	47	1	0.06
Neuropsychiatric hospitalization:				
Median age at first hospitalization	29	30	1	0.67
Median number prior hospitalizations	2	2	1	0.11
Median weeks prior hospitalizations	286	251	1	0.03
Type of hospital admission, %:				
Voluntary	45	41	1	0.11
Commitment	55	59		
Parents' marital status, %:				
Married and living	81	81	1	0.04
Other	19	19		
Brought up by, %:				
Both parents	56	60	1	0.11
Other	44	40		
Days, since last contact with relatives, %:				
0–16 days	51	49	1	0.03
17 days and over	49	51		
Employment:				
Social classification of last job, %:				
Lower middle class and upper lower class	30	48	1	3.64
Lower-lower-class	70	52		
Median number of jobs held in last 10 years	2	3	1	2.68
Median highest grade completed	12	12	1	0.44
Drinking behavior, %				
Heavy drinkers	27	32		
Social drinkers	46	49	2	1.48
Nondrinkers	27	19		
Police arrests, %:				
One or more	55	57	1	0.00
None	44	43		
Marital status, %:				
Single and never married	55	45	1	0.96
Other	45	55		
Current monthly income while hospitalized, %:				
0–$124	49	41	1	0.01
$125 and over	51	49		

matched on age, diagnosis, and length of hospitalization with the 75 persons from the volunteer-nonlodge group. It has already been shown in previous studies that matching on these characteristics equates patient groups on other demographic characteristics, a matter discussed earlier in this investigation.

Accordingly, each member of the volunteer-nonlodge group was matched with a member of the accumulated pool of 183 persons in the nonvolunteer-nonlodge group on age (within two years) and chronicity (exactly, in terms of membership in the three diagnostic subgroupings). Where more than one person in the pool of nonvolunteers could be matched with a volunteer, the person selected for matching purposes was chosen at random. In this way, two groups of 75 persons each were formed. Since only age was permitted in the matching process to vary within two years of the age being matched, a statistical evaluation of age was required. A chi-square test revealed no significant difference between the newly matched groups with respect to age ($\chi^2 = 0.00$, 1 df). Table 8.3 shows no significant differences on 18 other personal background characteristics after matching of the two groups. These two

TABLE 8.4
University Research Contract Form

1. I have freely consented to take part in a scientific study being conducted by :.............................

....

under the supervision of :..

Academic title : ....

2. The study has been explained to me and I understand the explanation that has been given and what my participation will involve.

3. I understand that I am free to discontinue my participation in the study at any time without penalty.

4. I understand that the results of the study will be treated in strict confidence and that I will remain anonymous. Within these restrictions, results of the study will be made available to me at my request.

5. I understand that my participation in the study does not guarantee any beneficial results to me.

6. I understand that, at my request, I can receive additional explanation of the study after my participation is completed.

Signed ....

Date..

Note:

1. If films, kinescopes, videotape recordings, photographs or audiotape recordings are to be used, a *Release Form* must be used in addition to this form.

2. If children are involved, a *Parental Consent Form* must be used in addition to this form and, where appropriate, a *Release Form*.

matched groups now differ only in the major characteristic that members of one group, when asked, volunteered to go to the lodge situation (and did not) and the other group, when asked, did not volunteer.

Since volunteering for scientific experiments is of such extreme importance nowadays, it may be informative to look at some examples of how permission to participate in the experiment is obtained in various settings. Table 8.4 presents the current form used at Michigan State University when persons volunteer for psychological experiments.

Thus, volunteering is a sampling problem that is especially important in social innovative experiments. Most new rehabilitative programs require that individuals volunteer to participate in them. The logical question that immediately arises is whether or not the volunteers are a representative sample of all the individuals experiencing the problem. In most contemporary social experiments this will not be a concern since *all* persons participating in the prototype and replicate models will be volunteers. Where this is not the case, an exploration of differences between volunteers and nonvolunteers can be undertaken by surveying the differences and similarities in their attributes or by establishing a nonvolunteer comparative group. Nevertheless, absolute probability levels leading to direct generalizations about the nonvolunteer group contrasted directly with volunteers is logically unattainable. Generalization can only logically be made to other volunteers. This is exceedingly important, especially with those new governmental programs that depend upon volunteers for their samples, because generalization about the success or failure of such programs for society—even when other appropriate conditions are met—can be considered applicable only to those who volunteer for them. If a well-conducted survey had established that only 10 percent of a problem population had volunteered for the experimental program, it should be obvious that such volunteers may not be representative of the problem population. Hence models that are satisfactory for these volunteers may or may not apply to the nonvolunteers, who, in this example, constitute 90 percent of the problem population.

Attrition

In most longitudinal studies there will be attrition of part of the sample both during the experiment and during the follow-up period. It is the researchers' responsibility to minimize the attrition as much as possible. Records should be kept of the amount and type of attrition that occurs during the experiment. Attrition tables can be later used to present this information in the results of the study. An example can be found in an earlier study when four types of therapeutic treatment—(1) group living

(GG), (2) group therapy (G), (3) individual psychotherapy (I), and (4) work (C)—were compared (Fairweather *et al.*, 1960). Table 8.5 presents the loss in sample and the reasons for the loss over the 24-month course of the experiment. Attrition can be minimized by setting up procedures for encouraging individuals to continue their participation in the program from the outset of the study. Thus, in longitudinal experiments it is always important to establish procedures to gain the participants' support regardless of what particular experimental conditions they might be participating in. This is one long-term advantage of informing participants about the experiment so that they can decide whether they want to volunteer.

Attrition not only occurs during the experimental period, it also occurs during the follow-up period, which may last for months or years. Usually losses can be minimized by good planning. Some examples of attrition with good and poor planning can make this point quite readily.

An example of a well-planned follow-up study was the research done by Whitney (1974). He had a sample of 61 juvenile delinquents and potential delinquents who participated in two different programs—the establishment of an automobile co-op for the innovative experimental condition and the usual program of assigned employment in various industrial settings as the comparative condition. Whitney was well aware that a loss in sample size could seriously impair his study, since the sample was quite small to begin with. Accordingly, he set up procedures for working closely with the persons from the outset which involved keeping records about them, particularly the location where they could be contacted at all times. As a result, Whitney did not lose a single person to attrition during the course of his follow-up period.

Another study shows the degree to which follow-up information can be maximized by keeping close interpersonal contact with the individuals who comprise the sample. In a study conducted by Fairweather (1964), 195 patients participated. Veteran's Administration social workers throughout the United States were alerted to the study and were informed when a follow-up ex-patient would enter their geographic area. The social workers then

TABLE 8.5
Reasons for Attrition by Experimental Group

	GG	G	I	C
Required major surgery		1		2
Discharged in less than 21 days	4		1	2
Developed more acute psychotic symptoms	1		2	3
Left without permission	2	2	1	1
Refused post-testing		1		2
Total	7	4	4	10

contacted the individual to make certain that he knew that a follow-up rating would be completed about him. The same social worker continued to work closely with the person followed throughout the experiment. Except for one death, only four persons of 195 were lost due to follow-up attrition. This small loss of the original sample during 6 months of community follow-up can readily be understood from this descriptive account of the tenacity with which the follow-up was pursued:

> This introductory discussion would not be complete without commenting about the extent to which the high proportion of returns was dependent upon the active participation of many people. Illustratively, one patient was interviewed at an airport in New York City after having just flown in from Puerto Rico. He was to return to Puerto Rico within 48 hours and this was known to the social worker prior to the plane's arrival through interview with relatives. Since the patient had been in Puerto Rico for the majority of the follow-up period, there was certain information which could be obtained only from him. This was done. On another occasion an entire family of brothers and sisters became involved in correspondence concerning an individual who could not be located. Through this cooperative effort he was finally found. These are only two examples of the cooperation and aid of others, both professional and family, which were repeated on many occasions throughout the follow-up period. It should be reiterated that the follow-up study could not have been completed successfully without this assistance.

Another way in which attrition of follow-up data can be minimized is in the choice of the dependent measures selected. For example, occasionally it is appropriate to use archival data (such as employment records) as an outcome variable. Often agreements can be reached with agencies charged with the collection of these data to release it for research purposes. This can be done in such a way that personal confidentiality is not jeopardized by obtaining an agreement from each participant upon entry into the program that such sources can be used if the person cannot be located later on. Drivers' licenses, social security numbers, permanent addresses of relatives, and other such sources can be recorded upon entry into the program and used for follow-up purposes if such agreements have been obtained.

High follow-up losses due to attrition are often experienced when adequate planning does not occur. Such high losses can be seen in the experiments of Jamison (1974) and Ives (1974). Jamison's loss was especially high. Persons participating in his program were seen for nutritional counseling concerning various types of physical illness such as anemia, low blood sugar, and so on.

A high percentage, in some counties as much as 70 percent, was lost for follow-up data-gathering purposes because they failed to return for additional meetings with their counselor. But it is very instructive to note here that no follow-up arrangements were made beforehand and no research personnel were assigned to have continuous contact with the individuals involved over the follow-up period. So far as one can ascertain, the persons' participating in the study felt no particular obligation to return for examination when additional follow-up measurements were due. The failure of adequate follow-up information in this study appears to be largely due to the lack of trained personnel who perceived it as their responsibility from the outset of the study to maintain close contact with persons in the sample during the entire follow-up period.

Ives's study also had a considerable loss due to attrition. Here, the participants were drug addicts who resented any kind of continuing relationship because of their past habits and the perceived possibility of getting into difficulty with the law. On the other hand, Ives did not have sufficient staff to overcome the logistic difficulties in maintaining continuous contact with this highly transient clientele.

Although clearly one sample differs from the other in terms of the difficulty of follow-up—ex-drug addicts contrasted with low-income persons who had no legal troubles—it is still important to recognize that losses due to attrition can be minimized when adequate plans are made from the very outset to involve the sample population and to obtain sufficient professional help to gain the follow-up information.

Thus, attrition can be greatly reduced through appropriate planning and actions on the part of the research staff. When this is done, the attrition rate can often be so small as to be negligible. On the other hand, when it happens that despite adequate planning the attrition rate becomes excessively high, it is most important that the experimenter compare the residual sample with the sample first drawn to discover whether any key variables now differentiate the persons remaining in the sample. If it can be concluded that the residual sample does not differ in any significant way from the original sample, one can make some *guarded* inferences about the results. On the other hand, should significant differences appear, it is highly likely that the residual sample is knowingly biased and the experimenter should be exceedingly concerned about the effects of sample bias on his or her results.

Stratification and Sample Size

When the research is concerned with a heterogeneous population, subgroups of which might respond differently to the created models, a sampling procedure that divides the population into these subgroups should be employed. This process is called stratification. In such a case, each subgroup may be treated as a separate population from which a representative sample is obtained. The experimenters may wish to divide the population into different age groups, different educational levels, or different degrees of social deprivation, if the evidence suggests that each subgroup may respond differently to the innovated models.

In a previous experiment (Fairweather *et al.*, 1960), the researchers' observations and other information about the mentally ill population indicated that neurotics, short-time psychotics, and chronic psychotics might respond differently to different treatments. The experimental sample was therefore subdivided into those three strata in order that the three different diagnostic groups could be independently compared. This sample stratification is presented in Table 8.6. It shows that the three diagnostic groups were signifi-

TABLE 8.6

Comparisons of Three Diagnostic Groups on Demographic Characteristics

Variable	N^a	PS	PL	Test of significance
Matching variables				
Mean age	36.09	34.41	33.31	$F = ...^b$
Mean weeks of prior NP hospitalization	25.34	20.47	111.22	$F = 45.91^d$
Concurrent variables				
% receiving tranquilizing drugs	37.5	56.3	65.6	$\chi^2 = 5.27$
Demographic variables				
Education				
Mean grade completed	11.03	10.34	11.09	$F = ...$
Race				
% White	81.3	65.6	81.3	
% Negro	18.7	34.4	18.7	$\chi^2 = 3.94$
% pensioned for NP illness	37.5	59.4	90.6	$\chi^2 = 19.46^d$
Mean age of first NP hospitalization	39.19	29.75	25.88	$F = 3.06$
Employment				
Mean % of time employed in past 10 years	79.22	83.50	51.09	$F = 17.02^d$
Mean weekly salary of last job	68.06	73.72	56.13	$F = 2.37$
Occupational status				
% professional-managerial	12.5	21.9	21.9	
% skilled trades, sales, clerical	34.4	18.8	18.8	$\chi^2 = 3.32$
% unskilled workers	53.1	59.3	59.3	
Marital status				
% currently married	28.1	46.9	6.2	$\chi^2 = 13.39^c$
% single or divorced	71.9	53.1	93.8	

a N—neurotics; PS—short-term psychotics; PL—long-term psychotics.
b The F ratio ... indicates that the within-group variance was greater than the between-group variance.
c 0.01 level of significance.
d 0.001 level of significance.

cantly different in the demographic characteristics of weeks of previous hospitalization, pension for mental illness, employment, and marital status. Furthermore, the results of the study showed that the chronic psychotics and neurotics made a significantly poorer community adjustment after treatment than the acute psychotics. Thus, by using stratification procedures, the demographic differences that appear in Table 8.6 were highlighted and a differential response to treatment by the three diagnostic groups was established. This example illustrates that increased information can often be found when a sample is stratified into subgroups. By combining matching procedures with stratified sampling techniques, the social innovative experimenter can achieve a great deal more information from small samples than can be obtained from simple random assignment. Further detailed discussion of stratified sampling procedures may be found in the book *Sampling Techniques* by Cochran (1963, pp. 86–153).

A problem for which there is no final and definitive solution, since an answer to it is dependent upon the influence of so many situational variables, is that of sample size. The experimenters are continuously faced with this problem. If all the population characteristics are known, an estimate of the sample size necessary to yield a statistic with a preselected level of statistical confidence can be obtained (Cochran, 1963, pp. 71–86; Snedecor, 1956, pp. 60–62). Usually, however, social innovative experimentalists do not have the type of information that permits them to estimate the sample size—particularly when they begin experiments with social problem populations. Therefore, they frequently must make an arbitrary decision about the size of the sample that is necessary for model comparisons to yield information with an acceptable degree of statistical confidence. When sufficient information about the population is not available to estimate the sample size required in the manner presented by Snedecor (1956) and Cochran (1963), it is suggested that the researcher have at least 50 matched participants in each of the models. This number is arbitrarily recommended because certain practical considerations, in addition to the statistical ones already mentioned, typically enter into the determination of sample size. When members participating in a model live in one dormitory, the size of the dormitory itself is a variable in the social model. A current experiment in a community dormitory indicates that 50 participants at any one time might very well be the upper limit for a social model where dormitory living is involved (Fairweather *et al.*, 1969). With two models, this provides a minimum sample of 100. Although the size of this sample is arbitrary, matched populations of at least 50 pairs or over usually yield sufficiently valid comparative and associative statistics. This is particularly true when initial survey material shows the sample to be representative of the parent population. The sample size, at least the minimum permissible size, should be determined prior to the onset of the experiment. Whatever the sample size, however, its representativeness is its most important characteristic.

Dissemination Research

The problem shifts in sampling when one moves from social model-building and evaluation to diffusion of a particular model that has been demonstrated experimentally to be a beneficial one. The general sampling problem in building social models is usually related to making the most of small sample size. In Ives's drug study (1974), the community lodge experiment (Fairweather *et al.*, 1969), and Whitney's delinquency research (1974) described in the last section, the samples were small and a great deal of time and effort was spent in insuring, as much as any individual can, that (1) the samples were representative of the problem group being considered, (2) the samples participating in each social model were equivalent (matching), and (3) different strata of the sample were defined and readied for later analyses. Thus, it is most often the case in social model-building and evaluation that the sampling procedures are extremely tedious so that every participant makes the maximum contribution to the data base of the experiment.

Dissemination experiments, by contrast, usually involve much larger samples. This varies, of course, depending upon whether the dissemination target is persons or organizations, the money one has available for securing a sample, the number of experimentalists and change agents that can be hired, and the location of the attempted diffusion effort. When the diffusion effort is limited to a small geographic area such as a small city or a sparsely populated county, the sample size may be relatively small. On the other hand, if the target population is individual persons and the diffusion is attempted on a national basis, fairly sophisticated and large samples can be drawn.

Sampling procedures where the population involved is *organizations* present a similar problem logically, but a different problem in terms of sample size. Here the target population is a particular type of organization that exists within the society. For example, if one is concerned about disseminating a new drug treatment model, the population for the diffusion effort may be all the drug treatment centers throughout the United States. A national population would also be involved if the dissemination experiment concerned itself with the adoption of models for public school systems, mental health units, and so on. In such cases it is necessary to take as representative a national sample as possible, although it should be obvious that such samples are often limited by cost and personnel factors.

As mentioned with small sampling procedures in the last section, the research team may wish to subdivide the sample into various strata. Thus, for example one can subdivide a city into different socioeconomic strata as defined by Warner (1960), Tryon (Krech, Crutchfield, & Ballachey, 1962), and others or one can divide a nation into different regions, SMSAs, cities, geographic areas and the like. Again, it cannot be overemphasized that the number and type of strata needed will be determined by the problem and by the knowledge that the experimenters have of the basic parameters of that problem population.

Sample size, of course, is a common issue when one attempts to begin the dissemination of an innovation. The prediction of the size of sample needed for a given confidence level is easy to compute when all the parameters of a problem are known. As mentioned earlier, an excellent discussion of this may be found in Cochran (1963). However, it is frequently the case that when experimenters begin to disseminate a particular innovation it is a problem of primary importance simply to define the target individuals or organizations where diffusion will be attempted quite aside from having any quantitative measures on the population parameters. For this reason, other factors such as cost, personnel available, in addition to the type of area one is trying to reach (city, county, state, or national) must be considered in determining sample size. It is usually necessary to make some compromises about the sample size in order to obtain a reasonable degree of accuracy from the dissemination results because of these factors. Thus, the ultimate selection of a sample is dependent upon size of the population, cost, personnel available, and so on. But even if all resources were unlimited, the sample size needed for a desired degree of confidence could only be an estimate based upon whatever knowledge about the target group the researchers may have at the time.

Some rules of thumb however seem appropriate. When the target population is individuals, the experimenters should attempt to stratify the sample on socioeconomic level, race, and other variables that may affect most disseminations to people. As an alternative, the study may concern itself only with those persons who represent the immediate target population, such as upper-, middle-, or lower-class persons; or, if the target population is organizations, the study may be limited to a region. Even so, when the diffusion sample is concerned with organizations, it is extremely important that as large a sample as possible be collected because as one goes through the different stages of approaching, persuading, activating, and diffusing the innovation as required in a dissemination experiment the possibility of a loss in organizations is exceedingly high. Thus, the experimenters will lose a number of organizations as they go through each of the successive phases.

Unless the sample is large to begin with, few organizations will remain for the activating and diffusing phases of the experiment.

This also brings to light a point of caution. It is often the case that researchers will attempt to persuade an organization in which the experimenters work to diffuse an innovation—sometimes one they have helped to develop. This of course limits the number of organizations to one. Beyond the problem of generalizations from a sample of one, which is logically untenable, it is also true that the likelihood of adoption by a single organization is extremely low—making this a risky operation. In fact it would almost be fortuitous if such a single organization did adopt the innovation.

This word of caution is especially appropriate to those persons who do not understand that adoption of a new innovation is a difficult process and should be perceived as a regional, national, or international experimental effort. Those who want a dissemination technique that will guarantee the adoption of a successful social model by their own organization usually are unaware of the low adoption rates that are obtained in the dissemination of almost *any* new social innovation—particularly those that require social role and status changes (Fairweather, Sanders, & Tornatzky, 1974).

Examples of the sampling procedures employed when individuals and organizations are used can now be presented. Lounsbury (1973) was interested in a sample of middle-class individuals from a city of around 150,000 people in a midwestern state. His study concerned the attempt to evaluate the use of different techniques in persuading persons to take action about ecologically related matters such as recycling of glass, reduction of energy use, and so on. To obtain his sample, Lounsbury reports the following procedure:

> Participants for this study were 185 female middle class (defined by membership in census tracts and blocks having above-average property values* for housing units) Smithville residents living in single-unit dwellings. Single-unit dwellings (e.g., a house) were selected for the experiment in preference to multiple-unit dwellings (e.g., an apartment house) because the occupants of single-unit dwellings are more likely to be personally responsible for the maintenance and costs of their utilities and solid waste disposal.
>
> Using 1970 census tract data, a form of two-stage cluster sampling (Cochran, 1963) of above-average blocks from above-average income tracts was accomplished with two units being chosen per block, on opposite sides of the block. The first stage of sampling involved selecting a random sample of above average census tracts in the Smithville metro-

* "In this context, 'above average' refers to the average property value for Smithville, as defined by 1970 census data—$17,800."

politan area. The second stage involved random sampling of above-average blocks in the selected tracts. Finally, houses were randomly selected from the blocks chosen in the second stage.

The Fergus (1973) study involved the sampling of personnel from organizations attending a workshop in order to learn techniques to implement a new form of patient governed nursing program. She set up different conditions of advocacy in order to discover which conditions yielded the greatest movement toward adoption of the nursing home innovation once the persons who had attended the conference returned home.

The workshop had been carried on for several years and information obtained from its records indicated that there was no known bias among individuals who came for the workshop at different times of the year. Therefore, Fergus decided her study would involve the sample that attended the workshop in June and August, because it was possible during those months to get the project funded and to make all the necessary arrangements for the training and experimental participation of the individuals who participated in the workshop. During this time, persons attending the workshop were from 36 nursing homes located in the eastern and midwestern United States. The sample was stratified on the basis of whether the nursing homes were privately run or were part of a state system. This was done because the organizational structure of nursing homes was quite different depending upon whether they were privately or publicly managed. This sample was then followed up with the different experimental techniques of implementation for a one-year time span.

The aspects of the Fergus study that were important for representative sampling are the following: (1) the assumption was made on the basis of previous evidence that the sample of July and August was no different than the sample that might be obtained at any of the other time periods when the program was in operation; (2) for inferential purposes, it was assumed that the sample of personnel participating from the nursing homes was representative of nursing home personnel that might be found throughout the areas where they were located; (3) although generalizations were only to be made about volunteers (all the personnel who attended from the various nursing homes had volunteered), it was hoped that later studies would show whether they differed from the nonvolunteers. However, even if volunteering differences were later found, there was an immediate interest in attempting to implement the nursing home among only volunteers because the act of volunteering for the workshop was an essential condition for any future replication of the experiment; and (4) the sample was stratified into privately and publicly administered nursing homes.

The Fairweather, Sanders, & Tornatzky (1974) study represented a different sampling problem than the preceding two studies from several points of view. First, it involved the *entire population of mental hospitals in the United States* except eight which were randomly discarded at the outset of the experiment. After the state or federal nature of each hospital and its urban or rural geographical location was ascertained, the hospitals were *randomly assigned* from four *strata* (urban-federal, urban-state, rural-federal, rural-state) to the experimental conditions of brochure, workshop, or demonstration program method of intervention and social status level of persons contacted (superintendent, psychiatry, psychology, social work, nursing, etc.). The state or federal nature of each hospital was easy to ascertain since this was determined by their management (federal or state government). The urban-rural nature of each hospital was arbitrarily defined by determining the distance to the nearest SMSA for each hospital. This distribution of SMSA size was divided at the median; hospitals located above the median size were arbitrarily categorized as urban while those below the median of the distribution were categorized as rural.

This sampling procedure, however, unlike that of the Lounsbury and Fergus study just mentioned, involved a *second stage.* This was because the outcome of the persuasion phase of the project yielded volunteer hospitals for a second phase of the study which involved the actual implementation of the lodge society under two new and different conditions of advocacy: one condition involved working directly with a social change agent (action consultant condition) and in the other information about implementing the lodge was provided by a written manual without face-to-face meetings with a social change agent (written manual condition). To achieve equivalent samples in each of these two conditions, hospitals were *matched in pairs* on their background experiences during the first phase of the study. For example, a hospital that was a state hospital in the brochure condition and in an urban community was matched with a hospital that had the same first phase identification (state-brochure-urban). *Twelve pairs* of hospitals with the same experimental background were formed and one of each was then *randomly* assigned to the social change agent and manual conditions. The unmatched hospital was randomly assigned and fell by such assignment into the change agent condition, thus yielding a final small sample of 13 hospitals in the change agent condition and 12 in the manual condition accounting for all 25 hospitals that had volunteered to participate in actually implementing a lodge society as a joint effort between their hospital and the community. A final phase involved a follow-up of all 255 hospitals one year after the end of the activation phase.

These three examples have shown that the proper population for dissemination experiments is either persons (Lounsbury) or organizations (Fergus; Fairweather *et al.*); sampling can be single (Lounsbury) or multiple stage (Fairweather *et al.*); it can be stratified (Fergus; Fairweather *et al.*), or unstratified (Lounsbury); the experiment can involve large or small numbers; and the conditions of sampling will vary depending upon the population with which one works and the stage of sampling (approaching, persuading, activation, diffusing). The essential condition of the sampling for dissemination is its representativeness and one usually seeks the smallest size sample that will give an adequate estimate of dissemination outcomes because of the cost involved. Here again sample stratification and matching are essential cost savers (more information per unit of cost). Special consideration must be given to matching on past experimental conditions prior to assignment to new conditions as one goes through the various phases of dissemination-approaching through diffusion, as shown in Figure 3.1.

In this chapter we have attempted to review issues of sampling as they relate to problems encountered in model building and dissemination research. Discussion was focused on representativeness, matching, stratifying, multi-stage sampling, sample size, and problems of volunteering.

CHAPTER 9

Measuring the Important Parameters

The experimenters must now prepare instruments with which they can measure the three attributes of the experimental process—participants, social situation, and outcomes.

INSTRUMENT CONSTRUCTION AND USE

Before instruments can be selected or created, however, it is essential that the researchers have an understanding of the concepts that are basic to measurement, particularly those that are used in the construction of scales. The general discussion presented here is liberally sprinkled with references so that the interested reader can easily find a more thorough presentation of the rationale and computational procedures of measurement.

It is most important that the investigations be cognizant of the fact that units of measurement for the data of social innovative experiments represent the entire spectrum of measuring scales. Generally viewed, there are four types of scales into which most social innovation data can be classified. They are the nominal, ordinal, interval, and ratio scales. Detailed definitions of these four types of scales appear in Stevens (1951) and Siegel (1956, pp. 22–30). An excellent basic discussion is available in Anderson (1971). They may be summarized as follows: Nominal scales are "naming" scales, which specify only membership in a category. Examples are diagnostic labels such as schizophrenic or tubercular and social group membership lists such as occupational groupings (lawyer or physician). No quantitative relation is defined between any of the categories. The only formal property of this scale is, equivalence within a category—that is, all members of a group are equivalent in membership. Ordinal scales do specify a quantitative relation among different categories (or points) of the scale, but are limited to statements of equivalence and inequality. Thus, of two values a and b on an ordinal scale, one may specify only the relations "equal to," "greater than," or "less than," with no statement of the distance between unequal values.

Any set of scores which may be ranked from least to most or best to worst makes an ordinal scale. An interval scale is formed when the distances between any two points are known for all values on the scale. Scales to measure temperature are of this type. A ratio scale is one which has an absolute zero point as well as all the characteristics of an interval scale. Examples are scales of mass and velocity.

Since social processes are real-life phenomena, they usually can only be measured with nominal or ordinal scaling. Indeed, it is questionable whether interval or ratio scales can empirically exist with most social data, at least as these variables are now conceived. Because of this, it is usually appropriate that the experimentalists plan to create nominal or ordinal scales. Of the information which the researcher utilizes, only standard psychological tests and other investigator-constructed questionnaires and some demographic information such as age may have actual interval or ratio measurement, and even here such precision of scaling is questionable. Because of this, the experimentalists need to categorize their information carefully so that scales appropriate for the data can be constructed. It is also important to note here that the classificatory nature of most social innovative data often requires the use of nonparametric statistical techniques, a subject more thoroughly discussed in Chapter 11.

The type of scale involved is only one of many considerations that have historically emanated from the construction of psychological tests when experimentalists enter the arena of measurement. While a detailed discussion of validity and reliability cannot be presented here, it is important to examine briefly their place in the measurement of social outcomes and processes. Excellent discussions of these measurement concepts as typically used in psychological test construction are available in Anastasi (1961, pp. 105–149), Ghisselli (1964, pp. 207–253, 335–369), and Guilford (1954, pp. 374–410).

Historically, the concept of validity has been given many different definitions which can be ranked from the very empirical to the very theoretical. In our discussion, the validity of an *outcome* measure will be considered separately from the validity of other measures, such as those of internal process, and so on. *The validity of an outcome measure in the field of social innovation is simply an empirical matter because it can be defined as the magnitude of its correlation with the social change outcome criterion.* As discussed in Chapter 2 and elaborated later in this chapter, the social change outcome criterion represents the consensus of a society's representatives about an acceptable solution to a given social problem. The social change outcome criterion, then, is the only valid criterion measure as far as society is concerned. Accordingly, the outcome validity of any other measure obtained during the course of an experiment can be ascertained by determining its correlation with this criterion.

Outcome validity for a social innovative experiment, therefore, concerns the extent to which any measure correlates with the outcome that society's agents are most interested in; for a social model experiment it might be employment for job training programs or recidivism reduction for criminal rehabilitative programs; for a dissemination experiment, it is the measure of model adoption. These correlations inform all interested parties about the relationship of any measure that might be taken during the course of the experiment with the measure that has the most important meaning to society's agents. Another type of validity, which we shall entitle *concept validity*, is involved in any social innovative experiment. It is more traditional and concerns the degree to which any assessment device measures what it purports to measure. The central question is: Do the created or chosen instruments actually measure the desired concept (morale, cohesiveness, aptitudes, and so on)? This form of validity is determined by conceptualizing different measures that logically appear to measure the construct in question and then determining through correlative techniques their interrelationships with an attempt to find a major defining dimension. The validity of each measure is its correlation with this defined dimension, which is usually ascertained through factor or cluster analysis described in Chapter 12.

Thus, there are two types of validity: outcome and concept. The outcome validity of any measure used in a social innovative experiment is determined by its correlation with the social change outcome criterion. On the other hand, concept validity is a slightly more complex matter. It is determined by two processes: (1) conceptualizing different assessment areas that appear to measure the concept and (2) finding their central dimension. For example, group morale might be defined by several different measures such as satisfaction with the group leadership, decision processes, peer relationships, and the like. Determining (usually by factor or cluster analyses) if there is a major dimension to which they all are related can then be accomplished. If there is such a central dimension, the concept validity of each measure is its correlation with this derived dimension. If there is not a central dimension, several independent measures of the concept should be used.

Reliability, another concept mainly developed from the creation of psychological tests, concerns the measuring instrument itself. More specifically, a measure's reliability is the degree to which the same scores would obtain if it were possible to repeat the measuring procedures under the same conditions. Empirically, the reliability of a given measure is computed through using various correlative techniques that are described in Chapter 12. Thus, the reliability of an assessment device is determined by the degree of association between distributions of scores. There are at least two general means of achieving these sets of scores and determining their reliability. The first is to secure two measures on the same sample under equivalent conditions and to determine the correlation between the two distributions; the second is to have a sample of raters for the same phenomenon and to utilize a statistic which computes the degree of consensus among the raters. A correlation coefficient is used in the first case and the coefficient of concordance, W, is a statistic that can be utilized for the latter purpose. A high reliability, represented by a correlation coefficient of .95, for instance, demonstrates that very similar scores are obtained when the measure is given under the same circumstances. For a highly reliable instrument, therefore, it is quite probable that the score determination obtained at one measurement would be approximately equivalent to those obtained on a second if no external interference (such as an effective experimental condition) intervened.

The concept of reliability, however, has a somewhat different meaning when applied to certain social process measures because of the nature of the measures and the social situation in which measurement occurs. When the measure is a test, for example, the reliability of that test can be determined by the method just mentioned. On the other hand, it is frequently the case that the measure is a behavior rating obtained in a real-life setting where the behavior itself occurs only once. In these circumstances the researchers cannot repeat the measure, so they use a second method—a consensus about the behavior that occurred in lieu of the usual correlation. In such cases, the "reliability" of the instruments, as far as experiments in social innovation are concerned, is more appropriately considered a consensus among judges. Because these different types of "reliability" are applicable to particular measures utilized in social innovative experiments, the concept of reliability will be discussed independently for each instrument along with a discussion of the measure itself later on in the chapter.

Equipped with an understanding of the concepts and computational procedures related to scaling, validity, and reliability, the experimenters are now faced with the pragmatic problems of constructing scales and utilizing them in collecting the research data. The selection or construction of measures depends, of course, upon the particular problem under investigation. The researchers develop measures that both describe and evaluate those outcome, participant, and social situational characteristics that are central to the problem at hand. It is most important therefore that the invesigators select or create measures appropriate to the problem under investigation, and that they not be rigidly bound to a set of measures simply because they have been frequently used and are available, or because they have high validity or reliability in other situations. After selecting the particular concepts they wish to measure, the researchers then explore the population of assessment devices that might profitably be used in the course of the experiment.

The population of items or measures, often referred to as the pool of scales or items, comes from many sources. The experimenters explore the literature because many measures pertinent to social problems have been developed for laboratory studies or other different but related situations. Another source of information for the collection of important measurable items is the worker in the field. In institutional settings, for example, the personnel who have daily contact with the inmates can often suggest important variables in the social situation or characteristics of the participants that scales could profitably be constructed to measure. Discussions with other professional workers and administrators is another source of potential items for measurement. Most important, however, is the observation of the participants and intimate acquaintance with their daily living situations which give the researchers their most pertinent sources of information for the selection or creation of items from which they can construct the scales. It is, however, from all these sources that the measuring devices are fashioned.

When scales that appropriately measure the attributes of the dimensions cannot be located, the researchers must construct them from their pool of items. They first decide, on a logical basis, which items will measure the research concepts. Items thought to measure the same concept are potential candidates for the scale. Once selected, all items are arranged so that the highest possible score for each item represents the highest value for the concept. Thus, if the scale is designed to measure productive work, each item should be arranged so that its highest score is given to that item response corresponding to the greatest production. Items can then be arranged in groups that logically measure the same concept. This group of items is called a scale. The scale score is the sum of the items comprising the scale. This is one method of constructing a scale. When it is created by grouping items that logically measure the same concept, it is usually referred to as a rational scale. A second typical method for constructing scales is more empirical. These empirical scales are created through discovering the interrelationships of the items in the pool. To do this, the sample of items is treated by factor or cluster analysis. Those items comprising a factor or cluster are then used as scales. A discussion of the creation of rational and empirical scales is presented by Guilford (1954, pp. 414–536) and Tryon (1966).

The scale construction method that has been found to be the most helpful in social innovative experimentation has been a combination of these two methods of scale construction—empirical and rational. After a pool of items has been obtained that logically represents the basic concepts with which the scale is concerned, a number of highly interrelated items are selected that express clearly the underlying rational dimension that one is attempting to measure. Using a cluster analytic technique—a discussion of which is presented in Chapter 12—these scale definers are preset in a cluster analysis so that they will define the cluster, which then becomes the scale. In this way, the experimenter (not the computer) determines the logical essence of the scale. However, the analysis determines the underlying relationships of the definers with all other items of information measured in the scale construction process.

This cursory exploration of scale construction does not, of course, concern itself with many of the details of scale construction such as the following. How many items should a scale contain? Are all items empirically, as well as theoretically, measuring the same concept? Are some items doing all the work in the scale? Can a scale be lengthened or shortened? What are the interrelationships among different scales?

Space does not permit a discussion of these detailed problems and some of the logical and statistical methods that have been developed to deal with them; however, the interested reader can pursue the discussion, in several well-known books. A thorough discussion of scale construction may be found in Ghiselli (1964), Guilford (1954), Nunnally (1967), Riley, Riley, & Toby (1957), and Torgerson (1958).

In addition to selecting the concepts, constructing the scales, and determining their reliability and validity, the experimenters must also be concerned about the measuring procedures. They are first concerned about the degree to which the measuring techniques themselves will differentially affect the processes being measured. It should, of course, be obvious that to keep the experimental conditions comparable, the measuring procedures utilized for one condition should be identical with those used in every condition to be compared.

Making the conditions of measurement comparable, however, does not insure that the naturalistic setting in which they are measured can be maintained—a condition necessary for maximum generalization from the experimental to comparable real-life situations. It is most important here that the techniques for obtaining the research information have as little effect as possible upon the natural living and working arrangements inherent in the experiment. This may be stated as *the principle of least interference.*

There are several techniques that the experimenters can employ to minimize the potential interference involved in the use of interviews, ratings, and other assessment devices. An interesting account of the ways in which measurement affects subjects, and techniques for reduction of these effects, is presented in *Unobtrusive Measures: Nonreactive Research in the Social*

Sciences (Webb *et al.*, 1966). In social model experiments the most important technique to reduce interference is the establishment of data-collection procedures as part of the model's normal operations at the outset so that the participants will not perceive the measuring techniques as interfering. An excellent example of attention to the principle of least interference may be found in the ratings completed by Goldman (1964, p. 53). Here, daily ratings were defined as an integral part of the model's procedures when they were established. Thus, little interference with ongoing social processes was attributable to them because, after the initial curiosity of the participants was satisfied, the rating procedures were accepted as a part of the daily routine.

An example of this principle of least interference in dissemination comes from the lodge dissemination experiment (Fairweather, Sanders, & Tornatzky, 1974). Here vital information about each hospital (255 were included in the study) was obtained from the *American Hospital Association Journal*. It contained several items of information about hospitals which might have been predictive of the diffusion of the lodge society. Some of the items were: number of personnel, size of budget, hospital census, staff-patient ratio, and the like. This crucial information about each hospital was available in the aforementioned publication at the time of the experiment so no intervention into the organizations was necessary. Other examples illustrating how pertinent information can be obtained without entering the social organization and formally getting measures is presented by Hodgkinson & Thelin (1971). They describe measures such as the ratio of faculty meetings to number of actions passed, whether or not the chairman smokes a pipe, and the percentage of faculty with degrees from the same institution, as representative examples of evaluative variables in higher education that can be unobtrusively obtained.

Interference with ongoing social processes can also be reduced if the researchers plan measurements as part of the tasks usually performed by the participants. It is desirable to limit measurement by interview or questionnaire—activities not usually associated with the naturalistic situation. However, when the measures are essential to the research and the necessary information cannot be derived from the usual behaviors of the participants, their use is legitimate. It cannot be overemphasized that any measuring procedure not essential to the completion of the usual role behaviors creates some interference with the naturalistic social processes. Albeit this interference is often minimal, it is important because it will limit the inferences that are applied to nonexperimental replicates where measuring techniques are not employed. Accordingly, the investigators should obtain their information whenever possible from measures that are interwoven into the fabric of real-life processes. An example can be given from the community study

(Fairweather *et al.*, 1969). In this case, ratings of the performance of the work crews were needed. Inspection sheets completed by the supervisor were required when every job was finished. These ratings were used by the crews as feedback information about their work and had a known utility because they were used to guide improvement in workers' performance. After the information was revealed to the crew, the ratings were retained by the staff as research records about the group's performance. This principle is also illustrated in a study conducted by Maynard in which rewards were associated with group performance in a naturalistic work situation. The feedback to the group on its performance occurred in the following way (Maynard, 1964, p. 65):

> As soon as the work of the groups had been evaluated on the Work Rating Scale, the psychologist computed the scores for each group and immediately posted it on the ward bulletin board. Usually all the scores were posted within an hour of the time the first group had finished and within a half-hour of the time the last groups had finished their work. The scores were posted in a way that displayed the cumulative reward gained by each group during the week . . .

When it is essential to use interviews, tests, and questionnaires for evaluation, the naturalistic conditions can be most adequately maintained by establishing the place where the tests or interviews are to be administered at some distance from the experimental situation. The hospital study gives an example of this (Fairweather, 1964, pp. 36–37):

> The paper-and-pencil assessment devices measuring patient change in the attitudes and perceptions . . . were administered when the patient entered and left the program. This testing was carried out in a specific building located approximately one block from the two research wards . . .

Particular attention has been given thus far to the concepts and procedures of instrument validity and reliability, scale construction, scoring techniques, and the procedures designed to obtain experimental data without unduly interfering in the naturalistic processes occurring in social innovative experiments. Now some of the common assessment devices used by social innovative experimentalists should be explored.

In any social model-building or dissemination experiment measures must be taken that quantitatively define and describe the participants, outcomes, and social situational variables as described in Chapter 3. A meaningful analysis and evaluation can only occur if measures are taken on all pertinent variables: those equated or held constant must be measured to assure that the experimental conditions are maintained over the longitudinal course of the experiment and those allowed to vary must be measured for comparative purposes.

The type of instrument or scale used for measuring any particular variable in the experiment must be suited to the object of the study and it must be consistent with the subject matter of the field experiment. Later in this chapter, examples of different types of scales will be presented in relation to the measurement of variables representing different parameters. Before going on to that task, it is important to discuss in some detail the measurement of those variables that are the outcome criteria in social innovation experiments.

MEASURING OUTCOMES

The social change outcome criterion for both model-building and dissemination research is typically a real-life behavior directly related to the solution of the problem being studied. In social model-building research the choice of items is to a large extent dependent on the social problem under consideration. Therefore, the experimenters need to choose criteria that a society's agents agree are a solution to the problem. For example, the social change outcome criterion for most rehabilitative programs—whether designed for the criminal, the chronic mental patient, or the physically handicapped— usually may be defined as adaptive social behavior. Items to measure such behavior deal with the amount and type of work, friendships, attained level of social skills, and so forth. In education, the social change outcome criteria are usually skills learned, grades completed, or other measures of academic achievement. In dissemination experiments, by contrast, outcome behaviors are typically actual movements toward adoption of the specific innovation. Thus, they might represent the different behaviors of the adoption processes, knowledge, persuasion, decision, communication, and action as described by Rogers & Shoemaker (1971). Measures such as participant satisfaction with their roles and future expectations are also important outcomes in some experiments. Outcomes are usually measured by questions asked in interviews, written questionnaires, behavior ratings, and other records of performance such as grades.

An example of some items from a questionnaire designed to assess the outcomes of models for the treatment of mental illness is presented by Wohl (1964, pp. 160–168).

The social change outcome criterion consisted of three areas of social concern about treatment effectiveness—namely, recidivism, employment, and the degree of illness. The questionnaire shows items assessing the criterion:

Name of respondent .... Date ....

Relationship to respondent ....: ....

Questionnaire

Please complete each of the following statements by checking the phrase that best describes how this person is getting along. Check only one of each set. An example is given below:

Example: This person came to the hospital because he was a

.... Clerk

.... Plumber

...X....... Person who needed help

.... Electrician

.... Salesman

The phrase to check is person who needed help. You will note a check opposite the term person who needed help.

Now please fill out the following items by checking the phrase which best tells how .... is getting along.

1. Since leaving the hospital, he(she) has:

    .... Remained out of the hospital and is not receiving treatment for nervousness.

    .... Been under a doctor's care for nervousness.

    .... Been back in a hospital for nervousness.

    Give date or dates ....

2. Since leaving the hospital, he(she) has:

    .... Worked full time (40 hour week).

    .... Worked about 30 hours a week.

    .... Worked some, but less than 10 hours a week.

    .... Been unemployed.

3. As I know him(her), he(she) usually behaves:

.... Very normally.

.... Usually normally, but with a few minor symptoms.

.... Generally normally, but some symptoms show he(she) is not quite well.

.... Not very normally and quite emotionally ill, but he(she) is able to get along.

.... Emotionally very ill and disabled. I believe he(she) will soon have to be hospitalized.

An example of measuring the outcome of the dissemination of a social model can be found in the lodge diffusion experiment. Movement toward lodge adoption was a highly complex task that consisted of a series of behavioral "steps" that could be measured. They are defined elsewhere by Fairweather, Sanders, & Tornatzky (1974):

1. Business. The adopted lodge—to be a viable replicate of the model— should have some form of employment activity for the ex-patient members.
2. Legal. Each lodge would have to establish some form of legal identity such as incorporation or a clearly defined but separate extension of the hospital.
3. Finances. Some source of maintenance funding, either external or internal to the hospital, would be necessary for the basic economic support of the lodge.
4. Patient group development. The group, or groups, of patients who would be lodge members would have to be developed as a cohesive, task-oriented functioning group, with stable leadership and performance.
5. Housing. A community residential facility would have to be located and acquired.
6. Coordinator and staff development. In-patient staff would have to re-allocate time priorities for the development of the patient groups. Some staff person or persons would have to be trained for and assume a coordinator's role.

Taken together, these tasks define virtually all the relevant *actions* necessary to activate and complete a lodge. An additional task was considered because it appeared to have considerable relevance to the adoption process and intrainstitutional social change:

7. Planning group development. Past experience showed that the six tasks mentioned above would be of such magnitude and diversity that they would have to be completed by a group of in-hospital staff. The seventh task, therefore, was concerned with the parameters of such a group: whether or not such a group developed and, if so, its viability as a cohesive problem-solving group.

Table 9.1 presents a summary of the types of scales typically used to measure some outcomes along with selected examples. A detailed discussion of the assessment devices with important references will be given in a subsequent section, "Procedures for Measuring the Variables of a Social Model."

TABLE 9.1
Types of Scales for Measuring Outcomes with Selected Examples

Type of scale	Examples of measures
Personal history	History of the participant as an organizational member
Behavior ratings	Checklist of psychiatric symptoms
	Checklist of criminal behaviors
	Measures of work performance
	Movement toward adoption of social model
Psychological tests	Social adjustment measures (personality tests)
Essay and open-end questions	Measures of satisfaction, morale, and self-regard
Attitude and expectancy scales	Measures of personal attitudes and expectancies
	Morale and cohesiveness measures
	Attitudes of community toward the innovation
Economic records	Records of financial productivity of the innovation
	Records of cost
Administrative records	Academic records of participants
	Medical records
	Prison records of participants
Research journal	Narrative accounts of events related to any of the outcome criteria of the experiment

MEASURING PARTICIPANT CHARACTERISTICS

In Table 3.2 the principal participant characteristics were listed as those pertaining to demographic information, personality, and intelligence. Demographic information is typically obtained through personal questionnaires and administrative records, such as clinical files and military histories. Personality characteristics are usually assessed through interviews with relatives, friends, and the participant; behavior in particular situations that reveals personality characteristics or behavior patterns; and psychological tests. Intelligence is often evaluated by school grades, performance on various aptitude and achievement tests, and awards received for outstanding academic performance. Table 9.2 presents the types of scales and some examples which

TABLE 9.2
Types of Scales for Measuring Participant Variables with Selected Examples

Type of scale	Participant variable examples
Personal history	Historical background before experiment
	History as an organizational member
Behavior ratings	Checklist of interpersonal behavior
	Amount of social activity
Psychological tests	Personality, aptitude, and preference measures
	Social adjustment measures
	Academic achievement tests
Essay and open-end questions	Autobiographical data
	Measures of satisfaction, morale, and self-regard
Attitude and expectancy scales	Measures of personal attitudes and expectancies
Administrative records	Academic records
	Prison records
	Medical records (drugs, illnesses, etc.)
Research journal	Narrative account of events related to participant variables

are most frequently used to measure the attributes of the participants. Discussions of these techniques for measuring participant characteristics are presented with examples in the section "Procedures for Measuring the Variables of a Social Model."

MEASURING THE SOCIAL SITUATION

Internal Processes

Table 9.3 presents a list of internal social processes that are typically measured. The type of *social organization* is measured by determining the table of organization for the model. The type of *work performed* is typically described and measured by the amount of productivity, organization of the work, individual or team work, and the status and role relationships among the work force members (such as supervisor and worker). *Group processes*, the dynamics of the internal social organization, are measured by assessing such important processes as group morale, leadership, and performance, usually by behavior ratings, questionnaires, and other scales. A small group bibliography by Raven (1961), a section of a book by Miller (1964, pp. 123–272), and a reference book by McGrath & Altman (1966) are excellent aids in selecting concepts and finding assessment devices for group processes.

TABLE 9.3
Types of Scales for Measuring Social Situational Variables
with Selected Examples

	Social Situational Variables	
Type of scale	Internal processes	External processes
Behavior ratings	Measure of interaction of group members	Interaction with members of outside community
Essay and open-end questions	Suggestions and comments on social model by members	Suggestions and comments on social model by others
Attitude and expectancy scales	Morale, cohesiveness, and expectancy measures	Attitudes of community toward model
Economic records	Monetary reward record (wages, fines, etc.)	Records of income from and output to community
Administrative records	Work performance rating Turnover of membership Table of organization	Visits by relatives and friends
Research journal	Narrative account of events related to internal processes	Narrative account of events related to external processes

The internal *fiscal processes* are a matter of bookkeeping. They include such items as income and costs. A helpful survey of methods to analyze such fiscal data—termed cost-benefits analysis—may be found in the work by Borus & Tash (1976).

External Processes

These processes, which are also presented in Table 9.3, are most frequently described by interviews and administrative records. The effect of the implanted model on the *neighborhood* is often evaluated through questionnaires. *Socioeconomic descriptions* of neighborhoods in which the models are located, as well as the relationship of the model to other community institutions, is frequently assessed by written questionnaires, interviews, census data, and community records. Examples of the types of scales used to describe and assess the social situation are shown in Table 9.3.

**PROCEDURES FOR MEASURING
THE IMPORTANT VARIABLES**

Tables 9.1, 9.2, and 9.3 illustrate that a selected number of scales are used in the measurement of outcomes, attributes of participants, and the social situation. It is now important to describe in detail each of these types of measuring devices and to present appropriate references so that the interested reader can pursue a further examination of them. For clarity, each type of measuring device is presented with special attention to the dimension or dimensions which it measures, the type of scale required by the data, the construction of rational or empirical scales, and the manner in which data can be collected. An example is given of several items from a representative scale. These examples and references are given to aid the experimenters in creating their own assessment devices. The first technique—the personal history—is common to all social innovative experiments.

Personal Histories

(1) *Dimension to which they apply:* Participants.

(2) *Type of scale:* Nominal, ordinal, and occasionally interval or ratio.

(3) *Securing the pool of items:* There have been many researches in different fields which have utilized extensive personal histories. Foremost among these is the United States Census questionnaire. A pool of items can be obtained by securing several different questionnaires that have been used in other experiments. For a helpful example, the reader is referred to the work by Hughes *et al.* (1960, pp. 443–544).

(4) *Creating or selecting instruments:* From the pool of items, the experimenters choose those that fulfill the experimental needs. The possibility of combining several items into rational or empirical scales is discussed elsewhere.

(5) *Techniques for scoring:* In order to score the items individually or to combine them into scales, it is necessary to be acquainted with the distribution of the items under consideration. For example, occupation, salary, and type of dwelling were used by Warner (1960, pp. 121–129) to construct a social status scale. Age may be used as its numerical value—for example, 10, 38. The type of scoring, therefore, will differ with the particular items depending upon whether they are from nominal, ordinal, interval, or ratio scales.

(6) *Procedures for obtaining:* Questionnaires that have been completed by the participants themselves, or by their relatives, friends, employers, and other individuals familiar with their backgrounds. One may also utilize records from schools, hospitals, employers, and so on.

(7) *Reliability:* In the case of historical information, the reliability of any item is enhanced when additional sources of information are utilized as a check against the informant. For example, school records, police records, and medical records may be compared with the information received from the interviewee. When the interviewee is the participant, it is also possible

to check the information received from him with parents, friends, relatives, and acquaintances.

(8) *Example:*

Historical Background

1. Name.. 2. Code No...............

3. Group.................. 4. ID No...................

5. Permanent address...

....

6. Age........................ Date of birth....................................

7. Race: W B Other

8. Marital status: Single   Married   Widowed
                     Separated   Divorced   Remarried

9. If married, occupation of spouse (specify):.............................

....

10. Education of spouse, highest grade completed:...........................

Specify any post-secondary training of spouse..........................

Behavior Ratings

(1) *Dimensions to which they apply:* Participants and social situation, internal and external processes.

(2) *Type of scale:* Nominal or ordinal.

(3) *Securing the pool of items:* Behavior ratings have been widely used in laboratory and naturalistic settings. Heyns & Lippitt (1954, pp. 370–404) describe such techniques. The Location Activity Index (LAI) developed by Hunter, Schooler, & Spohn (1962) and the Hospital Adjustment Scale (Ferguson, McReynolds, & Ballachey, 1953) are excellent examples.

(4) *Creating and selecting the instruments:* Scales are constructed as described on p. 205. Examples of creating behavioral rating scales can be found in Goldman (1964, pp. 45–77) and Maynard (1964, pp. 54–55).

(5) *Techniques for scoring:* Usual procedures for the scoring of scales as described on p. 205.

(6) *Procedures for obtaining:* Trained raters typically make their ratings in the naturalistic setting. An example of this can be found in Goldman (1964, pp. 45–77) and Maynard (1964, pp. 54–55).

(7) *Reliability:* Behavioral ratings sometimes have problems of reliability not encountered in psychological tests. Mainly they concern the degree to which the behavior is repeatable. In cases where the behavior is not repeatable, the usual method for determining reliability is the coefficient of concordance (W).

Here several raters evaluate the same behavior and the coefficient of concordance gives their percentage of agreement. It is also possible to compute a simple percent of agreement among raters (Maynard, 1964, pp. 54–55). In certain well-controlled situations where behavior is repetitious, reliability can be determined by the more common methods. Such a situation is described by Goldman (1964, pp. 51–55). Upon occasion the rater may wish to combine the reliability with the scale score itself—a technique developed by Fairweather *et al.* (1960, pp. 9–10).

(8) *Example:*

Social Activity Scale[a]

Observer.. Date...........................

Group...

....

Social Behaviors[b]

1	2	3	4	5	6	7	8	9
			Func.	P.S.	P.S.			
Name Path.	Sleep	Null	NS	Act.	Behav.	SG	2PG	3PG

[a] A discussion of the Social Activity Scale can be found in Goldman (1964, pp. 58–71).

[b] Description of behaviors:

1. Path—pathological
2. Sleep—sleeping
3. Null—unoccupied or apathetic
4. Func. NS—functional nonsocial
5. P.S. Act.—parasocial activities
6. P.S. Behav.—parasocial behavior
7. SG—social games
8. 2 PG—two-person interaction
9. 3 PG—three-person interaction

Psychological Tests

(1) *Dimension to which they apply:* Participants.

(2) *Type of scale:* Nominal, ordinal, or interval.

(3) *Securing the pool of items:* The experimenters may wish to use established psychological tests which can be obtained from the publisher. Certain personality questionnaires, self-sort personality devices, projective tests, achievement tests, intelligence tests, interest tests, and tests of occupational choice may be of value for the experimenter. Or the experimenter may create a pool of items from which he or she can construct their own questionnaire. Anastasi (1961) and Cronbach (1960) present thorough discussions of the different psychological tests.

(4) *Creating and selecting the instruments:* Usually the experimenters can find an existing psychological test that will fulfill their needs. If not, scales can be created with subscales if desired.

(5) *Techniques for scoring:* Most standardized psychological tests have a manual or a set of instructions which provides the experimenters with a description of the test, scoring techniques, and ways to interpret the test results. If an instrument is created, appropriate scoring techniques can be established for it.

(6) *Procedures for obtaining:* When testing the participants, it is important that procedures are established for administering the instruments in a consistent and sequential pattern.

(7) *Reliability:* Standardized psychological tests usually have information concerning the reliability of the tests in the booklet that accompanies them. If the experimenters create their own tests, one of the standard methods of determining the reliability of that test can be used.

(8) *Example:*

The Vocational Preference Inventory[a]

Developed by John L. Holland, Ph.D.

This is an inventory of your feelings and attitudes about many kinds of work. Fill out your answer sheet by following the directions given below.

(1) Show on your answer sheet the occupations which interest or appeal to you by blackening Y for "Yes."

(2) Blacken N for "No" for the occupations you dislike or find uninteresting.

(3) Make no marks when you are undecided about an occupation.

1. Aviator	31. Power station operator
2. Private investigator	32. Astronomer
3. YMCA secretary	33. Juvenile delinquency expert

[a]Information about the Vocational Preference Inventory may be found in Holland (1965).

Essays and Questions Requiring Verbal or Written Answers

(1) *Dimensions to which they apply:* Participants and social situation, internal processes.

(2) *Type of scale:* Ordinal and nominal.

(3) *Securing the pool of items:* Here again the researcher must determine what information is important and create questions to obtain it. The reader is referred to Vitale (1964, pp. 213–214) who discusses one instrument of this type.

(4) *Creating and selecting the instruments:* The experimenter chooses those questions that fulfill his or her experimental needs.

(5) *Techniques for scoring:* Verbal or written answers to questions or essays can be categorized in many ways. For example, the questions may be scored according to content. Procedures for this can be found in Berelson (1952), Cronbach (1960, pp. 65–66), and Anastasi (1961, pp. 564–590). This kind of analysis may be utilized for recorded tapes as well as questionnaires. Another type of scoring can be obtained by sorting the answers to the questions into prearranged categories from most to least characteristic (Block, 1961; Stephenson, 1953). If the responses are verbal, this procedure ordinarily requires a typescript of the recorded tapes. If the answers are written, the answer sheets themselves may be sorted. An example of scoring questions by the Q-sort method may be found in Vitale (1964, pp. 214–215). There are also methods that can be used for scoring tapes without typescript. For instance, Tryon (1941a, 1941b) has created a technique for raters to directly categorize observations of behavior which also can be used to determine scores directly from taped recordings.

(6) *Procedures for obtaining:* Data may be obtained by questionnaire or recorded interview. The training of interviewers is discussed by Hyman (1954) and Maccoby & Maccoby (1954, pp. 449–487).

(7) *Reliability:* The reliability of Q-sort techniques is discussed by Vitale (1964, pp. 214–215). Methods of obtaining reliability for the direct scoring of tapes can be found in Tryon's discussion (1941a, 1941b). Generally, the responses can be scored or ranked by several judges and the usual correlative methods of computing reliability applied.

(8) *Example:*

Name... Date....................
Group..
On this page, there is a three-part question. Please fill in each part as completely as possible.

(1) What aspects of the small-group program do you feel are beneficial to the group members?

(2) What aspects of the program do you feel are harmful to the group members?

(3) List below any ideas that you have which would make the program more helpful to group members.

Attitude, Expectancy, and Other Perceptual Scales

(1) *Dimensions to which they apply:* Participants and social situation, internal and external processes.

(2) *Type of scale:* Nominal, ordinal, or interval.

(3) *Securing the pool of items:* The pool of items may be secured from a number of researchers evaluating attitudes, expectancies, etc. Researchers may profitably use the references of Anastasi (1961, pp. 528–556), Sheriff (1965), and Miller (1964).

(4) *Creating and selecting the instruments:* Here again scales and subscales may be created by the rational or empirical methods described earlier.

(5) *Techniques for scoring:* Individual scores can be obtained by summing the items in the various scales.

(6) *Procedures for obtaining:* The testing procedures are the same as those used with psychological tests.

(7) *Reliability:* Reliability can be ascertained by the usual correlative techniques.

(8) *Example:*

Expectancy Scale

Name.. Date......................

Group...

Below are ten statements in which you are asked to guess how you will like your living situation in the community after you leave the hospital. Each statement can be completed in one of five ways. Please check the one phrase that most accurately reflects your guess about the future.

Example: I will like the food in the house where I reside in the community.

    X
.... A great deal

.... Quite a bit

.... Somewhat

.... Only slightly

.... Not at all

The person completing this question believed that he would enjoy the food in his community home a great deal.

Please complete the following statements by choosing the one phrase which most accurately reflects your guess about the future.

1. will like the place where I live.

.... A great deal

.... Quite a bit

.... Somewhat

.... Only slightly

.... Not at all

2. I will like the people with whom I live.

.... A great deal

.... Quite a bit

.... Somewhat

.... Only slightly

.... Not at all

Economic Records

(1) *Dimensions to which they apply:* Social situation, internal and external processes.

(2) *Type of scale:* Nominal, ordinal, interval, or ratio.

(3) *Securing the pool of items:* The items selected depend upon those aspects of the model's economic processes that are important to the social problem. Suppose, for example, the experimenters wish to determine the cost and the income of a social model where participants live and work. Following is a list of some items about which information will be needed: personnel, travel, equipment, supplies (food, office, etc.), rent, utilities, insurance, professional consultants (medical, legal, etc.), wages, other income, and bookkeeping costs.

(4) *Creating or selecting instruments:* From the list of economic items, the experimenters create scales that measure those economic aspects of the model in which they are interested. They may be interested, for example, in the economic position of individuals within the model, such as individual cost

or income. On the other hand, they may be interested in economic items for the entire model such as total expenditures or total income.

(5) *Techniques for scoring:* Scoring techniques here involve numerical representations of the monetary processes of a model. For example, ratios of income to output, individual income, group income, etc., can be presented in numbers.

(6) *Procedures for obtaining:* Detailed bookkeeping records for all costs and expenditures in research projects should provide the data for the construction of many of the scales.

(7) *Reliability:* Reliability is determined by the bookkeeping procedures. Exceedingly important here are periodic audits which should result in accurate records about the economic aspects of the models.

(8) *Example:*

Daily Expenditures

Date	Name	Lodging	Food	Medical	Personal	Other

Administrative Records

(1) *Dimensions to which they apply:* Participants and social situation, internal and external processes.

(2) *Type of scale:* Nominal or ordinal.

(3) *Securing the pool of items:* These records do not involve items in the usual sense. Rather, they are ordinarily frequency counts of records pertaining to health, for example—amount and type of medication, visits to physicians, and illnesses. Other records about such matters as friendships, recreational activities, and memberships in community social organizations are also classified here as administrative records.

(4) *Creating and selecting the instruments:* The experimenters choose those items of information that are important in describing the activities of the participants. If community models have been established for the criminal, the mentally ill, or school drop-outs, records concerning their relationship with the community may be important. If this is the case, the experimenters may be interested in the places (restaurants, lodges, or clubs) in the community visited by the participants. The table of organization and the social structure of the model are also important administrative records (Etzioni, 1961).

(5) *Techniques for scoring:* Usually a record for each individual can be

kept and scored on the amount of time spent in a selected activity or the frequency of such an activity—dinner engagements, for example.

(6) *Procedures for obtaining:* Health records may be obtained from the attending physician. Sign-out sheets may be utilized to record where a participant goes for recreation—for example, a bowling alley or the theater.

(7) *Reliability:* Here, the experimenter keeps records of his or her own which can be checked for accuracy with such information as physicians' reports and the participant-completed sign-out sheets. For each administrative record, it is important to establish checks on its accuracy.

(8) *Example:*

Tranquilizing Drugs

| Name | Dates | | |
	From	To	Amount
	Total:		

Research Journal

(1) *Dimension to which they apply:* All dimensions.

(2) *Type of scale:* Not applicable.

(3) *Measurement:* This is primarily a detailed account of the crises and other important events that occur during the course of an experiment. It describes the global operation as well as stages of development which are not covered by the formal measures. Critical incidents are reported here. For instance, one records here that members of the research team were replaced, the dates of new research phases, threats to the discontinuation of the program, and so forth. Certain critical incidents occur only once—such as a key researcher quitting—and these incidents are assessed in depth (that is, all information available from all sources is collected and collated). It is important here to gain as much information about the incident as possible. An example of the use of a research journal can be found in Vitale (1964, p. 239). Flanagan (1956) presents techniques for measuring and recording critical incidents.

(4) *Techniques for scoring:* Not primarily meant to produce formally scored items. The selected events that are recorded and described here may be categorized and scored according to frequency counts or content.

(5) *Procedures for obtaining:* Daily records of observed events, motion pictures, tape recordings, and on-line computers can all be used to portray the model in action.

EXAMPLES

The previous section presented the basic processes of measurement with which each social innovative field researcher is confronted. In order that the reader can fully appreciate the measurement techniques that are necessary in establishing and evaluating social models and in dissemination experiments, some examples are now given that represent the measurement that was taken in some selected researches.

Social Models

Since measurement of the various aspects of social models is inextricably related to social model outcomes, it is now necessary to clarify what experimental hypotheses are and how they are related to social outcome.

Usually the experimental hypotheses are stated in terms of the comparative effectiveness of the model's outcomes. Since the social innovative experimenters propose only models designed to improve the social position of their participants, the experimental hypotheses are always stated in a manner which predicts that the innovated model or models will be more beneficial to their participants than the usual social practice (control condition). In the simplest case there are two models. One is the usual social practice (control condition) and the other is an innovated one. Here the general experimental hypothesis is that the experimental model will result in significantly more beneficial outcomes than the usual social practice. When several models have an equal opportunity, in the judgment of the experimenters, to improve the social position of the participants, the experimenters may hypothesize that all new models will produce significantly better outcomes than the usual social practice. On the other hand, when several different models are involved, the experimenters may predict that each new model can be rank-ordered in terms of its potential beneficial effects. Thus, they may predict that the first new model will do better than the usual social practice, the second will do better than the first, and so on. In any case, it should be clearly evident that the hypotheses are stated in such a manner that the innovative experimental models are always predicted to yield more beneficial outcomes than the current social practice (control condition). This is true because experiments in social innovation are designed to accord their participants a more rewarding role in their society. Thus, the social innovative experimenters cannot entertain the hypothesis that any new model will result in no change or a worsening of the participants' social position. All hypotheses are therefore one-sided, a matter discussed further in Chapter 13.

In planning the measurement of an experimental endeavor, it is necessary to link the measurement by both area and instrument to the hypotheses that are made about the prospective outcome processes of the social models under consideration.

In order that the reader can follow the process of the linkage between hypothesis and instrument creation or selection as well as measurement of other essential aspects of social models, we have chosen two social model-building experiments. The first experiment concerns the creation of an automobile cooperative established by Whitney (1974). The second model presents an examination of the measurement procedures of the lodge project. These two projects have been specifically chosen in order that the reader can follow the creation of hypotheses and their linkages to instruments in a simple and complex experiment.

The delinquency experiment

A rather straightforward and relatively unfettered experiment was used by Whitney (1974) to compare the effects that employment and ownership of an automobile cooperative would have upon the adjustment of juvenile delinquents when contrasted with the traditional parole program of placing juvenile offenders in jobs where they work for others, usually in relatively low status positions. Whitney's problem review had led him to the following hypotheses:

> The cooperative compared with the usual job placement program will reduce the occurrence of juvenile offenses; it will improve the academic performance of those in school, and will increase length of steady full-time employment.

In addition to these hypotheses Whitney also wanted to study the internal social processes of the cooperative automobile repair program so that he could better understand the effect that morale, individual popularity, and the like had upon individual and group performance.

In order to achieve matched participants to randomly assign to the models it was necessary for Whitney to obtain background information by an historical questionnaire. This he entitled the Participants In-Take Form; it is presented in Table 9.4. It is important to note here that *all* of the measuring instruments created or selected by Whitney were short and easy to complete, since Whitney was very aware of the dislike that most of his participants would have for reading and completing lengthy forms.

In order to test the first hypothesis about the beneficial outcome of the cooperative as contrasted to the typical work program on recidivism (social

TABLE 9.4
Participant Intake Form

Interviewer ....   Date: ....
                                                                                                                        (Month)(Day)(Year)

Name: ....

Address: ....

Telephone: ....

Sex: Male.................................... Female.......................................

Age: (circle)   14   15   16   17   18   over   Birth date: ....
                                                                                             (Month)(Day)(Year)

Ethnic origin: Black...
                 Mex-Amer...
                 Indian ....
                 White ....
                 Other (Specify)..

Marital status: Married ....   Dependents ....
                  Single ....
                  Separated ....

Family income: Less than $3,000...
                 $3,000–4,999 ....
                 $5,000–6,999 ....
                 $7,000 or more..................................

Nearest relative: Relationship...
                    Address...

Referred from: Outreach staff (Specify)...
                 Agency (Specify) ....
                 Police ....
                 Court ....
                 Other (Specify) ....

Educational status:
    Highest grade completed: 7   8   9   10   11   12   13   14   +
    In school, full-time.................................... Where? ....
    In school, part-time .... Where? ....
    Out of school.................................... Reason ....
                                                             (truant, suspended, drop-out)

Number of times suspended or expelled: 0   1   2   3   4   5   +

Correctional history:
    Has not been arrested   ....
    Arrested, but not adjudicated   ....
    Arrested and adjudicated   ....
    Arrested, on probation   ....
    Arrested, on parole   ....
    Arrested, institutionalized   ....
    Institutionalized, out   ....
    Reason for arrest:..
    ....

Automotive mechanic experience: (list)

1. ....
2. ....
3. ....

Employment history: (List jobs for past two years, where, and immediate supervisor)

1.. How long? ....
2.. How long? ....
3.. How long? ....

What do you plan to do for employment in the next two years?

....

....

How do you feel about owning and operating an auto repair shop in Smithville?

....

....

In addition to having a job would you be willing to spend one (1) night per week to improve your community? Yes.................... No....................

Comments by interviewer on individual's prospects:

....

....

....

....

Module: 1 2 3 4 5

Auto experience: None.................... Little.................... Much....................

change outcome criterion), employment, and education, Whitney used two sources of information. First he had all participants complete a follow-up every 90 days for the 360-day follow-up period. Secondly, he had access to police records—i.e., the recorded police arrests—and school records. The follow-up form is presented in Table 9.5.

Whitney was also interested in studying the group processes of the co-operative. He was particularly interested in the popularity of various members which other studies (Sanders, McDonald, & Maynard, 1964) had shown to be related to leadership, the morale of the members, and their individual performance on the job. The reliability and validity of the scales he chose had been established in earlier studies on similar populations (Fairweather, 1964; Fairweather *et al.*, 1969). He chose a simple sociometric rating scale to measure the popularity of each person in the cooperative. It is presented in Table 9.6, the morale scale is presented in Table 9.7, and the job behavior scale is presented in Table 9.8. The latter is divided into two subscales. The first 14 items measure the worker's job performance and the last 12 items his or her social adjustment on the job.

TABLE 9.5
Follow-up Form

Name: ....   Date: ....

Outreach worker: ....   (Month) (Day) (Year)
Module: **0   1   2   3   4   5**

Number of weeks client has been in Y.D.C. ....

School status:
....   Continued in School—Full-time
....   Name of School.............................
....   Continued in School—Part-time
            Name of school....................................
....   Truant (reason) ....
....   Suspended (reason) ....
....   Dropped out (date and reason)..
            ....
....   Graduated (date and school) ....
            ....
....   Other (specify)...
            ....

Employment status:
....   Unemployed
....   Employed (full-time and place) ....
....   Employed (part-time and place) ....
....   Y.D.C. Work-intern (place) ....

Correctional record:
....   Not been arrested
....   Apprehended, not arrested
....   Arrested, but not adjudicated
....   Arrested and adjudicated
....   Arrested, on parole
....   Arrested, on probation
....   Arrested, court ward
....   Other (specify)

If arrested, explain details of arrest and results of arrest:
....
....
....

Recommended supportive services:
....   Psychological counseling
....   Psychological testing
....   Medical treatment
....   Social counseling—group
....   Social counseling—individual
....   Academic training
....   Vocational training
....   Other (specify)

Referred to following sources for services ....

Explain results of services (if possible):

....

....

Referred to other program:
.... Police
.... Court (ongoing)
.... School
.... Family
.... Social agency (specify) ....
.... Other (specify) ....
Explain results of referral (brief) ....

....

TABLE 9.6
Popularity Scale

Directions: Below there are seven items, one for each member of the group. Please rate each member, excluding yourself, on the scale as to how much you like or dislike them. (CIRCLE YOUR ANSWER)

Names:

....A. (1) Do not like at all (2) Mildly dislike (3) Dislike just a little (4) Neither like nor dislike (5) Like just a little (6) Mildly like (7) Like very much

....B. (1) Do not like at all (2) Mildly dislike (3) Dislike just a little (4) Neither like nor dislike (5) Like just a little (6) Mildly like (7) Like very much

....C (1) Do not like at all (2) Mildly dislike (3) Dislike just a little (4) Neither like nor dislike (5) Like just a little (6) Mildly like (7) Like very much

....D. (1) Do not like at all (2) Mildly dislike (3) Dislike just a little (4) Neither like nor dislike (5) Like just a little (6) Mildly like (7) Like very much

....E (1) Do not like at all (2) Mildly dislike (3) Dislike just a little (4) Neither like nor dislike (5) Like just a little (6) Mildly like (7) Like very much

....F (1) Do not like at all (2) Mildly dislike (3) Dislike just a little (4) Neither like nor dislike (5) Like just a little (6) Mildly like (7) Like very much

....G (1) Do not like at all (2) Mildly dislike (3) Dislike just a little (4) Neither like nor dislike (5) Like just a little (6) Mildly like (7) Like very much

It will be noted that Whitney did not measure external social processes. This occurred because he was limited in finances and research staff and therefore limited his measures to those variables directly related to the hypotheses and others that he considered most important. However, he did keep a research journal in which all interactions with the neighborhood and other significant persons in the society were recorded as well as critical events that occurred in both social models throughout the experiment. It should also be noted that Whitney tried all instruments out prior to using them in the experiment proper.

TABLE 9.7
Morale Scale

Name.. Shift.................................... Date..

Below are listed several statements with which you may agree or disagree. There are five possible ways you might react to each statement. Please put a check mark in front of the one response which most adequately expresses your feelings.

1. I would just as soon have my present job as any other job that I know about.
   ....Strongly agree ....Agree ....Undecided ....Disagree ....Strongly disagree

2. I am perfectly happy with my present position in the group.
   ....Strongly agree ....Agree ....Undecided ....Disagree ....Strongly disagree

3. I have a lot of training or skills that could be used better by the group.
   ....Strongly agree ....Agree ....Undecided ....Disagree ....Strongly disagree

4. Even if it were not for matters of training and experience, I would rather be in my present position with this group than in any other position with any other group.
   ....Strongly agree ....Agree ....Undecided ....Disagree ....Strongly disagree

5. Is your group manager good at figuring out easy ways to do things when the group has work?
   ....Very good ....Pretty good ....Sometimes ....Usually no ....Not good

6. Does your group manager usually help to settle arguments among the men under him?
   ....Almost always ....Often ....Sometimes ....Rarely ....Never

7. How often does your group manager help the members out in personal matters?
   ....Almost always ....Often ....Sometimes ....Rarely ....Never

8. When the men or women in your group do something wrong, is your group manager able to handle the situation?
   ....Almost always ....Often ....Sometimes ....Rarely ....Never

9. All of the members in my group work as hard as they can.
   ....Almost always ....Often ....Sometimes ....Rarely ....Never

10. All of the members in my group cooperate with each other.
    ....Almost always ....Often ....Sometimes ....Rarely ....Never

11. So far as overall performance is concerned, I would rank my group as:
    ....One of the best
    ....One of the next best
    ....Somewhere between the best and worst
    ....A poor group
    ....The poorest group

TABLE 9.8
Job Behavior Scale

Worker's name ....   Group ....

Rater's name ....   Date ....

1. ....The worker makes few errors.
   ....The worker makes many errors.
2. ....The worker seldom needs prodding to get job done.
   ....The worker usually needs prodding to get job done.
3. ....The worker rarely needs help.
   ....The worker often needs help.
4. ....The worker follows directions on the job.
   ....The worker does not follow directions on the job.
5. ....The worker works for extended periods of time.
   ....The worker fails to work on a task for any reasonable period of time.
6. ....The worker abides by job rules and regulations.
   ....The worker violates job rules and regulations.
7. ....The worker usually profits from constructive criticism.
   ....The worker usually does not profit from constructive criticism.
8. ....The worker seldom becomes upset by failure.
   ....The worker usually becomes upset by failure.
9. ....The worker usually does not complain about the tasks that are given him.
   ....The worker usually complains about tasks that are given him.
10. ....The worker usually applies self to task.
    ....The worker usually does not apply self to task.
11. ....The worker works with average accuracy.
    ....The worker's work is often inaccurate.
12. ....The worker works constantly on the task.
    ....The worker rarely works on the task.
13. ....The worker reports regularly to work.
    ....The worker often fails to show up for work.
14. ....The worker usually profits by his mistakes.
    ....The worker repeats his mistakes over and over again.
15. ....The worker does not do or say anything which is disturbing to others.
    ....The worker sometimes says or does things that disturb others.
16. ....The worker is courteous and considerate, showing a normal concern for the feelings
    of others.
    ....The worker is discourteous and often shows no concern for the feelings of others.
17. ....The worker is reasonably friendly and agreeable.
    ....The worker is usually unfriendly and disagreeable.
18. ....The worker often speaks to others.
    ....The worker rarely speaks to others.
19. ....The worker is usually happy.
    ....The worker is usually sad.
20. ....The worker takes pride in the quality of his work; i.e., shows work or talks about
    work to others and/or supervisor.
    ....The worker does not take pride in the quality of his work.
21. ....The worker seldom finds fault with others and/or their work.
    ....The worker often finds fault with others and/or their work.
22. ....The worker pays attention to the work and activities of others.
    ....The worker does not pay attention to the work or activities of others—is in a world
    of his own.

TABLE 9.8 *contd.*

23. ....The worker makes some worthwhile suggestions about tasks.
............The worker makes no worthwhile suggestions about tasks.
24. ....The worker usually accepts constructive suggestions from the supervisor.
............The worker seldom accepts constructive suggestions from the supervisor.
25. ....The worker is not usually disturbed by constructive criticism.
............The worker is usually disturbed by constructive criticism.
26. ....The worker seldom finds fault with his work.
............The worker often finds fault with his work.

The lodge society

The evaluation of the lodge society was accomplished by creating an autonomously operated living-working situation as a new social model for discharged mental patients, particularly those with long hospitalization, and contrasting it with the traditional community health program available to such people (Fairweather *et al.*, 1969). The hypotheses for the lodge society were as follows:

"A community social sub-system which provides a place of residence and work for mental patients will increase time out of the hospital, increase employment, and enhance personal self-esteem when contrasted with a traditional program using those community facilities usually available to mental patients (such as visits to mental hygiene clinics while living at home, sheltered workshops)." In addition to the specific outcome criteria there was an extreme interest in understanding the social processes of the new society, how it affected its various members, what its historical growth curve appeared to be, and how it interacted with both individuals and organizations in its neighborhood and with significant others.

To specifically test the hypotheses about reduction of recidivism, improved employment, and personal enhancement, a questionnaire containing these and other items of interest was developed. This was completed by an individual who knew the ex-patient intimately, and was supplemented with a form for the patient to complete. These forms were completed every six months for a four-year period. To expand upon this evaluation, interviews were held every 90 days with members of the lodge society and all failures from both models were interviewed if they returned to the hospital.

Background materials for matched volunteer patients assigned to the two different social models were obtained through the use of an extensive *personal history* form. Their own perceptions of themselves with regard to their futures were evaluated by *expectancy questionnaires* indicating each person's expectations for his own future. Additional information about the effects of volunteering was obtained by administering an expectancy questionnaire concerning the extent to which each individual desired to go to the lodge prior to his entry.

The social processes of the lodge were explored through a series of measures completed every 90 days for the four-year duration of the lodge society. They included scales of a *sociometric choice, role clarity, group acceptance, group attraction,* and *group satisfaction* which were designed to study the group dynamics of the society. The work aspect of the society was examined through forms evaluating the *group performance* on each job and the perceived value of the *work training* program which had been established for lodge residents, the number and type of *jobs* obtained, and a *check list of tools* and equipment used on each job. The administration of the lodge society was studied through the use of a *daily report* issued by the lodge member who was designated as manager for the day, a *visitor's log,* a *log recording departures* to local community individuals and organizations, and *reports of medication taken.* An evaluation of the group decision-making processes was made by obtaining and rating *tape recordings of periodic meetings* held between staff and lodge members, the executive committee meetings of the lodge management group, and meetings held to evaluate the progress of the lodge society every 90 days. The economic aspects of the lodge were studied through the use of its *accounting* records.

Of course, the lodge was embedded in a neighborhood where its members interacted daily with persons from the neighborhood and organizations near the lodge as well as with other persons from the community with whom there was continuous contact. *Questionnaires* and *interviews* were created to accomplish the measurement of the external processes. Some questionnaires were created to evaluate the relatives' attitude toward the lodge; others to evaluate the attitude of persons who used the janitorial and gardening service as clients, immediate neighbors, and associates of the lodge members. *Interviews* were held every 90 days with lodge members and with the persons who had contact with the lodge through job or organizational relations such as the house physician, vendors who brought milk and food to the lodge, and so on.

A particular hospital was linked with the lodge by providing the mental patients who were to become the members of it. The patients came from a program in the hospital designed to teach the members how to perform as groups. In order to evaluate the effectiveness of this pre-community training, several *group process measures* were obtained in the hospital setting which measured the *leadership, decision making, work performance,* and each person's *task and personal improvement* during the course of participating in these hospital-based decision-making groups. *Administrative records about the amount of medication* and entry and exits to the program were maintained within the hospital setting.

Needless to say, the reliability and validity of each of these questionnaires, interviews, behavior ratings, and administrative records were completed in accordance with the procedures recommended in the previous section for the different types of instruments involved. A summary list of these instruments by type is presented in Table 9.9.

TABLE 9.9
Lodge Assessment Devices

Outcomes
  Questionnaires for:
    Respondent evaluation of patient adjustment
    Patient evaluation of his own adjustment
  Interviews for:
    Periodic evaluation of lodge by members
    "Failures" from all experimental groups
Participant characteristics of members
  Questionnaires for:
    Personal history
    Expectancies about future
    Expectancies about the community lodge
Internal social processes

Of the lodge	Of the hospital
Group—process ratings	Group—process ratings
Sociometric	Leadership
Role clarity	Group performance
Acceptance of members within group	Work
Attraction to group by member	Patient improvement (notes
Satisfaction with leadership	exchanged between staff and
Research journal	patients)
Daily description of group and critical events	Administrative records
Work ratings	Medication reports
Job inspection	Entrances and exits from ward
Training program	
Administrative records	
Daily report by member in nightly charge of lodge ("OD")	
Visitor's log	
Departure log	
Medication reports	
Number and type of jobs obtained	
Tool and equipment check sheets	
Tape recordings	
Staff-member precommunity group meetings	
Staff-member community evaluation meetings	
Executive committee meetings of members	
Fiscal processes	
Accounting books	

External social processes of the lodge
  Questionnaires for:
    Relatives' attitudes towards lodge residents
    Client evaluation of janitorial and gardening service
    Neighbors' and associates' evaluation of lodge members
  Interviews for:
    Periodic evaluation of the lodge by those closely associated with it (physician, vendors, etc.)

Although the interested reader can clearly see that an actual list of the instruments developed would be far too extensive to be presented here, it is important to recognize that many different types of instruments are necessary to measure a complex social program. This, of course, is made even more difficult when measures are repeated every 90 or 180 days for a four-year period as occurred with the lodge. Nevertheless with adequate planning such measurements can be made.

Dissemination

The same format will be followed in presenting measurement for dissemination experiments as that developed in the social model section. First, a relatively simple research will be presented showing the relationship between the hypotheses and the actual instrument created for the purposes of measuring the important and selected variables. A second dissemination study will then be presented which will present many areas of measurement describing the instruments created without presenting the instruments themselves. The intent of discussing the latter experiment is to present a more complete picture of a longitudinal dissemination experiment.

The environmental experiment

From an earlier presentation, it will be recalled that Lounsbury (1973) was concerned with persuading citizens to conserve energy and otherwise become alert and active in the ecological movement. He designed an experiment in which he attempted to evaluate the effectiveness of different conditions of persuasion in motivating persons to engage in energy saving and recycling action. To accomplish this, he created a newsletter entitled *Eco-Action* in which he specified certain behaviors that persons could take to improve the quality of the environment (recycle glass, etc.). Lounsbury formulated the following hypotheses:

> 1. An information dissemination approach in the form of an Eco-Action Newsletter will be more effective in involving citizens in environmental action than no systematic effort.
> 2. Those conditions in which the subjects are contacted by a change advocate will display greater participation in environmental action than conditions not receiving personal contact by an advocate.
> 3. Participants in the send-to-neighbors conditions will be more involved in environmental action than persons not in these conditions.

In order to test these hypotheses he created two different conditions for disseminating the information through which he attempted to stimulate further personal action. They were: (1) telephoning some persons at pre-arranged times contrasted with others who did not receive calls; (2) sending the letter to some neighbors of the persons who originally received the news-letter contrasted with others whose neighbors did not receive the letter. He also created a standardized, naturalistic control condition in which no specific information was given.

The measures created to test hypotheses 1 and 2 were contained in a behavioral checklist entitled "Current Activities" to measure the adoption of environmental practices (social change outcome criterion) outlined in the newsletter. The questionnaire is presented in Table 9.10.

TABLE 9.10
Current Activities

For each of the following environmentally related activities (1 through 9) indicate how often, during the last three months, your household has been practicing these activities by circling one of the six numbers following the activity. The numbers, ranging from 1 to 6, stand for:

1—Never
2—Once in a great while
3—Sometimes
4—Frequently
5—Almost always
6—Always

	Never	Once in a great while	Sometimes	Frequently	Almost always	Always
1. When needed, take paper to a recycling station (or have it picked up by a voluntary group) .	1	2	3	4	5	6
2. When needed, take glass to a recycling station (or have it picked up by a voluntary group) .	1	2	3	4	5	6
3. When needed, use a compost heap to dispose of organic materials such as food scraps, lawn clippings, leaves, etc.	1	2	3	4	5	6
4. Use unnecessary electrical appliances such as electric can openers, electric combs, electric hedge trimmers, electric manicure sets, electric pencil sharpeners, electric swizzle sticks, and electric toothbrushes .	1	2	3	4	5	6
5. Use enzyme presoaks such as Biz or Axion when doing laundry	1	2	3	4	5	6
6. Buy food products with unnecessary plastic packaging such as individually wrapped (slices) cheese, frozen food packaged in cooking pouches, and plastic-wrapped meat	1	2	3	4	5	6
7. Use less detergent when washing clothes than the manufacturer suggests	1	2	3	4	5	6

8. Measure out the amount of detergent for clothes
   washing with a measuring cup or some other device   1   2   3   4   5   6
9. Make an active effort to turn off unneeded lights
   around the house   1   2   3   4   5   6

The following items (10 through 13) also apply to your household for the last three months:

10. When you put gas in your car, approximately what percent of the time do you use low-lead gas?
    0%   10%   20%   30%   40%   50%   60%   70%   80%   90%   100%
    (CIRCLE ONE)
11. Approximately what percent of the beverage bottles you buy are returnables?
    0%   10%   20%   30%   40%   50%   60%   70%   80%   90%   100%
    (CIRCLE ONE)
12. If you buy returnable beverage bottles, do you usually return them to the store?
    YES   NO
    (CIRCLE ONE)
13. When you use your electric or gas-operated clothes washer and dishwasher, approximately what percent of the time do you run only on full loads?
    0%   10%   20%   30%   40%   50%   60%   70%   80%   90%   100%
    (CIRCLE ONE)

For each of the following environmentally related actions (14 through 18), indicate whether or not you or some other member of your household has, during the last six months, done it by circling one of the two choices (YES or NO) following the action.

14. Placed a brick (or stoppered container) or bent the float rod in the water
    tank of your toilet to conserve water when flushing   .   .   .   .   YES   NO
15. Requested information from an environmental action group (or some
    other organization) on how to save on your utility bills   .   .   .   YES   NO
16. Joined or sent in a contribution of a local environmental action group   YES   NO
17. Joined or sent in a contribution to a national environmental action group   YES   NO
18. Switched to fluorescent lighting for at least one lamp or light fixture   YES   NO

19. In the space below, list any other environmentally related activities which you or any other member of your household have done or have been doing on a regular basis during the last three months:

....

....

A second scale entitled "Current Outlook Survey" was created by Lounsbury in order to assess demographic information about the persons involved and their households. Table 9.11 presents this survey.

Lounsbury was also interested in assessing the reaction to the content of the newsletter and the diffusion of its content. To do this, he created a scale entitled the "Eco-Action Newsletter." That scale is presented in Table 9.12.

TABLE 9.11
Current Outlook Survey

The purpose of this survey is to obtain information about the concerns that different people have for current issues, especially environmentally related issues. There is no need for you to put your name on this survey. Please fill out all the items.

Thank you in advance for your cooperation!

General Information

1. What is your sex?   Male   Female   (CIRCLE ONE)
2. What is your marital status?   Married   Single   (CIRCLE ONE)

   If married, how many children do you have?   1   2   3   4   5   more

   (If more, specify how many ....)   (CIRCLE ONE)
3. In what year were you born? ....   (WRITE IN)
4. What is your occupation? ....   (WRITE IN)

   If retired, what was your occupation? ....   (WRITE IN)

   If married, what is your spouse's occupation? ....   (WRITE IN)
5. What is your religious affiliation?

   Protestant   Catholic   Jewish   None   Other   (CIRCLE ONE)

   If other, please specify ....   (WRITE IN)
6. Do you have any brothers or sisters?   Yes   No   (CIRCLE ONE)

   If yes, how many? ....

   If yes, were you the:
   - (a) first born
   - (b) second born
   - (c) third born
   - (d) fourth born
   - (e) other (specify ....)

         (CIRCLE ONE)
7. What was the size of the city or town you grew up in (6 to 16 years old)?
   - (a) rural (no city or town)
   - (b) 1–1,000 people
   - (c) 1,000–10,000 people
   - (d) 10,000–100,000 people
   - (e) over 100,000 people
   - (f) cities of different sizes

         (CIRCLE ONE)
8. What was the last grade of school you completed?
   - (a) 8th grade or less
   - (b) some high school
   - (c) high school graduate
   - (d) some college
   - (e) college graduate (4-year degree)
   - (f) some post-graduate work
   - (g) an advanced degree

         (CIRCLE ONE)
9. What was the income of your household last year?
   - (a) less than $5,000
   - (b) $5,000–$10,000
   - (c) $10,000–$15,000
   - (d) $15,000–$20,000
   - (e) more than $20,000

         (CIRCLE ONE)

10. How many days did you spend on vacation trips last year?
    (a) less than 1 week
    (b) 1–2 weeks
    (c) 2–3 weeks
    (d) 3–4 weeks
    (e) more than 4 weeks
           (CIRCLE ONE)

11. Approximately how many hours out of a typical day in this month did you spend out-of-doors?
    (a) less than 1
    (b) 1–4
    (c) 4–8
    (d) more than 8
           (CIRCLE ONE)

12. How many cars do you have in your household? .... (WRITE IN)

13. How many other motorized transportation vehicles do you have (including motorcycles, snowmobiles, scooters, dune buggies, etc.)?

.... (WRITE IN)

14. What magazines, newspapers, and periodicals does your household take on a regular basis?

....

....
                                      (WRITE IN)

15. What type of dwelling do you live in?
    (a) house
    (b) duplex
    (c) apartment
    (d) mobile home
    (e) dormitory
    (f) other (specify ....)
           (CIRCLE ONE)

16. How many years have you lived in Ingham County?
    (a) less than 1 year
    (b) 1–2 years
    (c) 2–4 years
    (d) 4–6 years
    (e) 6–8 years
    (f) more than 8 years
           (CIRCLE ONE)

17. How many years have you lived at the current address?
    (a) less than 1 year
    (b) 1–2 years
    (c) 2–4 years
    (d) 4–6 years
    (e) 6–8 years
    (f) more than 8 years
           (CIRCLE ONE)

18. Concerning the dwelling you live in, do you:
    (a) own it
    (b) rent it
    (c) other (specify ....)
           (CIRCLE ONE)

TABLE 9.11 *contd.*

19. How is your place of residence heated?
    (a) electric
    (b) gas
    (c) oil
    (d) coal
    (e) wood
    (f) other (specify ....)
        (CIRCLE ONE)

20. In your household, who is usually responsible for:
    20.1 Trash disposal?
         Husband   Wife   Both   (CIRCLE ONE)
    20.2 Grocery shopping?
         Husband   Wife   Both   (CIRCLE ONE)
    20.3 Purchasing small household appliances?
         Husband   Wife   Both   (CIRCLE ONE)
    20.4 Doing the dishes?
         Husband   Wife   Both   (CIRCLE ONE)
    20.5 Clothes-washing?
         Husband   Wife   Both   (CIRCLE ONE)
    20.6 Taking care of the lawn and yard?
         Husband   Wife   Both   (CIRCLE ONE)
    20.7 Minor household repairs?
         Husband   Wife   Both   (CIRCLE ONE)
    20.8 Subscribing to magazines and periodicals?
         Husband   Wife   Both   (CIRCLE ONE)
    20.9 Automobile maintenance?
         Husband   Wife   Both   (CIRCLE ONE)
    20.10 Turning off lights?
         Husband   Wife   Both   (CIRCLE ONE)

In addition he wanted to investigate the perceptions of the individuals who received the telephonic contact (which he called "Prod-calls") encouraging them to take environmental action. Seven items entitled "Miscellaneous" were used to measure these perceptions. They are presented in Table 9.13.

He also wanted to explore whether the attitudes toward current issues of the persons contacted changed. To evaluate this, he constructed a 26-item attitude scale concerned with general attitudes toward environmental degradation and action. It is presented in Table 9.14.

Through the use of these scales, Lounsbury tested hypotheses 1, 2, and 3 listed above. He also was able to investigate quantitatively the personal demographics of the individuals involved in the sample and what was present in their households, to assess any change in attitudes that might have occurred as a result of the use of the newsletter, and to further discover the perception that individuals had about the continuing phone calls that were used in trying to enlist their support in environmental action.

TABLE 9.12
The Eco-Action Newsletter

The Eco-Action Newsletter

The following questions concern the Eco-Action Newsletter you have been receiving in the mail.

1. In general, how interesting do you find the newsletter?
    (a) Not interesting
    (b) Slightly interesting
    (c) Fairly interesting
    (d) Very interesting
    (e) Extremely interesting
        (CIRCLE ONE)

2. In general, how helpful do you find the suggestions set forth in the newsletter?
    (a) Not helpful
    (b) Slightly helpful
    (c) Fairly helpful
    (d) Very helpful
    (e) Extremely helpful
        (CIRCLE ONE)

3. Who has been reading the newsletter?
    (a) Yourself
    (b) Your spouse
    (c) Your children
    (d) Your neighbor (or neighbors)
    (e) A friend (or friends)
    (f) People with whom you work
    (g) Other persons (specify ....)
        (CIRCLE ONE *OR MORE*)

4. Who have you been talking about the contents of the newsletter to?
    (a) Nobody
    (b) Your spouse
    (c) Your children
    (d) Your neighbor (or neighbors)
    (e) A friend (or friends)
    (f) People with whom you work
    (g) Other persons (specify ....)
        (CIRCLE ONE *OR MORE*)

5. What other areas would you like to see covered in the newsletter that have not been so far?   (WRITE IN)

....

....

6. We have a number of extra copies of the first 5 issues of the Eco-Action Newsletter. If you would like to have a copy of an issue (or issues) sent to someone you think would be interested in reading it, please write their name, address, and which issue you would like them to receive in the space below, and we will send it to them (free of charge).

Name and address   Issue no.

....

....

....

....

TABLE 9.13
Prod-Call Evaluation

Miscellaneous
  In general to what extent do you think each of the following terms describes how you feel
about the contact we made with you by phone?

a. Interesting	1. Not at all	2. Somewhat	3. Quite	4. Very	(CIRCLE ONE)
b. Helpful	1. Not at all	2. Somewhat	3. Quite	4. Very	(CIRCLE ONE)
c. Sincere	1. Not at all	2. Somewhat	3. Quite	4. Very	(CIRCLE ONE)
d. Uninformative	1. Not at all	2. Somewhat	3. Quite	4. Very	(CIRCLE ONE)
e. Annoying	1. Not at all	2. Somewhat	3. Quite	4. Very	(CIRCLE ONE)
f. Unfriendly	1. Not at all	2. Somewhat	3. Quite	4. Very	(CIRCLE ONE)

Other comments : ....

....

....

....

The lodge dissemination experiment

As a final example of the types of instruments developed for assessing the parameters of a dissemination experiment, instrumentation of the lodge dissemination study is presented. The hypotheses listed in question form were as follows (Fairweather, Sanders, & Tornatzky, 1974):

1. Are organizations more likely to change if persons contacted about the change hold high, middle, or low social status positions in the selected hospital?
2. Are hospitals with lengthy "chains of command"—such as federal hospitals—easier or harder to change than hospitals with shorter "chains of command"—such as state hospitals?
3. Are hospitals located in urban areas, where jobs are more clearly defined, more or less likely to change than hospitals that are rural and where, typically, job-definition rigidity does not exist?
4. Are active approaches, such as demonstration projects, used in persuading hospitals to change more likely to influence those organizations to adopt new practices than less active approaches, written material and verbal workshops?
5. Are change agents actually necessary? Is the effective role of the change agent simply to present new information or, to be effective, should it be a much more broadly defined role including some knowledge of group structure, leadership, and motivation?

6. Are organizations that are more bureaucratic and in which leaders made decisions without consulting their underlings more likely to change than more participative organizations?

7. Are hospitals that have better communication systems more likely to change than hospitals that do not?

8. Is there any relationship between the various phases leading to adoption: that is, are the methods of attempting to persuade hospitals actually related to what happens in the adoption phase?

9. Are hospitals more financially able to change more likely to do so? Are hospitals with more facilities more likely to change than those with few?

10. Are hospitals that have more well-educated staffs more likely to change than hospitals that do not?

11. Are demographic characteristics, such as the region in which the hospital is located, related to change?

13. If so, is diffusion related to a general innovativeness in hospitals or any other characteristic of those organizations?

14. Are there any characteristics of the superintendent that lead to social change? For example, is the cosmopolitanness of the leader, as mentioned by Rogers and Shoemaker (1971), related to change?

The measuring instruments created to test these hypotheses were described in the following manner:

There were a large number of assessment devices used over the four years of this project in an attempt to measure the many aspects of social change. First of all, there was a telephone questionnaire completed at the time the interviewer first contacted a person in the hospital with whom he discussed the lodge possibility. This individual, of course, was randomly selected for social status (superintendent, psychiatrist, psychologist, social worker, or nurse). There was also concern about how effective the different conditions of persuasion were, that is, to what extent did the individuals who received the brochure, who participated in the workshop, or who established the demonstration model see this experience as satisfying and as influencing the hospital. These instruments were entitled the brochure effectiveness questionnaire, the workshop effectiveness questionnaire, and the demonstration model effectiveness questionnaire. Information was also obtained on another form about the effectiveness of the persuasive technique (brochure, workshop, demonstration ward) for those individuals who did not actively participate in the condition but were members of the same hospital staff.

TABLE 9.14
Attitudes Toward Current Issues

Attitudes Toward Current Issues

The purpose of the following items is to survey general attitudes toward current issues, especially environmentally related issues. Please read the following statements carefully and indicate how much you agree or disagree with each of the statements below. Agreement or disagreement can be indicated by circling one of the six numbers following the statement. The numbers, ranging from 1 to 6, stand for:

      1—Strongly disagree
      2—Disagree
      3—Slightly disagree
      4—Slightly agree
      5—Agree
      6—Strongly agree

Thus, if you strongly agree with a statement, circle the number 6 (e.g., 1 2 3 4 5 ⑥). Or to cite another example, if you're not really certain, but you think you slightly disagree with a statement, circle the number 3 (e.g., 1 2 ③ 4 5 6). Please circle one number for each statement. PLEASE DO NOT SKIP ANY STATEMENT.

There are no right or wrong answers to any of these questions.

	Strongly disagree	Disagree	Slightly disagree	Slightly agree	Agree	Strongly agree
1. If mankind is going to survive at all, environmental pollution must be stopped	1	2	3	4	5	6
2. People should use less detergent than the manufacturer recommends to help preserve water quality	1	2	3	4	5	6
3. The news media have exaggerated the ecological problem	1	2	3	4	5	6
4. Putting a brick in one's toilet to conserve water is a dumb idea	1	2	3	4	5	6
5. Overpopulation is a major source of environmental problems today	1	2	3	4	5	6
6. It seems like a waste of time to try to conserve electricity by turning off unneeded lights around the house	1	2	3	4	5	6
7. People with new cars should use low-lead gas	1	2	3	4	5	6
8. People should buy (and return) beverages only in returnable containers	1	2	3	4	5	6
9. I am worried about future children's chances of living in a clean environment	1	2	3	4	5	6
10. Having a lot of money may not bring you happiness, but it sure helps	1	2	3	4	5	6
11. People should avoid buying unnecessary plastic packaging found in such food products as individually wrapped (slices) cheese and frozen food in cooking pouches	1	2	3	4	5	6
12. Although polluted environments may smell bad or be unsightly, they are usually not dangerous or harmful to health	1	2	3	4	5	6
13. Every couple in America should try not to have more than two children	1	2	3	4	5	6

14. It seems silly to attempt to conserve natural resources by running only *full* loads in dishwaters, and clothes-washers and dryers   1   2   3   4   5   6
15. I enjoy taking long walks   1   2   3   4   5   6
16. Personally, I would rather have astroturf than real grass in my front lawn   1   2   3   4   5   6
17. People should recycle used glass and paper . .   1   2   3   4   5   6
18. We shouldn't worry about environmental problems because science and technology will solve them before very long   1   2   3   4   5   6
19. I wish I could spend more time out-of-doors .   1   2   3   4   5   6
20. All endangered species of animals should be pro-tected so that they won't become extinct . .   1   2   3   4   5   6
21. I would like to be a millionaire   1   2   3   4   5   6
22. If possible, one should join or support financially an ecology center or action group to help solve the environmental crisis   1   2   3   4   5   6
23. I don't mind seeing billboards when I drive along highways   1   2   3   4   5   6
24. The solution to pollution starts in the home . .   1   2   3   4   5   6
25. There is nothing wrong with using electric can openers, electric pencil sharpeners, and electric manicure sets   1   2   3   4   5   6
26. Leaves and food scraps should be composted when-ever possible   1   2   3   4   5   6

Finally, in the persuasion condition there was a decision-making questionnaire that contained such items as who made the final decision, the degree to which the staff was involved in the decision, etc. A social status questionnaire was given to determine what the relationship was between hospitals that had very well-organized hierarchical social structures and those that did not upon the decision-making process.

There was, in addition, a voluminous amount of information obtained about the particular hospital itself. This concerned such information as the population density of the state and area where the hospital was located, the number of psychiatric beds in the hospital and in the state, the salaries and training of professional persons, etc.

After the persuasion phase was completed, those hospitals that had agreed to establish the lodge were divided into those that received ex-tensive written instruction as to how a lodge could be established, and those that received the consultation of an expert in helping them actively pursue their work on the lodge. The action consultants who visited the hospitals gathered descriptive information about the hospital itself, in-cluding such diverse items of information as its social climate, physical plant, and the staff's reaction to the consultant. In addition, other in-formation about the implementation phase was collected every ninety days through follow-up telephone calls. In these calls to the twenty-five volunteer hospitals questions were asked about their progress in implementing the lodge. The social change outcome criteria was measured by movement toward adoption.

Finally, recordings were made of each session the hospital planning group had with the action consultant. This supplied an ongoing description of the internal workings of the small groups that had been designated by each hospital to help establish the lodge. From the outset, each experimenter had a research journal which he took on his trips. In it he made notes about critical incidents that occurred and other items of information.

The summary of the assessment devices is presented in Table 9.15.

TABLE 9.15
Assessment Devices

Questionnaires:
    about the initial contact of the research staff with the hospitals
    workshop effectiveness
    brochure effectiveness
    demonstration ward effectiveness
    biographical information
    diffusion processes
    decision-making processes
    90-day follow-up of volunteers
    attitudes about social status
    attitudes about mental illness
Demographic information:
    characteristics of the hospitals
    characteristics of the state in which hospital is located
Conference discussions:
    interview about the persuading and activating processes
    recordings of social action consultant sessions
Research journal:
    critical incidents and observations

In this chapter we have presented the way in which the central dimensions of social innovative experiments can be conceptualized and measured. Our attention now turns to how these instruments and the research plan itself can be administered.

CHAPTER 10

Administering the Research Program

Once the planning for the experiment has been completed, and the research program is placed in action, problems arise that are associated with actually fielding the research. All of the planning necessary for arranging the experiment has been described and discussed in the preceding chapters. However, these are preliminary to actually carrying out the research itself. This is clearly a case where the old saw about the "best laid plans of mice and men" is surely true. Program and interpersonal problems that emerge as the research progresses must be solved "on the spot" or the extensive time spent in planning will have been for naught. A discussion of the administration of planned field research in both social model-building and dissemination experiments should help the reader become aware of the problems that emerge in the daily management of a research program.

Procedures to establish the administrative commitments necessary to carry out an experiment, to establish a research team, to select the experimental problem, to define and describe the models that are to be compared, to choose the areas of measurement and create devices to assess them, to select the appropriate evaluative techniques, and to set forth the hypotheses to be tested were presented in Chapters 3 through 9. All that remains of the planning phase now is the development of an experimental plan for scheduling all experimental processes.

SOCIAL MODELS

The Experimental Plan

It is clearly necessary to make a comprehensive plan for the entire experimental program. Such a plan specifies the manner in which procedures are to be carried out and prepares a time schedule for their execution. It shows the times for the beginning and ending of the different phases of the research program—the planning, action, and evaluation phases. The plan also contains a timetable for measurement and the introduction of new experimental

247

procedures. An example of such a plan can be found in the lodge study referred to earlier. It is presented in Table 10.1.

Inspection of this plan highlights one of the difficulties of all such plans— it is difficult to plan for everything. The notion that we are trying to convey is that the research should articulate *as much as possible* who is supposed to do what, when, and how. If possible, the plan in Table 10.1 should have listed the actual people responsible for each of the tasks. When this is un- known, a job description for each task should be created. The issue of what the requirements are for particular research roles is extremely important in real-life researches. The lodge experiment gives a further example of why this is important. One of the research questions of the community lodge experiment concerned the degree of professional leadership required for the operation of a community model whose participants were discharged chronic mental patients. To explore the amount and type of professional supervision required, it was decided that leadership of the working–living situation would be changed three times. For the first eight months of operation, the super- visor would be a well-trained psychologist with several years' experience working with mental patients. At the end of the 8 months, he would be replaced by a less experienced psychologist who had not yet completed his training. Finally, at the end of 16 months of operation, he would be replaced by a lay leader who had no previous experience with mental illness. The three leadership periods in the action phase were scheduled in the research plan presented in Table 10.1. An evaluation of the professional requirements for lodge leadership could not have been accomplished without these switches. Social innovative experiments ordinarily will require such introductions of planned experimental change at prearranged times during the course of the experiment.

The preceding example illustrates the necessity to fully describe and elaborate upon each specific detail of the research procedure in the final research plan. It is also usually necessary to plan the size sample needed for the experiment prior to the onset of the action phase. It often happens that the use of naturally occurring open human groups for social models prevents establishing beforehand a date at which the sample size will be reached. Accordingly, the size of the sample is determined during the planning phase of the experiment and sampling is discontinued at the moment when the participant who represents the predetermined number enters the experi- mental model—a matter discussed in Chapter 8.

The timing of all measurements and research innovations, as well as the beginning and end of the different phases, should carefully follow what has been determined in the final research plan. This is important because later comparisons between models should not be unduly influenced by unplanned events. As a last important facet of the research plan, all of the researchers

TABLE 10.1
General Plan for an Experiment Comparing a Community Lodge
and Traditional Community Treatment Models

Program phase	Time scale	Research activity
Residual of planning	minus 4 months	Trial of assessment devices under model field conditions
	minus 3 months	Modification and perfection of assessment devices Establish preliminary reliability of assessment devices
	minus 2 months	Establish location of both models Preliminary testing of the samples
	minus 1 month	Draw initial samples for both models Preliminary meetings for participants of both models
Initiate models	0 months	Initial testing for both models First professional supervisor of community model begins operations
Action	plus 6 months	First general testing of both models First follow-up measures for both models
	plus 7 months	Start training of second professional supervisor for community model
	plus 8 months	Change to second professional supervisor of community model
	plus 12 months	Second general testing of both models Second follow-up measures for both models First measures of community and hospital attitudes toward both models
Action	plus 15 months	Start training of nonprofessional supervisor for community model
	plus 16 months	Change to nonprofessional supervisor of community model
	plus 18 months	Third general testing of both models Third follow-up measures for both models
	plus 24 months	Fourth general testing of both models Fourth follow-up measures for both models Second measures of community and hospital attitudes to both models
Close models	plus 28 months	Final measures of community attitudes which were impractical while models were in operation Stop all data collection except for follow-up data Begin scoring, tabulation, and analysis of data gathered to date
Evaluation and dissemination	plus 30 months	Fifth follow-up measures for both models Begin planning phase of next experiment
	plus 42 months	End write-up and publication of experiment Continue planning phase of next experiment

whose roles involve interaction with the participants should rehearse their required behaviors. To do this, it is important to simulate the new social organization that is being planned. This, of course, is difficult to accomplish because the new social model has not yet been established and roles that are pertinent to it cannot be exactly duplicated in another social situation. Nonetheless, it is necessary to do the best one can to simulate the conditions existent in the social innovation prior to its inception so that any radical changes that might be necessary can be made prior to the establishment of the new social model.

The establishment of the lodge society provides a rather clear example of the processes involved. In that particular social model, ex-patients were to operate their own society, including a work and living arrangement in the community. But many of the prospective members had never had the experience—often because of long and frequent hospitalization—of taking responsibility for planning their own lives. For this reason, they functioned in problem-solving groups while they were in the hospital prior to their move to the community. In these hospital-based groups they were given problems that involved the types of activities that they would be faced with once they completed their move to the community. These problem-solving sessions provided training for and simulation of the problem-solving decisions that would have to be made once they arrived in the community setting. Whenever it is possible, the research team should *try out new roles and social processes* so that they can be corrected when necessary prior to the establishment of the innovated social model. When this is done, the possibility of model failure is reduced.

It is also necessary to establish the validity and reliability of measurement devices by actual field trial during this pre-experimental period. An excellent example of the corrective effect of trying out the instruments and practicing rating is presented by Goldman (1964, p. 49).

> However, the social behavior that we sought to measure was not all represented in the LAI, and so plans were made to alter the instrument. In the course of making practice observations, it also became apparent that, although the over-all technique was well suited to our needs, the fact still remained that many of the scoring techniques had been developed with a patient population apparently far more immobile and considerably less active than our own. To put it more succinctly, the observer all too often could not keep pace with our patients' movements and social activities. Thus reconstruction and modification of the LAI was in order and, consequently, a new scoring and procedural manual was written by the psychologist-observer.

It is clear that this practice aided in improving the instrument as well as preparing the rater for the action phase of the experiment.

Much of the trial period for practicing with assessment devices and role playing may be done in the ordinary social research by carrying out pilot studies prior to the onset of the experiment proper. Such full-scale pilot studies are usually not feasible with social innovative experiments, because social models cannot be set up to be used for a few days or weeks and then abandoned. Therefore, practicing the research roles, determining the reliability and practicality of using the instruments, and role simulation usually must be done with the experimental population in situations that are not identical with the experimental models that will later be created. Because the control condition in social innovative experiments is usually existing societal practice, it is advantageous to try out the experimental procedures in one of these settings that *will not* be used in the actual experiment. Since there will be no opportunity to try the procedures in the new models once they are created, it is very important that every experimental procedure be tried and perfected in these unused control situations prior to the action phase. All assessment devices should be tried, timing should be agreed upon, and roles should be rehearsed during the planning phase so that the experimental procedures go smoothly when the new models are activated. The piloting and pre-testing of social roles, measurement instruments, and so on, has the obvious advantage of making the experimental plan more accurate and the experimental procedures more valid.

Other examples of research plans can be seen in the experiments of Whitney (1974) and Beck (1973). It will be recalled that Whitney's experiment involved the creation of an automobile repair cooperative owned and operated by juvenile delinquents which was compared with a matched comparative group receiving individual employment with typical industries (automobile manufacturing companies, etc.). His research plan appears in Table 10.2. Whitney's plan shows the activities, dates during which they would be accomplished, and who is responsible for each activity.

Another research plan was designed by Beck, who created and evaluated consumer groups that were organized to speak for their own health care and were contrasted with a matched group that did not receive the group training. Her experimental plan is presented in Table 10.3.

It should be noted that even though Whitney's plan (Table 10.2) assigned the research tasks to persons with particular research project roles, most of these assignments were to actual persons. It is important in the experimental plan to name the persons who will carry out each task. Often a highly complex social experiment involves some specialization of roles. An experimental plan should therefore not only specify time frames for task accomplishment,

TABLE 10.2
Whitney's Experimental Plan

Task	Time began	Expected date of completion	Individuals responsible
1. Approval of agreement with Y.D.C.	10/16/72	10/31/72	Project Director
2. Approval of business location	10/23/72	11/10/72	Project Director Employment Coordinator
3. Agreement with co-op and auto trainers	11/16/72	11/17/72	Project Director Employment Coordinator
4. Selection of subjects	10/23/72	11/10/72	Project Director
5. Job placement for control group	11/10/72	11/17/72	Work-Intern Supervisor
6. Assignment of small groups for control	11/17/72	11/20/72	Project Director
7. Co-op training	11/1/72	12/15/72	Jack Smith
8. Assignment of small groups for experimental group	11/3/72	11/6/72	Project Director
9. Order equipment	11/10/72	11/17/72	Project Director
10. Bi-weekly meetings for control group	11/20/72	2/28/73	Project Director
11. Legal agreements and insurance, workmen's compensation, etc.	12/1/72	12/15/72	Project Director Lawyer
12. Rennovation of building	11/10/72	12/29/72	All co-op members
13. Begin auto training	12/15/72	1/15/73	College
14. Advertisement	12/15/72	1/15/73	All co-op members
15. Install equipment	upon its arrival		All co-op members
16. Business questionnaire	1/15/73	1/22/73	Project Director
17. Evaluation and monitoring	continuous		Project Director
18. Open for business	2/1/73	continuous	All co-op members
19. Group discussions for experimental group	3/1/73	5/31/73	Project Director
20. End of research project	—	10/1/73	—
21. Analyze data	10/1/73	11/1/73	Project Director
22. Write up results	11/1/73	12/1/73	Project Director
23. Final report to sponsor	1/15/73	—	Project Director

but personnel allocation. The function of the experimental plan is to serve as a constant reminder to the research staff of upcoming research activities and to present a time schedule for their completion. Unless a research plan is devised and followed, there will almost inevitably be wasted effort, measurements that are not completed on time, and considerable confusion among team members. This is a particularly important problem in social innovative research because data that are not collected at the appropriate time are lost forever in such longitudinal research. If a deadline is missed, it cannot be retrieved. A research plan helps insure that such losses will not occur and that the research will proceed in an orderly and systematic fashion.

TABLE 10.3
Beck's Experimental Plan

Program phase	Time scale	Research activity
Residual of planning	minus 6 months	Trial of survey device under model field conditions
		Modification and perfection of survey device
	minus 5.5 months	Administer pre-experimental survey to all agency members
		Recruit volunteers for training program
		Conduct preliminary analysis of pre-experimental data
	minus 3.5 months	Recruit additional volunteers
		Assign volunteers to training and comparison groups
		Notify volunteers of respective assignments
		Trial test of meeting interaction device under model field conditions
Initiate models	0 months	Initiate Experiment Phase I
Evaluation and dissemination action	plus 2 months	Assessment of Phase I progress within training group
		Initiate Phase II
	plus 4 months	Assessment of Phase II progress within training group
		Initiate Phase III
	plus 6 months	Assessment of Phase III progress within training group
		Terminate experimental period
	plus 7 months	Administer post-experimental survey to all agency members
Close models	plus 12 months	Collect attendance data for post-experimental period
		Begin post-experimental data analysis
		Begin planning phase for next experiment
	plus 16 months	End write-up and publication of experiment

Emergent Problems: The Correlates of Action

Almost all naturalistic experiments will require some changes when the research begins. Social model experiments are particularly vulnerable to such problems.

Initial adjustments

On a designated day, the participants are placed in the models and the programs designated for each of the social models begins. The practiced roles for participants and staff alike can now be put into effect. This formally begins the action phase. It will usually be accompanied by the need for some revision in plans because *unforeseen events will occur*. As an example, on the initial day of activating the community lodge, 15 chronic mental patients were moved from the hospital to a community dormitory. Here they were expected to operate a janitorial and gardening service. Many had performed such jobs in the hospital for a number of years and it was therefore expected that they would immediately begin work in this capacity in the community setting. It was soon apparent, however, that the hospital training they had received did not adequately prepare them for community work; accordingly, a training program—not part of the initial experimental plan—was devised to correct this deficiency. This is but one of the many changes that had to be made as the model began to function, but the basic plan of a self-governing society including operating a business and maintaining the members of the model was not altered.

Innovated models can have new roles that cannot be tried prior to the experiment. In such cases it will be necessary that the specific behaviors required for such roles evolve during the first several weeks of the action phase. An example can be found in the evolution of the social worker's role in the small-group program of the hospital study. It was recognized in the planning phase that a social worker's role would be needed to deal with relatives and the community. The precise manner in which this role could be integrated into the small-group program could not be clearly understood before the model was placed in operation. The role therefore evolved in the first few weeks of the action phase. Blochburger & Lewis (1964, pp. 259–261) give the following account:

> The social worker's role gradually evolved in the program as it pro-
> gressed. . . . Not until about six weeks after the program's beginning did
> it become apparent that the social worker would have a unique and
> specialized function in the system. As the time neared when patients
> were ready to make leave plans after having completed the requirements
> of the program, the question arose as to how their plans should be
> evaluated. . . . An evaluation of the leave plans frequently involves inter-
> views with family members; it seemed appropriate for the social worker
> to assume this function. Some plans required referral to other com-
> munity agencies, such as employment offices, welfare agencies, and
> out-patient rehabilitation centers, many of which have a working
> relationship with the Social Work Service of the hospital. Also, some
> plans included the use of programs directly under Social Work Service
> administration, such as foster home care and follow-up supervision by
> social workers in the field office. . . . In retrospect, the evolution of the
> social worker as evaluator of group-approved plans came about rather
> naturally and smoothly. Once the roles were established, it was possible

to refine the procedures and become engaged in a maximum effort to help the patients obtain the benefits that the system offered.

Adjustments often need to be made in the first days of the action phase so that the planned model can fulfill its intended goals. It is probable that some adjustments will have to be made when any innovated programs are placed in action. It is important, therefore, that the research plan allow for some flexibility in the initial days of operation so that such needed changes can be accomplished. The changes that are needed and the procedures necessary to implement them should be recorded in detail as research data.

The process Whitney went through in creating an automobile cooperative for juvenile delinquents is an excellent example of the adjustments that often must be made to make the social model function properly. About these early adjustments, Whitney (1974) states:

> Many people did not have a business attitude in working. Therefore a lot of time had to be spent on developing appropriate job behavior; developing the fact that this was a business and not an agency; that as a business certain types of behavior must be controlled when working in the program. . . .
>
> It had to be stressed time and time again that it was a business and individuals had to display appropriate behavior. For example, a customer would walk in and individuals would be horse-playing, cursing, or talking in a very loud manner. These types of behaviors detracted from the business and caused great concern among many customers. Therefore many weekly meetings were spent merely in telling the individuals about appropriate behavior. . . .
>
> Another major problem associated with the new model is concerned with keeping equipment to do the work. During the first two months of operating the business, the equipment disappeared at a very rapid rate. Individuals who were employed here did not feel or understand that the equipment was necessary in order for the employees to have a job and to satisfy the customers—the equipment was theirs and they were stealing from themselves. To correct the situation, every time a part was missing the money to pay for it would be taken out of everyone's check. The result of doing this . . . was that the equipment started being returned, primarily because individuals who did not take equipment were not willing to pay for the missing equipment . . .
>
> Another major problem associated with the behavior of participants in the model that detracted from the business was getting to work on time. Many of the young people did not think of getting up at eight

o'clock in the morning at the beginning of the operation of the co-op. Many times when I went down to open the garage I was the first one there. I had to call individuals up; go pick up those that lived near in order for them to come to work. Soon a policy was set in a group meeting that all persons attended. They decided that if an individual was late or absent three times that he would be suspended or not paid for the total days missed . . .

Beck's innovative consumer advocate model also required some initial adjustments before it became organized and was functioning properly. About this initial adjustmental period, Beck (1973) has written:

The problems that emerged in the beginning of the experiment were with some incompatibilities between the plan of the research and what the consumers would actually let happen. In this research there was a general plan of action which the volunteers agreed to, such as carrying out periodic meetings and how they would be conducted. But the main theme of the new model was that the consumers would be encouraged to conduct the program as they wished so that as the consumer group training program began these incompatibilities became obvious. The first problem to emerge was in group development. The researchers were trying to let the natural leadership of the group develop. One member decided that he was going to turn the autonomous group meeting into his own political platform and try to rearrange the way in which the program was run. A great deal of hostility developed over this but eventually, after some of the group left and after disrupting several meetings, the group voted against his plan and about the fourth meeting he left.

During the action phase of the experiment, the operation of the model is continued without change except for the adjustments needed at the beginning and those innovations that are part of the experimental conditions, such as the planned changes in leadership mentioned in Table 10.1.

External interference

Many types of interference can occur during the course of an experiment that could alter the model's operation and therefore destroy the experimental conditions so assiduously developed and established by the researchers. The investigators must be aware of such sources of interference and be prepared to invoke the administrative agreements which were made during the planning phase to prevent interference with the models after the action phase has begun. Again, social model experiments are particularly vulnerable to outside interference. Some sources of interference that may occur when models have been activated are worthy of brief discussion.

First, a successful research may arouse the interest of the scientific and lay communities. Interested individuals may wish to visit the models to see their operation at first hand. This is a particular problem when working with populations like the mentally ill, in whom the public is beginning to have a much greater interest. Permitting such visits may destroy the operation of the models, because it introduces new social variables that, ordinarily, are not planned for at the outset of the experiment and may not be present in any replicates that might be created. Frequent visits would, in fact, change the models themselves. To prevent such intrusions, the researchers may need to request support from their research institute to prevent visits that could in any way interfere with the experimental conditions.

Another source of interference may be publicity. It often happens that new programs gain early publicity that either raises false hopes or prematurely records failure. In either case it has an effect upon the participants in the various models. This effect may prevent direct future application of the experimental model because such publicity will probably not be given to the replicates which are established as service programs. This is particularly true of new programs that excite interest, because once the novelty of the program has disappeared the interest of the curious wanes. From an experimental point of view, such publicity can be devastating because the results obtained may not be attributable to the social model but rather to the attention paid the participants. Placebo effects are well-documented in other research situations (Frank, 1961, pp. 65–74). Accordingly, it is exceedingly important to avoid this source of extraneous interference. Social innovative experiments are especially vulnerable to excessive publicity because the protection accorded researchers when they are carrying out laboratory studies is usually not accorded the social innovative experimentalists, particularly when their work is in the community. It is very important that the agreements about publicity reached with newspaper people and other interested persons prior to the onset of the experiment are honored.

Such interference often occurs when the new social model is perceived as meeting a social need even though, from a scientific point of view, it is still in the process of being evaluated and could, in fact, still be a failure. The lodge society provides an example of this emerging problem. The lodge society was a self-governing society established by formerly hospitalized patients. It was located in a lower socioeconomic area of a west coast city. The society owned and operated its own business and it eventually became a monetary success. Because of its obvious financial success, persons living in the area often entered the business office requesting employment. Although these visits were recorded as research information, the neighborhood residents could not be absorbed into the lodge work force because of logistic and methodological issues. The pressure for admission did not stop there. The parents of other mentally ill persons contacted the lodge, asking for admission of their relatives. Of course the effect upon sample bias and the resulting inability to evaluate the outcomes of the lodge would have occurred if such admissions had been permitted. This would *not*, of course, prevent the researchers from trying other means of obtaining employment and residence for such persons.

On the other hand, different forms of interference can occur from the neighborhood if the social model is perceived as a failure or as undesirable. It is commonplace these days to read in the newspapers that a "halfway house" for drug addicts, ex-prisoners, the mentally ill, and other socially marginal groups, has been closed because of a negative reaction by the neighbors. This can often be prevented by careful planning and an awareness of the external social factors mentioned in Chapter 3 that might impinge upon the social model; where such planning has been unsuccessful, every attempt should be made to carry out the research as planned despite opposition. If the opposition becomes so intense that it interferes with the daily operation of the social model, the research project will of course have to be abandoned. Information from this first failure can often be used in picking subsequent sites so that the probability of failure will be minimized. Often researchers have an unrealistic faith in the humanitarian aims of others and neglect to do their homework in laying the political groundwork for possible controversial community programs. Appropriate agreements among the citizens, social administrators, and researchers as procedurally described in Chapter 6 can be of great aid in reducing the probability of failure.

Preventing outside interference is sometimes difficult, particularly when the interested people are in some way associated with the funding of administration of the research program. Nonetheless, it is the responsibility of the researcher to try to prevent alterations in the experimental conditions. This is most important because future social models about which the researchers wish to generalize from the prototype model will usually not be accompanied by the interest which new models create. For maximum generalization, therefore, naturalistic conditions must be preserved if at all possible.

Personnel issues

Another source of interference may be turnover among staff personnel. This is a recurring source of difficulty because of the longitudinal nature of social innovative research. For this reason, it is important to establish procedures at the outset of the experiment for the training of new personnel who might be needed as replacements for those members who probably will leave. It is especially important that the effects of personnel changes are minimized during the action phase because role constancy is an essential experimental condition. Procedures for training new personnel should be included as an integral part of the planning phase. An example of training a new rater during the course of the action phase of the experiment is given by Goldman (1964, p. 53):

> The second observer was to become the sole rater during the last six weeks of the program, since commitments would take the original observer from the ward scenes.
> ... the second observer also needed to be equally familiar to the patients on both wards. Approximately ten days of instruction and practice were instituted in order to provide a fair test of reliability of the instrument and to insure a similarity in rater technique. Both judges independently rated 280 patients during 7 separate recreational periods ... in no case did the average rater agreement fall below 90%.

Loss of research personnel sometimes arises because they are not suited for the roles that are created in the new social model. Even though every attempt should be made to select persons who will feel comfortable in the new social positions by role playing prior to the experiment wherever possible, there still remains the probability that some individuals cannot meet the role requirements. Notes taken from the lodge research journal record such an instance in the following manner (Fairweather *et al.*, 1969):

> The original two men whom we hired for the job were Mr. Hawkins, a retired Marine (Corps) Major, and Mr. Edwards, a former quarry worker who had been partially disabled as a result of a back injury. Both of these men came to work together for the first time on Tuesday, the first of June—Monday being a holiday. It became very apparent over the next week—over the week, that is, of June 1st—that Mr Hawkins was not at all comfortable in the job that we were asking him to do. He made several arrangements during the first week which made it quite clear that he saw himself as being primarily an office man and organizer and sort of the brains of the outfit, while Mr. Edwards, the second man, took over the outside work—that is, the delivery of crews on jobs and the inspections and so forth. This impression became stronger and stronger as the week progressed in spite of several conferences

which the two of them, myself, and Bob (Dr. Watkins) had altogether, and the extended discussions during those times of the lay leaders taking on the entire job which I was then doing by myself. Although Bob and I both stressed this with Mr. Hawkins and Mr. Edwards, Mr. Hawkins obviously continued the kind of behavior which aimed him toward taking over the inside, or office aspects of the job, and leaving the other to Mr. Edwards. This became so obvious that by Monday, the 7th of June, Mr. Hawkins seemed quite depressed about the kind of job he was getting into and I discussed it with him on the morning of the 7th. He told me then that he was evaluating the job and that perhaps it had been more than he had bargained for. I told that to Bob on that same night—the night of the 7th—and the following morning as Bob requested me to do, I sent Mr. Hawkins in to speak to Bob. The upshot of meeting with Bob was that . . . Mr. Hawkins was terminated as of June 11. Over the past six days, it had become increasingly apparent that he had been dissatisfied with the janitorial and gardening aspects of the work. It would seem that he perceived these as low-status jobs and did not appreciate the overall rehabilitative intent of the project, although every precaution was taken in describing these aspects of the job to him prior to and subsequent to employment. He stated in final interview, "You did not tell me that I would be mainly running a janitorial and gardening service." This may have more generalizable elements. It occurs to me that people with high-prestige ambitions, who are found predominantly in the more well-educated groups, are poorer risks in administering rehabilitative projects than people from the lower socioeconomic groups.

In this example the retired major was so uncomfortable in the new position that he was replaced in the research project by an individual who was able to perform adequately as required by the research plan.

In other instances some retraining may be necessary and maybe effective if the person wishes to continue in the new role even though he or she is having trouble with the new assignment. Whitney (1974) describes such a situation:

The second problem associated with maintaining and operating the model was the fact that we had to find a good management person— a person with very good skills in automotive repairs. This was difficult because we really didn't have enough money to pay a well-qualified person. Most individuals in this particular area that we were looking for were employed elsewhere in jobs ranging from $12,000–$14,000 and we are asking for someone to commit a lot of time and energy, one who could get along with the young people, and would also have automotive repair skill. We finally took an individual who had skills in automotive repairs but, it turned out, did not understand the purpose of our organization. The fact that we were running a cooperative and not a profit making organization was difficult for him to grasp. He tended to carry over many behaviors he had developed to deceive the customers by telling them repair work was necessary when they didn't need it and in general being dishonest. So I had to re-educate him in the purposes of the cooperative, the emphasis on training, the emphasis was not on making money, but on making sure the kids learned the skills and could do things without his assistance. In the beginning he wanted to do all the work and have the kids stand around and watch him. The kids were not getting trained. These problems were solved, however, by continuously stressing that if he wanted a job here he would have to be responsive to the needs of this organization.

It is also possible that certain research procedures will need to be altered during the course of the experiment. This often happens if any of the experimental techniques begin to interfere unduly with the naturalistic processes that are being investigated. In the community lodge program, for example, weekly discussions with the participants were part of the initial research plan. These were structured discussions where the group was asked questions concerning their satisfaction with the organization and their roles. By the end of six months, all information about the developmental phase had been collected and it soon became apparent that the group discussions were interfering increasingly with the work and living situation of the participants. Accordingly, they were discontinued.

Abrogation of administrative agreements

If the original negotiations for the administrative agreements were completed with persons who have since left or if there was "lukewarm" acceptance of the project in the first instance, attempts to "sabotage" the research project may occur. As was pointed out in Chapter 6, the drawing up of administrative agreements does not mean that they necessarily will be honored. This involves a ceaseless effort of discussion, cajoling, etc. Ives' (1974) drug research is an excellent example of a successful "sabotage" effort. The persons administratively responsible for the drug agency were only reluctantly persuaded to permit the establishment of the new drug model which gave the released addicts a significant voice in their program. Because the top administrators of the drug program were not in sympathy with any approach that permitted the ex-addicts to participate in decision making, the experimentalist was never permitted to fully activate this condition. Ives was permitted to establish a home in the community for the ex-addicts, but the essential experimental condition of ex-addict participation in developing and managing the home was not realized. This form of "sabotage" is direct and open. The research team must decide at this point whether or not there is any value in continuing the project. Ives decided that sufficient information could be gained so that continuation of the project was warranted. There was, of course, no way in which the initial hypotheses could be tested.

Beck (1973) faced a similar situation, but managed to preserve the experimental model. She reports constant harassment from the agency that sponsored the project once they clearly perceived the benefits that were accruing to the consumers. Beck describes the harassment in part in the following statement:

> The major interference with our study was not that things turned out so dramatically different from what we planned but that we constantly had to defend the integrity of what we were doing. For example, we constantly defended the fact that the agency couldn't touch the research money—that the money was *our* research grant and it was going to be spent as our grant said it was. The research group was set up to carry out the terms of the grant and they (the agency) couldn't tell us how it could be spent. It was a constant harassment day by day by day of what could and could not be done and the fact that they would just as soon we left and went away and didn't come back. So we won but we got very tired . . .
>
> The truth is that the agency really didn't want a research effort to begin with. Consequently they were constantly looking for us to make some slip-up so that they could catch us and give us a negative report. The thing I would caution others about is make sure you're cleaner than clean. This means all of your financial arrangements have to be in order. No slip-up in any way on your auditing because that is the first thing they will get you on, and the second one is on personnel. You can't take too much time off or that sort of thing.

Another form that resistance to carrying out the initial agreements can take is the refusal of the agency or organization with which the arrangements have been made to continue to support the *sampling* plan needed for successful completion of the research effort, a matter discussed in Chapter 8. It will be recalled that Ives (1974) was continuously threatened with either the loss of new members to the autonomous drug program or with an unwillingness on the part of the drug agency to assign participants to the program at random as in the initial agreement.

In contrast, Whitney (1974) found that popularity of the new program can lead to difficulties in following the prearranged sampling procedures. He reports this problem in the following way:

> Whenever a spot became vacant in the experimental model I would immediately get four or five referrals from the agency staff who wanted to place their clients. This occurred after the initial random assignment of clients. The agency persons appeared unaware that randomization procedures had been and were continuing to be used and that there was already a waiting list for individuals who had volunteered to participate in the experimental subsystem. This did cause some problems in my relationship with the agency but since the signed administrative agreements specified that random assignment would occur I had the authority to reject their request for placing their clients. All these problems developed because this was the only program the agency had established as its own employment operation and therefore it was looked upon as a desirable place where individuals could get training, learn skills and get financial reimbursement.

Throughout the course of the action phase, sources of interference that require the experimenter to ask for the execution of the agreements made prior to the onset of the study will appear. Upon occasion, for example, it may be necessary to ask for maintenance of the agreement made about sampling. It is quite common that a sample is readily available at the outset of the study, but after several months of experimental action the initial sampling procedures are placed in jeopardy because the institutions involved have forgotten about them or other needs have arisen which interfere with existing sampling agreements. If this occurs, the experimentalists should advise the administrators who have agreed to the sampling procedures of this change and request a return to the original procedures. It cannot be overemphasized that it is the ultimate responsibility of the investigators to maintain the constancy of the social models during the action phase.

It is not uncommon that new and interesting processes will occur during the course of the experiment which were unknown or unforeseen at its beginning. The researcher should design new instruments to measure these processes as they occur. Although adequate planning may reduce these unforeseen events to a minimum, in longitudinal experiments of several months or years duration, new processes that should be fully described will emerge.

When these changes occur, it is most important that new data collection procedures are arranged to measure them. The new procedures should require as little change as possible in the research plan. Also, occasionally one event occurs as a unique experience. In such a case, as much information as possible should be obtained about it. This might be called *information saturation*, because special attention is given all aspects of any incident that occurs once and is not likely to be repeated. In the community lodge project, for example, one of the researchers left the research program. All information concerning his relationship with the lodge group, his reasons for leaving, and the group's interaction with him were accumulated prior to the time he left, so that the information could be studied later in great detail.

During the action phase, there are usually planned changes that are scheduled to occur at designated times for which extensive planning must be done. For instance, in the hospital study, the staffs were switched from one model to the other at a prearranged time. "To equate the number of days each of the two staffs spent in the two treatment programs, the staffs changed treatment programs half way through the experimental period, a procedure which later was entitled 'the staff switch.' Through this procedure, each staff spent an equivalent amount of time in the two experimental programs" (Fairweather, 1964, p. 33).

As another example, Table 10.1 shows that three different supervisors were introduced to the community model at the planned times. In addition there are the continuous ratings, interviews, and testing which are scheduled for given dates, also shown in Table 10.1. These scheduled activities require extensive staff preparation so that all aspects of the move could be carried out with a minimum of interference with the daily activities of the social model. These research activities must be executed at the appropriate times with the least interference possible in the processes of the model.

Problems of data gathering

There are, of course, many problems pertaining to the collection and storage of data which emerge during the action phase. As far as data collection is concerned, it is important to establish check sheets to make certain all data are obtained from each participant at every time of measurement. To minimize collection errors, a check sheet for each participant can be created and all incoming data can be recorded on the sheet as they arrive. Preventing errors is particularly important in longitudinal research where repeated measures are used, because data that are not collected at the designated time cannot be retrieved. Another source of error is incomplete forms. To reduce the number of incompletions, it is important that all responses to questionnaires, tests, and so on be reviewed while the respondents are still present so that they can complete whatever items they have missed. Furthermore, the administrator of the tests can reduce such deletions by being available to give additional instructions when necessary. This is exceedingly important with marginal populations, many of whom may be uneducated or emotionally disturbed. Also, adequate storage space for the collected data needs to be provided. Here, it is most important that all information be clearly labeled and appropriately filed so that the data can be readily located when scoring is to be done. It is important that all researchers associated with the experiment coordinate their activities so that the preparation of measuring devices and the collection and labeling of the data can continue concomitant with the operation of the models. To accomplish this, each researcher should be made responsible for particular aspects of the research so that all data collection continues without interruption. It is also important, when possible, that some of the data be scored during the action phase. Scoring manuals can be created for each instrument and used by the research staff to begin scoring the vast accumulation of data.

Other problems in the collection of data may be associated with the field conditions of the research itself. Thus, persons who are not on the research team but who sometimes are responsible for data collection can show little interest in data collection. This often occurs when the research team is limited by financial resources and finds it necessary to enlist the support of other persons or agencies. In such circumstances a member of the research team *must* monitor the data-collection process in order to make certain that data are collected on time and in the appropriate manner. When adequate data collection does not occur, the researcher must take action to collect the research information under the most appropriate conditions possible at that time.

Whitney (1974) discusses this problem as it affected his research and the action he was impelled to take:

Another problem associated with operating the automobile cooperative as a business was the fact that I had to obtain research data and follow-up reports on the clients. This was a very simple procedure in dealing with the participants of the cooperative since many of those had become personal friends and I saw them daily. They did consult with me and felt they could talk with me concerning their problems with the courts or police, home, school, etc. However the problem did arise in trying to collect data and follow-up information for the control participants. Originally the experiment was designed so that the parent youth organization would be using the same type of follow-up as I did in the cooperative and it could therefore be used as comparative data. The agreement was that the youth organization's outreach component would be responsible for obtaining client follow-up of those persons in the control model. But I found I had to spend a lot of my time making sure that clients were being followed up, making sure that each client had an outreach worker and that the outreach worker was actually obtaining the follow-up information. In the final analysis I had to go back and verify all follow-up reports for all persons. This is a very time-consuming task.

The follow-up data-collection problem facing Whitney was also a difficult problem for Beck (1973). Although she was able to keep her follow-up data loss to a minimum, she reports the difficulty in the following statement:

The other problem that occurred with the research effort as a whole surfaced in the filling out of questionnaires by some of the other members of the organization who were not in the experimental model. This was especially true with the follow-up questionnaires. Some of the more vocal anti-consumers made remarks in open meetings that they didn't have the time to fill out 'all of this kind of stuff,' that they had no knowledge of what the group was trying to do and certainly didn't want 'to spend any time on it'.

Termination of Models

Eventually, it will be necessary to stop the operation of the models when the action phase of the experiment has been completed. Planning for termination of the models is part of the experimental plan. The future of the participants after termination of the action phase also needs to be considered as part of this plan. For example, the community lodge program was continued as a private business by the discharged patients themselves upon completion of the action phase of that experiment. When the model is located in the community and the action phase is completed, it is also necessary to cancel residential leases, make arrangements for the cessation of insurance coverage, dispose of the work tools, and so forth.

The experimenters thus must close down the entire operation. This is often difficult to do, particularly when the research has been successful with marginal people. For this reason, the researchers should make plans from the outset of the project about how they will continue the operation of the prototype social model if it is successful and how they will close it down if it is not. An example of how such a transition can take place with a successful model is given in this account of the phase-out plan for the lodge society (Fairweather *et al.*, 1969):

> When the end of the research phase of the lodge project was five months away, the research staff began planning for its autonomous future. Most appropriately, the lodge would be closed at the conclusion of the lease agreement with the owner of the motel in five months' time, when all members would have to become self-sufficient. Accordingly, this time was used to decrease gradually the amount of research financial support given the lodge, in order to determine how the men would react when they were required to increase support for themselves through their own resources.
>
> Initially, the plan was to reduce by half the amount of money contributed by the research budget for food. A similar reduction in research money to pay for telephone, utilities, gas and oil for the work trucks, laundry, postage, equipment maintenance and repair, work clothing, and other supplies was also planned. The plan required that by the time the lodge was closed, the members would be paying every expense for operating the lodge dormitory and the business. The plan also called for discontinuing research funds given to the men for medication and periodic visits to the local physician. Needy members would have to visit local outpatient or mental hygiene clinics, where the cost would be very minimal or where the costs could be paid by the men from their own resources. The plan expected members would assume the cost of the lodge by contributing from all their sources of income—wages from the business, pensions, compensations, and Social Security disability funds. Of course, the plan assumed that the amount each individual should contribute would have to be determined by the members themselves.
>
> In order to facilitate an easy transition to this more autonomous phase, the research staff set out to determine the various medical resources in the community that might be available to the members, the members' financial guardianship status, and the actual monthly costs for the lodge and the business. As a result of this survey, it was decided to extend increasing financial responsibility to the lodge members during the first three months of the five-month period, with the group paying the entire costs of the lodge during the final two-month period. Thus the members would experience two months of autonomous operation before the lodge buildings had to be vacated according to the lease agreement. Based upon lodge costs, the schedule for increasing financial responsibility was established as shown in Table 10.4.

TABLE 10.4
The Plan for Financial Autonomy

Time	Percent lodge members pay of total costs	Percent research project pays of total costs
1st month	20	80
2nd month	49	51
3rd month	78	22
4th month	100	0
5th month	100	0

Estimated lodge costs as shown in Table 10.4 included eventual payment by the members for the lay coordinator's salary, all food costs, the cost of the lodge lease, and the cost of leasing work trucks. Finally, the plan specified that eventually members must pay for all medical costs incurred by them. In order to facilitate member payment, it was decided to establish a bank savings account where money contributed by members for payment of their expenses during the five-month period could be deposited.

After the Action Phase

Even after the action phase has been completed, some data continue to be collected. Follow-up information often needs to be obtained from the participants (who had been in the models for several months or years) after these models have ceased operation. This is particularly important when evaluating the permanence of the models' outcomes upon the lives of the participants. In models designed for marginal people, such as the chronically mentally ill and long-term criminals, the experimenters are often interested in recidivism or other effects which may occur after the models are no longer in operation.

As soon as the model's operations have been terminated, the scoring and analysis of the data begin. When possible and if staff permits, some of the scoring may already have been done during the data-collecting phase. However this may be, it is now necessary to complete scoring and prepare the data for computer analysis. Often the data may be placed on optical scanning sheets, which enables a relatively automated punching of cards from which the analyses are made. If it is impossible to do this because of the nature of the data, computer keypunch sheets must be prepared. The data are then treated according to the plan established for data analysis in the planning phase.

However, certain decisions—the use of parametric or nonparametric comparative methods, for example—depend upon the empirical distributions of the data. Many of these distributions will be unknown at the time the data analyses were planned. Therefore alternative forms of analysis must have been set forth in the research plan—usually parametric and nonparametric alternatives—and now those methods appropriate to the collected data will be used in the analyses. The experimenters make decisions about whether the data meet the assumptions for parametric statistics or whether missing- or nonmissing-data computer programs are to be used. Such decisions are typically made after the data are collected because the experimenters may not know the nature of the data prior to the experiment. In such a case, their choice of a particular method is made when the data are at hand so that they can choose the most appropriate method.

When the data have been analyzed by the appropriate comparative and relationship techniques described in Chapters 11 and 12, the researchers must determine from these analyses and their own experiences the inferences which can properly be made from this information, a subject reserved for Chapter 13. If the inference can be made that one of the new social models is more beneficial to the problem population than existing social practice, an experiment in implementing the new social model is begun.

DISSEMINATION

When the results of an experiment are positive, it is the responsibility of the research team to utilize them in advocating an experiment to implement the new social models on a regional or national basis. In addition, the experimentalists must give society's representatives all of the information they have and even supply members of the research team to aid in establishing such programs, for it is the researchers' responsibility to society to aid its members in putting beneficial new social models into effect on a day-to-day service basis. It is not only the experimenters' proper responsibility to innovate and evaluate new programs, but it is also their responsibility to disseminate successful models, a philosophical and logical position presented in Chapter 3.

The problems of activating and carrying out dissemination researches has some similarities and some differences with the initial social model-building experiments. The similarities involve the basic research aspects common to all field researches—selecting a research team, choosing the sample, selecting the areas of measurement, creating the assessment devices, setting forth the hypotheses, and data collection and processing. All these activities are common to both social model-building and dissemination researches. Problems emerging in these areas are often very similar. When they are not, a separate discussion of each area has been arranged in the preceding chapters.

Experimental plans are just as necessary in dissemination experiments as they are when social models are compared. Keith (1974) created a rather simple experimental plan in an attempt to persuade organizations to use the services of a community program operating out of a university. Some organizations in the community were given different types of experimental treatment in order to evaluate their effects upon adoption and interaction with the new university-based program. Keith's experimental plan is presented in Table 10.5. A perusal of Table 10.5 shows the similarity of Keith's dissemination plan with the social model experiments shown in Tables 10.1, 10.2, and 10.3.

TABLE 10.5
Keith's Experimental Plan

Operations phase	Project time frame Time frame	Activity
Preparatory planning	— 2 months	Development of standarized communications instrument for (1) introductory letter and (2) telephonic contact Development of workshop format (discussion, media, lectures, etc.) and materials Development of instrumentation materials, pre-testing, and reliability testing of instruments
	— 1 month	Have judges select sample of organizations Determine reliability of ratings Finalize development and testing of workshop materials and operational plans
Initiate operations action	0 month	Send introductory letters to organizations
	+ 1 week	Make telephonic contact with organizations
Terminate operations	+ 3 weeks	Completion of workshop. Obtain decisions from participants regarding possible subsequent interaction with Ecological Psychology unit
Analysis of data	+ 4 weeks	Score, code, and tabulate data Begin analysis of results
Write-up of research report	+ 8 weeks	Completion of data analysis Begin write-up of report
Completion of research project	+ 18 weeks	Completion of write-up Disseminate results to appropriate target audience

However, most dissemination experimental plans are much more complex. The reader will recall that the lodge study implementation required extensive planning throughout the various phases of implementation. This complex experimental plan involved the four stages of approaching, persuading, activating, and diffusing. The complex nature of the plan and its design are presented in Table 10.6. The reader will see that no time scale was featured because the complex and unique nature of the experiment made such estimates difficult, if not impossible, to make at the time the plan was devised.

TABLE 10.6
The Lodge Dissemination Experimental Plan

I. Send letters to 50 Department of Mental Health Chiefs
II. Approaching phase
A. Brochure condition
    1. Researcher calls hospital telephone information for chief and his name.
    2. Hospital contact is then called to obtain a decision about sending a roster of hospital personnel so that brochures can be mailed by name.
    3. A structured interview is conducted over the telephone with the contact pertaining to his: (a) attitudes toward mental illness, (b) a "yes" or "no" decision about entering the persuasion phase, (c) information about how the decision was made, and (d) who made the decision.
    4. If a decision cannot be obtained upon initial call, arrangements will be made for a second call.
    5. If the decision is NO, the hospital is placed in the nonvolunteer group.
    6. If the decision is YES, the hospital is placed in the Brochure Condition of Persuasion phase.
B. Workshop condition
    1. Researcher calls hospital telephone information for chief and his name.
    2. Hospital contact is then called to obtain a decision about holding a workshop at the hospital.
    3. A structured interview is conducted over the telephone with the contact pertaining to his: (a) attitudes toward mental illness, (b) a "yes" or "no" decision about entering the persuasion phase, (c) information about how the decision was made, and (d) who make the decision.
    4. If a decision cannot be obtained upon initial call, arrangements will be made for a second call.
    5. If the decision is NO, the hospital is placed in the nonvolunteer group.
    6. If the decision is YES, the hospital is placed in the Workshop Condition of Persuasion phase. Date when the workshop will be held is agreed upon.
C. Demonstration ward condition
    1. Researcher calls hospital telephone information for chief and his name.
    2. Hospital contact is then called to obtain decision to hold demonstration at the hospital.
    3. A structured interview is conducted over the telephone with the contact pertaining to his: (a) attitudes toward mental illness, (b) a "yes" or "no" decision about entering the persuasion phase, (c) information about how the decision was made, and (d) who made the decision.
    4. If a decision cannot be obtained upon initial call, arrangements will be made for a second call.

TABLE 10.6 *contd.*

5. If the decision is NO, the hospital is placed in the nonvolunteer group.
6. If the decision is YES, the hospital is placed in the Demonstration Ward Condition of Persuasion phase. Date when the demonstration ward will be established is agreed upon.

III. Persuading phase (volunteers)

A. Brochure condition

1. When rosters from hospitals are obtained, a letter is sent to professional staff about establishing the community treatment program.
2. Two days after the letter is sent, the brochure and postcard questionnaire about their interest in establishing the lodge program are sent to professional staff.
3. Follow-up postcard questionnaires are sent to staff who have not returned the first card.
4. After a response is received, a questionnaire about the effectiveness of the brochure is sent to hospital staff.
5. Each contact is then called for a decision about the community treatment program. At this time a structured interview is held on the telephone about : (a) what the hospital's decision is, (b) how the decision was made, and (c) who made the decision.
6. If a decision has not been reached at the time of the initial call, arrangements are made for a second call.
7. If the decision is NO, the hospital becomes a nonvolunteer for activation.
8. If the decision is YES, the hospital enters the activation phase.

B. Workshop condition

1. When a date is set by us for holding the workshop, arrangements are continued by telephone with the hospital contact.
2. After completion of the workshop, postcard questionnaires about interest in establishing a community treatment program are distributed to professional staff and a supply is left for those not able to attend the workshop.
3. While at the hospital for the workshop, questionnaires about the effectiveness of the workshop will be completed. Those not attending will receive a different type of questionnaire later.
4. While at the hospital for the workshop presentation, a roster will be obtained so that follow-up postcard questionnaires can be sent to those not responding.
5. Each contact is then called for a decision about the community treatment program. At this time a structured interview is held on the telephone about : (a) what the hospital's decision is, (b) how the decision was made, and (c) who made the decision.
6. If a decision has not been reached at the time of the initial call, arrangements are made for a second call.
7. If the decision is NO, the hospital becomes a nonvolunteer for activation.
8. If the decision is YES, the hospital enters the activation phase.

C. Demonstration ward condition

1. When a date is set for establishing the demonstration ward, arrangements are confirmed by telephone with our contact at the hospital.
2. While at the hospital for establishing the demonstration ward, a roster is obtained for postcard questionnaire follow-up to be initiated one month later.
3. Two months after completion of the demonstration ward, a postcard questionnaire about their interest in establishing a community treatment program is sent to the professional staff.
4. Different questionnaires about the effectiveness of the demonstration ward are sent to those who were involved in the demonstration and to those who were not.

5. Each contact is then called for a decision about the community treatment program. At this time a structured interview is held on the telephone about: (a) what the hospital's decision is, (b) how the decision was made, and (c) who made the decision.
6. If a decision has not been reached at the time of the initial call, arrangements are made for a second call.
7. If the decision is NO, the hospital becomes a nonvolunteer for activation.
8. If the decision is YES, the hospital enters the activation phase.

IV. Adopting phase
  A. These hospitals are matched in pairs for background experimental experiences and randomly assigned to one of two conditions—a condition where the hospital staff itself will attempt to activate the lodge through a written manual and a condition where activation will be attempted through a social action consultant's visits to the hospital.

V. Diffusing phase
  A. All 255 hospitals in the sample are interviewed to ascertain if any dissemination of the lodge has occurred in the two years since the hospital had its last contact with the research team.

However, future experimental plans, even when researches are very complex, should contain a time estimate for each phase. A perusal of these dissemination plans shows that as with the experimental plans for social models there is a clear necessity for meticulous planning and accurate timing. Longitudinal field experiments in dissemination no less than those in social model building require an experimental plan which is similar to a blueprint and which is followed for the duration of the experiment.

As mentioned in Chapter 6, the administrative agreements for dissemination experiments very often are with individuals or organizations that are spread over a wide geographic area. The researchers are thus much more reliant on persons in field settings who are not on the research payroll to carry out some of the aspects of the research program. One primary difference between carrying out dissemination research in a broader setting compared with a research in one location close to the research team headquarters, as occurs in social model comparative experiments, is that the prototype model must be duplicated and its constancy maintained so that outcomes will be approximately the same in the replicates as they were in the initial model-building comparative experiment.

Accordingly, many difficulties arise during the course of carrying out implementation experiments that are often a function of the number of replicates and geographic factors. Since the initial models are now being replicated throughout a city, county, state, region, or nation, the problems of excessive publicity, who can participate in them, and the like are replicated over and over again. It cannot be overemphasized that one of the foremost problems in implementation research is the creation of *absolute* replication so that the results that obtain in the original experiment will occur again in the replicates. The researchers have the most difficulty when those carrying out the implementation of the new social models are not attending to the plan for implementation. When this occurs, the major parameters of the initial model are not often replicated and the results emanating from them are unpredictable. A clear example comes from the lodge diffusion study. In that study, it was necessary that ex-mental patients become responsible for governing their own small society which included control of their money, discipline of their members, and the creation of an entire self-governing society. It was a very common experience during the course of implementing lodges throughout the nation that the involved mental health professionals, who had been trained to supervise and make decisions for mental patients, found this new autonomy too deviant from their typical dominant role. Accordingly, it was often necessary for the experimenters on field site visits to point out to the local staff that they were assuming too much responsibility for the program and needed to return decision-making power to the lodge members. When this problem was noticed and called to the attention of the local groups, the necessary changes were sometimes difficult to accomplish. These changes were made somewhat easier when it was found that once they were made the high morale and level of performance observed and measured in the prototype lodge became obvious to the staff members in the replicates.

A second problem of importance in implementation experiments is that certain minor modifications may need to be made to fit local conditions. This must be done without altering the conditions essential to the success of the social model. Here again the lodge implementation experiment can serve as an example. Some minor changes were made in the lodge society to meet local conditions but only when they did not alter the form or shape of that society. For example, the prototype lodge created a gardening and janitorial service which it owned and operated. When the lodge was replicated in other areas of the country, it was sometimes impossible to establish a business; so therefore, employment in small groups often replaced a member-owned business as the work of the organization. Constant observation and feedback from these groups during the period of their formation and organization into work groups with different tasks clearly showed that as long as the basic autonomy and decision making of the members was maintained the type of work performed was more a matter of individual and group preference than a necessary condition for social model success.

A third and extremely important problem inevitably emerges in implementation experiments because the research team is dependent upon various persons in different organizations throughout the implementation experiment for carrying out various aspects of the research. Fergus' (1973) research can serve as an example of this problem. She trained change agents in a workshop and depended on them for aid in implementing the new nursing home program after they returned to their own installations. About this experience, she said:

> At the workshop I had asked for the names of three people who would be interested in implementing the ideas and who could be contacted for telephonic consultations. The plan was that these three people would become committed to the program and would form a core-planning group which would place in action the ideas taught at the workshop. Finding and keeping this core group of people working together was a difficult thing. What happened was that if a person became disinterested in the program after this initial commitment, he or she would refer me to another individual saying they were not the appropriate person to call anymore. That was one kind of problem.

Another difficulty that Fergus often found was the inaccessibility of these local "change agents." About this matter she has written:

> Another difficulty was the inaccessibility of staff to receive the phone calls. It was difficult sometimes to reach people because they were reported to be "on vacation," "at a meeting," "they were not on the ward," or "they were somewhere else." I often had to make several calls back again—I learned to make person-to-person calls very quickly.

Experiences such as this led the researchers (Fairweather, Sanders, & Tornatzky, 1974) who conducted the national lodge experiment to conclude that perseverance in carrying out an implementation was one of the keys to successful completion of such a research About this matter they stated:

> The first principle of social change that seems of major importance is the principle of hard work and tolerance for confusion. If there is a single general notion from our data and experiences that we would like to impart to the reader it is that effecting institutional innovation is a highly complex multivariate phenomenon; that it takes a long time to achieve; and that the payoff is often minimal when weighed against the effort expended. Looking back over the five years of effort that this action research program has involved we are left with perceptions of both positive and negative accomplishments. On the plus side, it was possible to establish the lodge in other locales, and in this sense the program was successful both in effecting change, and in demonstrating that a social innovation developed through an action research program

could be replicated. In a more negative note, those who were members of the research team will also remember the meetings that came to naught, letters that stimulated nothing, telephone calls unreturned, and promises unkept. The intent here is not to sound the horn of alarm about institutional resistance to change, but to introduce reality to the prospective change experimentalists.

CHAPTER 11

Comparing the Experimental Conditions

The major purpose of establishing social models as alternative solutions to important social problems is to compare their effectiveness in alleviating those problems. Even though the paramount comparison is made on the principal social change outcome criterion, it is essential that comparisons be made on other outcome variables involving the internal and external social processes of the models. Additionally, in social innovation research, experiments aimed at discovering the essential conditions for dissemination need to be carried out with each successful model. Thus, both social model and dissemination experiments use comparative techniques to portray an understandable and meaningful picture of the research outcomes. These techniques for conveying the results of comparative experiments may generally be categorized as *narrative-descriptive, graphical,* and *statistical.* Since both social model and dissemination experiments use the same comparative techniques, this chapter will present both experimental comparisons under the rubric of experimental conditions. It should be clearly understood that the use of the term "condition" applies to both social model and dissemination experiments. When discussing social model comparative analyses, the term "experimental conditions" refers to the *models themselves.* When the discussion involves dissemination experiments, the term "experimental conditions" refers to the *different techniques* involved in the dissemination process (different conditions of persuasion, for example). The reader should keep this definition of experimental condition in mind while reading this chapter. The first part of this chapter will present the different comparative methods for contrasting experimental conditions. The last section presents examples from both model-building and dissemination experiments.

NARRATIVE-DESCRIPTIVE TECHNIQUE

It may come as a surprise that narrative-descriptive techniques are listed as a way of describing the outcomes of a social experiment. Most scientific writings use the sparsest of prose, however, we feel that longitudinal experimental social innovation involves such a richness of information and wealth of detail that these intricacies must be understood. Thus, unlike the cursory writings for scientific journals, narrative-descriptive accounts are *essential* in longitudinal studies where different social processes are involved. Graphs and statistics, the more formal comparative methods, cannot capture the dynamic qualities of social processes, particularly those involving changes over time. For example, in the small-group study referred to earlier (Fairweather, 1964), the complex development of a small-group ward program could not be adequately portrayed without extensive descriptive narration. At the outset of this experiment, several questions were asked by the experimenters. Some of the questions formulated at that time were the following: What type of work can the individuals perform? Can they be trained to improve their performance? What level of organization is required? Can they leave the living-working situation and take a normative work role in society? What work roles develop?

Clearly, any two different models could yield different results as answers to these questions. Although scales of measurement were developed to answer each of these questions comparatively, the total work situation had a history that needed complete and accurate narration in order to clearly present the entire comparative picture. An example of a descriptive comparison of the two models in this study is presented by MacDonald (1964, p. 97):

> A second comparative example concerns the manner in which staff members were discussed by patients. . . . On the traditional ward, staff members were rarely disturbed by the criticism of patients. . . . On the small group ward patients evidenced far more spontaneity and affect in discussing a staff member . . . and this consequently, led to much discussion . . . during the staff meeting that followed.

A second example is given by Tipler & Rankin (1964, p. 252):

> The first great change all personnel felt was the complete silence on the traditional ward. We had grown accustomed to activity and discussions from the patients and it was like another world on the traditional ward. We had plenty of time to read patients' charts and to become familiar with their behavior. We had to relearn the traditional communication patterns and adjust to the role of, giving support, reassurance, and assistance in a one-to-one relationship again.
>
> The large-group meetings were a complete change. Here the patients

were more quiet and many slept through the meetings. During this period of readjustment, we began to question our own usefulness and had a feeling of being superfluous. The patients accepted the staff change without undue concern.

Descriptive accounts that comparatively present the many facets of experimental social models represent only one use of narrative descriptions. Very often they are used to describe social processes and interpersonal relations that cannot adequately be presented by graphs and statistics. An example comes from the lodge experiment where former mental patients were in the process of developing their own self-governed society (Fairweather *et al.*, 1969). The personal problems that are encountered when peers make decisions about their fellows was recorded in this incident:

> Mr. March, who was again working overtime in the office to keep things shipshape, made a really extraordinary speech to me. It was mainly about the issues of personal freedom and the difficulty of having to judge other persons under difficult circumstances. He was speaking specifically about the case of Mr. Ring, saying how much he regretted the eventuality now open about Mr. Ring—that he would have to leave the lodge. And how much he regretted this, especially because he saw the value of the lodge to people like Mr. Ring and knew very well that he had very slim chances outside of the lodge. But still, how complicated this was by the fact that all the other men at the lodge had to be protected also and that it was more important to save the lodge as an institution for the benefit of the greater number of men than it was to risk it being harmed by keeping Mr. Ring. It was a speech, I think, that was full of awareness of the difficulties of making a decision like this on a very high intellectual level. It seemed to confirm the extent to which Mr. Marsh has become a very capable holder of the job of business manager.

Reports of the problems faced when carrying out a dissemination experiment also greatly enhance an understanding of the manner in which the experimental conditions have been completed. Presenting the lodge program to a number of hospitals was accomplished by comparing the persuasion outcomes achieved by brochures, workshops, and demonstrations (Fairweather, Sanders, & Tornatzky 1974). A description of the change agent's experience in a representative hospital in the workshop condition was presented in the following manner:

Upon arrival at the contact's office (director of nursing) there was no one to meet me other than the secretary who seemed vaguely aware that I was supposed to be there. After about one-half hour, the director of nursing appeared, excusing herself by stating that she had had to attend a general staff meeting. After formal introductions, she took me next door to nursing education where she essentially "dragged me" into the hands of three nursing education supervisors who immediately started catering to my needs. They were all obviously well aware of my arrival and what I was going to be doing at the hospital. Preparations had been made to hold the workshop in a very old auditorium in which the lighting and ventilation were poor and where no one could smoke. Nevertheless, a lectern was provided, a carousel 35 mm projector and screen were provided as well. No sound system was needed as the acoustics were surprisingly good and the audience turned out to be painfully small. The workshop was attended by about twenty people, mostly nurses, social workers, and vocational rehabilitation personnel. No M.D.'s or Ph.D.'s attended nor did I meet one while I was at the hospital. In fact, I was not even introduced to the hospital director or the assistant hospital director during my stay. Neveretheless, the workshop went well although we did not break down into the four small groups as usual after the workshop because of the size or rather lack of size of the audience. I conducted it as one small group with me acting as the leader and the group discussing all parts of all four of the usual small group topics and questions. The response was surprisingly good considering the small-ness of the group. The group was not overly enthusiastic but neither were they lethargic. The lodge proposal seemed a bit sophisticated for them but they grasped it as they did have some experience with halfway houses and foster home care, etc. Only one person was in attendance from the community.

The hospital and grounds were moderately run down. The grass was not well manicured, and the buildings were quite old. The interiors were poorly lighted and quite dingy although some attempts had been made to improve conditions by the hanging of new fluorescent fixtures. Although dingy and old, the interiors were fairly well kept and clean. Some patients were roaming around in typical hospital garb. The hospital was located in a rural part of the town, more accurately the country, which did not even appear to be part of the city. Although the majority of buildings were old, there were a group of buildings near the entrance to the hospital (one-half mile from the main section) that were new and modern. They were used for vocational rehabilitation and the criminally insane. They also housed a very handsome cafeteria-dining room for the staff. The director of nursing did say that one of the reasons for the poor attendance at the workshop was that a conference was being held at the hospital with the new personnel director for the state. This situation, according to her, developed after the workshop was first established.

Narrative-descriptive accounts of social models are especially important to the dissemination process. If one or more of the models significantly benefits the problem population, it will be necessary to embark upon an experiment attempting to get the model adopted on a broader scale—usually a state, region, or nation. The narrative-descriptive account of the social model is important in this process because persons with a variety of educational and personal backgrounds will need to be involved in the change effort, and they will need to understand the model being disseminated. Since many individuals will not be versed in scientific writing and statistical methods, it is especially important that the new model and its benefits are accurately and simply described to this diverse audience. Unlike publications for scientific journals whose audience is mainly other scientists (whose educational background and interests are usually similar to the experimenters), the results of these social experiments will be used by administrators, members of the problem population, service personnel, and others. Because of this diverse audience, the results of social innovative experiments must be clearly described in the simplest and most communicative manner possible. Thus, the narrative-comparative account provides a descriptive picture of the experimental conditions, and these descriptions can highlight differences between the conditions as well as giving a clearer view of their social processes. Frequently, the narrative is punctuated by graphs or statistics where such techniques contribute to the clarity and completeness of the comparative picture. But whatever graphs and statistics are presented, the experimenter should be aware that narrative-descriptive accounts are a paramount feature in communicating the experimental findings.

GRAPHICAL TECHNIQUES

Graphical presentations of differences are another way of describing the results of an experiment. Because of the static nature of most statistical methods, graphical presentations often need to be used to show the longitudinal nature of the differences. Such graphs reveal time trends. Suppose, for example, that weekly measurements were taken for each experimental model for two years. Let us further assume that the data can only be ranked (ordinal scale) and that the experimenters wish to compare the model for the two-year time span. A nonparametric test, as described later in this chapter, might be used to compare the cumulative scores for the entire two years, but this statistic would not show the weekly fluctuations of the scores. There may, for example, be a reversal of scores during some weeks of the two-year period which would not be apparent from the single statistic computed from the cumulative data. A graph of the weekly scores would quickly reveal any such reversals. Figure 11.1 presents illustrative graphs from the small-group study just mentioned (MacDonald, 1964, pp. 90–93) showing two trends over time whose cumulative scores both yielded significant statistics. It is quickly apparent that the time trends are quite different. In the first graph the differences are decreasing whereas in the second they are increasing with time. It is important to point out here that certain parametric statistics have been created for testing such time trends. However, as mentioned later in this chapter, the experimental data, particularly that of the real-life social change outcome criterion, rarely meet the rather stringent assumptions required for the use of these trend analyses. Graphs are therefore often used in social innovative experiments in lieu of more formal parametric trend analyses. They are

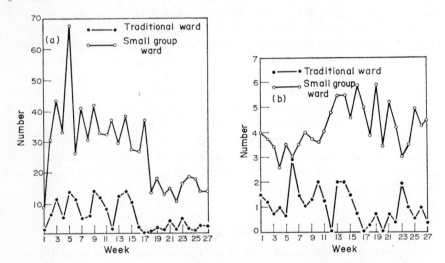

Fig. 11.1. Different time trends for two sets of comparative data that both yield significant overall statistics. (a) Set 1. Mean number of times two or more patients were speaking at once for each treatment program. (b) Set 2. Mean number of topics with eight or more discussants for each treatment program

particularly useful in clarifying model comparisons when nonparametric analyses are performed on cumulative data, as was the case with the graphs presented in Fig. 11.1.

Other types of graphs can be used to present differences or similarities between experimental conditions in a precise and simple manner. These graphs are quite useful with social innovative data when the information is divided into two, three, or four distinct categories. Bar graphs are most often used for this purpose. Figure 11.2 shows a bar graph of the treatment

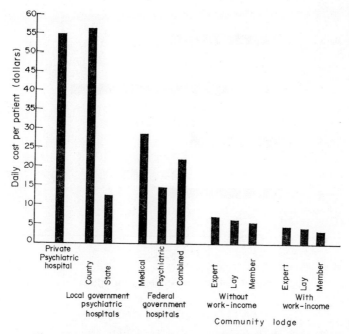

Fig. 11.2. Mean daily cost per person for alternative treatment settings in California Bay Area, 1964–66

costs of participants in the lodge and traditional social models (Fairweather *et al.,* 1969). These differences clearly are very great, and a graphical presentation is an excellent way of conveying the power of the data to the nonscientific reader.

As mentioned earlier, graphs can also be used to enhance the reader's understanding of the social processes. Figure 11.3 presents information about post-hospital living arrangements of participants in the control condition of the lodge research. The length of time released patients stayed with friends or relatives with whom they had intended to live after being released is presented by each bar. A clear pattern of residential wandering is portrayed by the graph. Graphical representations of research data is particularly suited to experimental social· innovation because of the longitudinal nature of the studies and because real-life data often can be expressed only on nominal or ordinal scales. Furthermore, graphs can present the data in such a simple manner that communication is enhanced. The interested reader may pursue a detailed discussion of the use of graphs elsewhere (Guilford, 1956, pp. 18–24; Moroney, 1956, pp. 19–33).

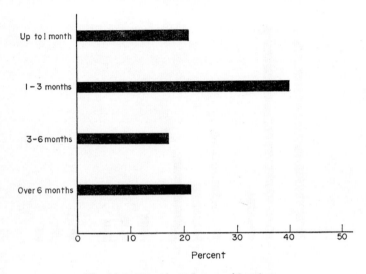

Fig. 11.3. Duration of stay with others

STATISTICAL TECHNIQUES

This section on statistical techniques is included to serve as a brief overview for those not familiar with them and as a quick general review for those who are. It is hoped that this general introduction will encourage those who are not familiar with statistical methods to pursue a detailed knowledge of them from appropriate sources. On the other hand, even though it will seem rudimentary to those familiar with statistics and their use, it is our hope that the quick review presented here will better prepare the informed reader for the more complex uses described in later sections of the chapter.

Differences between experimental conditions are usually not as extreme as those shown in Figs. 11.1 and 11.2. When this is the case the experimentalists use the more formal statistical methods to test hypotheses about differences between them. These comparisons are made by testing statistical hypotheses. It is important that the social innovative experimentalists have an understanding of the logic of testing statistical hypotheses. The interested reader may pursue a thorough and rigorous discussion of this matter in Lehmann (1959).

As an integral part of the planning phase for the experiment, the researchers should state their ideas about the outcomes of the models in the form of hypotheses. These hypotheses can then be subjected to test through the use of the appropriate statistical methods. The directional nature of any hypotheses for the statistical tests of social models differs from that for dissemination research. Social model comparison experiments have one unique characteristic that differentiates them from many other social researches with respect to the hypotheses one is testing. This concerns the *direction* of the hypotheses. Comparative hypotheses about the outcomes of the social models are always stated in terms that predict that the created experimental models will be more beneficial to the participants than the model that society may be using currently (the control social model). Social innovative researchers never entertain an hypothesis that predicts that the created models will have no effect or will have a harmful effect compared to the usual social practice (control), a matter discussed more fully in Chapter 13. In statistical parlance, this is termed a one-sided hypothesis and it has considerable effect in determining the inferences that can be made from the resulting statistic. Such situations give rise to one-tailed tests of significance discussed more fully in Chapter 13.

Dissemination experiments, on the other hand, usually use the more conventional two-sided hypotheses. This is because the results will be used whatever the outcomes of the experiment. Essentially, the purpose of these experiments is to discover what conditions give the highest yield in terms of adoption of the social innovation. Therefore, no technique that is not directly applicable to this effort is entertained and none is hypothesized to yield better results than any other technique. For this reason, the two-sided (null) hypothesis is the predictive statement of choice.

In order to test a statistical hypothesis for a particular experiment, the researchers choose the method most appropriate to their problem. When classified in terms of the data, there are two general types of statistics — parametric and nonparametric. The differences between these two types of statistics involve the assumptions the researchers can logically make about some very basic properties of their data. Parametric statistics — although usually considered more powerful and sensitive — require that the experimenters make more stringent assumptions about the nature of the research data than do nonparametric statistics. They also require more rigid suppositions about the distributions of the data and the units of measure. In general, parametric statistics require interval or ratio scales with normally distributed populations whose variances are homogeneous, whose data are based on independent observations, and whose scale scores are additive. Nonparametric statistics, on the other hand, require that the researchers make fewer assumptions about their data. They are sometimes called "distribution-free" methods because they make no assumption about the population parameter involved and therefore are applicable to data that can only be categorized (nominal) or ranked (ordinal). Nonparametric statistics usually require less computational time than parametric statistics when small samples are used, an important consideration if computers are not readily available.

Statistical methods usually compare the central tendencies of the distributions of scores from the various conditions, or they compare the distributions themselves. The mean and the median are the most common measures of central tendency. The mean is used when the score distributions are normal. It is simply the average score.

An example of two distributions with different means is presented in Fig. 11.4. Differences in sample means are usually tested using parametric statistics. The median, on the other hand, is the middle score of a distribution. If, for example, one has 11 scores and ranks them from highest to lowest, the sixth score in the ranking is the median. This measure of central tendency is less influenced than the mean by extreme scores and by odd-shaped distributions. Medians are usually compared by nonparametric methods. An example of two distributions with different medians is presented in Fig. 11.5 Sometimes the data are divided into so few categories

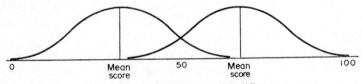

Fig. 11.4. Two score distributions with different means

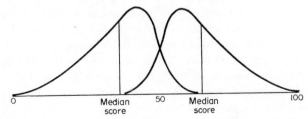

Fig. 11.5. Two score distributions with different medians

that it is only feasible to compare the shape of the distributions. An example of such a distribution can be found in Fig. 11.10. Usually nonparametric techniques are used to compare the differences between such odd-shaped distributions.

Nonparametric Techniques

Nonparametric techniques are the most useful comparative statistics for social innovative researchers because their data rarely meet the assumptions for parametric statistics. Frequently, data from different academic disciplines can only be categorized and such information is amenable to nonparametric techniques only. In this regard, it often occurs that raters can only judge the relatively greater or less than value of an item; for example, more or less work is done, more or less effort is shown, and so forth. For a detailed discussion of the assumptions and use of parametric contrasted with nonparametric techniques, the interested reader is referred to Siegel (1956, pp. 18–34), Moses (1952), and Edwards (1960, pp. 111–114).

This presentation of statistical methods is not intended to be exhaustive, but rather to furnish the reader with a general understanding of the conditions under which those methods that seem to have the most promise for use in evaluating social innovative experiments can be applied. For those interested in a thorough discussion of the underlying assumptions, mathematical derivations, along with some computational examples of the techniques presented here and of others that are available, the reader is referred to the reference works of Hollander & Wolfe (1973); Conover (1971); Edgington (1969); and Wilcoxon & Wilcox (1964).

The use of nonparametric techniques for comparative statistical analysis requires a single score per participant, regardless of the statistic employed. This fact should be kept in mind during the ensuing discussion of such techniques since the subsequent discussion of parametric techniques will include the use of statistics involving more than one score per participant.

Two conditions with matched participants

Suppose the experimentalists wish to compare two conditions with matched participants when they have only one score per individual. This is frequently the case when the data are from ordinal or nominal scales and the researchers combine several repeated measurements into one cumulative score. Such a situation exists when, for example, repeated behavioral ratings or questionnaires are obtained. Let us further assume that matched sampling techniques, as presented in Chapter 8, have been used. Several nonparametric techniques are applicable in this situation. The *sign test* is commonly used when each of the matched pairs, one of whom participates in each condition, can be compared with each other in terms of having a more-than or less-than value on the comparative score (ordinal scale). In using the sign test it is not necessary to consider the size of the differences between the scores of the matched pairs but only the directionality (greater or less than). Thus, in analyses where the scores for the matches pairs can only be arranged in greater- or less-than comparisons, the sign test is an excellent technique.

On the other hand, the experimenter may not only be able to compare each score of the matched pair in a differential manner, but, at the same time, the scores may also reveal the magnitude of the differences. Thus, for example, it may be possible to state that one of the paired scores is not only greater than the other, but that the difference between them is greater or less than the difference between another pair of scores. When this is the case, the *Wilcoxon signed rank test* for paired replicates may be used. When the experimenters can assign direction (greater or less than) and specify the magnitude of the differences between any two scores (interval scale), and when the distributions are symmetrical though not normal, a more powerful test—the *Walsh test*— can be used. There are, of course, other nonparametric tests for matched pairs when only one score per participant is available, but the experimentalists will find the three described here especially applicable to social innovative experiments.

Two conditions without matched participants

It sometimes happens that the experimenters cannot establish appropriate sampling procedures to create matched pairs. Upon occasion it is so difficult to establish sampling techniques from which to create the matches that it is necessary for the researchers to utilize simple random assignment for the conditions. Although the advantages of matched samples are numerous, as elaborated in Chapter 8, the practical problems involved in creating sampling pools and the like are sometimes too great to warrant their use. Then, the experimenters compare conditions without matching the participants.

When these data fall into two categories (such as employed or unemployed, married or single), *Fisher's exact probability test* can be utilized. The *chi-square technique* is another test that can be used for unmatched, random samples. It is perhaps the most commonly used of all non-parametric techniques when the data are divided into discrete categories. Thus, for example, the hospital study compared the effect of the small group and traditional treatment model with the chi-square technique (Wohl, 1964, p.

164). The data for each model can be divided into two, three, or more discrete categories, provided certain assumptions about the minimum number of scores in each cell can be met.

Another commonly utilized technique when the data yield distributions of scores is the *median test*. Note again, here, that no assumption about normality of these distributions needs to be made; however, they must have a distribution so that a median (central point) can be determined. In these cases, the common median for the scores of both sets of conditions is located and a two-way table comprised of those in each condition falling above or below the common median is established.

When the data fall on an ordinal scale—that is, when they can be arranged in rank order—the *Mann-Whitney test* can be used. In this case, advantage is taken of the fact that an ordinal rather than a nominal scale exists. Data that fall on an ordinal scale can be compared by the *Wilcoxon rank sum test* for unpaired replicates. In this test ,the scores for all conditions are first ranked and then compared by using the sums and the averages of the ranks.

When the distributions of the data are sufficient to yield cumulative frequencies, the *Kolmogorov-Smirnov test* can be used to compare the two distributions. At least ordinal scales are necessary to compute the statistic. Another test for two conditions with unmatched participants yielding ordinal data is the *Wald-Wolfowitz test*. This test compares any differences in the central tendencies or distributions of the data for the conditions.

More than two conditions with matched participants

It is frequently the case, however, that the experimentalists wish to compare more than two conditions at one time when they have one score per participant. At the same time, the data may be from ordinal or nominal scales. It is therefore necessary for them to use a nonparametric technique. The data for an analysis may form a nominal scale or it may be dichotomous. In such a case, the *Cochran Q test* can be used. If the data comprise an ordinal scale, the most common and useful technique for these comparisons is the *Friedman test*. Essentially, this technique requires data that can be ranked for matched participants as far as the conditions are concerned. For illustrative purposes, suppose that 100 matched participants were randomly assigned, 25 to each of four conditions. Each condition would then have 25 matched participants. There are thus 25 groups of four matched subjects—one in each of the four conditions that can be ranked 1, 2, 3, and 4. These ranks are used to compare the conditions.

It is also possible to use the Friedman test to compare the interaction effects when different types of participants are involved in the experimental conditions. This technique is very useful with group data when one wishes to compare group scores.

More than two conditions without matched participants

The *chi-square test* is most commonly used for this purpose. It tests the difference between frequencies within a category. The chi-square table can have several rows and columns. The columns could be the conditions to be compared and the rows could be the categories of participants, such as high school and college students. The only difference between the comparisons of three or more conditions and the two conditions comparison is an increase in the number of columns from two to the number of treatments that the experimenters wish to compare. Data for the chi-square test are ordinarily categories comprising a nominal scale.

The *median test*, like the chi-square test, can be extended to compare more than two conditions. Here the measurement needs to be at least of rank order (ordinal scale). The median of the scores from all conditions is located and a 2 (above and below the median) by N (number of conditions) table is constructed from which the statistic is calculated. As mentioned earlier, this is the test for differences between the medians of the distributions for the conditions.

The *Kruskal-Wallis test* can also be used to compare more than two conditions. Here the distributions must be continuous (not necessarily normal) and the measurement on an ordinal scale. All participants in all conditions are ranked from highest to lowest score, then the conditions are compared on the rank scores. This test is concerned with the probability that the different conditions have different distributions of scores.

Despite their utility, there are some difficulties with nonparametric statistics that must particularly concern the social innovative experimentalists. Usually the repeated measures have to be summed into one score because there is no adequate nonparametric technique for repeated measures of the same participants. When this is the case, as it often is, the computation of the nonparametric statistic can be combined with graphs portraying the degree to which the computed statistic represents a constant difference over time.

Parametric Techniques

Occasionally the experimenters have parametric data—that is, the data are normally distributed (as shown in Fig. 11.4), they are independent measurements, and the conditions' score distributions have homogeneous variances. If this is not the case, it is still possible in some instances to transform the original scores into distributions whereby these assumptions can be made. At any rate, when such assumptions can be met, parametric statistics are the statistics of choice. There has been a rather intense discussion about the degree to which these assumptions need to be met before parametric statistics can reasonably be used. For those interested, reference is made to a discussion by McNemar (1962, pp. 374–375) and to Norton's study, presented by Lindquist (1953, pp. 78–86). As a general guideline, however, the scales should be interval or ratio before parametric statistics are applicable. For those interested in a thorough discussion of the underlying assumptions, mathematical derivations, along with some computational examples of the methods presented here and of others that are available, the reader is referred to books written by Edwards (1960); Lindquist (1953); McNemar (1962); Walker & Lev (1953); Winer (1962); and Snedecor (1956).

Although it is uncommon for social innovative data to be suitable for parametric tests, where such tests are applicable they are the statistical tests of choice not only because they are the more powerful tests but also because they offer statistical designs that can yield more information. This is particularly true when the scores are repeated measures on the participants or when before-and-after measures (pre and post) are a part of the evaluation.

Parametric techniques are concerned with testing for the significance of the differences between the means (central points) by use of the variances of the conditions' distributions. A normal distribution with the mean and standard deviation is shown in Fig. 11.6. The variance is the square of the standard deviation. A discussion of the mean, standard deviation, and variance can be found in Edwards (1960, pp. 33–43) and McNemar (1962, pp. 20–35). Let us now examine the parametric techniques that seem to be most useful to the social innovative experimentalists.

Two conditions with one score per participant and matched participants

The most common technique used for this purpose, when each participant has one score, is the *t-test*. There are computational differences when the samples are matched and when they are not matched.

Two conditions with one score per participant and without matched participants

The statistic of choice is again the *t-test*. Its logic and the inferences are the same as the t-test with matched pairs, but there is a difference in computation.

*More than two conditions with one score per participant and
matched or unmatched participants*

The most common statistical methods developed for these comparisons
are the *analyses of variance*. These analyses are used to test the significance
of the differences among the means (central points) of the score distributions

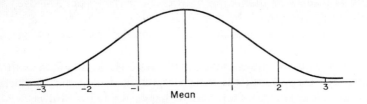

Fig. 11.6. The relationship of the mean to 1, 2, and 3
positive or negative standard deviations

of the conditions by using the variances of those distributions. Instead of
t-tests of significance, they yield *F-ratios*. The comparison makes possible a
probability statement about the differences among conditions. As long as
the matching procedures presented in Chapter 8 are followed, the same
statistical design can be used for both matched and unmatched samples.
Matching procedures are designed to make the variances of the several
distributions equal, and they are, as with other statistics, more efficient designs. There are simple *analyses of variance* which are used only to compare the differences among the conditions.

There are other more complex designs which yield more information.
Frequently it is possible for the researcher to use a more complex design
simply by planning more adequately for the statistical treatment of the data.
One of the analyses most useful to the social innovative experimenter
involves a comparison not only of the effects of the conditions but also of
their effects upon different classes of participants. Let us assume that the
researchers wish to compare the effects of three conditions on three types of
participants. They may, for example, have three different marginal groups—
mentally ill, Job Corps members, and paraplegics—who are participating in
equal proportions in three different conditions of employment. By use of a
multiple classification design, the researcher can find not only the effects of
the conditions but also whether the conditions have a differential effect upon
the three groups. The important point here for the experimenters is that the
investment of more time in planning the design and the sampling procedures
may yield important information not attainable by using more simple
procedures.

Another useful type of analysis of variance is the *factorial design*. This is a design on which the conditions and a second independent variable can be ordered so that they represent points along a continuum. Let us consider the researcher who wishes to compare three conditions, each representing different degrees of freedom from control by societal authorities. The three models might be those applicable to criminal rehabilitation, and therefore they could be arranged so that they represented little, some, and much autonomy from parole agents. At the same time, three criminal groups representing different degrees of institutionalization—short, middle, and long termers—might participate in all three models. In such a case, the design would include three points (little, some, much) upon two dimensions (institutionalization and autonomy), the results of which could be analyzed in a factorial design.

The advantage of the factorial design is that it not only compares the effects of the conditions and the effects upon the different participant groups, but it also reveals any interaction effects. An interaction effect occurs when participants in the categories respond in a differential way to the conditions. For example, the group with "little" institutionalization might show great benefit from the autonomous model and little benefit from the autocratic model, while the "much" institutionalized group might show the opposite of this. These interactions effects cannot be evaluated unless a design appropriate for them is developed.

Other complex analyses of variance designs can be used, but they have only limited applicability in social innovative experiments. The factorial analysis of variance designs, for example, need not be restricted to two dimensions. It is possible to construct designs with several dimensions which yield increased information. But such very complex designs are typically too unwieldy for the practicalities of social innovative research. It is therefore usually the experimenters' choice to conduct two or three simpler experiments instead of one very complex experiment. When the complexities of a single design are so great, they may obscure some results or become so unwieldy that they are unfeasible to establish in the real-life setting.

An excellent example of this occurs in a *Latin Square design*, where all participants, in the ordinary design, would be required to participate in each model for an equal number of days—a condition not only impractical but also not lifelike because most naturalistic social groups are open so that their members can come and go. As another example, certain *randomized block designs* require that participants spend equal time in each model and it is then assumed that the individuals' experience in one does not affect their experiences in the others. Certain assumptions in complex designs that have been primarily developed in other fields (agriculture, for example) are sometimes untenable in social innovative experiments. However, there are infrequent occasions when quite complex designs can be used. The interested reader is encouraged to pursue an extended discussion of them which may be found in the references mentioned at the beginning of this section.

Two or more conditions with two scores per participant (*pre and post measurement*) *and matched or unmatched participants*

This is called the method of *covariance* and is a very useful method in social innovative research when two of the same measures are obtained on each participant. This occurs most often when measures are taken as participants enter the model and when they leave. Covariance analyses are particularly relevant in experiments where it is difficult if not impossible to equate the participant in the experimental model for initial scores on the desired assessment device. Consider, for example, the experimenters who wish to compare the conditions on behavioral change. When the participants enter the models, they are rated on a behavioral outcome scale and given a score. This measurement procedure is repeated when they leave the model. Under these conditions, however, the participants in each model could generate different relationships between the behaviors at entry and the behaviors at exit. By using a covariance analysis, the participants' scores can be adjusted for these differences.

This method, therefore, is most often used to equate statistically participants in the models when a known uncontrolled variable can affect the outcome. By using this technique, outcome differences found between the models at the end of the experiment can be attributable to the differential effects of the model and not to differences in the initial level of performance or the influence of uncontrolled covariates. The usual analysis of covariance requires an equal number of participants in each condition, but Kempthorne has devised a method for treating conditions with unequal numbers. Since this is a common occurrence in naturalistic settings, it is a very valuable method. A thorough discussion of the *linear hypothesis method* of covariance analysis with an unequal number of participants in the conditions may be found in Kempthorne (1952, pp. 28–67).

Two or more conditions with repeated scores on each participant and matched or unmatched groups

Whenever the appropriate assessment of a social innovative phenomenon requires several of the same measures on the same participants and the data are parametric, the statistic of choice is an F-ratio as found in what has become known as a *repeated measurement design* or a *trend analysis of variance*. A discussion of analysis of variance when there are repeated measures on the same person can be found in the references listed at the beginning of this section. There is one major difficulty in using the common repeated measurement and trend analysis designs for social innovative experiments. The requirement that the same participants continue to be measured during the course of the experiment cannot be met typically. Most naturalistic research takes place where changing membership often occurs. Accordingly, the longitudinal nature of such experiments makes the requirements of equal numbers of the same people for the entire course of the experiment usually unattainable. Nonetheless, when these requirements can be met, trend analyses are powerful comparative tools for the social innovative experimentalists.

The social innovative experimenters should use the most appropriate statistics available to compare the created social models and dissemination techniques. It is very likely that a mixture of all comparative methods will and should be utilized. Wherever graphs or narrative discussions give a more meaningful description and comparison, it is important that they be used. Furthermore, very often the data do not meet the assumptions for parametric statistics and hence nonparametric techniques are the most useful. Where appropriate, the more powerful parametric statistics are the statistics of choice. Where inappropriate, the researcher should not hesitate to use the newer and currently less well-developed nonparametric techniques. The paramount feature of the comparison must be that inferences from the results are clearly warranted and that the comparative evaluations are presented to the reader in a readily understandable manner.

Parametric and nonparametric techniques as applied to experimental social innovation have been presented briefly in the foregoing discussion. Table 11.1 gives a summary of these methods. This cursory review of comparative methods would not be complete without emphasizing that the interested reader should pursue more detailed discussions of them in the references provided and other important sources available. Certainly, many of the statistical classics should be in the social innovative researchers' library. It is always necessary that a statistician be a consultant to the research team, particularly during the planning phase of the social innovative experiment—a matter more fully considered in the discussion of the team approach in Chapter 5. It cannot be overemphasized that although it is the experimenters' ultimate responsibility to select the most appropriate comparative methods to evaluate their data, it is equally their responsibility

TABLE 11.1

A Summary of Nonparametric and Parametric Statistical Tests Applicable to Social Innovative Experiments

Experimental condition	Nonparametric statistics Scale			Parametric statistics Scale
	Nominal	Ordinal	Interval	Interval or ratio
Two conditions with matched participants	Sign Wilcoxon Signed Rank		Walsh	t
Two conditions without matched participants	Fisher Chi square	Median Mann-Whitney Kolmogorov-Smirnov Wald-Wolfowitz Wilcoxon Rank Sum		t
More than two conditions with matched participants	Cochran Q	Friedman		One score per participant: Analyses of variance Simple type Multiple classification Factorial design Latin square design Randomized block design
More than two conditions without matched participants	Chi square	Median Kruskal-Wallis		Two scores per participant: Analysis of covariance Repeated scores per participant: Analysis of variance Trend analysis

to seek out the best consultation available. If this chapter on comparative methods does nothing more than make the researcher aware of the multitude of comparisons needed in social innovative experiments, and the resultant need for extensive experimental planning, it will have achieved its goal.

From the outset of the experiment, plans should be made to use computers for analyzing the voluminous data collected for the social innovative experiment. There are many comparative statistical techniques—particularly of the parametric variety—that have been programmed for computers. The Biomedical Computer Programs (Dixon, 1965) of the University of California at Los Angeles provides one outstanding example; SPSS (Statistical Package for the Social Sciences) (Nie *et al.*, 1975) is another. All major universities have computer centers which the experimenters can use, provided the proper arrangements are made in advance as an integral part of the planning for an experiment. And the consultative advice of the statisticians and the computer programmers is an invaluable aid to the experimentalists.

The use of many different comparative methods in the longitudinal social innovative experiment, as well as the need for extensive planning (particularly with statisticians and computer experts), reveals that social innovative experiments require statistical programs rather than a statistic. But such programs cannot be complete until newer statistical methods are developed to meet the particular needs of the experimentalist doing research in social change. There is an urgent need for further development of nonparametric techniques—particularly where repeated measures on the participants are obtained—for use in evaluating social innovative experiments.

EXAMPLES FROM SOCIAL MODEL AND DIFFUSION EXPERIMENTS

The preceding section should have given the readers an overview of the comparative methods available to them for their experimental endeavors. However, it does not show the manner in which these various techniques can be put together for actual comparative evaluation. It should be quite obvious by now that many of the techniques presented in the first section will need to be used in a single research. In order to focus the readers' attention on the relationship between the problem and the design of a comparative field experiment, examples will be given in which different comparative techniques are used. Each experiment presented here is incomplete since only a selected few comparative techniques are given for each one. A complete overview of all experimental results for those experiments is presented in Chapter 13 where the topic shifts to experimental inferences. The following examples, therefore, present designs that have been found to have special value in social innovative comparative research. For this reason they have been selected for presentation here in abbreviated form.

Social Models

The comparison of two models

An excellent example of a comparison of two social models is presented in the experimental work of Beck (1973). The reader will recall that Beck established two social models in an attempt to discover their comparative effects upon the participation of the users of medical services in planning health programs. One model included the creation of small cohesive groups that not only gained information about medical services and their application but the group members also were trained to become advocates for their own cause. A second model was a classical educational model of informing people of the various avenues open to them without training them to become cohesive group members. The two models are described in Chapter 4. A simple schematic of the social model design is presented in Table 11.2.

TABLE 11.2
Beck's Two Social Model Design

Model 1	Model 2
Autonomously trained consumer support group	Traditional participant group
(Trained for group autonomy and consumer legitimacy)	(Engaged in usual consumer activities like consumer meetings)

The results of Beck's study were presented using many of the techniques described in the previous section. She presented a *narrative description* of the processes involved in forming the autonomous group, including an extensive discussion of the developmental processes that occurred in the consumer group program. For example, in describing some of the members' activities in the autonomous consumer support model she said:

> The members themselves also suggested several ways of developing more effective consumer participation: the use of name tags, personal

introduction of members who join a committee, and a thorough orientation of new members to a committee and of all members to committee issues as they arise. They discussed ways of recruiting more dedicated consumer members and ways of placing them on the more powerful committees. They also frequently discussed how they themselves could participate more effectively in current events in their respective committees . . .

Beck also used graphs to show time trends. An example can be found in the development of the autonomous group during the time the coordinator minimized her role. Beck presented this change of increasing frequency of talking in *graphical form* by comparing member and nonmember performance in a common group meeting. The graph presented in Fig. 11.7 shows that while both members and nonmembers increased their discussion, the members of the autonomous group showed a consistently higher speaker frequency of talking than the nonmembers with a concomitant reduction in coordinator input. Beck also presented a number of other graphs which illustrated the time related phenomenon of group development.

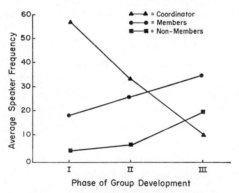

Fig. 11.7. Average speaker frequency by phase of group development

Finally, Beck presented several t-test comparisons of different aspects of the small-group functioning in areas such as those of the amount of information learned, identifying themselves as a constituency, influence and power, role and task distribution, interpersonal processes, psychological membership, personal importance, and task environmental issues. An example with significantly higher means by the group trained for autonomy and consumer legitimacy on four of these tests of significance is given in Table 11.3.

TABLE 11.3
Comparisons of Traditional and Autonomous Models

	Traditional model		Autonomous model		Degrees of freedom	t—test
	Mean	Standard deviation	Mean	Standard deviation		
General information	1.87	0.48	2.25	0.33	18	2.10*
Staff names used	1.55	0.42	2.40	0.52	18	4.03**
Committee names used	1.32	0.49	1.78	0.68	18	2.36*
Chairmen names used	1.58	0.33	2.40	0.52	18	2.27**

$* = P < 0.05.$ $** = P < 0.01.$

While the problem of inferences from a large number of tests of significance will be discussed in Chapter 13, it should be clear from this comparison that many different types of comparative techniques were used to present the results of this longitudinal field experiment.

The comparison of two models with a stratified sample

Tucker (1974) believed that improvement in reading could occur among poor readers (defined by him as those who were in senior high school—13 to 19 years of age—and who could only read at a second-through fifth-grade level) if they became more interested in the subject matter presented for learning. He was particularly concerned about black students who were often criticized by white teachers for speaking in black dialect and not learning standard English. Seizing upon the idea that this could be an advantage as well as a handicap, Tucker decided to establish a learning program where children would first learn to read stories in black dialect, take a comprehensive exam over the story in the same dialect, later learn to read the story in standard English and take a final test in standard English. The control condition used the same amount of time but all their time was devoted to the standard English form which is commonly used in a class-room. Tucker was also interested in the degree to which these two methods of learning to read would affect black and white students so he stratified his sample into these two racial groups. The design is shown in Table 11.4. As with Beck's study, Tucker too used a series of different comparative techniques. Since Tucker took measures both before the learning situation, during it, and afterward, he used a number of time-ordered tests of significance. For example, he used a *covariance* analysis in those instances where he had only pre- and post-scores, and a *repeated measures* analyses on those measures where assessments were made on a weekly basis. An example of

TABLE 11.4
Tucker's Experimental Design

	Model 1	Model 2
Black students	Black students Dialect reading followed by standard English	Black students Standard English only
White students	White students Dialect reading followed by standard English	White students Standard English only

one covariance analysis can be seen in Table 11.5 and the significant part of a repeated measures analysis in Table 11.6. Tucker illustrated the differences found in the treatment and control conditions by graphs such as the one shown in Fig. 11.8.

In addition Tucker quoted the comments of some of the participants as a way of illustrating the positive reaction of some of the students. An example concerns students' reaction to the story about Malcolm X.

TABLE 11.5
Analysis of Covariance for Vocabulary Test Scores

Source of variation	Degrees of freedom	Mean square	F—ratio
Learning condition	1	1318.06	41.97*
Race	1	8.63	0.27
Interaction: LC × R	1	5.16	0.16
Error	55	31.41	

$* = p < 0.001.$

TABLE 11.6
Repeated Measure Analysis of Variance on Weekly Reading Test Scores

Source of variation	Degrees of freedom	Mean square	F—ratio
Between subjects			
Learning condition	1	278.80	47.70**
Error	58	6.52	
Within Subjects			
Time	9	25.84	18.02**
Interaction	9	5.87	4.10*
Error	52	1.43	

$* p < 0.01.$ $** p < 0.001.$

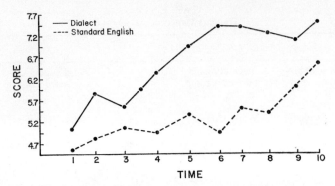

Fig. 11.8. Means of the dialect and standard
English conditions at the ten time periods

"I dug the story about Malcolm, Shine and Stag. I wish we had things like that in our other classes;" and
"If there was a class like this at my junior high school I'd go every day and not play hookey."

Tucker's use of narrative-descriptive information, graphs, and different tests of significance gave a clear and precise picture of the outcomes of this particular study.

The comparison of more than two models with a stratified sample

Fairweather *et al.*, (1960) wished to compare the effectiveness of four different mental health treatment models. To accomplish this, four different treatment methods were created: one in group living (GG); another in group therapy (G); a third in individual therapy (I); and a fourth was simply rehabilitative work (C). A schematic of the experiment is shown in Table 11.7. These four treatments were compared with three different patient groups—neurotics, short-term psychotics, and long-term psychotics. A narrative description was given of the four programs. An example is the following quote:

In the first treatment program, a rehabilitation team provided each patient with an individual *work assignment* and planning for post-hospital living. This group constitutes the control group for the study and will be referred to as Group C. For the second group (Group I), the treatment program consisted of an individual work assignment, in-dividual psychotherapy, and departure planning outlined by the

TABLE 11.7
Four Treatment Models with a Stratified Sample

	Individual psychotherapy	Group psychotherapy	Group living	Work only
Neurotics	Individual psychotherapy (neurotics)	Group psychotherapy (neurotics)	Group living (neurotics)	Work only (neurotics)
Short-term psychotics	Individual psychotherapy (short-term psychotics)	Group psychotherapy (short-term psychotics)	Group living (short-term psychotics)	Work only (short-term psychotics)
Long-term psychotics	Individual psychotherapy (long-term psychotics)	Group psychotherapy (long-term psychotics)	Group living (long-term psychotics)	Work only (long-term psychotics)

rehabilitation team. The treatment program for the third group (Group G) included an individual work assignment, group psychotherapy, and departure planning by the rehabilitation team. For the fourth group (Group GG), the treatment consisted of a group work situation, group living situation, and group psychotherapy.

Upon their arrival on the ward, members of the C, G, and I groups were interviewed by a counseling psychologist and given individual work assignments. In addition, the G and I groups were given therapy appointments. Groups C, G, and I were responsible for ward housekeeping for a period of two weeks. This was done on a rotating basis.

The GG group lived together in a single ward dormitory. Their work assignment was to produce a hospital newspaper every two weeks. Each afternoon at 1 o'clock they reported to a room which had been set aside as the newspaper workroom. Here, under the supervision of a staff member, they had the total responsibility for running the newspaper: they made decisions about the content of the paper, the reporting of the articles, its reproduction, and all other matters relating to the administration and design of the paper. The first hour of each afternoon was devoted to a discussion of their work. In addition, they received group therapy and were responsible as a group for the housekeeping in their dormitory.

A large number of measures were used to compare background information about the patients in the four different treatments. An example of using a mixture of parametric (F-ratios) and nonparametric (chi square, χ^2) statistical tests can be seen in Table 8.1 which was presented earlier in the sampling discussion of the background comparisons for the participants in the four treatments. Chi-square tests were used when the assumptions for parametric statistics could not be met.

In addition, several outcome measures including the social change outcome criteria of follow-up recidivism and employment as well as other follow-up behaviors, time in treatment, change on selected psychological tests (MMPI scale scores, ward behavior scale, interest test scores, self-concept and projective devices) were completed. Throughout the course of the study, 73 tests of significance were computed, using various parametric statistics (F-ratios and t-tests) as well as selected nonparametric tests (Friedman's test, and chi-square tests). This combination of narrative description and tests of significance presented the results of this longitudinal study in a readable manner to those interested in its outcomes.

The comparison of social models with multiple time measures

Social models for different conditions evaluated at different moments in time were completed by Fairweather *et al.*, (1969). In this study a new small society was established by ex-patients as described in Chapter 2. Certain patients volunteered to participate in the experiments and others refused. Additionally, some of the volunteers were in the lodge condition and others in the usual community mental health treatment (control condition) depending upon where they fell by random assignment. This raised the need for two types of designs: one that would compare the lodge society against its control, and another that would attempt to evaluate the effects of volunteering itself. To accomplish this, the design was established in two separate phases. The first phase dealt with the lodge comparisons and the second with the volunteering comparison. Both designs had one comparison condition in common. The manner in which these two designs were accomplished for the stratified sample of nonpsychotics, psychotics from zero to four years of previous hospitalization and psychotics of over four years hospitalization is shown in Table 11.8. Several chapters of narrative in the published version of this experiment were used to describe the movement of the lodge from a regulated to a self-governing society. An example is given below:

> The difference in the atmosphere between this place and the hospital is very striking for someone who steps into it cold and with no preparation, as I have done. It really has the feeling of a going

business, with none of the "marking time" mood of the hospital. In trying to analyze why it produces this impression, I've decided that at least one reason is that the lodge is far more subject to contingencies set by the outside community than is the hospital. The simple fact of sending groups of men out to do productive work in the community for wages has generated a whole series of behaviors which are in contrast to those in the hospital. Because the men at the lodge are engaging in a whole series of activities which are necessary to operate in the community as a business, there is a general atmosphere of purposefulness. The men are engaged in meaningful tasks which will produce a money reward in the society at large. This activity, plus the general absence of "busy work" or "work as therapy" hospital standards, generates the atmosphere I have described.

Throughout the course of the five-year experiment, voluminous data were collected including measurements about the participants' time in the community and employment (social change outcome criteria), other follow-

TABLE 11.8
Design for Evaluating the Lodge Society and Volunteering

Diagnostic group	Model 1 Volunteer lodge	Model 2 Volunteer traditional community
Nonpsychotics	Nonpsychotics lodge	Nonpsychotics traditional community
Psychotics, 0–4 years	Psychotics (0–4 years) lodge	Psychotics (0–4 years) traditional community
Psychotics, over 4 years	Psychotics (over 4 years) lodge	Psychotics (over 4 years') traditional community

Diagnostic group	Model 2 Volunteer traditional community	Model 3 Nonvolunteer traditional community
Nonpsychotics	Nonpsychotics volunteers	Nonpsychotics nonvolunteers
Psychotics, 0–4 years	Psychotics (0–4 years) volunteers	Psychotics (0–4 years) nonvolunteers
Psychotics, over 4 years	Psychotics (over 4 years) volunteers	Psychotics (over 4 years) nonvolunteers

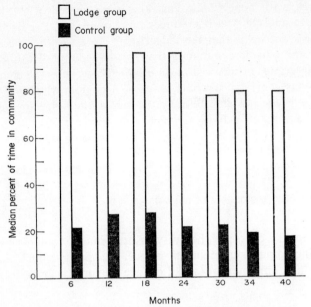

Fig. 11.9. Comparison of lodge and control groups
on time in the community for 40 months of follow-
up

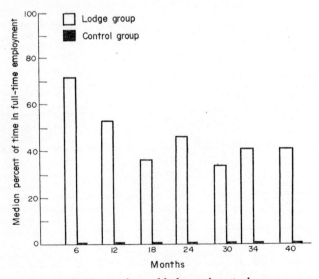

Fig. 11.10. Comparison of lodge and control groups
on employment for 40 months of follow-up

up measures, self-satisfaction, group membership, social processes within the hospital, social processes within the new lodge society, and so on. And graphs were often used. Two bar graphs, used to compare the lodge society with its control treatment on time in the community and employment, are presented in Fig. 11.9 and 11.10.

Appropriate statistical tests including chi-square analyses, analyses of variance, covariance analyses, and time trend analyses were applied to all the data.

Most of the analyses were completed by chi-square since the data were often nonparametric in nature. The results also included analyses of the effects of volunteering and of diagnostic groupings at different moments in time. The extensive presentation of comparative statistics, graphs, and narrative description presented the results of the lodge society in a book which clearly described and compared the effects that the lodge society and its volunteer traditional control condition had upon those who participated in them (Fairweather *et al.*, 1969).

Clearly, these examples do not exhaust the possibilities of the various permutations and combinations of narrative-descriptive, graphical, and statistical techniques that can be used in any evaluative program designed to compare various social models. It does, however, give examples that begin with relatively simple two-model comparisons and go through multimodel designs with comparisons made at different time periods. It is the hope of the authors that the flexible use of these techniques can be perceived by interested experimentalists.

Diffusion Experiments

One-time advocacy aimed at individuals in a two-dimension control experiment

Lounsbury (1973) was interested in the problem of helping individuals change their behavior so that they would be more willing to recycle glass and newspapers, conserve energy, and in this and other ways preserve the quality of their environment. In attempting to persuade people to adopt more conservation-minded techniques, he created a design in which a newsletter describing how conservation could be achieved was sent to a representative sample of households in a midwestern city. He also sent copies of the newsletter to some of the neighbors and not to others. In addition he called some persons in the sample encouraging them to read the newsletter (prod condition) while others he did not (no-prod condition). His design is presented in Table 11.9.

TABLE 11.9
The Experimental Design used in Lounsbury's Study

	Additional phone calls	
Place newspaper sent	Prod	No-prod
Send-to-neighbors	Send-to-neighbors prod	Send-to-neighbors no-prod
Do not send-to-neighbors	Do not send-to-neighbors prod	Do not send-to-neighbors no prod No treatment Do not send-to-neighbors

Narrative-descriptive accounts of the problems involved in the study were given. An example of this can be found in the discussion of those individuals who left the study.

At the first contact, some participants refused for no stated reason while other participants gave excuses such as the following: "I don't have the time," "I can't be bothered," "My husband won't let me," "My son just broke his arm so I can't," and "I don't want to be involved." Also, several husbands answered the door at the first contact and flatly refused to allow their wives to respond to the survey.

TABLE 11.10
Analysis of Variance of some Selected Environmental Action Variables

Variable	Source of variation	Degrees of freedom	Mean square	F—ratio
CA 1	Prod	1	7.31	1.94
Recycling paper	Send	1	14.25	3.79[a]
	Prod × Send	1	1.07	0.28
	Within Cell	135	3.77	
CA 2	Prod	1	11.30	2.82*
Recycling glass	Send	1	1.01	0.47
	Prod × Send	1	5.20	1.28
	Within Cell	135	4.05	
CA 3	Prod	1	6.98	1.77
Composting	Send	1	2.26	0.57
	Prod × Send	1	6.10	1.55
	Within Cell	133	3.93	

[a] Indicates that the mean of the no-send-to-neighbors conditions was significantly ($p < 0.05$) greater than the mean of the send-to-neighbors conditions.
* $p < 0.05$

To evaluate the study further, Lounsbury used a large number of analyses of variance. Table 11.10 presents a few examples of the analyses used in his study. From the analyses and narrative information presented in this study, Lounsbury was able to present a comprehensive evaluation of sending or not sending newspapers to neighbors in the study as well as to all participants in the experiment under prod and no-prod conditions. The potential contribution of such techniques for environmental action could thus be evaluated.

Advocacy aimed at individuals and groups in a one dimension stratified by two organizations design

Fergus (1973) became interested in promoting a new form of milieu therapy for nursing homes which involved greater participation by resident members. She also was aware that there were many different types of geriatric facilities including those run by private organizations and those located in state hospitals. Additionally, other research had convinced her that the number of people within an organization promoting an innovation might influence its adoption. Accordingly, she designed an experiment in which different numbers of people (0, 1, 3) in nursing homes and hospitals were subjected to the same promotional effort of the new program.

The design is presented in Table 11.11. Fergus used narrative description

TABLE 11.11
The Fergus' Experimental Design

Organizations	Number of staff receiving consultations		
	0	1	3
Nursing homes	Nursing homes No staff	Nursing homes One staff	Nursing homes Three staff
Hospitals	Hospitals No staff	Hospitals One staff	Hospitals Three staff

in presenting her results. For example, she described the type of consultations that were given to the organizations in the different experimental conditions as follows:

> Five consultations were given to each of the organizations (nursing homes and hosptials) in the two experimental treatment conditions. These consultations were conducted by a person-to-person call to each of the recipients once every two weeks. . . . The content of the telephone consultation consisted of: (1) introducing oneself as associated with the milieu training staff, (2) questioning what had been initiated

after return from the workshop or last consultation, (3) encouraging information dissemination to other staff, (4) encouraging creating a group of interested staff, (5) suggesting that meetings be set with interested staff on a regular basis, (6) encouraging that specific tasks be delegated to begin action toward adoption, and (7) offering to answer any questions staff may have had. The length of the consultations was not limited and ranged from approximately 30 seconds to 30 minutes.

The statistical comparative results of the experiment were presented in several different F tests and chi-square tests depending upon whether the assumptions for analyses of variance could be met. When she could, an F test was completed. When she could not, chi-square was used. A total of 23 chi-squares and F tests were completed to test the major hypothesis and 124 others were used for exploratory tests of the data as spinoffs from the various hypotheses. An example of an analysis of variance is shown in Table 11.12. Fergus also used graphs to show some of the comparative results as shown in Fig. 11.11 Through this presentation of narrative-descriptive information, graphs, and tests of significance, Fergus presented a readily understandable picture of the results of her study.

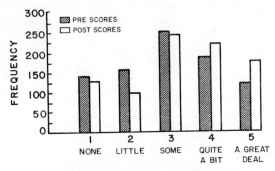

Fig. 11.11. Pre- and Post-scores for initiation of behavioral change

TABLE 11.12
Comparison of the Number of Staff Receiving Information

Source of variation	Degrees of freedom	Mean square	F—ratio
Institutions	1	0.0075	0.003
Treatment	2	0.2582	0.1031
Interaction	2	0.5488	0.2191
Error	30	2.500	

*Multiple advocacy techniques aimed at organizations in a
timed series of phases*

A national experiment was designed to advocate the use of the lodge program described in the previous section. This five-year experiment involved 255 mental hospitals in the nation. The design of the experiment was broken down into three separate phases. The first phase included approaching and persuading the various organizations with an eye toward convincing them to adopt the new mental health lodge program. The design of that phase of the experiment with the number of hospitals in each cell can be seen in Fig. 11.12.

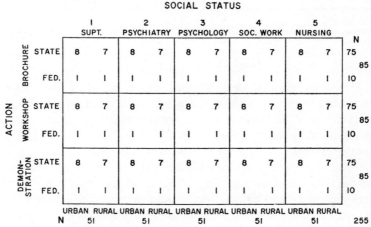

Fig. 11.12. Experimental design showing the social status, action, urban-rural, and state-federal variables

It will be noted that the major dimensions to be evaluated concerned the social status of entry into the mental health organization (i.e., whether it makes any difference in terms of yield if one approaches persons high or low in the hierarchy); whether or not the yield is affected most by approaching through a written technique (brochure), verbal technique (workshop), or action technique (demonstration); if the yield of persuaded hospitals is affected by whether they are more bureaucratic (federal) or less (state) or whether or not they are from urban or rural areas. The comparative results were presented in a number of chi-square tables, one example of which is shown in Table 11.13.

The adopting phase of the study was a second experiment which involved the random assignment by match of the 25 hospitals that agreed to proceed with the adoption of the lodge society. The sampling technique is described

TABLE 11.13
Comparison of Passive-Active Modes of Presentation

| | Mode of presentation | | | | | |
| | Brochure | | Workshop | | Demonstration Ward | |
Change score	(N)	(%)	(N)	(%)	(N)	(%)
1. No change	26	30	17	20	64	75
2. Permitted persuasion attempt	55	65	58	68	12	14
3. Persuaded to change	4	5	10	12	9	11
			$\chi^2 = 69.39*$ (4 df)			

* $p < 0.001$.

as follows:

Therefore, it was decided that those hospitals that had been persuaded to establish the lodge would be divided into matched pairs on the basis of their previous experimental exposure, and then randomly assigned to either a written or action consultation approach to implementation. One group of hospitals would receive a written manual that clearly described each step in the movement from the hospital into the community, while a second group would receive periodic visits from an action consultant who would aid them in carrying out the move into the community. By comparing the progress made in movement toward adoption by those hospitals receiving the manual with those having active consultation one could clearly evaluate whether an action consultant was necessary and what the processes of these different forms of consultation happened to be. These two conditions (written and action consultation) constituted the major dimensions of the Adopting Phase of the experiment (Fairwether, Sanders, & Tornatzky, 1974).

They are shown in Table 11.14.

TABLE 11.14
The Design of the Activating Adoption Phase of the Experiment with
Volunteers from the Preceding Persuasion Phase

Manual (organizations received a manual with written directions for establishing a lodge)	Change agent (organizations received consultations from a lodge advocate who helped them create a lodge society)

An example of a nonparametric test to compare social change agent advocacy with a written manual is shown in Table 11.15.

TABLE 11.15
Comparisons of Selected Mean Task Accomplishment Scores for
Action Consultation and Manual Conditions

Task	Action consultant	Manual	T—value
Business	4.58	3.08	0*
Legal	4.79	3.13	0*
Finances	5.17	4.00	1**
Mean omnibus change score	33.71	25.96	3**

* $p < 0.05$.   ** $p < 0.005$.

After the adoption phase was completed, the diffusing phase began. This was essentially a follow-up of all 255 hospitals in the study to find out how much spontaneous diffusion had occurred during a two-year interval since the last hospital had been contacted. The amount of diffusion for hospitals with different adoption histories is shown in Table 11.16.

TABLE 11.16
Amount of Diffusion by Hospitals Showing a Differential Responsiveness
to Adoption During the Preceding Phases of the Experiment

Willingness to adopt lodge in original experiment	Knowledge		Persuasion		Decision and/or confirmation	
	(N)	(%)	(N)	(%)	(N)	(%)
1. Turned-down-cold	36	84	14	14	2	2
2. Foot-in-the-door	79	68	32	27	6	5
3. All-the-way	5	20	5	20	15	60

$\chi^2 = 15.70$* (4 df)

* $p < 0.001$.

Throughout the presentation of the experimental results of all phases of the study, the description is punctuated with narrative-descriptive information about letters, discussions, and the experiences of the social change agents. An example of correspondence encountered during the experiment is presented below:

Dear . . . .
Well, it looks like they had gotten over the last major hurdle prior to moving out into the community—it will be a major accomplishment in and of itself and one not to be underestimated. Let me say that the

experience you have recently had was very reminiscent of my experience with the prototype lodge. I received a great deal of vicarious gratification from what you reported on the telephone yesterday.

The major purpose for my writing at this time is to confirm our visit to the psychiatric institute for the move to the community during the week of July 6. As the time approaches, if you find this date to be inappropriate, please let me know. Please continue to keep me informed of the project as we are very, very excited about the impending move.

Sincerely,

A reply received from the hospital contact in early June read:

Dear . . . .

This is to confirm our move into the lodge. We are definitely moving on July 6 and will look forward to seeing you then.

I may be in Chicago for the weekend of July 4 and 5 and, if so, would like to ride back on the plane with you. If you could, I would appreciate it if you could let me know what flight you are taking. If I am down there, I'll meet you at the airport.

Sincerely,

An example of the narrative description is found in the notes of the research team (Fairweather, Sanders, & Tornatzky, 1974), reporting the following on the actual move into the community.

Wednesday, July 8: The lodge was operating nicely by this third day. The carpenter had finished with the remodeling and painting. The lodge contracted with the carpenter to pay for materials and his time spent in painting. Some of the labor was donated to the lodge. The place is pretty well cleaned up now except for some of the bedrooms.

Thursday, July 9: The lodge continued to do well and is more and more autonomous. There was a big drinking party the night before among five of the lodge members. Apparently they made a lot of ruckus and kept people awake so that the executive committee met and decided that there would be no drinking in the rooms and that one fellow who got in particularly bad shape would not be able to drink at the lodge at all for a period of time. They called this their restricted list. Some people at this point were talking about wanting to leave the lodge and look for work. The lodge members supported this and offered to let the persons stay and look for work and housing from the lodge. I clued them in: they should not be paid if they did not go to work, and that they ought to set up a sick leave and time off policy. The ideas stressed the fact that the lodge is a business and that members do not just get a work pass anytime they don't feel like going to work.

A testimonial dinner was held for all connected with the lodge tonight. Members of the lodge were not there since they were pushing the 'therapeutic community' concept, i.e., separate lives and autonomy for patients. It was lots of fun and a good experience for all.

Friday, July 10: The lodge continued to be in good shape. Their training was excellent and the program is running smoothly. No incidents or evidence of extreme anxiety. The hospital contact told me that he was somewhat surprised since they had really gotten frightened as the date to move neared.

By presenting a description of the experimental conditions and some selected comparisons of these several model-building and diffusion experiments, we have attempted to show the reader how different evaluative techniques are used in simple and complex social innovative experiments. Furthermore, we have attempted to present the point of view that in longitudinal experiments a series of different types of information and statistics may be used repeatedly or diversely to present a comprehensive comparative view of the different social models or dissemination efforts. For a more thorough understanding, it is important to go beyond the comparative data and examine the involved social processes, presented in Chapter 12, and a comprehensive review of all comparative and social process information used in making inferences, as presented in Chapter 13.

Understanding the Social Processes

After the comparisons mentioned in the preceding chapter have been completed, the experimentalists are in a position to use associative techniques to understand more fully what aspects of the social models or dissemination efforts are providing the outcome results in the first instance. This may be done whether or not significant differences have been found in the experimental conditions being compared. Usually the experimenters will want to study the social processes of successful models in considerable detail, so associative analyses are typically carried out when the comparative analyses yield significant differences. Although the problem of inference is delayed until the next chapter, whether or not there is a knowledge payoff in understanding the social processes of a failure depends upon the information the experimenters are interested in obtaining. The researchers, therefore, will have to decide whether or not to proceed with correlative analyses if their comparative analyses do not yield significant results.

Before presenting some examples of the study of social processes through the use of correlative techniques, it is important for the researchers to have in mind the various correlative devices from which they may choose those that are most important to their particular analyses. The following section is included for this purpose. Although this review may be perceived as far too elementary for many readers, it is designed to refresh the reader's memory about the logic and types of correlations in order to set the scene for later sections dealing with simple and complex associative analyses.

There are typically a large number of measurements made during the course of any social innovative experiment, only a few of which were presented for each study in the comparative analyses examples given in Chapter 11. The investigators usually should not only try to find the relationships that may exist among them, but they should also explore these relationships during the passage of time. Furthermore, they should determine whether or not the relationships among the many variables are different for the several social models or experimental dissemination conditions. For example, when a social model comparative experiment is conducted, the experimentalists usually should attempt to explore the internal processes of the model by finding the relationships among group processes and outcomes. When there is a dissemination experiment, they will also often need to find the relationships among adoption outcomes and dissemination processes. They will therefore need methods to determine these relationships and, when desired, to compare them.

CORRELATIONS

The methods to determine these relationships are generically classified as the correlative methods. A correlation shows the degree of association between any two variables. The value of a correlation can vary from 1 to –1. A correlation of 1 exists when there is perfect positive agreement between any two distributions of scores. For clarity, in illustrating a hypothetical 1 and –1 condition, the rank correlation (rho) can be used. Figure 12.1 shows the straight line formed by the points from two hypothetical sets of rank-order scores for the same participants. The reader will note that the individuals involved have the same rank order on the two sets

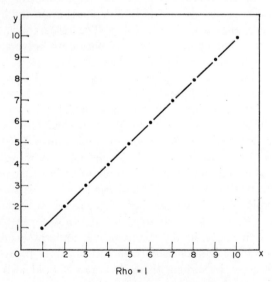

Fig. 12.1. Regression line placed through the points (x,y) for a rank correlation of 1

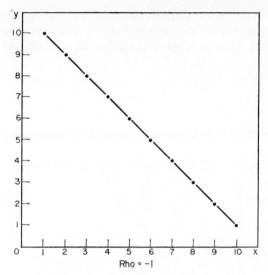

Fig. 12.2. Regression line placed through the points (*x,y*) for a rank correlation of –1

of scores. This is a perfect positive agreement which results in a rank correlation (rho) of 1. A correlation of –1, on the other hand, exists when the two distributions of scores show a perfect inverse relationship. Figure 12.2 shows the regression line resulting from two distributions whose plotted points are exactly the opposite—namely, the highest score on one distribution goes with the lowest score on another. This graph illustrates the –1 rank correlation between the sets of scores on two variables.

The line drawn through the points in Fig. 12.1 and 12.2 is commonly called the regression line. In the case where high scores on one distribution go with the high scores on the other, the slope of the regression line is positive and so is the value of the correlation; when an inverse relationship exists (when the high scores on one distribution go with the low scores on the other), a negative correlation and a negative slope of the regression line obtain.

It must also be clearly understood that correlations show relationships and do *not* reveal causation even in the rare instance where a correlation of 1 or –1 exists. It cannot even then be directly inferred that one set of scores causes the other or vice versa. The preceding hypothetical graphs shown in Figs. 12.1 and 12.2 are for the "pure" case; the experimenter usually will not have data in which there is perfect agreement. Rather, experimental data usually represent points that are at varying distances from the regression line. In these instances, the line of best fit (regression line) is placed through the points. Figure 12.3 presents a graph showing a plot of points where

Fig. 12.3. Regression line and plot of points (*x,y*) for a positive correlation

the correlation is positive. The graph shows that the regression line—the line of best fit—is the line which reduces the sum of the squares of the distances between the points and the regression line to a minimum.

It is most important that the reader grasp the following points about correlations:

(1) A correlation represents a line of best fit between the plot of the points of any two measures.

(2) With the usual correlation, this is a straight line.

(3) The basic data for computing a correlation are simply variables measurable on a continuous scale. Ordinal scales are therefore necessary and sufficient for computing a correlation.

(4) Correlations do not reveal causation but the degrees of association between two variables.

(5) The statistical symbol for a correlation is r.

These statements describe general theoretical notions for correlations.

For purposes of understanding the various types of correlative techniques, the following brief descriptions are offered.

When both variables are truly dichotomous, the experimenter may compute a *phi coefficient*, r_ϕ. On the other hand, if the researcher has dichotomous data for which he or she assumes underlying continuous distributions, he or she should compute a *tetrachoric correlation*, r_t. Upon occasion, the researcher has only data that can be categorized in two, three, or more categories—such as high-, middle-, and low-income groups. When this is the case, a *contingency coefficient*, C, may be computed. It is a measure of the degree of association but is not technically considered a correlation.

Sometimes the experimenter will find that one of the distributions is dichotomous while the other is continuous. The experimenter should compute a *point biserial correlation*, r_{pb}, if he or she assumes the dichotomous variable to be truly discrete, and a *biserial correlation*, r_b, if he or she assumes that a continuous variable underlies the dichotomous data.

Frequently the social innovative experimentalist has rank-order data. Examples of two rank-order distributions which resulted in 1 and −1 correlations were given in Figs. 12.1 and 12.2. When this is the case, a *rank correlation* (rho) can be computed. When there are several rank-order distributions (a frequent occurrence if several raters rank the same data), a *Kendall coefficient of concordance*, W, is computed. It shows the degree of agreement among all of the raters. The computational procedures and use of W are fully discussed in Hollander & Wolfe (1973) and Conover (1971). The most commonly used measure of correlation, however, is the *Pearson product moment correlation*, r. This is frequently used when data are measured on an interval or ratio scale.

While the preceding discussion has presented the correlational techniques by classifications of data, it would also be possible to classify them by their relationship to each other. Thus, the Pearson product moment correlation, phi, and the point biserial correlation are all forms of r, whereas the tetrachoric correlation and the biserial correlation are estimates of phi and the point biserial correlation, respectively.

There are other correlational methods that the experimentalists may need upon occasion. The two most important are the *partial correlation* and the *multiple correlation*. A partial correlation is computed when the experimentalists wish to correlate two variables while eliminating the effect of a third. A multiple correlation is computed when the researchers wish to correlate one variable with a group of other variables. There is also the rare occasion when a plot of two variables to be correlated reveals that their relationship is not linear. The plot forms a curved instead of a straight line. In such a case, it is appropriate to find the degree of association by determining the curved line that best fits the data. This is accomplished by computing the *correlation ratio, eta* (η). For a discussion of the different kinds of correlations mentioned here, of partial and multiple correlations as well as eta, the reader is referred to Ghisselli (1964), Guilford (1956), McNemar (1962), Glass & Stanley (1970), Marascuilo (1971), and Kerlinger & Pedhazur (1973).

FACTOR AND CLUSTER ANALYSES

Although the social innovative experimenters occasionally have the need to compute independently a correlation—whether product moment, partial, or multiple—they are usually interested in multivariate analyses. They are methods by which the intercorrelations among a large number of measures can be determined. These multivariate procedures are the social innovative researchers' most important methods to study relationships and processes because most experiments have many measures that are often repeated during the course of the experiment, and it is necessary to find their inter-relationships. There are two commonly used methods of multivariate analysis—factor and cluster analysis. Both are based upon the computation of individual correlations just described.

Factor analysis had its roots in England where it was an extension of the early development of the Pearson product moment correlation co-efficient. Much was contributed to its development by Spearman (1927), Burt (1941), Thomson (1940), Holzinger & Harman (1941), and Hotelling (1933). Factor analysis was later more fully developed by L. L. Thurstone. In 1947 he published a book, *Multiple Factor Analysis: A Development and Expansion of the Vectors of Mind*, which became a commonly used text. Cattell (1946) later presented methods for determining the factor structure among tests, persons, and occasions. The basic idea of factor analysis is that a vector can be placed through a subset of the interrelated variables and this vector represents a dimension of measurement to which each variable is related. This dimension can therefore replace the separate variables so that the researcher can deal with a reduced number of variables without loss of generality. Of course, there can be few or many dimensions depending upon the con-figurations of the correlations. If a large number of score distributions are intercorrelated, it is possible that they would form several relatively independent clusters of measures. The relationship of each variable to any dimension is the *factor loading* on that dimension. The dimensions (factors) themselves may be interrelated or independent.

Many and varied themes have been played upon the basic ideas of factor analysis. Thurstone (1947), for example, believed that factor structure revealed the basic dimensions of the variables under investigation. Other factor analysts, however, believe that factor analysis shows that certain variables go together or are interrelated. Thus, "factor structure" may be dependent upon one or many determinants such as the construction of the scales, the measurement situation, and basic dimensionality. An excellent and readable presentation of the development, logic, and methods of factor analysis can be found in Fruchter's book *Introduction to Factor Analysis* (1954).

Computer programs are available for the vast amount of work required in factor analysis. This is especially important for experimenters who wish to use these methods because the time required to compute a single factor analysis by hand is exceedingly great. The social innovative experimentalists will usually have to compute many. Computer programs for factor analysis are a part of the analytic techniques available in many university computer centers.

The thorough and complete development of the method of *cluster analysis* by Tryon (1958, 1959, 1966) and his associates (Tryon & Bailey, 1966, 1970), along with the associated computer programs, gives the social innovative researchers their most useful multivariate method. Cluster analysis has the same premises as factor analysis concerning clusters of interrelated variables and it is, in fact, a more global method because it also incorporates factor analysis as a special case. Tryon makes no assumption that the clusters represent dimensions or basic variables. Rather, he assumes from the outset that these interrelationships have to be explained from the knowledge of the experimenters about their subject matter.

This cluster method or, more accurately, series of methods, is usually the most appropriate technique in studying the relationships and processes of social models. These methods combine factor and cluster analyses and, in addition, arrange them "in tandem" when required by the researcher. Thus, the experimenter may make several analyses in sequence. The procedures can be arranged so that each new analysis in the sequence is derived from the preceding one. For example, the structure of one cluster analysis may be compared with the structure of a second cluster analysis in a single computer procedure. Two separate operations are involved here—the computation of the two cluster analyses and then the comparison of the cluster structures found. The computer can be programmed to perform the first operation (cluster analysis) and the second operation (comparing them) on the same computer run.

The BC TRY cluster system provides many uses of practical and theoretical significance to social innovative research. The principal uses for the experimentalist are the following:

(1) It may be used to reduce a large number of measurements on variables to a small number of clusters which have sometimes been termed dimensions.

(2) Different cluster analyses can be *compared* through the use of an unusual correlative technique. This is especially important when studying social processes because cluster analyses of data collected at different moments in time can be compared and developmental patterns revealed.

(3) It is possible to compare individuals rather than scores on various social, behavioral, and perceptual variables.

(4) It can be used for sampling purposes. Where there are a large number of variables of individuals, the BC TRY system provides a method for randomly selecting by computer individuals or variables that are unbiased samples of a particular population.

The cluster analysis results (the computer printout) provide the researchers with a great deal of information that is important to them. Most important to the social innovative researcher are the following:

(1) Where the data are normal, it provides a set of means for each variable.

(2) In such cases it also provides the standard deviation for each variable.

(3) It provides intercorrelational matrices. This is important because researchers can obtain the relationship of any variable with any other variable from this matrix. One should note here that the hand computation of a single correlation may take as much or more time than the machine computation of an entire cluster analysis.

(4) It provides the clusters—that is, the correlation of each variable with every cluster in the analysis.

(5) It provides a correlation matrix of the derived clusters.

(6) It provides geometric drawings of the cluster. This is an important feature for those who more easily grasp geometric concepts.

(7) In the case where more than one cluster analysis has been accomplished, it provides a comparative analysis of the cluster structure coming from the separate analyses.

(8) After the clusters have been determined, each individual in the sample can be assigned on the "printout" a score on each of the derived clusters. This is an important time-saving device because the researcher is provided with new scores for each individual in the sample on each cluster. Such data can then be used for comparative purposes.

(9) Cluster analysis has also been programmed for missing data. In

naturalistic settings, individuals usually enter and leave the models so quickly that missing data are a present and recurring problem.

This is a very brief description of some but not all of the important information researchers can obtain from a cluster analysis.

All of the correlative techniques, from simple to complex, are tools the experimentalists need to employ in understanding the social processes of the social models that have been compared. This is typically accomplished at the end of the experiment because the experimenters do not have information on all of the measures for the same individuals—a condition necessary for the computation of correlations—prior to the completing of the experiment. For this reason, correlational analyses in field experiments most often follow comparative analyses. Used judiciously and appropriately, they can be of inestimable value to the social innovator when used jointly with the comparative techniques presented in Chapter 11. Our attention now turns to how the associative techniques are actually used in specific experiments.

THE USE OF ASSOCIATIVE TECHNIQUES

In the last chapter the comparative statistics that hinged upon the use of narrative-descriptive techniques, graphs, and statistical comparisons were presented. However, these techniques do not stand alone as methods used to understand the social processes that occur in any longitudinal social innovative experiment. Important relationships among the many participant and social situational variables can be most clearly understood from the computation of correlations or by finding their dimensions from factor or cluster analyses. In the examples now to be presented, simple correlative analyses and the several uses of cluster analysis will be given. Cluster analysis created by Robert C. Tryon and his associates is the authors' choice of the complex associative techniques available since it is a highly versatile package and the most useful, consisting of several programs which present the experimenters with a great deal of flexibility in studying the processes operative in a social experiment. The following examples will be taken from both social model and dissemination experiments, since experimentalists will find that cluster analyses are useful in understanding the social processes in both types of experiments.

Correlational Analysis

Sometimes a few correlations can be computed that reveal important relationships among variables considered to be central to a particular

TABLE 12.1

Intercorrelation Matrix for Tucker's Experimental (Bilingual) Group on Pre-test and Post-test Variables

Measures	1 Voc Pre	2 Voc Post	3 Comp Pre	4 Comp Post	5 School Pre	6 School Post	7 Parent Pre	8 Parent Post	9 Teacher Pre	10 Teacher Post	11 Self-concept Pre	12 Self-concept Post
1. Pre vocabulary		0.96	0.85	0.77	-0.02	0.15	0.07	-0.28	0.00	0.39	-0.20	0.29
2. Post vocabulary	0.96		0.81	0.80	0.07	-0.10	0.07	-0.13	0.09	0.22	-0.13	-0.15
3. Pre comprehension	0.85	0.81		0.79	0.15	0.18	0.26	0.26	0.06	0.41	-0.04	0.15
4. Post comprehension	0.77	0.80	0.79		0.05	-0.05	0.17	0.00	0.07	-0.13	-0.12	0.07
5. Pre attitudes toward school	-0.02	0.07	0.15	0.05		0.14	0.00	0.00	0.24	-0.10	-0.02	0.00
6. Post attitudes toward school	0.15	-0.10	0.18	-0.05	0.14		-0.30	0.30	0.25	0.49	0.05	0.20
7. Pre attitudes toward parent	0.07	0.07	0.26	0.17	0.00	-0.30		0.38	0.38	-0.08	0.18	-0.03
8. Post attitudes toward parent	-0.28	-0.13	0.26	0.00	0.00	0.30	0.38		0.01	0.66	0.15	0.67
9. Pre attitudes toward teacher	0.00	0.09	0.06	0.07	0.24	0.25	0.38	0.01		0.45	0.03	-0.19
10. Post attitudes toward teacher	0.39	0.22	0.41	-0.13	-0.10	0.49	-0.08	0.66	0.45		0.35	0.47
11. Pre self-concept	-0.20	-0.13	-0.04	-0.12	-0.02	0.05	0.18	0.15	0.03	0.35		0.58
12. Post self-concept	0.29	-0.15	0.15	0.07	0.00	0.20	-0.03	0.67	-0.19	0.47	0.58	

TABLE 12.2

Correlation Matrix of Hospital Variables and Follow-up Items

Measures	Ward behavior	Job behavior	Drugs (on)	Time in treatment	Finney scale	Not re-hospitalized	Employed full-time	Well most of time	Talks to others	Has friends	Not a problem drinker
Within hospital assessments											
Ward behavior		0.12	0.04	-0.26	0.50	0.04	0.28	-0.32	0.23	0.14	-0.47
Job behavior	0.12		-0.10	0.22	-0.14	0.02	-0.06	0.08	-0.22	0.11	-0.41
Drugs (on)	0.04	-0.10		0.10	0.22	-0.02	-0.07	-0.11	-0.19	-0.19	0.18
Time in treatment (long)	-0.26	0.22	0.10		-0.20	-0.30	0.08	-0.04	-0.23	0.07	0.24
Finney scale	0.50	-0.14	0.22	-0.20		0.42	0.75	0.09	0.20	0.29	-0.54
Follow-up											
Not rehospitalized	0.04	0.02	-0.02	-0.30	0.42		0.66	0.59	0.09	0.12	0.29
Employed full-time	0.28	-0.06	-0.07	0.08	0.75	0.66		0.57	0.30	0.46	0.14
Well most of time	-0.32	0.08	-0.11	-0.04	0.09	0.59	0.57		0.46	0.50	0.60
Talks to others	0.23	-0.22	-0.19	-0.23	0.20	0.09	0.30	0.46		0.51	0.06
Has friends	0.14	0.11	-0.19	0.07	0.29	0.12	0.46	0.50	0.51		-0.08
Not a problem drinker	-0.47	-0.41	0.18	0.24	-0.54	0.29	0.14	0.60	0.06	-0.08	

study. In the experiment of teaching reading through Standard English, and the bilingual methods of black dialect and Standard English, Tucker (1974) had some measures of comprehension and vocabulary mastery as well as some measures of attitudes towards self, parents, teachers, and school. He computed a correlational analysis to discover the degree to which these various important outcomes were interrelated for both the control and experimental condition. Both intercorrelational matrices showed essentially the same pattern. The experimental model's inter-correlational matrix is presented in Table 12.1.

A glance at this table indicates that the pre and post vocabulary and comprehension results are highly interrelated while both are only marginally related to attitudes toward parent, school, teacher, and the students' self-concept. The attitudes themselves show no specific pattern of high interrelationships. This finding clearly indicates the surprisingly multivariate nature of the outcome criteria.

In an experiment evaluating different types of treatment for hospitalized mental patients completed by Fairweather *et al.* (1960) a large number of measures of adaptation were taken both within the hospital and six months (follow-up) after the patients had left the hospital. A correlational analysis of these measures was later completed by Forsyth & Fairweather (1961). It is presented in Table 12.2. This table shows that remaining in the community after hospitalization is related to being employed, being perceived as being well (the follow-up form was completed by other persons who know the ex-patient), and behaviorally adapting in group psychotherapy sessions—Finney Scale (Finney, 1954). But just as important, reduction in recidivism was not significantly related to ward or job behavioral adjustment while in the hospital, drugs taken in the hospital, time spent in treatment, or to other community behaviors such as communicating with others, friendships, or drinking behavior. The multivariate nature of outcome criteria and the lack of relationship between hospital and community situations seem clear enough from a study of Table 12.2.

Cluster Analysis

Determining dimensionality

In another social model-building experiment, Fairweather and his associates (1964) again compared persons participating in the program on a wide variety of outcome criteria. The question of the relationships

TABLE 12.3
The Eight Clusters

Cluster	*Loading*

Cluster 1—Post-hospital Adjustment
1. Follow-up
   - a. Remains out of the hospital (social change outcome criterion) — 0.82
   - b. Has socially supportive living situation — 0.71
   - c. Is frequently employed — 0.45
   - d. Is frequently employed in low-status job — 0.43
   - e. More frequently talks to other people — 0.41
2. Treatment prior to discharge
   - a. Fewer days in experimental treatment program — 0.80
   - b. Fewer weeks of hospitalization during lifetime — 0.47
3. Group processes measures
   - a. Has fewer penalties imposed by task group — 0.40

Cluster 2—Social Interaction
1. Recreation hour behavior
   - a. Frequently engages in social activity — 0.95
   - b. Frequently engages in social interaction with other patients — 0.89
   - c. Talks frequently — 0.81
   - d. Frequently faces room — 0.41
2. Frequently chosen by others on the picture sociometric as a person one would
   - a. Plan to go out with — 0.53
   - b. Live on same street with — 0.49
   - c. Like to work with — 0.49
   - d. Like as a close friend — 0.49
   - e. Seek out if help was needed — 0.48
   - f. Stop to talk with — 0.46
   - g. Say hello to — 0.45
   - h. Recognize — 0.42
3. Group meeting behavior
   - a. Makes many speeches — 0.45
   - b. Spends time in speaking — 0.45
   - c. Makes problem-oriented speeches — 0.45
   - d. Frequently talks to group at large — 0.44
   - e. Frequently talks to other patients — 0.42
4. Group processes measures
   - a. Frequently seen as a helpful task group member by staff — 0.43
   - b. Frequently seen as a helpful task group member by patients — 0.42

Cluster 3—Positive Attitudes about Treatment Program
1. Biographical evaluation of treatment program
   - a. Frequently perceives program as leading to personal gain — 0.85
   - b. Frequently would choose same ward — 0.84
   - c. Frequently assesses treatment program as positive — 0.55
   - d. Perceives the total treatment program as helpful — 0.45
2. Staff and ward regulation attitude questionnaire
   - a. Postively evaluates ward regulation — 0.72
   - b. Positively evaluates pass policy — 0.62
   - c. Positively evaluates ward doctor — 0.53
   - d. Positively evaluates staff nurse — 0.53
   - e. Positively evaluates money policy — 0.53
   - f. Positively evaluates aides — 0.50

TABLE 12.3 *contd.*

Cluster	Loading
Cluster 4—Affective Involvement in Treatment Program	
1. Biographical evaluation of treatment program	
a. Positive feelings during process of treatment program	0.79
b. Negative feelings upon entry	0.74
c. Gives general positive evaluation of treatment program	0.50
d. Has strong affective involvement in treatment program	0.41
Cluster 5—Behavioral Nonconformity during Group Meeting	
1. Group meeting behavior	
a. Frequently leaves group meeting early	0.81
b. Frequently enters group meeting late	0.79
c. Frequently whispers	0.42
Cluster 6—Social Preference	
1. Frequently chooses others on picture sociometric as person one would	
a. Plan to go out with	0.87
b. Like to work with	0.86
c. Seek out if help was needed	0.84
d. Live on same street with	0.82
e. Stop to talk with	0.74
f. Say hello to	0.73
g. Recognize	0.69
h. Like as a close friend	0.66
Cluster 7—Aspirations and Status	
1. Job interview aspiration scale	
a. Perceives self as having high-status job	0.90
b. Perceives self as being willing to accept only high-status job	0.83
c. Expects high-status job at discharge	0.67
d. Expects to have high-status job five years after discharge	0.56
e. Expects to be advanced in job status	0.52
f. Held high-status job prior to hospitalization	0.41
Cluster 8—Tranquilizing Medication during Hospitalization	
1. Greater total amount of medication received	0.94
2. Greater number of days medication received	0.81
3. Greater mean daily dosage	0.74
4. Greater number of dosage changes	0.57

among the criteria which had been used (what might be called its dimensionality) was determined through a variable (V) cluster analysis. Table 12.3 shows that eight clusters (dimensions) were found and Table 12.4 shows that they are relatively independent. It will be noticed, for example, that the post-hospital adjustment cluster (1) is correlated .24 with social interaction which is its highest positive relationship, while correlating –.23 with amount of tranquilizing medication, the highest negative relationship. The remaining correlations with the five other clusters vary between these two extremes, showing the relatively low relationship of post-hospital adjustment with such common behaviors as

TABLE 12.4
The Correlations Among the Eight Clusters

Cluster	1 Post-hospital adjustment	2 Social interaction	3 Positive attitudes about treatment program	4 Affective involvement in treatment program	5 Behavioral nonconformity in large group meetings	6 Social preference	7 Aspirations about status	8 Tranquilizing medication
1. Post-hospital adjustment		0.24	0.20	0.18	-0.01	0.02	0.08	-0.23
2. Social interaction	0.24		0.10	0.15	0.05	0.17	0.35	-0.20
3. Positive attitudes about treatment program	0.20	0.10		0.16	-0.08	0.22	-0.10	-0.03
4. Affective involvement in treatment program	0.18	0.15	0.16		0.12	0.21	0.05	-0.02
5. Behavioral nonconformity in large group meetings	-0.01	0.05	-0.08	0.12		-0.04	-0.08	-0.02
6. Social preference	0.02	0.17	0.22	0.21	-0.04		0.01	-0.13
7. Aspirations about status	0.08	0.35	-0.01	0.05	-0.08	0.01		-0.11
8. Tranquilizing medication	-0.23	-0.20	-0.03	-0.02	-0.02	-0.13	-0.11	

social interaction and positive attitudes about the treatment program. The relationships are very close to zero with social preference, personal aspirations, and group conformity. As with the earlier mental health treatment study just mentioned and Tucker's study, this experiment clearly shows the complexity and often the independence of outcome measures, and thus the need to attend to several dimensions at one time.

Another example of the use of associative techniques comes from Lounsbury's dissemination research (1973). Lounsbury cluster-analyzed his information about persuading individuals to change their habits toward environmental action. With 40 variables concerning attitudinal, demographic, and diffusion correlates of environmental action, he found two clusters as shown in Table 12.5. About this cluster analysis. Lounsbury said the following:

TABLE 12.5
Cluster Analysis of Attitudinal, Demographic, and Diffusion Correlates
of Environmental Action

Cluster	Loading
Cluster 1. *Personal Sentiments and Diffusion*	
More favorable perception of the newsletter as interesting and helpful	0.85
More favorable attitude toward concern for environmental quality	0.56
More favorable attitude toward concern for environmental action	0.55
Greater number of types of persons talked to about the contents of the newsletter	0.55
Greater number of types of other persons who read the subject's copy of the news- letter	0.54
More frequently uses less laundry detergent than the manufacturer recommends	0.46
Cluster 2. *Environmental Action and Demographics*	
Has lived longer at current address	0.67
More frequently recycles paper	0.56
Spent more days on vacation trips last year	0.53
Being older	0.48
More frequently recycles glass	0.44
Has lived longer in Ingham County	0.36

Two relatively independent clusters emerged. The correlations between the two oblique cluster domains was .12. The first cluster contains several measures of participants personal sentiment—toward the newsletter and toward environmental quality and action—and two measures of the diffusion of the contents of the newsletter. Only one environmental action item (using less detergent than the manufacturer recommends) clustered with the above items. The second cluster contained two positively loaded environmental action items (recycling glass) and (recycling paper), along with four other variables having to

TABLE 12.6
Variables Comprising the Clusters of Each Time Period

Cluster	Time period								
	I (0 days)	II (90 days)	III (180 days)	IV (270 days)	V (360 days)	VI (450 days)	VII (540 days)	VIII (630 days)	IX (720 days)
1. Group Cohesiveness									
Cohesiveness	×	×	×	×	×	×	×	×	×
Morale	×	×	×	×	×	×	×	×	×
Attraction to group		×	×	×	×	×	×	×	×
Satisfaction with leader	(×)	(×)	×	×	×	×	×	×	×
Expectancies		(×)	×	(×)	(×)	(×)	(×)	×	×
Choice of others	×	×	(×)	×	(×)	×	×	(×)	×
2. Group Performance									
Performance				×	×	×	×	×	×
Reward	×		×	×	×	(×)	×	×	×
Problem input				−		−	−	−	×
Information input				×		×	×	×	×
Information input ÷				×		−	−		×
Total input				×	×	×	×	×	
Percent turnover of membership				×	×	×	×	×	×
Variance of performance			−	(×)	−	×	×	(×)	×
Variance of reward			−	×		−	×	×	−
3. Leadership and Role Delineation									
Leadership		×	×	×	×	×	×		×
Role clarity		×	×	×	×	(×)			×
Acceptance by group		×		×	(×)	(×)	×		
Diagnosis and chronicity						(×)	×		
Time in group			×	(×)		(×)			

do with time—the respondent's age, number of years lived at the current address and in Ingham County, and number of days spent on vacation trips last year.

Conspicuously absent from these two clusters are the majority of the 14 environmental action and 16 demographic variables used in the analysis. Considering them separately, it was found that of a total of 224 different correlations between a demographic and an environmental action variable, only four were significant at the p less than .01 level.

Thus, Lounsbury was able to show empirically that environmentally positive attitudes and behaviors are relatively independent and are significantly related to only a very few other environmental activities.

Comparison of social process dimensions over time

A large number of measures of group performance were taken during the course of the development of groups who were later to go into the community lodge society (Fairweather, *et al.*, 1969). These measures were taken every 90 days for a period of 720 days, or nine consecutive 90-day periods. They were then cluster analyzed at each 90-day interval. Three basic dimensions were found and the degree to which they developed over time is portrayed in Table 12.6. The X's indicate the appearance of that variable in the cluster at a loading indicating that it is strongly associated with the cluster; (X) denotes a weakly associated variable, and –X a negatively related variable. A glance at this table shows that group cohesiveness develops very quickly and maintains its stability throughout the 720-day period. On the other hand, it is equally obvious that group performance is much slower to develop and begins its stability at about 180 days after groups have been formed and by 270 days is quite consistent in the measures that constitute it. Leadership and role delineation develop early and are quite consistent. The lack of relationship between these dimensions is shown in the Table 12.7, which again shows behavioral performance is relatively independent of group cohesiveness and leadership, at

TABLE 12.7
Correlations Among the Three Clusters

Cluster	1 Group cohesiveness	2 Group performance	3 Leadership and role delineation
1. Group cohesiveness		0.13	0.19
2. Group performance	0.13		0.00
3. Leadership and role delineation	0.19	0.00	

least in these hospitalized action groups. Beyond the independence, the multivariate nature of outcome criteria is again indicated.

The degree to which these three dimensions were influenced by the hospital situation was explored when the groups moved from the hospital into the community setting. There the time periods for analysis were lengthened from 90 to 180 days. These social processes were again measured and compared. Table 12.8 presents the cluster analyses for 180, 450, and 720 days, three representative points throughout the course of the measurement period. As can be seen from Table 12.8, group cohesiveness remains

TABLE 12.8
Variables Comprising the Clusters at Each Block of Time in the
Community Lodge Situation

Cluster	I (180 days)	II (450 days)	III (720 days)
1. *Group cohesiveness*			
Cohesiveness	×	×	×
Morale	×	×	×
Attraction to group	×	×	×
Satisfaction with leader	×	×	×
Time in the group	×		
2. *Group performance and leadership*			
Leadership	×	×	×
Performance	×	×	×
Sociometric choice by peers	×	×	×
Acceptance by the group	×	×	×
3. *Residual dimension*			
Reward	− ×	×	
Diagnostic category		×	

a single and viable dimension with great consistency over time; however group performance and leadership now merge into one dimension. The authors reasoned that the difference in relationship between leadership and group performance occurred because of situational differences between the hospital and community settings. They argued that during the course of the first experiment in the hospital, patient leadership of an autonomous type could rarely develop because of overriding hospital rules, which left the major decisions to the hospital professional staff. Thus, the patient group leadership that developed was token leadership that could not directly affect the performance of the group. However, in the cooperative lodge society, leadership was, in fact, delegated to the ex-mental patients who lived in the community and operated the society. Given the first-class citizenship responsibilities associated with lodge membership, leadership became essential to good performance. This is why leadership appears as a separate dimension in Table 12.6 (the hospital group) and is integrated with performance in Table 12.8 (the community group).

O-typing profiles of groups

Another aspect of cluster analysis is that which Tryon calls O-typing. Through this technique groups of persons who show similar profiles of cluster scores are located and defined. It will be recalled that Ives (1974) conducted a study in which he compared two different treatments for drug

TABLE 12.9
The Three Drug Clusters

Cluster	Loading
Cluster 1. Outcome	
1. Greater number of dirty urines	0.69
2. Shorter time in the program	0.33
3. Heroin	
a. Greater time mainlining heroin	0.82
b. Longer time spent clean	0.69
c. Greater cost of habit	0.38
d. Tendency to support habit illegally	0.46
4. Less optimistic expectations for treatment	0.77
5. Greater amount of time spent in jail after beginning illegal drug use	0.44
Cluster 2. Drug Behavior	
1. Greater number of drugs used	0.91
2. Drugs	
a. More frequent use of marijuana/hash	0.76
b. More frequent use of hallucinogens	0.68
c. More frequent use of narcotics	0.67
d. More frequent use of CNS depressants	0.65
e. More frequent use of CNS stimulants	0.75
f. More frequent use of cocaine	0.53
g. More frequent use of alcohol	0.42
3. Tendency to be younger	0.48
Cluster 3. Institutionalization	
1. Institutional history	
a. Older at first institutionalization	0.43
b. Greater number of institutionalizations	0.56
c. Higher probability of being reinstitutionalized	0.41
2. Greater number of residence changes	0.42
3. Tendency to be female	0.42
4. "Middle class"	
a. Tendency to be white	0.82
b. Parents have a higher occupational code	0.54
5. Older at first illegal drug use	0.45
6. Tendency to be married	0.38
7. Tendency to have been born and raised in the same town	0.33

TABLE 12.10

Correlations Among the Oblique Cluster Domains

Cluster	1	2	3
1. Outcome		0.09	−0.09
2. Drug behavior	0.09		−0.01
3. Institutionalization	−0.09	−0.01	

addicts with heroin users and non-users. In the course of the experiment he collected a considerable amount of data which was later cluster-analyzed, yielding measurements on outcome, drug behavior, and institutionalization. Table 12.9 presents the cluster dimensions. Table 12.10 shows them to be quite independent. Nine different types of addicts emerged from an O-analysis profile based upon these three dimensions.

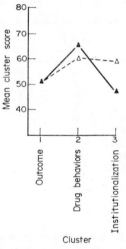

Fig. 12.4. Two O types similar on outcomes

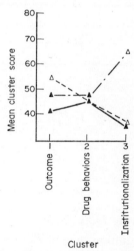

Fig. 12.5. Three O types similar on drug behaviors

For purposes of illuminating the use of profile typing, two O types from Ives' study have been selected that are similar on one cluster but quite different on others. Figure 12.4 shows that the two O types achieved approximately the same outcome scores; they are fairly similar on drug behaviors, but somewhat dissimilar on past institutionalization, with the persons in one O type having considerably less institutionalization than the other. This type of comparison is particularly useful when the experimenters wish to examine more closely the profiles of persons who achieved similar outcomes. For example, they may want to discover if there are subgroups with differentiating features in personal history or on other measures.

By comparison, Fig. 12.5 shows three other O types from Ives' study that are quite similar on drug behaviors, quite different on outcomes, and some are different on institutionalization—the figure shows that two of the groups look quite similar on institutionalization contrasted with one group that accounts for most of the difference. This type of result is particularly important if the experimenters are interested in groups having similar drug behaviors and wish to discover whether they are different on other dimensions. In this case the dimension of similarity is drug behaviors and the dissimilarity is on outcomes and institutionalization.

TABLE 12.11

Comparison of Task Groups on the Number and Percentage [a] of Patients in Each Cluster Group when chosen by Others (Patient as a Social Object)

Cluster Group	1		2		3		4	
	N	%	N	%	N	%	N	%
1	0	0	0	0	1	11	8	89
2	1	11	3	33	2	23	3	33
3	1	14	5	72	0	0	1	14
4	7	100	0	0	0	0	0	0
5	3	42	2	29	0	0	2	29
6	1	17	4	66	0	0	1	17
7	0	0	4	80	0	0	1	20
8	1	20	0	0	1	20	3	60
9	0	0	0	0	3	100	0	0

[a] The chance percent of patients is 25 in each task group.

Clustering individuals

In addition to exploring groups of persons who have similar cluster score profiles, it is sometimes important to look at their interpersonal relationship structure. When social models have been compared, the experimenters may wish to know whether the formal organization of the models affects the participants' perception of others. Application of cluster analysis to this problem is presented in a small-group ward study (Cressler, 1964, pp. 103-121). An eight-item picture sociometric was given to all individuals in the sample. These items were then scored in such a manner that each individual was given a score on the degree to which he preferred to associate with members or nonmembers of his task group. Cluster analyses were performed on these sociometric scores. The preference for members of their own task group is shown by the percentages given in Table 12.11. For example, cluster group 4 was comprised *only* (100%) of members of their own group (task group 1). Thus, working together in this experiment is highly related to perceived social desirability. By use of this cluster technique, the size of the perceptual groups and an individual's affiliation with them can be determined.

Redefining outcomes (*pre-set analysis*)

It often occurs during the course of a social experiment that the experimenters wish to know what clusters are formed that are directly related to the social change outcome criteria about which they are concerned. Very often in the actual V analysis (factor analysis) which is used to define dimensionality, the social change outcome criteria appear in the middle of the cluster or as a poorly defined cluster variable. Yet, even though the blind empirical V analysis has given them an inconspicuous status, it is still often the experimenters' interest to define the dimensions in terms of outcome. For this reason, Tryon developed a pre-set analysis. In this way outcomes that are extremely important to the experimenter can be defined and pre-set in the cluster analysis so that other measures will cluster around them to the extent that they are intercorrelated. In the Ives' experiment just mentioned, for example, he was interested particularly in outcomes related to readily observable and definable variables, such as urine analyses through which evidence of heroin use could be established. He was also interested in persons who used a great deal of drugs and in defining what the correlates of excessive usage were. In addition he was concerned about whether or not institutionalization for drug addiction was related to high usages of drugs. The clusters themselves and their interrelated variables were presented in Table 12.9 and 12.10. It was through this method of pre-set analysis that Ives was able to define more clearly these three dimensions of his study that were extremely important to him.

Ives' example was taken from a social model comparative experiment (different drug treatments). The same form of pre-set analysis often occurs in dissemination experiments as well. Occasionally there is one variable—usually the social change outcome criterion of innovation adoption—that is so important a theoretical construct that it is necessary to discover what would be related to it if it were the *key defining variable* in the cluster. Such a case occurred with the social change outcome criterion of movement toward lodge adoption, measured in the lodge dissemination experiment (Fairweather, Sanders, & Tornatzky, 1974). The movement toward lodge adoption could be scored in several steps that eventually resulted in lodge

TABLE 12.12
The Change Cluster

Variable	Loading
I Pre-Adoption Communication and Decision Making	
1. Greater number of professional staff involved in decision to implement the lodge	0.55
2. Greater personal satisfaction among the hospital staff about the decision to implement	0.45
3. Greater number of persons talked to, and talked to more often, at time of initial contact with the hospital	0.44
II Communication with the Consultant	
1. Greater number of calls and letters during implementation period	0.88
2. Greater number of spontaneous calls to consultant during implementation period	0.78
3. Greater number of letters to the consultant during implementation period	0.56
4. Longer telephone conversations with consultant at time of second follow-up during adoption	0.54
III Reduced Status and Prestige Hierarchy	
1. Greater likelihood that hospital superintendent will be a nonspecialist M.D. or public health person than a psychiatrist	0.55
2. State salaries for psychiatrists are relatively low	0.49
3. Hospital perceives less difference in prestige between superintendent and other staff members	0.43
IV Superintendent Characteristics	
1. Superintendent agrees that patients are in many ways like children	0.51
2. Greater career geographic mobility for the hospital superintendent	0.48
3. Greater number of career job moves for the hospital superintendent	0.44
4. Superintendent feels that ex-patients are no more dangerous than the average citizen	0.43
V Hospital Effectiveness and Capability	
1. Quick turnover of patients in the hospital	0.53
2. More favorable staff-patient ratio throughout the state	0.52
3. More favorable staff-patient ratio in the hospital	0.52
4. Decision to implement (as perceived by the contact) was not affected by availability of funds	0.46
VI Delegation of Authority	
1. Greater number of people attending first action consultation meeting	0.57
2. Lower status person is the contact at time of first follow-up during implementation	0.46
3. Lower status person is the contact at time of third follow-up during implementation	0.43
VII Demonstration Ward Development	
1. Starting the demonstration ward later than the second follow-up after the consultation	0.74
2. Starting the demonstration ward later than the first follow-up after the consultation	0.50
3. Starting the demonstration ward later than the third follow-up after consultation	0.49
4. Starting the demonstration ward later than the fourth follow-up after the consultation	0.49
5. Having a demonstration ward	0.43

adoption. The pre-set analysis yielded the "change cluster" presented in Table 12.12.

This table shows that 26 items arranged in seven conceptual categories (pre-adoption communication and decisionmaking, etc.) were associated with institutional adoption of the lodge society. Their particular contribution to adoption would, of course, have to be determined by future experiments.

In this chapter we have attempted to show how correlative techniques can be used in understanding the social processes of social models and dissemination efforts. The manner in which such information can be combined with comparative information to make appropriate inferences is the burden of the next chapter.

CHAPTER 13

Permissible Inferences and Publication

Now that we have reviewed the various types of comparative (narrative-descriptive, graphical, nonparametric, and parametric tests of significance) and associative (correlations, factor and cluster analyses) analyses, it is important to turn our attention to how these various "bits and pieces" can be used to explore the validity of a social model or a dissemination experiment. This question involves thought processes that are similar to those required of a musician or artist who selects the various notes or makes certain brush strokes in an effort to create a work of art. In their own way the socially involved scientists must accomplish similar creative acts not only in designing and carrying out innovative programs but also in using the many evaluative techniques that are available to tell the story and give the picture of the particular research effort. This permits them to determine the conclusions that can be drawn from the results and whether or not there is logical as well as statistical significance.

Unlike experiments with a single test of significance, the inferences stemming from social model and dissemination experiments come from the many sources of information that have been collected during the course of the longitudinal experiment. It is thus inaccurate to speak of an evaluative statistic for social research. Rather an evaluation *program* is a more accurate term. Inferences are based upon a variety of evaluative techniques including observations made during the weeks, months, or years of the experiment and information that is displayed in graphs to show time trends, from both parametric and nonparametric statistical tests and from associative statistics, particularly factor and/or cluster analyses. All of the information from these various sources needs to be integrated into a comprehensive picture of the experiment which forms the background material from which the inferences must be made.

While it should be quite obvious that statistical tests of significance provide the most objective evaluation of outcome, it is equally true that such

343

tests are enhanced and made more understandable by historical events, time trends, and the relationship of the various outcomes to other events that have occurred during the course of the experiment.

The necessity to use information gained from actual observation in making adequate inferences from the statistics and other research data should be clear enough. Since numbers are themselves devoid of meaning, it should be obvious that a statistic does not "tell" the scientists anything. It is only the statistic or a series of them in the context of the experimentalists' knowledge of the field of investigation that gives meaning to the research information. Thus, an in depth knowledge of a particular problem is absolutely essential to a proper interpretation of the experimental information which the researchers must use as a basis for generalization. For this reason, the evaluation of these social experiments is a rather complex affair that needs to be viewed as an exercise in logic.

Since the inferences that one can make about social model and dissemination experiments are based upon knowledge accumulated over a period of time, it is important to view all of this information and put it in perspective prior to making inferences from it. The reader should keep the need for this wholistic approach in mind while reading this chapter. For purposes of instructional clarity, the chapter is organized into a two-part presentation. The *first* is a general review of some of the bases for the generation of logical inferences; the *second* is a presentation of the process of logical inference through the medium of selected experiments.

INFERENCES

After the analyses have been completed, the researchers make inferences from them by integrating them with their own experiences. They make inferences from all of the information accumulated during the course of an experiment. Thus, tests of statistical significance obtained from the analyses of the data are only one type of information from which the generalizations can originate. They are, however, the most unbiased source if they are properly applied. To understand this more completely, it is necessary to recall that statistics are used to test the hypotheses set forth in the initial research plan. Provided the statistical tests indicate a significant difference, they will allow the experimenter to reject the hypothesis that the several means, medians, or distributions of the experimental conditions—depending on the data and the nature of the tests—were derived from the same population. If the statistical hypothesis is rejected—that is, if the two or more statistics are not likely to have been derived from the same population—then the experimenters *infer* from them and all other experimental information what could most likely have brought about the differences in the derived statistics. Provided all experimental conditions have been met and there is no contrary information, they usually infer that the differences between the statistics represent the differential effects of the created experimental conditions.

The experimenters, however, must be aware that any differences in these statistics that they attribute to the conditions constitute only an inference. That is, it is simply a probability statement. The experimenters test the statistical hypothesis by use of probability tables that are typically found in statistical methods books. These tables allow the researchers to find a level of statistical significance for the particular test employed, such as the *t* test, F ratio, or chi square. This level of significance may be defined as the probability that the two or more comparative statistics were derived from the same population. Thus, when the level of significance is arbitrarily set at .01, the experimenters may say that the obtained difference between the means, medians, or distributions would occur only rarely—that is, one time in 100 by chance alone. If the experimenters accept this probability level as significant (an arbitrary decision), they may reject the hypothesis that the computed statistics were derived from the same statistical population.

Social Models

In social model experiments, the researchers are always testing the hypothesis that the newly created model or models produced better results for the selected social problem than the control condition—the usual social method of handling the problem. This is a statistical one-sided hypothesis mentioned elsewhere. Assuming that any measure used in the experiment will yield a higher score when the social position of the participants is enhanced, the experimenters are only interested in the statistical hypothesis that the innovative experimental model or models receive a higher mean score, median score, or distribution of scores than the usual social practice (control model.) This hypothesis is tested by a statistical test of significance.

Theoretically, each test of significance is drawn from a population of such tests. This population of tests typically forms a normal curve; when the computed statistic falls in an arbitrarily selected area under this curve, the experimenters may reject the statistical hypothesis. The social innovative experimenters would thus reject the hypothesis that the mean score, median score, or distribution of scores of the innovated model is equal to or less than such scores for the control model.

One-sided hypotheses and their tests of significance as applied to social innovative experiments can be illustrated with the *t* test. In such a case, the experimenters will have two mean scores: one for the experimental model and one for its control. They are interested in testing the hypothesis that the mean score for the experimental model is equal to or less than the mean score for the control. Assuming that they accept the .05 level of significance, a *t value* falling in this area in a theoretical distribution of *t values* may be used as sufficient evidence to reject the hypothesis that the mean score of the experimental model is equal to or less than the mean score of the control model. If their other experimental data support this finding, they can infer from this rejection that the mean score for the experimental model is significantly greater than the mean score for the control. Figure 13.1 shows that the *t value* must be of sufficient magnitude to fall in the shaded area under

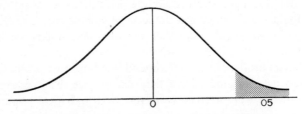

Fig. 13.1. The social change experimentalists' one-tailed test of significance for the statistical hypothesis that the mean of the experimental model $(m_em) \leq$ the mean of the control (m_c) against the alternative $m_em > m_c$. If the computed t falls in the shaded area, the statistical hypothesis $m_em \leq m_c$ can be rejected

the curve. Thus, it is only the one side of the distribution of tests of significance that the social innovative experimenters are interested in using. One-sided testing changes the common usage of most probability tables. The .01 level becomes the .02 level, the .025 becomes the .05, and so on. An excellent discussion of one- and two-tailed tests of significance has been presented by Jones (1952). Other discussions can be found in Edwards (1960, pp. 94–97) and McNemar (1962, pp. 61-69).

Suppose that the experimentalists are able to reject the statistical hypothesis that the obtained statistic for the experimental model is equal to or less than the same statistic obtained for the control model. Before making inferences about the effectiveness of the models, they first must attempt to synthesize the results of the statistical tests of significance with other sources of information available to them. Statistical tests alone are not sufficient evidence for the experimenters interested in social change. Not only must they require a more stringent level of statistical significance than experimenters in other fields before proposing any changes, but they must also combine the data analysis with information gained through observation, discussion, and pursuit of the total problem. They thus add to the evidence from the statistics the information that has arisen from their own experiences.

As far as the tests of significance are concerned, it is most important that a stringent level of significance be adopted because inferences made from such an experiment might be used by the agents of society to instigate social changes. The ethical experimentalists would not wish to support social change unless their results clearly suggest that such changes would appear to benefit significantly the population under investigation. Since the usual social practice with which the experimental models are compared has been assiduously developed by society's agents over many years, it would be foolhardy to recommend a change in the manner society has developed to handle its problem unless a better solution has been manifestly demonstrated. This suggests that in statistical terms a probability level of at least a .05 should be established as the acceptable level for recommending changes. It should be adopted because social changes are distasteful to many individuals and should not be recommended unless they are clearly warranted. The selection of a .05 level of statistical significance is, however, perfectly arbitrary. The acceptance of any level of significance as representing the point at which the hypothesis will be rejected is determined by the weight of many factors such as the data involved, the problem selected, the sample characteristics, and even the personality of the researchers.

Suppose, now, that the experimenters are able to infer from collating all their experimental information that one or several of the experimental models produces a more beneficial outcome than the usual social practice. They are then faced with making a second inference that concerns the degree to which this beneficial solution can be a solution to the problem in a society. The degree to which the solution found in the model can be generalized to solve the existing problem in society depends upon three conditions:

(1) how representative the model's sample is of the problem population in a society;

(2) how representative the model's social context is of the social context in which the problem is typically found in a society; and

(3) how representative the social change outcome criterion is of a society's consensus about a solution to the problem.

The representativeness of these three components of generalization may be presented geometrically as the dimensions of a cube. In Fig. 13.2 the numerical values of these dimensions represent the percentage of representativeness on each of the three dimensions. Thus, zero is no representativeness; .50 is 50% representativeness; and 1.00 is 100% or perfect representativeness. The volume of each of the three cubes, which is represented by the shaded area, shows the degree to which the experimental solution is a valid solution for a society—that is, the degree to which it solves the general social problem. Cube (a) shows that when the sample perfectly represents the problem population, when the social context within which the model is implanted is perfectly representative of the social context of the problem in a society, and when the selected social change outcome criterion perfectly represents a consensual solution to the social problem, there is complete generalization from the experimental solution to the solution for a society. Cube (b) shows a dramatic drop of 50% generalizability when two dimensions are perfectly representative and one dimension is only 50% representative. Cube (c) shows a drop of 87.5% in generalization when each of the three dimensions are only 50% representative. These cubes, even though theoretical, dramatically illustrate the caution with which the experimenter should approach the problem of generalizing from the experimental situation to the society at large.

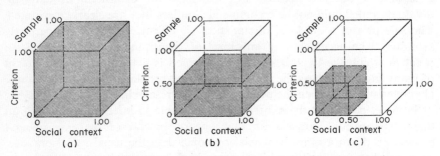

Fig. 13.2. Shaded portions of the cubes represent the degree to which an experimental model is a solution for a society's social problem. (a) When perfect (100%) representativeness exists on the three dimensions; (b) when perfect representativeness exists on two dimensions with 50% representativeness on the third; (c) when 50% representativeness exists on the three dimensions

Figure 13.2 shows that one of the important facets in making inferences is the representativeness of the sample. In this respect, the important characteristics of the sample were defined while the sample was being obtained, and these sample attributes should now be contrasted with comparable national characteristics. For example, the researcher concerned with a sample of public school children between the ages of 6 and 12 would have ascertained many of the attributes of this population through the detailed historical questionnaire and other defining measures obtained during the planning phase of the experiment.

The representativeness of this experimental sample can now be ascertained by checking the distributions of the defining variables with those of the national statistics, if available. When such national statistics are not available or are likely to be unreliable, the experimentalists should begin a compilation from their own sample so that generalization in future experiments can be made more accurately. In any event, the researchers should attempt to ascertain the representativeness of their sample by every means at their disposal. They should also clearly present the characteristics of their sample as well as comparative national data, where available, in the publication of the experiment, so that other experimentalists can determine the degree of similarity between the research sample and others that they may wish to use in the future.

There are other characteristics of the participants that the experimenters also need to consider. Suppose that the children participating in such educational models are volunteers. The generalizations then would necessarily be limited to children with the same attributes who are also volunteers. This is an increasingly important problem in social innovative experiments as discussed in Chapter 8. At the very least, the same descriptive information about nonvolunteers should be obtained and their characteristics should be compared with those of the volunteers before generalizations are made.

Finally, before generalizing, failures in the models as well as successes should be examined carefully. Any differences between participant failures and successes must be explored before the experimentalists can reasonably generalize from their results.

The degree of permissible generalization is also contingent upon the social context in which the experimental models were implanted. In the educational example just mentioned, the experimentalists not only must consider the degree to which the sample is statistically similar to the general student population, but they must also be concerned about where the elementary schools are located. Let us assume that the sample of children comes from a lower-lower socioeconomic area as defined by a social class index such as the one developed by Tryon (Krech, Crutchfield, & Ballachey, 1962). The experimenters will have to limit generalizations to similar socioeconomic and political areas.

Prior to generalization, the researchers must also consider the degree to which the social change outcome criterion used in the experiment represents a consensual solution to a society's problem. The situational specificity of many of the measures typically used in social innovative experiments has been found in various studies (Fairweather *et at.*, 1969; Forsyth & Fairweather, 1961). Such measures, including the social change outcome criterion, may not only be unrelated in the same situation but their relationships may change in different situations. It is therefore most important that the experimenters make their inferences only about the same or similar situations where similar criteria and samples are likely to be used. Because of the empirical nature of social innovative experiments, it is most important that generalizations be used as the basis for further experiments, so that new models can be continuously established and compared.

Let us assume, in the grade school example just given, that the responsible agents of society interested in academic achievement define the social change outcome criterion as school grades. The experimentalists will collect many measures during the course of their experiment, one of which will be the social change outcome criterion—in this case, school grades. For example, they may use scores on academic achievement tests, or on intelligence tests, or various measures of social adjustment in addition to school grades. They must then find the correlations between these measures and the social change outcome criterion before generalizing about the effectiveness of the models. Should the experimentalists find that achievement test scores were correlated only .30 with grades—the social change outcome criterion—they would point out this relatively low relationship in predicting school achievement to those responsible for admission policies or other educational procedures. Whether or not there would be a continued interest in collecting achievement scores would have to be determined at this point.

All these types of information must be considered before the experimenters can generalize. They must carefully consider the representativeness of the sample, the social context in which the research occurred, the degree to which the social change outcome criterion represents a society's consensus about problem solution, and the negative cases in formulating their research generalizations. To make such inferences, it is necessary for the researchers to synthesize the results of all their experiences with the vast amount of data collected and the various statistical analyses. It is this general synthesis of all sources of information from which the inferences about the research results are made and from which new experiments can arise.

Dissemination

If the experimenters discover that two or more models yield significantly beneficial results contrasted with the natural social condition, a subsequent experiment should be used to compare the beneficial models. Following the logical process of repeated attempts at problem solution, the experimenters eventually should be able to find one social model that yields more beneficial effects than the naturalistic social condition or any other social innovative model that has been tried. When this occurs, the experimenters can make the inference that the beneficial results from this model would also obtain if it was created and implanted in social circumstances similar to those extant at the time and place of the prototype comparative experiment. A dissemination experiment follows this inference.

The dissemination experiment is established to accomplish two interrelated goals. One is to further disseminate the new social model. In this regard each newly implanted model can be considered a *replicate* of the initial social model. Usually it is not possible to set up the entire prototype comparative experiment again, with a naturalistic social model control and random assignment of participants to the different conditions. Instead, the experimenters usually create several different replicates of the prototype social model in their dissemination effort. When replicates are established under conditions where the researchers can only collect information from the new replicates themselves (random assignment and adequate controls cannot be achieved), the experimenters usually use quasi-experimental techniques to compare the replicates of the prototype social models with the naturalistic social model control in the geographic area where the implant occurs. If on this comparison the first replicate yields essentially the same results as the prototype model did when it was contrasted with its control, the initial inference about the generalizability of the prototype model may be considered empirically validated. The confidence that researchers can place in the empirical validity of the prototype model increases with every replicated social model that shows similar results to those found in the initial experiment. If the researchers cannot get information from an ongoing social program that can be contrasted with the outcomes of each newly implanted social model, they should contrast the new implant with the control social model against which the prototype model was initially compared. If marked deviations from the outcomes for the replicates under either of the aforementioned comparative conditions of the prototype model occur, the generalizability of the results are thrown into question. If additional replicates show similar questionable results, the initial controlled experiment with the prototype model will need to be repeated in its entirety because, assuming an .05 level of significance, a one in 20 chance outcome may have occurred in comparing the prototype experiment. Such an improbable occurrence would yield invalid results.

Assuming that repeated replicates yield results sufficiently similar to the original comparative experiment so that continued dissemination of the social model is warranted, a dissemination experiment aimed at a state, regional, or national audience ensues. Inferences will need to be made from this dissemination experiment. They are those having to do with the outcomes (adaption yield) of the different conditions of approaching, persuading, activating, and diffusing as outlined in Chapter 3. Typically these demand the use of *two-way* tests of significance and the usual test of significance probability levels found in standard statistical texts can be used directly rather than converting the probability levels to one-tail tests, just mentioned with regard to comparing social models. The essential question for a dissemination experiment becomes: to what degree do the different implementation techniques such as written, verbal, and action approaches effect the actual adoption rate of the new model. As with social model-building experiments, if an experimental dissemination condition shows that significantly different results (more adoptions) can be obtained by using it in the activation of a model, that condition is used in future dissemination attempts. In such cases, the successful technique when used again can be contrasted with the percent of successes found in the sample of the initial study. If no significant differences occur between these percentages, the technique for replicating can, at the very least, be considered a logical success. And if similar adoption rates obtain as more and more attempts to disseminate occur, more and more confidence about the use of the particular dissemination technique will have been gained. On the other hand, when repeated attempts to use an implementation technique found in one experiment yield significantly different results than those found in the initial study (adoption rates are consistently lower), less and less confidence can be placed in the first discovered condition of implementation and a complete replicate of the initial study is required.

These logical difficulties in generalizing from one experiment simply stress the probabilistic nature of inferences. The experimenters must always be aware that they are dealing with probabilities. Even though probabilities are set high—for example, one in a 1000—it is still possible that the one in a 1000 chance of drawing an incorrect inference has occurred. It is therefore important that the researchers do not over-generalize from their data. They should also understand the need for replication and they should be aware that every replication with similar findings increases the probability that the results of the initial experiment were accurate.

The probabilistic nature of the statistics used may be somewhat complicated when two or more social change outcomes are used in one experiment. When this occurs, the researchers are faced with making inferences from a series of statistical tests. Viewing the total number of statistical comparisons as a pool of statistical tests, the question for the researchers becomes: What is the chance probability of obtaining the observed number of significant tests of significance (.05 or .01, or any other agreed-upon level) from the actual number of tests computed? If the tests are *independent* (outcomes are unrelated), one can discover the chance probability by use of the binomial model as described by Jones & Fiske (1953). Sakoda, Cohen, & Beall (1954) have created two graphs presenting the chance probability of obtaining a particular number of significant statistics at the .05 and .01 level from the number of statistics calculated in a given experiment. These graphs are presented in Figs. 13.3 and 13.4. A study of these figures shows that n represents the number of significant statistics and N the number of calculated statistics.

In the case where the experimenters are using either the .05 or .01 level of significance, the probability level of obtaining n significant statistics from N calculated statistics is found in the graphs by tracing the intercept of the two lines formed by n and N and reading the point of interception on the right-hand scale of the figure. For example, where the number of statistics calculated is 10 (N) and the number found to be significant at the .05 level is 4 (n) the intercept is on the .001 curve. Thus, the probability of obtaining 4

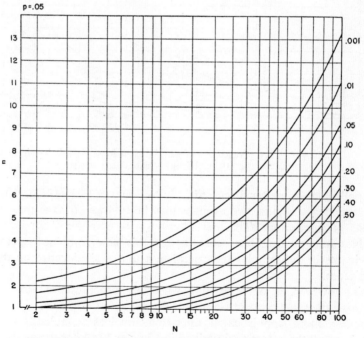

Fig. 13.3. Chance probability of obtaining at least *n* statistics significant at the .05 level from *N* calculated statistics

tests of significance at the .05 level when 10 tests have been computed is .001, or one chance in a thousand.

However, another common problem that the researchers will face in using multiple tests of significance occurs when the different measures are *not independent*. In such a case the graphs shown in Figs. 13.3 and 13.4 are

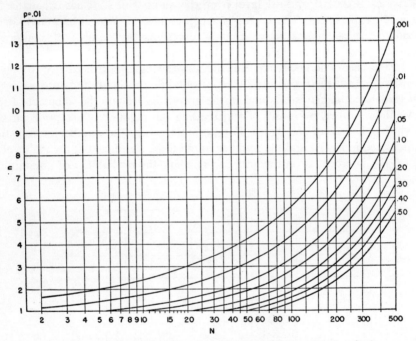

Fig. 13.4. Chance probability of obtaining at least *n* statistics significant at the .01 level from *N* calculated statistics

not applicable—a matter discussed fully by Jones & Fisk (1953). When lack of independence occurs, two avenues may be followed for the total number of tests of significance. The first solution is to combine these interrelated variables into an omnibus score, assign this new combined score to all participants in the sample, and complete a test of significance on the combined score.

This, however, is only possible when all measures are also logically measuring the same concept—a matter discussed in Chapter 9.

Another more sophisticated approach involves completing a cluster analysis on all the scores as described in Chapter 12. After the analyses, new cluster scores for each independent cluster can be computed and assigned each participant and a new test of significance can be computed separately for each cluster. In this case all related variables will be contained in one cluster and if the comparative analyses are completed only on independent clusters (zero or close to zero correlations with every other cluster), independence will have been achieved and the tests of significance can be completed on demonstrably independent dimensions. Figures 13.3 and 13.4 are applicable to these cluster-defined independent dimensions. Where the experimenters have selected a level of significance as .05 or .01, and the calculated statistics are independent, these two figures can be of time-saving help to them. Where the levels are *not* .05 or .01, and the statistics are independent, the experimenters should use the binomial model as described by Jones & Fiske and mentioned above.

Beyond these problems of data inference from a series of statistical tests, each experiment also generates new ideas that cannot be experimentally tested in the research itself. While these notions are often interesting and provocative, they become hypotheses for future researches and are not themselves established empirical facts. The researchers should clearly delineate the inferences that can properly be made on the basis of their research information from those general ideas they develop that may serve as hypotheses to be tested in future experiments. Generalizations from social innovative experiments not only result in the publications of scientific journal articles or books, but also may be used to change the lives of many individuals. Under these conditions, it is more desirable to be conservative about generalizations from any single experiment.

Some researchers will *not* be successful. All parties in the research effort should clearly recognize this possibility of failure at the outset. Information showing that certain models probably do not benefit their participants is just as important as information demonstrating that some do. All information, whether negative or positive, can be useful in planning the next innovative experiment.

The Inferential Process

The inferential process is essentially a process of logic. It concerns the permissible statements that can be made from the data and the knowledge gained through observations during the course of an experiment. The manner in which inferences can be made from the data presented in a series of experiments will now be reviewed for three selected researches. In Chapter 2 the series of longitudinal field experiments leading to the development and dissemination of the lodge society were briefly discussed. However, at that time no experimental data analyses were presented showing clearly the information upon which the experimenters' conclusions were drawn. This section will present the three crucial experiments leading to the establishment and evaluation of the lodge society. This presentation is intended to *illustrate* how research material is integrated into a holistic picture from which inferences are made about the social problem being studied and the generalizations that can be made from them. Although some information about these three experiments has been presented piecemeal in past chapters, it will be synthesized in this section so that the reader can perceive the total picture from which the inferences emanated.

Working examples

The first such study involved a comparison of four psychotherapeutic programs—group living (GG), group therapy (G), individual therapy (I), and a work alone situation (C), with three different patient groups: neurotics, short-term psychotics (hospitalized less than one year), and long-term psychotics (hospitalized for more than one year). A discussion of the four treatment conditions can be found on pages 302–3; the design is shown in Table 11.7; Table 8.1 shows that the persons participating in each of the four treatment groups were very similar on a large number of background variables. This sample similarity is important when making inferences because it permits the experimenters to assume that the persons participating in the four groups were themselves sufficiently similar so that any social model outcome differences can be attributed to the models and not their participants. The *social change outcome criteria* consisted of two post-hospital follow-up measures—rehospitalization and employment. A comparison of the experimental conditions and diagnostic classifications is presented in Table 13.1. Other behavioral follow-up outcome measures (friendships, communication, etc), personality and vocational interest test scores, and within-hospital behaviors are also compared in Table 13.1. When a significant difference exists, it appears in the table as an S along with its probability level (.05 for example). NS in the table indicates a nonsignificant difference—the differences did not reach the .05 level of significance.

First let us explore the differences between treatments. A glance at Table 13.1 shows that out of four tests of significance on the social change outcome criterion, significant differences occurred only at six months in employment. The percentage of employment at six months by treatment groups was Group Living 42%; Group Therapy 33%; Individual Therapy 45%, and Work Only Control 8%. None of the other follow-up behaviors, personality tests, or social behaviors significantly differentiated the treatment at six months.

TABLE 13.1

Comparison of the Four Treatment Models and Diagnostic Groups on Several Measures of Change

Area of measurement	Between treatments	Between diagnostic groups	Interaction
Outcome			
Social change outcome criteria			
Follow-up behavior			
6 month rehospitalization	NS	S(0.01)	NS
18 month rehospitalization	NS	S(0.01)	NS
6 month employment	S(0.05)	S(0.01)	NS
18 month employment	NS	S(0.01)	NS
Other follow-up behavioral outcomes			
Friendships—6 month	NS	S(0.01)	NS
18 month	NS	S(0.01)	NS
Communication—6 month	NS	NS	NS
18 month	NS	NS	NS
General adjustment—6 month	NS	S(0.05)	NS
18 month	NS	NS	NS
Excessive drinking—6 month	NS	S(0.05)	NS
18 month	NS	NS	NS
Anti-social relations—6 month	NS	NS	NS
18 month	NS	NS	NS
Problem behavior—6 month	NS	NS	NS
18 month	NS	NS	NS
Degree of illness—6 month	NS	S(0.05)	NS
18 month	NS	S(0.05)	NS
Cost (days in treatment)	S(0.05)	S(0.001)	NS
Tests			
Personality I (MMPI)	NS	NS	(S)
Personality II (TAT)	NS	NS	NS
Vocational interests (HVPI)	NS	NS	NS
Behavior			
Social behavior on ward	NS	NS	NS

(S) Significant on two or more of the MMPI Scales.
S   Indicates a statistical significance with the probability level indicated.
NS Indicates a nonsignificant statistical test.

At 18 months, none of the social change outcome criteria or other behavioral outcomes reach the .05 level of significance. The one advantage accruing to the three therapy groups at six months—that of employment— appears to be short-lived since this advantage disappeared in the next 12 months. Table 13.1 also shows that personality and vocational interest test behavior did not change significantly under the different treatments nor did social behavior on the ward at 18 months continuing the six-month trend. Going now to cost of treatment, the groups have significant differences in days in treatment as shown in Table 13.1. The mean number of days for each treatment is shown in Table 13.2. The most days in treatment (assuming an

equivalent cost per day per individual to remain in the hospital) is attributable to individual therapy and group living. So far as treatments are concerned, then, if there are significant differences between them it occurs only
in employment at the end of six months and has disappeared by 18 months.
This result itself is extremely shaky since only one test of significance out of
18 tests yielded a significance at the .05 level. To attain these poor results,
the cost is very high, at least for those treatments involving individual
psychotherapy and group living in contrast to the work-alone situation.

TABLE 13.2
Mean Days in Treatment

	GG	G	I	C	Mean
N	119.5	65.4	117.8	86.0	97.18
Ps	78.6	61.4	129.8	89.5	89.83
Pl	172.3	163.9	191.1	92.5	154.95
Mean	123.47	96.90	146.23	89.33	

Turning now to the difference between diagnostic groups, the researchers
see a totally different picture. Table 13.1 shows clear differences between
diagnostic groups where significant differences obtain at the .05, .01, and
.001 level. Recidivism and employment (the social change outcome criteria)
are significantly different for the groups at six and 18 months (.01 level).
Other follow-up criteria show a relatively similar picture with significant
differences at the .01 level for friendships at six and 18 months, degree of
illness at the .05 level at six and 18 months, and general adjustment and
excessive drinking at the .05 level at six months. Nonsignificant differences
obtain on personality and vocational inventories and social behavior on the
ward. Table 13.3 presents the percentage of the most adaptive responses for
the three diagnostic groups on the significant outcome criteria. Again, the
cost for different treatment groups is significant, as shown in Table 13.1,
with the highest cost borne by the most chronic group, as shown by their
longer periods of hospitalization (Table 13.2). Table 13.3 shows that the
long-term psychotics were the most poorly adjusted group on both social
change outcome criteria (out of the hospital and employment), they had
fewer friends, and they were not problem drinkers. In terms of rehospitalization, the nonpsychotics were more similar to the long-term psychotics than
to the short-term psychotics. On two other follow-up measures (getting along
satisfactorily and well most of the time) the short-term psychotics again
appear to be making a much better adjustment than the neurotics or long-
term psychotics at six months. Thus, in all categories the short-term psychotics showed the most adaptive percentages. Table 13.3 shows that the

same adjustmental picture continues for 18 months. By that time only 27.6% for the long-term psychotics and 44.4% of the neurotics remained out of the hospital, whereas 71% of the short-term psychotics had not been rehospitalized. Areas of employment, friendships, and degree of illness show similar trends for the long-term psychotic. Generally, then, it seems clear that highly significant differences do obtain between the three diagnostic groups on the social change outcome criteria of rehospitalization and employment as well as on other follow-up behaviors and cost. The most maladaptive group is the long-term psychotic followed by the nonpsychotic, with the short-term psychotic showing the best adjustment.

TABLE 13.3
Percentage of Success on Significant Outcomes by Diagnostic Groups

Outcome	Neurotic N	Short-term Psychotic PS	Long-term Psychotic PL
Follow-up 6 Months			
Social Change Outcome Criteria			
Out of hospital	50.0	87.5	40.6
Employed full-time	34.4	40.0	9.4
Other follow-up behavior			
Some friends	62.5	75.0	37.5
Getting along satisfactorily	53.1	81.3	59.4
Well most of the time	53.1	84.4	59.4
Not a problem drinker	65.6	90.6	90.6
Follow-up 18 months			
Social Change Outcome Criteria			
Out of hospital	44.4	71.0	27.6
Employed full-time	40.7	51.6	14.3
Other follow-up behavior			
Some friends	65.0	71.0	28.0
Well most of the time	57.7	58.1	32.1

Table 13.4 shows a cluster analysis of 120 of the variables used in the study. They produced seven clusters which are relatively independent as shown by the correlations between the clusters in Table 13.5. The two social change outcome criteria (rehospitalization and employment) are highly interrelated as shown by loadings of (.96) and (.73) in Cluster 1 (Table 13.4) and are related to the Family Group Therapy Behavioral scale (.66) (Finney, 1954), which is a measure of interpersonal relationships in psychotherapy settings. Other areas of measurement such as test scores (MMPI, HVPI and other demographic characteristics) are relatively unrelated to follow-up behavior (Table 13.5). Finally Table 13.6 shows that high correlations exist between six- and 18-month follow-up.

TABLE 13.4
Criteria of Patient Adjustment

The Seven Clusters			
Cluster 1		**Cluster 4** (*continued*)	
a. Follow-up, employed full-time	(0.96)	c. No service connected pension	(0.69)
b. Follow-up, well most of time	(0.73)	d. Nonpsychotic diagnosis (upon	
c. Follow-up, was not rehospitalized	(0.73)	admission)	(0.60)
d. Adaptive Finney scale score	(0.66)	e. Few total weeks of previous	
		hospitalization	(0.57)
Cluster 2		f. Older age upon admission	(0.52)
a. Adaptive MMPI CS[b]	(0.98)[a]	g. Fewer number of previous	
b. Low MMPI—F	(0.92)	hospitalizations	(0.51)
c. Low MMPI—P1	(0.89)		
d. Low MMPI—SIM[a]	(0.88)	**Cluster 5**	
e. Low MMPI—Pa	(0.86)	a. Maladaptive follow-up drinking	(0.86)
f. Low MMPI—Sc	(0.82)	b. High HVPI 9 (Mf-masculinity)	(0.77)
g. High ideal-self Q sort correlation	(0.82)	c. Nonpsychotic diagnosis upon	
h. Low MMPI—D	(0.80)	admission	(0.64)
i. High MMPI—Es	(0.75)	d. Low HVPI 7 (Control)	(0.60)
j. Low MMPI—Hy	(0.73)	e. Few total weeks of previous	
k. Low MMPI—Hs	(0.64)	hospitalization	(0.57)
l. Few previous arrests	(0.51)	f. Adaptive ward behavior	(0.55)
		g. Low HVPI II (Infrequency)	(0.53)
Cluster 3		h. Low MMPI—Welsh R[d]	(0.51)
a. High HVPI 5 (Verbal activity)	(0.94)		
b. High HVPI 12 (Responds like		**Cluster 6**	
others)	(0.91)	a. High service discharge rank	(0.83)
c. High HVPI 4 (Conformity)	(0.87)	b. High gain in service rank	(0.75)
d. High HVPI 6 (Emotional)	(0.87)	c. Low HVPI 11 (Infrequency)	(0.63)
e. High HVPI 8 (Aggressiveness)	(0.87)	d. More education completed	(0.59)
f. High HVPI 3 (Responsibility)	(0.86)	e. Few service courts-martial	(0.56)
g. High HVPI 9 (Mf-masculinity)	(0.73)	f. High socioeconomic status	(0.56)
h. High HVPI 2 (Intellectuality)	(0.72)		
i. High HVPI 1 (Physical activity)	(0.63)	**Cluster 7**	
j. High HVPI 10 (Status)	(0.53)	a. Few previous arrests	(0.82)
		b. Few jobs held in past	(0.64)
		c. Few service courts-martial	(0.61)
Cluster 4		d. Maladaptive job behavior in	
a. Older age at first hospitalization	(0.96)	hospital	(0.60)
b. Older onset age	(0.96)		

[a] MMPI is Minnesota Multiphasic, HVPI is Holland Vocational Preference Inventory.

[b] In addition to the usual MMPI scales, configural interpretations of the MMPI and HVPI were obtained. George S. Walsh and John L. Holland, experts on each of these tests, were asked to place each test profile into an adaptive or maladaptive group in terms of the expected follow-up adjustment of each patient. These two scales were designated, respectively, as MMPI Configural Scoring (MMPI-CS) and, similarly, HVPI-CS.

[c] SIM is the MMPI scale of Inner Maladjustment (Simon, 1952).

[d] MMPI Welsh A and R refer to Welsh's (1956) Anxiety and Repressions scales.

TABLE 13.5
Intercorrelations Between the Cluster Domains

	Follow-up	MMPI	HVPI	Neurotic-Psychotic	Psycho-pathic	Achieve-ment	Con-formity
Follow-up		0.26	0.12	−0.04	0.09	0.17	0.07
MMPI	0.26		−0.03	0.12	0.03	−0.07	0.36
HVPI	0.12	−0.03		0.02	0.32	00	0.18
Neurotic-Psychotic	−0.04	0.12	0.02		0.31	−0.20	0.09
Psychopathic	0.09	0.03	0.32	0.31		−0.27	0.04
Achievement	0.17	−0.07	00	−0.20	−0.27		0.27
Conformity	0.07	0.36	0.18	0.09	0.04	0.27	

TABLE 13.6
Intercorrelations Between Six Months and
18 Months Follow-up Rating

Follow-up Area	Correlations
1. Out of hospital	0.93[a]
2. Employed full-time	0.77[a]
3. One or more friends	0.53[a]
4. Frequently talks with others	0.37[a]
5. Getting along adequately	0.60[a]
6. Easy to get along with	0.57[a]
7. Usually well	0.59[a]
8. Not a problem drinker	0.88[a]
9. No anti-social legal violations	0.93[a]

[a] Significant at 0.01 level.

Putting together all of the aforementioned information, what inferences appear warranted from these results? First, it appears that the treatments are *not* generally producing significantly different results, particularly when community adjustment of the psychotherapeutic treatment conditions is contrasted with the work-only control. The only variable that significantly differentiated the four treatments was employment at six months and this difference disappeared by 18 months. A global score attained by combining the nine follow-up behavior areas is presented in Table 13.7. As should be expected, at six months the global scores show no significant differences between treatments in regard to follow-up behavior. Thus, the general ineffectiveness of the four therapy programs when contrasted with the control seems clear even at six months. This lack of difference appears all the more significant when one considers the cost differential. The work-only condition appears to produce about equivalent results to any of the more expensive therapeutic treatments at significantly less cost. The picture becomes more elaborated as we look at the difference between diagnostic groups. Here, highly significant differences obtain on the social change outcome criteria and several other follow-up behavioral outcomes. These differences also obtain when the follow-up measures are combined into a global score as shown in Table 13.7.

Generally it can be said that chronic psychotics show the poorest overall adjustment followed by the neurotics who typically fall somewhere between the short-term and long-term psychotics in follow-up adjustment. The isolation of a major mental health problem in terms of hospital chronicity appears to have been accomplished. The long-term psychotics show a 72% return rate to the hospital within 18 months and are followed by almost 56% of the neurotics, while the short-term psychotics have a much better community adjustment pattern (71% remained out of the hospital).

TABLE 13.7
Chi-square Comparison of Treatments and Diagnoses on Global
Follow-up Scores at Six Months

Between treatments	Between diagnoses	Interaction: treatment X diagnoses
2.15 (3 df)	21.75[a] (2 df)	4.38 (6 df)

[a] Significant at 0.001 level.

From these results, it seemed clear that the concentration of future efforts should be in the direction of providing more adequate services for chronic and neurotic patients who appear to be the major problem from a participant point of view. The low relationships found among the seven clusters shows that follow-up behavioral adjustment in the areas of rehospitalization and employment is relatively unrelated to almost all measures that occurred within the hospital, demographic historical variables, and other follow-up behaviors except for the behaviors in a group psychotherapy situation as revealed in the Finney scale (1954). Finally, six months of follow-up treatment in an institutional setting would seem to yield valid results because of the high correlations found between six and 18 months of follow-up.

These inferences were then used as a basis for establishment of a second experiment. The correlation of the Finney scale indicated that behavior in close interpersonal group settings within the hospital might lead to more adaptive community behavior. Coupled with a knowledge of a number of other small-group experiments that showed group membership helped to maintain the group's members in difficult situations, it seemed important to launch an experiment to discover the effects that group membership might have on adjustment. The direct goal of such an experiment would be to discover whether small problem-solving groups of patients could be formed in hospital settings and, if this could be done, whether such participation would influence follow-up outcome behaviors. After an initial study showed that small groups of chronic patients could perform reasonably well without staff supervision (Lerner & Fairweather, 1963), a small-group treatment program was established and compared with the

TABLE 13.8
Comparison of Treatments on Demographic Characteristics

Variable	Small group	Work only	df[1]	Test of significance
Mean age	37.95	36.51	1 and 187	$F = 1.24$
Race, %:				
White	84	75	1	$X^2 = 2.30$
Other	16	25		
Military service, %:				
Service-connected pension	53	58	1	$X^2 = 0.47$
No service-connected pension	47	42		
Military service, 0–2.9 years	46	41	1	$X^2 = 0.47$
Military service, 3 years and over	54	59		
Neuropsychiatric hospitalization:				
Mean age at first hospitalization	28.97	28.44	1 and 186	$F = 0.16$
Mean number prior hospitalizations	3.03	2.48	1 and 184	$F = 3.81$
Mean weeks prior hospitalizations	149.37	154.05	1 and 187	$F = 0.07$
Family:				
Mean number of children in family	4.27	4.09	1 and 168	$F = 0.12$
Mean ordinal number	2.73	2.61	1 and 167	$F = 0.08$
Parents' marital status, %:				
Married	36	35	1	$X^2 = 0.04$
Other	64	65		
Brought up by, %:				
Parents to age 18	59	50	1	$X^2 = 1.40$
Other	41	50		
Employment:				
Mean number of jobs held	4.24	3.74	1 and 178	$F = 0.76$
Mean social classification of last job[2]	1.97	1.88	1 and 181	$F = 0.17$
Mean monthly salary of last job	270.01	250.82	1 and 176	$F = 0.47$
Mean number of months employment during last 10 years	54.22	49.56	1 and 173	$F = 0.55$
Mean highest grade completed	10.48	10.52	1 and 186	$F = 0.01$
Drinking behavior, %:				
Drinkers (heavy)	32	30	1	$X^2 = 0.10$
Nondrinkers (none or social)	68	70		
Marital status, %:				
Single	39	46		
Divorced or separated	32	29	2	$X^2 = 2.55$
Married or widowed	29	25		

[1] df for F-ratios vary slightly owing to missing data.
[2] According to Coleman's classification (see Chapter 8).

TABLE 13.9
Comparison of Treatment Models and Diagnostic Groups on Several Measures

Area of measurement	Small group vs Work only	Diagnostic groups
Social Change Follow-up Outcome Criteria		
rehospitalization	NS	S(0.001)
employment	S(0.05)	S(0.05)
Other Follow-up Outcome		
friendships	S(0.05)	NS
communication	S(0.05)	NS
appraisal of illness	NS	NS
drinking behavior	NS	S(0.05)
nature of residence	NS	S(0.01)
membership in community groups	NS	NS
involvement in leisure time	NS	NS
Other Areas of Treatment		
Cost		
days in treatment	S(0.05)	S(0.001)
Change during treatment		
social behavior	S(0.001)	NS
interpersonal choice	S(0.05)	NS
satisfaction with program	S(0.05)	NS
attitudes toward mental illness	NS	NS
attitudes toward staff	NS	NS
expectations	S(0.001)	S(0.05)
passes and visitors	NS	NS
medication (drugs)	NS	S(0.01)

TABLE 13.10
Comparison of Treatments and Diagnostic Groups on Number of Days
in Treatment

Source of variation	Mean	Degrees of freedom	F-ratio
Between treatments		1	4.37*
Small-group ward	109.01		
Traditional	149.96		
Between diagnostic groups		3	6.79**
Nonpsychotic	77.85		
Psychotic, 0–2 years	102.05		
Psychotic, 2–4 years	138.60		
Psychotic, over 4 years	174.10		
Interaction: treatments × diagnostic groups		3	1.12
Residual		187	

* Significant at 0.05 level.   ** Significant at 0.001 level.

"work-only" condition. This was again used as the control condition since the experiment just presented found that it was the least costly and yielded very similar results to the more expensive psychotherapeutic treatments.

Table 13.8 shows that the two samples participating in the two experimental programs (small group and work only) were very similar. No background information variables differentiated the two groups so that differences found between treatments can logically be attributed to them. Table 13.9 summarizes the between-treatments and diagnostic group comparisons. Since *all means were in the more adaptive direction for the small-group program*, Table 13.9 shows that post-hospital employment was significantly greater for the participants in the small-group program. However, rehospitalization continued at almost the same rate regardless of treatment. Those who participated in the small-group program were also able to make more friends and to have better communication patterns after leaving the hospital, but they did not show significant differences contrasted with the work-alone control situation on five other follow-up variables (appraisal of illness, drinking behavior, nature of residence, membership in community groups, and involvement in leisure time). The cost was significantly lower for the small-group program as shown by the significant differences in days of treatment presented in Table 13.10. A mean of 109.01 days obtained for the small-group program and 149.96 days for the work-alone control. Table 13.9 also shows that the small-group program affected behaviors and perceptions during treatment. It brought about improved patient social behavior, greater satisfaction with the program, a higher degree of interpersonal choice, and more positive expectations about the future. It did not change attitudes toward mental illness and staff directly and no differences between the number of passes and amount of medication can be attributed to it.

TABLE 13.11
Comparisons of Treatments on Significant Follow-up Items

Area of measurement	Small-group	Work only
	%	%
Employment		
Employed some of the time	54	38
Unemployed	46	62
Friendships		
Alone most of time	35	49
Gets together with friends regularly	65	51
Verbal communications with others		
Never talks	4	9
Rarely talks	18	25
Sometimes talks	28	36
Often talks	50	30

Thus, the small-group program appears to improve employment, friendships, and communications once the people have reached the outside, but it does not reduce recidivism, degree of illness, or improve membership in community groups. The program is accomplished at a considerably lower cost than the control because fewer days are spent in treatment and it creates a social situation for improved interpersonal relationships as shown in social behavior, interpersonal choice, and expectations. Furthermore, six tests of significance out of 16 tests are significant (three at the .05 and three at the .001 level of significance), an unlikely chance occurrence as shown in Figs. 13.3 and 13.4, so that the overall program is relatively successful with regard to these variables. The differences between the two treatment programs on the follow-up areas of measurement that were significant can be seen as percentages in Table 13.11. Figure 13.5 gives an example of the significantly greater participation in group meetings occurring in the small group program contrasted with the work-only control condition while the patients were in the hospital.

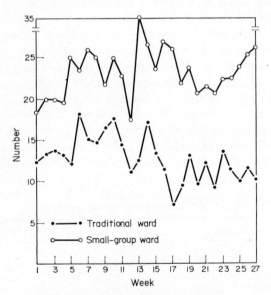

Fig. 13.5. Mean number of patients participating per session for each treatment program

Table 13.12 shows that the diagnostic groups also responded to the treatment programs significantly differently. It shows the same rehospitalization problem encountered in the previous study—chronic psychotics and neurotics are returning at over a 50% rate within 6 months and unemployment is higher with the most chronic groups. Drinking behavior is a significantly greater problem for the neurotics while supervised living is most common among the chronic psychotics. Differences between the diagnostic groups also appeared in expectations (Table 13.9) with the most chronic having the least positive perception of the future. Thus, the diagnostic groups again show the same trend as that observed in the first study. Fifty-eight percent of the most chronic psychotics were back in the hospital during the first 6 months of follow-up, the two-to-four-year psychotics showed a 51% return, the neurotics showed a 56% return. Only 20% of the less-than-two-year psychotics returned. Significant differences between drug usage as shown in Table 13.9 are elaborated in Table 13.13. It shows that during hospital treatment, the three psychotic groups had a significantly higher medication than the neurotics with the two most psychotic groups taking the greatest amount of drugs. Costs were different between the groups, with the more chronic warranting the greatest cost because of their greater number of days of hospitalization and higher medication dosages as shown in Tables 13.10 and 13.13.

A cluster analysis of 120 different measures was presented earlier in Chapter 12 (Table 12.3). It shows that remaining out of the hospital is most highly related to having a socially supportive living situation in the community (.71), community employment (.45), and a short stay in the

TABLE 13.12
Comparisons of Diagnostic Groups on Significant Follow-up Items

Area of measurement	Non-psychotic	Psychotic 0–2 years	Psychotic 2–4 years	Psychotic over 4 years
	%	%	%	%
Rehospitalization				
In hospital some time	56	20	51	58
Remained out of hospital	44	80	49	42
Employment				
Employed some of the time	72	54	33	38
Unemployed	28	46	67	62
Drinking behavior				
Drinks a lot and gets into trouble	22	3	10	4
Drinks a lot but stays out of trouble	11	8	13	4
Drinks once in a while	22	39	49	45
Never drinks	45	50	28	47
Nature of residence				
Living in hospital, dorm, or home care	10	10	26	43
Living in other situations (e.g. small hotel)	32	25	32	19
Living with parents, relatives, or friend	37	47	32	29
Living with wife	21	18	10	9

TABLE 13.13
Comparison of Diagnostic Groups on
Mean Daily Dosage[a]

Comparison	Mean
Between diagnostic groups	
Nonpsychotics	110
Psychotic, 0–2 years	170
Psychotic, 2–4 years	240
Psychotic, over 4 years	220

[a] In approximated milligrams of chlorpromazine
to the nearest 10.

hospital. It is related also to being a more cooperative task group member in the hospital setting. The rest of the variables created an additional seven clusters of social interaction, attitudes toward treatment, involvement in treatment, behavioral nonconformity, social preference, aspirations and status, and level of tranquilizing medication. None of these are highly related to follow-up behavior, which again confirms the findings of the earlier study showing a lack of relationship between within-hospital measures and community measures as well as between perceptions and behaviors. The low relationships were shown earlier in Table 12.4 of Chapter 12. This is especially important since the correlation between social interaction and post-hospital adjustment is .24 despite the Finney scale's cluster loading of .66 found in the follow-up cluster in the earlier study. This throws into doubt the question of a high relationship between social behavior in hospital and its relationship to community adjustment.

What are the permissible *inferences* from this study? One of the two social change outcome criteria (employment) differentiates the treatment groups at the .05 level of significance, with the highest percentage of employment being shown by those who participated in the small-group treatment program. Two of the seven other follow-up behaviors (friendships and communication) also significantly differentiate the two programs in favor of the small-group treatment. Other areas of treatment were also affected. Significant benefit obtained in favor of the small-group program within the hospital in terms of cost, social behavioral change, interpersonal choice, satisfaction with program, and expectations. The cluster analysis for this experiment presented in Table 12.3 shows that only two of these (interpersonal choice and social behavior) are interrelated measures. If we combine them into one global score which is significant, we then find that we have four tests of significance that reach at least the .05 level in other areas of measurement. Thus, there are a total of seven significant tests of significance (follow-up employment, friendships, communication, cost, within-hospital interpersonal choice and social behavior, satisfaction, and expectations). They are relatively independent. Table 13.9 shows that the seven occurred out of 17 computed since social behavior and interpersonal choice were combined into one. Figure 13.3 shows that seven significant tests of significance out of 17 tests would occur less than one time in a thousand (.001) by chance. The inference that the small-group program is a general success is warranted.

The diagnostic groups show significant differences in both the social change outcome criteria (employment and rehospitalization) as shown in Tables 13.9 and 13.12. Since these two criteria are interrelated as shown in the cluster analysis (Table 12.3), an omnibus score combining the two was computed. It yielded a chi square of 13.78 with three degrees of freedom, which is significant beyond the .001 level of significance. When one glances at the percentage of rehospitalized and employed, as shown in Table 13.12, it is clear that the most chronic psychotics and neurotics are making the worst adjustment.

Tables 13.9 and 13.12 show that in the two other follow-up areas—drinking behavior and nature of residence, the diagnostic groups showed significant differences. Since the cluster analysis for this experiment presented in Table 12.3 shows that these outcomes failed to appear in the clusters even though they were included in the analysis, it is obvious that they are relatively independent.

By contrast, the within-hospital measures for diagnostic group comparisons (Table 13.9) shows three tests of significance reaching significance— cost (.001), expectations (.05), and medication (.01).

Thus, seven tests of significance reached the .05 and .001 level of significance out of 17 calculated, since social behavior and interpersonal choice had been combined into one score (Table 13.9). Such results would occur by chance alone only five times in one hundred according to Fig. 13.3, which is clearly an underestimate since two of the seven tests of significance reached the .01 level and one was significant at the .001 level. It appears, therefore, that not only does chronicity affect lowered community adjustment rates, it also is associated with poorer within-hospital adjustment.

Summarily, then, the small-group program in contrast with the work-only control significantly improves the follow-up outcomes in employment, communication, and friendship behaviors but does not significantly reduce rehospitalization. It is significantly quicker and cheaper than the work-alone condition and results in a more adequate overall hospital adjustment. *But the diagnostic group comparisons, with over 50% of the persons returning to the hospital in the nonpsychotic and two most chronic psychotic*

*group categories, suggest that even though a statistical significance exists a
logical social model significance may not.* The logical question is whether or
not an over 50% return rate during six months is an acceptable percent of
return to treatment planners despite the other advantages of the small-group
program. The experimenters found this high return rate unacceptable and
were, in addition, particularly struck with the high correlation as shown in
the cluster analysis of this study (Table 12.3) between recidivism and a
supportive situation in the community which was also related to being
employed. This led the experimenters to raise another research question: If
the small-group hospital program were followed by a supportive community
situation, where employment was available, would the recidivism rate be
reduced? This idea seemed all the more desirable in view of other information gained from relatives who often stated that they would not accept discharged patients in their homes even though the staff and fellow patients
believed they could make an adequate adjustment in the community.

This question led the researchers to design a new experiment where the
small-group program in the hospital was linked with a supportive community living and working situation (lodge). Persons who volunteered to go
to the lodge were assigned by match to a small-group community condition
followed by the community lodge. This total social system was then
contrasted with persons having the small-group experience and going into
traditional community treatment settings—the experimental condition in
the experiment just discussed which had been found to be significantly more
beneficial than the work-only model. Patients participating in the two social
models were matched so that equivalent groups would go through each
program in order that inferences could not be attributed to different
samples but to the two social models. A comparison of the samples'
participants in the lodge and traditional aftercare models is seen in Table
13.14. This table shows both samples are relatively equivalent in demographic
characteristics upon entry into the two social models, since not a single background item significantly differentiates the participants of the two models.

Table 13.15 presents the comparative results of the experiment. It shows
that highly significant differences in rehospitalization and employment occur
from six through 40 months. Eight of those significant differences were at
the .001 level, three at the .01 level, and three at the .05 level. Thus, all tests
of significance for every six-month period between the lodge society and
traditional community programs comparing recidivism and employment
were significantly different. In each case the higher percentage of employed
and the lower recidivism rates were obtained with the lodge society.

These highly significant differences are seen in graphical form in Figs.
11.9 and 11.10 in Chapter 11. Since the total number of days spent in the

TABLE 13.14
Comparison of Lodge and Nonlodge Groups on Demographic Characteristics

Area of measurement	Volunteer lodge group	Volunteer nonlodge group	df	x^2
Median Age	41	43	1	3.50
Race, %:				
White	81	80	1	0.00
Other	19	20		
Military Service, %:				
Service-connected pension	41	54	1	1.93
No service-connected pension	59	46		
Military service, 0–122 weeks	49	49	1	0.00
Military service, 123 weeks and over	51	51		
Military rank, buck private	28	29	1	0.00
Military rank, PFC or higher	72	71		
Neuropsychiatric Hospitalization:				
Median age at first hospitalization	27	29	1	1.11
Median number prior hospitalizations	2	2	1	0.01
Median weeks prior hospitalizations	233	262	1	0.06
Type of Hospital Admission, %:				
Voluntary	44	46	1	0.01
Commitment	54	54		
Parents' Marital Status, %:				
Married and living	12	18	1	0.50
Other	88	82		
Brought up by, %:				
Both parents	42	55	1	1.49
Other	56	54		
Days since Last Contact with Relatives, %:				
0–89 days	64	64	1	0.00
90 days and over	36	36		
Employment:				
Social classification of last job, %:				
Lower middle class and upper lower class	21	29	1	0.95
Lower lower class	79	71		
Median number of jobs held in last 10 years	2	2	1	0.34
Median Highest Grade Completed	11	12	1	0.32
Drinking behavior, %:				
Heavy drinkers	35	26		
Social drinkers	39	48	2	1.52
Nondrinkers	26	26		
Police Arrests, %:				
One or more	59	57	1	0.04
None	41	43		
Marital Status, %:				
Single and never married	64	54	1	1.19
Other	36	46		
Current Monthly Income while Hospitalized, %:				
0–$101	53	47	1	0.44
$102 and over	47	53		

TABLE 13.15
Comparison of Lodge and Traditional After-care Models

Area of measurement	Lodge vs Traditional	Area of measurement	Lodge vs Traditional
Social Change Outcome Criteria		Respondent Evaluations:	
Days in the Community		Association with friends	
6 mo	S(0.001)	6 mo	NS
12 mo	S(0.001)	12 mo	NS
18 mo	S(0.001)	18 mo	NS
24 mo	S(0.001)	24 mo	NS
30 mo	S(0.05)	30 mo	NS
34 mo	S(0.05)	36 mo	NS
40 mo	S(0.05)	40 mo	NS
Employment		Verbal communication	
6 mo	S(0.001)	6 mo	NS
12 mo	S(0.001)	12 mo	NS
18 mo	S(0.001)	18 mo	NS
24 mo	S(0.001)	24 mo	NS
30 mo	S(0.01)	30 mo	NS
34 mo	S(0.01)	34 mo	NS
40 mo	S(0.01)	40 mo	NS
Other Follow-up Items			
Patient Self-evaluation		Appraisal of symptom behavior	
Satisfaction with living conditions		6 mo	NS
6 mo	NS	12 mo	NS
12 mo	NS	18 mo	NS
18 mo	NS	24 mo	NS
24 mo	NS	30 mo	NS
30 mo	NS	34 mo	NS
34 mo	NS	40 mo	NS
40 mo	NS		
		Drinking behavior	
Satisfaction with leisure activity		6 mo	NS
6 mo	NS	12 mo	NS
12 mo	NS	18 mo	NS
18 mo	NS	24 mo	NS
24 mo	NS	30 mo	NS
30 mo	NS	34 mo	NS
34 mo	NS	40 mo	NS
40 mo	NS		
		Activity level	
Satisfaction with community living		6 mo	NS
6 mo	NS	12 mo	NS
12 mo	S(0.05)	18 mo	NS
18 mo	NS	24 mo	NS
24 mo	NS	30 mo	NS
30 mo	NS	34 mo	NS
34 mo	NS	40 mo	NS
40 mo	NS		

TABLE 13.15 *contd.*

Area of measurement	Lodge vs Traditional	Area of measurement	Lodge vs Traditional
Social responsibility		Leisure activity	
6 mo	NS	6 mo	NS
12 mo	NS	12 mo	NS
18 mo	NS	18 mo	NS
24 mo	NS	24 mo	NS
30 mo	NS	30 mo	NS
34 mo	NS	34 mo	NS
40 mo	NS	40 mo	NS

TABLE 13.16
Clustered Measures in the Two Community Situations

Cluster[a]	Lodge	Shared variation %	Cluster[a]	Traditional	Shared variation %
1. Community tenure and employment (10)		21	1. Community tenure and residential status (8)		12
2. Individual satisfaction with hospital and community living (25)		25	2. Community social behavior (19)		38
			3. Individual satisfaction with community living (17)		17
3. Community employment level and residential status (6)		16	4. The older psychiatric patient (2)		5
4. Alcoholic conviviality in the community (10)		16	5. In-hospital attitudes toward ward and community living (8)		11
5. Community social behavior (18)		14	6. Community employment (7)		7
6. Community leisure activity (4)		8	7. Prior military service (2)		5
			8. Service-connected disability income (2)		5

[a] The number in parenthesis after each cluster name represents the number of variables included in that cluster.

hospital were significantly fewer for the lodge society, the difference in cost was significantly lower for each follow-up period as can be seen in summary form in Fig. 11.2 which can be found in Chapter 11. In it the low costs of the lodge are contrasted with the higher costs of other programs in the area. Beyond these comparisons, eventually the lodge became self-supporting.

Table 13.15 also shows that differences between the lodge society and traditional community situations to which mental patients usually go did not produce differences in the ex-patients' satisfaction with their living conditions and their adjudged adjustment by the persons' with whom they lived. Reference to Table 13.15 shows that only one test of significance reaches the .05 level of significance out of 70 calculated for other follow-up

TABLE 13.17
Correlations Between Clustered Measurement Domains

Lodge situation

Clusters	1	2	3	4	5	6
1. Community tenure and employment		-0.05	0.43	-0.06	0.37	0.06
2. Individual satisfaction with hospital and community living	-0.05		-0.15	0.14	0.14	0.22
3. Nonfamily group living situation	0.43	-0.15		0.11	-0.02	-0.26
4. Alcoholic conviviality in the community	-0.06	0.14	0.11		-0.09	-0.01
5. Community social behavior	0.37	0.14	-0.02	-0.09		0.30
6. Community leisure activity	0.06	0.22	-0.26	-0.01	0.30	

Nonlodge situation

Clusters	1	2	3	4	5	6	7	8
1. Community tenure and residential status		0.06	-0.06	-0.12	-0.08	0.29	0.24	0.22
2. Community social behavior	0.06		0.25	-0.18	0.34	0.41	0.00	0.07
3. Individual satisfaction with community living	-0.06	0.25		-0.04	0.40	0.12	-0.08	-0.06
4. The older psychiatric patient	-0.12	-0.18	-0.04		-0.06	-0.09	0.20	-0.22
5. In-hospital attitudes toward ward and community living	-0.08	0.34	0.40	-0.06		0.07	-0.06	-0.07
6. Community employment	0.29	0.41	0.12	-0.09	0.07		0.08	-0.04
7. Prior military service	0.24	0.00	-0.08	0.20	-0.06	0.08		0.17
8. Service-connected disability income	0.22	0.07	-0.06	-0.22	-0.07	-0.04	0.17	

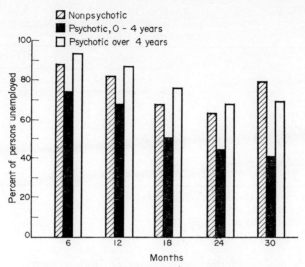

Fig. 13.6. Percent of persons in nonlodge diagnostic groups unemployed for 30 months of
follow-up

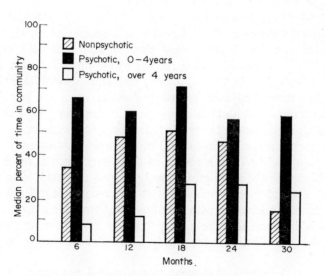

Fig. 13.7 Percent of nonlodge diagnostic groups on
time in the community for 30 months of follow-up

TABLE 13.18
Diagnostic Group Comparisons for Lodge and Nonlodge Models on Time
in Community and Employment[a]

Source of variation	Follow-up time periods (months)				
	6	12	18	24	30
Traditional Model					
Social Change Outcome Criteria:					
Cumulative days in community	18.70[d]	12.08[c]	10.50[c]	4.93	4.38
Full-time employment	14.53[d]	7.30	6.40[b]	3.17	3.38
Lodge Model					
Cumulative days in community	2.96	2.07	0.76	0.62	1.04
Full-time employment	2.98	0.62	1.16	0.64	0.60

a — Table contains chi-square values with 2 df.
b — Significant at .05 level
c — Significant at .01 level
d — Significant at .001 level

measures. A review of the mean scores of both groups for these other follow-up items shows that significant differences did not obtain *because* all scores for both models were so very high. Simply being out of the hospital— regardless of social model—was apparently enough to cause high satisfaction scores, etc.

When the cluster analyses for each of the two social models were completed (their summaries are in Table 13.16), it was found that high correlations existed among the different time measures of 12, 18, 24, 30, 34, and 40 months, although the several clusters were relatively independent (Table 13.17). If we combine time periods (6 months, 12 months, etc.) into one so that both days-in-the-community and employment have one score, there are then three significant tests of significance when cost is included at a .001 level of significance. Thus significance is reached on all three social change outcome measures. Using Fig. 13.4 for a very conservative approximation, it is clear that such results will occur rarely by chance (.001).

It seems quite clear from a review of these experimental results that the lodge coupled with the small-group ward program did result in less frequent hospitalization and more employment at lower costs. It did not, however, result in greater satisfaction with post-hospital living nor more communication, friendships, and the like simply because most persons regardless of social model participation were highly satisfied with simply being out of the hospital.

The diagnostic groups that went to traditional programs tell the same story as shown before. On the social change outcome criteria, including days in the community and full-time employment, significant differences obtained for 6, 12 and 18 months as shown in Table 13.18. The chronic psychotics make a significantly poorer adjustment as shown in Figs. 13.6 and 13.7. On the other hand, no differences between the diagnostic groups on the social change outcome criteria of time in the community and employment appear in the lodge society as also shown in Table 13.18. Difference on other follow-up items of satisfaction were generally not significant for diagnostic groups in either of the two models due to the improved satisfaction for all persons out of the hospital as mentioned earlier.

What are the *permissible inferences* from the aforementioned research information about the lodge society? It seems relatively clear that the problems of recidivism and unemployment are greatly reduced by use of the lodge social model contrasted with traditional community mental health programs. Furthermore, differences between diagnostic groups that are prevalent in the control condition in the lodge study, and a hallmark of previous studies (chronic psychotic patients adjust less well), is markedly reduced by the lodge society. It has disappeared completely in employment and recidivism. The cost of the lodge society was much lower than contrasting services and eventually persons in the lodge society become self-supporting. Again, the relative independence of outcome measures re-emphasizes the need to designate some outcomes as social change outcome criteria and to continue to measure several dimensions simultaneously.

Two replicates of the lodge, one in a rural and one in an urban area, were soon established and their results were very similar to those found in the prototype lodge. A national dissemination experiment was then carried out as described in Chapter 2. What seems clear from these experiments, when all results are reviewed simultaneously, is that a beneficial social model for mental patients who have been hospitalized for more than two years has been discovered, validated, and implanted.

This section of the chapter has dealt with the problem of permissible inferences from the information gained in social experiments. As the reader can clearly see, it is a difficult procedure requiring a logical integration of a great deal of material. But it is this integration of information that permits dissemination action to be taken and hypotheses to be made for subsequent studies so that more beneficial models can be created and evaluated.

PUBLICATION

After inferences have been made from a synthesis of all the research data, it is necessary to publish the results of the study. It is the obligation of the research team to report in detail all aspects of the experiment. Members of the research team should write about those aspects of the experiment that are most familiar to them. It is the research team leader's responsibility to carry out the agreements about publication made at the outset of the experiment and to be certain that they are followed as closely as possible. Although the researchers should write about those aspects of the experiment with which they have been most directly concerned, it should usually be the team leader's responsibility to edit all reports in order to reduce repetition and to make the final presentation as simple and understandable as possible. Here the leader must attempt to preserve each individual writer's style, at the same time integrating the separate writings into a meaningful whole.

It is possible that the writing phase of the project may result in some tension among research team members. This can occur because professional prestige is frequently accorded those who complete scientific writing. If any conflict does arise among members of the team, it is likely to take the form of some authors perceiving others as being in a more favourable position than they. Some authors may perceive their writings as unalterable. Accordingly, they may be unwilling to make changes, even when their writing appears poor or does not fit into the remainder of the presentation. For this reason, agreements are made about authorship prior to the experiment (as mentioned in Chapter 6). Therefore, the editor's role and those of the various authors should be clearly set forth and agreed upon before the experiment is carried out. If possible, such contracts should be in writing and signed by the various members of the research team so that they can be referred to at a later date if needed. When possible, these agreements should include topical area of writing, location of authors' names, editorial prerogatives, and the like.

In all aspects of publication, it is the editor's responsibility to try to meet each author's needs to the extent possible in such team endeavors. The editor must, however, have the final voice in determining the form of the manuscript because in such a team effort one uncooperative author can write a chapter or section so out of harmony in style and content with the remainder of the publication that it can seriously detract from the publication of an important longitudinal research. While the editor (who is usually the research team leader) must attempt to preserve each individual's style and assigned area of writing, it is also necessary for each writer to be aware of the total document and, accordingly, to write with the publication's overall organization in mind.

The results of social innovative experiments typically should be presented in one publication rather than in a series of shorter articles. This is necessary because interested readers should be able to explore all facets of the experiment in one manuscript. It is also important that initial drafts of the manuscript be read by individuals who are capable of editing them from their points of view. This procedure helps clarify communication by checking with others the degree to which the authors are clearly presenting the research program. However, the recommendations that come from others should be accepted or rejected by the editor or author solely on their merits in terms of increasing the communication of the experimental findings.

Such experiments can usually be published in book form. It is important for the researcher to explore all avenues of book publication and to select a publisher who can best present the publication to the audience that the experimenters wish to reach. It is a primary responsibility of the social innovative experimentalists to publish so that the results are available to all interested persons. The final document should present a clear description of the sample, with the participants described in terms of their defining characteristics; a clear and lucid description of the models including all roles; a description of the internal processes and the external processes; comparisons of the models on the social change and other outcome criteria; a presentation of relationship and process analyses; and, finally, a description of all phases of the research.

It is also important, particularly when the populations are marginal people (such as the mentally ill and criminals), that the participants' names be deleted from the manuscript. Anonymity should be a feature of any research. This is of special importance with marginal group members, many of whom might be personally embarrassed by revelation of their names, despite the fact that they are willing participants in created social models. This procedure merely emphasizes respect for the wishes of the participants.

THE NEXT EXPERIMENT

During the preparation of the manuscript and while synthesizing the results of the experiment, the researchers may begin to plan their next experiment. Since social innovative experiments are mainly empirical in nature, such researches will usually proceed in step-wise fashion—each being built upon the results of the immediately preceding one. The first studies are, of course, more broadly conceived than those that occur later. For example, the lodge project established that recidivism rates may be reduced and employment increased when a particular type of community living-working situation is provided for previously hospitalized mental patients. The next experiment might create different community models for comparative purposes, because the value of at least one model located in the community for these chronically hospitalized participants has already been experimentally established and replicated numerous times with similar beneficial results. Succeeding experiments with other models might well be organized around different social tasks and group compositions.

The same is true of the national dissemination experiment (Fairweather Sanders, & Tornatzky, 1974). Future experiments concerned with establishing new conditions for dissemination generated from the initial experiment need to be done. It is inherent in the experimental process to proceed from gross to finer comparisons. Each succeeding experiment thus contributes new and more refined knowledge to the solution of the social problem under consideration. As the final step, the experimental processes involved in the planning of a new experiment can now begin. The most beneficial conditions in the preceding experiment can now become defined as the control conditions for a new experiment and the methods for experimental social innovation will be started in a new cycle from planning of new social models through their implementation.

CHAPTER 14

An Institutional Context for Research and Training: The Center for Experimental Social Innovation

PROBLEM OF INSTITUTIONALIZING EXPERIMENTAL SOCIAL INNOVATION

Let us consider the methods for social problem solving that we have presented in this book and the demands that it engenders upon the surrounding society. First of all, we have argued for the utilization of an actual field experimental research approach. This type of research necessitates the establishment and monitoring of two or more experimental social models designed to solve a particular social problem. Another requirement of the approach is that the experimental comparison must be longitudinal; thus, the experimental models must be continued unmolested over a long period of time. A third requirement of the methodology is that the experimenters have complete access to each of the models for outcome and process measurement. The final, perhaps most important, aspect of this approach is that by a succession of comparative evaluations of innovated models, a model will be found that will be adjudged most effective on the basis of empirical comparative data in solving the selected social problem. This model should replace the current operational practice. The logical outcome, therefore, of a "successful" social model experiment is another major experimental effort aimed at disseminating the new program found to be beneficial. Considered together, these bare essentials of experimental problem solving demand a great deal of control over programs, a long-term commitment, a plethora of administrative agreements, and a future commitment to implement and disseminate those solutions found to be beneficial.

It is assumed that such research must be located in some organizational unit or center. The question that is being addressed in this section is where (organizationally speaking) could a proposed center for research be located? In other words, what would be the best way to maximize the resources necessary for such problem-solving research? What combination of talent, money, commitment, and control would be best for such work? We are considering anew, and at a higher level, the problem of *linkages* that was dealt with briefly in Chapter 6. In the former chapter we considered the problem from the experimenters' point of view: obtaining administrative agreements for a single research. In this chapter we will present a more general utopian plan. What we will do is pose a question and give our answers. The question is: Given no bars to funding and other necessary ingredients, what would be the ideal type of administrative and fiscal arrangements possible in order to maximize the problem-solving capacity of a center for experimental social innovation? Such an ideal center would have seven principal features: (1) *democratic organization*, (2) *freedom of inquiry*, (3) *longevity*, (4) *operational control of social models*, (5) *dissemination ability*, (6) *training opportunities*, and (7) *multidisciplinary orientation*.

Democratic Organization

Throughout this book, the authors have expressed the point of view that no social experiments are permissible that are not humane and democratic. The humanitarian aspect of the research is a rather individualistic one and can be achieved by the researchers simply refusing to become engaged in the creation, evaluation, or dissemination of any social model that may not be perceived as beneficial to the problem population. The democratic aspect of this experimental approach requires that the researchers, societal administrators, and the problem population be cooperatively involved in planning and carrying out social innovative experiments. The center, therefore, would provide the meeting ground for discussion and planning among these three groups. It would be essential to its basic social problem-solving orientation that all three groups have adequate representation in the research planning of the center. Not only would such an approach enhance the problem-solving ability of such a center, it should prevent the sterile and dictatorial norms that must inevitably develop when an "elite" group of any type (scientists included) alone plan the social experiments for the society. Such a singleminded and authoritarian approach would undoubtedly fail quickly in a society that is committed to the democratic process.

Freedom of Inquiry

Perhaps the most necessary aspect, and one of the most difficult to define, would be a robust freedom of inquiry in the hypothetical center. Historically, the best research has been that which is unencumbered by political considerations and administrative interference. This has been one of the difficulties in research units that are "captive" of their respective service agencies. What this means in operational terms is that the center would not approach any existing social programs as sacrosanct and would need to have the mandate in power and resources to implement any type of new experimental model the three groups mentioned above had agreed upon as desirable. Thus, a given research would not be bound by the prevailing norms of the agency in which it is done.

Longevity

As freedom of inquiry operates, there obviously needs to be some guarantees of longevity for the center. It is clear that the operation of an active experimental social innovation (ESI) center would engender considerable controversy and opposition, particularly from agencies whose practices were questioned by the experiments being done. What would be needed is long-term funding so that the institute's survival would not be continuously threatened by dissident groups whose practices might be found not to be beneficial by experimental inquiry. In addition to long-term funding, bipartisan political rapport should be established by the center not becoming the spokesman of any particular political or ideological viewpoint. It should be perceived and receive its support solely on the basis of its objective evaluative scientific endeavors.

Operational Control of Social Models

As has been mentioned throughout this book, it is essential that experimental social innovation be accomplished in a way in which the research team has control over the experimental social models involved. To accomplish this, the research unit cannot be too separated administratively from the program units which it is evaluating. This has been one of the consistent difficulties of many program analyses and evaluation units. Our ESI center would have direct access to the operation of a limited and agreed-upon number of service programs.

Dissemination Ability

As has been outlined in Chapter 3, this is probably the single most neglected area of most social researchers. It is our contention that a good portion of this neglect results from the fact that there is no institutionalization of dissemination activity. Whenever a new experimental program is found to be effective, subsequent dissemination is essentially a haphazard process. In our proposed ESI center this would be changed considerably. Any experimental social model found to be beneficial would immediately be moved into an experimental dissemination effort. Considerable resources and staffing would need to be available for dissemination experiments of the appropriate scope and magnitude.

Training Opportunities

It has been our experience over the past several years that a new generation of socially conscious experimenters has yet to arrive. At the present time there are only a handful of graduate training programs in this country which are fully committed and involved in training field experimental researchers. The output of these programs is negligible. Thus, any experimental social innovation center that was established should have a training component in order to add to its own staffing needs and to increase the net supply of individuals trained in this methodology.

Multidisciplinary Orientation

Such an experimental social innovation center must be able to bring its methodology to bear on a number of different social problems. In this sense it cannot be bound to any particular discipline or training background, nor to any particular programmatic focus. Historically, the attempt to address social problems through categorical aid and organizational units has been a failure. Most problems do not simply come under the rubric of a single discipline or organization. Nor are most problems so simple that they can be classified as psychological, political, and so on. Usually they cut across disciplines. Those in the center must be able to employ experimentation across such rigidly defined categories as social welfare, corrections, mental health, and so on.

LOCATION OF AN ESI CENTER

As we see it, there are four potential locations for the proposed experimental social innovation unit. They are: (1) the university, (2) private industry, (3) government, and (4) a location between all three.

The University

In many ways this would seem to be the ideal location for such a research unit. The university has a long history of involvement and commitment to scientific inquiry and research. Given the uncertain nature of any public funding, the contemporary public university has established itself as a fairly independent unit. For example, the utilization of independent boards of trustees that are marginally subservient to political pressures has contributed to the longevity of the university and its various subunits—one of which could be an ESI unit. In addition, the institution of faculty tenure would also afford some protection for ESI center staff and contribute to the resolution of the longevity issue. Another advantage of locating in a university setting would be the clear opportunities for establishing the necessary training programs. Only the university as an agent of the society has a clear mandate and the legitimacy to offer higher educational training of the sort needed for complex research efforts. Establishment of graduate training programs focused on experimental social innovation would be clearly desirable.

However, there are many disadvantages to a university setting. One is the simple fact that historically universities rarely have been willing to involve themselves in community activities. There is a long history of controversy over the appropriate role of "applied" research in the usual academic context. It is presently unresolved and it is not likely to be fully resolved for some time if, indeed, it ever is. Coupled with this is the pervasive norm of disciplinary chauvinism within a university setting. Typically, departments and academic units stake out areas of knowledge and establish inviolate fiefdoms. There is often a very limited degree of interaction among academic units within the university. All this, of course, would be to the detriment of multidisciplinary, problem-focused research. Accordingly, a center would have to be established independent of the various departments so that it would not become embroiled in interdepartmental conflict while at the same time interacting with their personnel for specific disciplinary expertise.

But the *principal* difficulty with the university as a setting for problem-solving experimentation is its impotence in respect to control of operational programs. Since it is totally separated from any actual service programs in the community, it can only gain control by "buying its way in." Thus, in order to establish alternative social models, a resource unit located at the university would have to obtain external funding to cover both research *and* service activities. While this is possible in some situations, it is extremely difficult in most university settings. Often research and contract money is funneled through state or local service agencies and it is virtually impossible for researchers to obtain access to these monies while operating from a university setting. For example, it would be extremely difficult to do experimental research on prison systems unless one had direct access to an existing correctional department. It would be unlikely that a funding agency would fund a university-based researcher to establish temporarily a prison for research purposes. This problem of lack of operational control of social agencies is also related to real difficulties in fielding dissemination experiments. Typically, the university does not have access to or legitimacy in agencies that can disseminate new social programs. The university would be perceived as an outsider and resultant dissemination would suffer. Historically, the only exception to this general rule has been the long-term role of the state university in agricultural extension activities. Here the university has operated as a dissemination unit for many decades and has exerted a significant impact on practice in this area. However, it should be pointed out that the extension model has necessitated the establishment of a wide-range dissemination apparatus and the painstaking gaining of credibility among potential users of innovation information. A similar process would be required if that model were to be applied to social innovation activities.

Private Industry

A second potential location for an ESI center would be in the private sector of the economy. In fact, since the war on poverty began, we have witnessed the establishment of several hundred private consulting and research organizations. All of these in a sense have set themselves up to address social problems. Needless to say, the fallout from these organizations has been less than encouraging. These private research units have had little influence on the course of social innovation in this country primarily because they usually become captives of the funding organizations they depend on and consequently they often become identified with governmental units such as the defense department and others.

Typically, the vehicle which is used to involve such organizations is the *contracting* mechanism. Thus, private research units contract to perform a certain service, evaluate a program, or develop a new social product. While there are many obvious advantages from a research management point of view to this type of an arrangement, there are several disadvantages. The foremost is the agency subservience mentioned above. Since the life blood of the unit is "soft money," freedom of inquiry is considerably compromised. To the extent that the unit must show a profit in order to survive, it will typically propose researches that are palatable for funding agencies. Often these are of negligible impact and imagination. It is much easier to fund safe projects that promote agency policy rather than innovative ones that question it. The development over the past decade of hundreds of products for primary and secondary education, most of undemonstrated utility, is an example of such a practice. Similarly, the police hardware explosion fostered by extensive funds available from the Law Enforcement Assistance Administration has had less than maximally desirable impact on the social problems relative to criminality.

It is obvious that longevity is jeopardized by such a process. The private research unit essentially lives from contract to contract. It is constantly at the whim of the funding priorities at the federal, state, and local level and social practices of agencies. Coupled with this is the difficulty that private research units have in establishing operational control of social programs in the context of an experiment. Although operational control of social programs could clearly be specified via the contracting mechanism, they typically are not. This is for the simple reason that such specifications would often make a proposal less palatable to a funding agency. Occasionally, multiple contracts are let out on a single project which complicates the program control. This has been researched in some detail in the case of the Head Start evaluation.

In turn, dissemination experiments of a private research unit are compromised by what is salable in the contracting and grant market. Obviously a fairly forceful and moderately disruptive dissemination activity would be resisted by those in positions of power who grant money. Finally, of course, the private research unit has extreme difficulty in fostering any type of a training operation. It often does not have ready access to the intellectual resources of the university, nor does it have legitimation in developing formalized training programs recognized outside its own bailiwick.

Government

There are many obvious advantages for establishing an experimental research unit in the context of government. More than any other combination discussed thus far, government provides the opportunity for the creation and *clear control of experimental social models* in the context of a research program. Many good program evaluation researches were those accomplished "in-house" by operational agencies. Another manifestation of this type of "in-house" activity is the increasing utilization of legislative program evaluation analysis units. Finally, over the past several years we have seen continuing growth of staff capability at the executive level of government. The growth of PBBS systems of fiscal allocation in the past years is a testimonial to this trend.

There are several issues that can be raised, however, about the inclusion of the establishment of research units that are subservient to different governmental groups. One of the principal issues involves the freedom of inquiry. Most "in-house" government research units have limited if any freedom in selecting researches that need to be done. There is very little opportunity to establish innovative types of experimental models as required by the ESI methodology. Another issue concerns longevity. Although clearly there is opportunity for "hard" money support of a research unit in the context of government, and the additional security afforded by the Civil Service system, there is always the problem of being part of a political football game and having one's funding cut summarily. Part of this problem might be resolved by trying to obtain bipartisan support from different political and ideological factions.

Another issue concerns both the operational control of agencies and their dissemination capability. Depending upon where in government an ESI center might be located, either or both of these functions might suffer. For example, while an "in-house" research unit that is part of a state agency (such as a state department of mental health) could have considerable power in controlling various experimental models, there might be considerable difficulty in dissemination and implementation activities. To the extent that results were found which would be embarrassing to existing practice, these results might be buried in file cabinets selected for this purpose and the research unit would be prevented from implementing its new beneficial social model throughout the state system. This is a common occurrence in research units that are totally subservient to an operational agency. It also might be pointed out that if a research unit were located within a state agency, this might mean that research activity would be fragmented among the different agencies, with the necessity for a different research unit within each state department. From the standpoint of a multi-disciplinary problem-focused orientation, such an approach is extremely undesirable.

In contrast, if a research unit were an arm of the legislative branch of government, it might have the real difficulty of gaining operational control over experimental social models that would have to be created and activated. Presently, legislative analysts have some power to get access to materials and records, but their ability in gaining temporary *control over programs* is extremely limited. In turn, dissemination capability would be somewhat hampered in a research unit totally under the purview of the legislative branch. While on the one hand it could clearly provide funding for dissemination activity through appropriations, such activity might be resisted by executive operational units.

Finally, of course, we come to locating a research unit in the context of the executive office. This might, for example, be within the confines of the office of the governor. Some of the advantages are obvious. It would clearly be possible to establish an ESI center which would have access to, and potential control of, social models in any operational unit. However, there would be some problems with longevity. To the extent that ESI unit becomes perceived as the arm of a partisan administration, its longevity is contingent upon the political survival of that administration. Thus, for example, the war on poverty was perceived as the Johnson program and was only partially continued in subsequent administrations. Freedom of inquiry might also be somewhat limited because all researchable questions would need to be cleared by prior administrative authority. If there were no research options for the ESI center that were politically supported, its mission would be somewhat jeopardized.

Finally, it should be clear that locating the research center in any context of government would eliminate training opportunities of a professional nature. Training would consist exclusively of staff development activities and so on. With complete isolation from the university degree-granting apparatus, it would be difficult to continue to train a new generation of social experimenters.

The "In-between" Solution

Two of the three aforementioned alternatives—with the exception of the private sector—seem to have both positive and negative aspects. It appears, however, that the ideal location for an experimental social unit would be in organizational space that *lies between and overlaps various aspects of government and the university. The best organizational form seems to be one that involves funding and legitimacy by the executive, legislative, and operational units of government and of the university.*

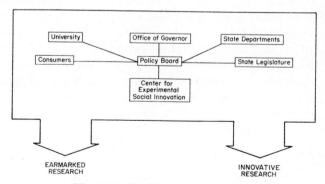

Fig. 14.1. The in-between solution

In Fig. 14.1 we have outlined the structure of one type of center that would be considered. The model that we present here would be particularly appropriate for operation at the state level. A similar structure might be considered for the federal or county level. As can be seen, we have included a *Policy Board* which would have representatives from the governor's office, the state legislature, involved state departments, the university, and representatives of various citizens' or consumer groups in order to articulate the "users'" point of view. Correspondingly, it is expected that *financial support* for the center would come from all these units (with the exception of the consumers). The logic for such a funding vehicle is to insure some degree of bipartisan and cross-institutional support so that the unit has legitimacy. In turn, it is expected that funding from each of these participating institutions would be of a long-term nature in order to give the unit some type of longitudinal security.

The question might be raised about how freedom of inquiry could be maintained in such a setting. One of the vehicles that might be used to accomplish this goal would be to divide research done by the center into *contracted research* and *innovative research.*

Contracted research would be done at the behest of participating government agencies. For example, the legislature might want to compare two different types of welfare systems. In essence, the center would contract with the legislature to form this type of experimental analysis. Additionally, a department of mental health might wish to have the unit compare experimentally a number of alternative post-hospital treatment programs. This, too, could be accomplished. In this sense the ESI unit might be equivalent to a normal type of research unit in the private sector. However, freedom of inquiry might be maintained through a simple vehicle. Thus, contracted research would be charged a certain percentage of cost overhead. This *cost overhead* money could then be used by the center to field *innovative research*, or research which is not in response to a specific request by a governmental agency. Clearly, such a funding scheme would have to be established in enabling legislation for the center.

If one looks at the organizational diagram shown in Fig. 14.2, how operational control of experimental subsystems could be maintained can readily be grasped. As can be seen, the center is organized into functional units corresponding to social problem areas *and* not coincidentally roughly corresponding to the functional organization of state government. Each one of these functional subcomponents would be headed by an assistant director of the center who would in turn have administrative status within the affected state departments. Thus, for example, the assistant director of the correctional research area would also be an *Assistant Director of Programs* within the agency, and possibly within a Department of Social Services, and so on. This would hopefully enable and legitimate operational control of experimental social models and a fairly comprehensive dissemination plan.

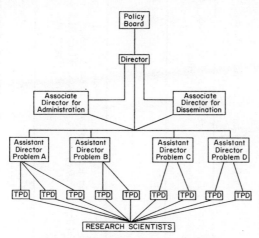

Fig. 14.2. Organizational diagram

Such a center should be established so that the director and several staff members would have faculty status within the university. If research center members were granted tenure, it would assist in longevity of the center and enable the creation and administration of a training program. Thus, center staff could teach small seminars for individuals in graduate and postgraduate training, and also make use of the university for more formalized classroom training for students, use of computer facilities, and the like. There are other advantages that a university affiliation would permit. To the extent that the center would be exclusively affiliated with state level agencies, it would be prevented from embarking on national level dissemination activities. Affiliation with a university could correct this limitation by supporting the obtaining of extramural grants and contracts in order to create a national dissemination effort.

The Policy Board shown in Fig. 14.1 would essentially have two purposes: (1) reviewing research and (2) the more informal objective of providing legitimacy and bipartisan support. Such a unit might operate in the following manner. At the regular meeting time of the board, impending research proposals would be reviewed. These proposals would be a combination of contracted and innovative research that would need to be approved by the board at these meetings. In order to insure that there will be no

CHARACTERISTICS

LOCATION	Freedom of inquiry	Longevity	Operational control of subsystems	Dissemination ability	Multidisciplinary orientation	Training opportunity
University	Excellent	Good	Poor, no direct access to programs	Poor to Fair no access again	Fair, disciplinary chauvinism	Excellent
Private industry	Poor to Fair, necessary to maintain profits	Poor to Fair	Poor, contracting mechanism insufficient for control	Fair	Good	Poor
Government	Varies, poor if research is "captive"	Excellent under civil service	Excellent, if located in operational dept, only Fair from legislature	Good, if located in dept, Poor to Fair elsewhere	Poor, if located in single dept, Good, if located in legislature	Poor
"In-between"	Good to Excellent	Good to Excellent	Good to Excellent	Good to Excellent	Good to Excellent	Good to Excellent

Fig. 14.3. Comparison of function of ESI center locations

frivolous or excessive rejection of researches, a voting procedure might be arranged so that it would be difficult to veto a research proposal. For example, a rule might be established that a *two-thirds* majority of board members would be needed in order to reject a proposal. Using such a procedure, a workable balance of power might be established between the research unit and each of the involved units of government.

Thus far we have discussed the external relationships in organizational form of the proposed experimental research unit. In order to get a better appreciation of the advantages and disadvantages of the various inter-organizational formats, the reader is directed to Fig. 14.3, in which the various alternatives are presented and their advantages and shortcomings are set forth. The intent has been to convey the delicate and fragile nature of the administrative arrangements necessary to establish a fully functioning experimental research unit. In subsequent sections we will deal with the issues of internal staffing and structure of the research unit.

INTERNAL ORGANIZATION AND STAFFING OF THE RESEARCH CENTER

The internal organization of the center would be designed to place two conflicting tendencies in equilibrium. One is the necessity to maintain a *task-oriented* high level of productivity, and the second concern is to provide an atmosphere for *creative autonomy*. When one looks around at various research units, institutes, or academic departments, one typically finds that one of these two orientations is primary. Either the unit is structured in a hierarchical bureaucratic manner with fairly rigid task and disciplinary specialization or the unit is organized along the lines of the individual investigators. The first alternative sacrifices scientific creativity for productivity; the second model sacrifices project-oriented productivity for individual creativity.

One organizational solution to this dilemma is to combine both features within the same organizational unit. As we have discussed briefly and presented in Fig. 14.2, it is assumed that the research unit will be divided into several broad problem areas each headed by an assistant director. In this organizational form, the assistant directors, assisted by a small professional staff assigned directly to them, would have the responsibility to develop both contracted and innovative research thrusts in their general area of interest. The vehicle through which the actual research could be accomplished would be the *Project Team*. Thus, below the organizational level of assistant director would be a *large cadre of research scientists* who would not be assigned to any particular social problem area. These research scientists would provide a pool of research expertise which would be "recruited" by each of the center assistant directors to work on a given project. For example, if an assistant director in the area of mental health wanted to develop a research project in the area of residential treatment for childhood schizophrenia, he would let it be known that such a research project is in the planning stage and would develop a small group of volunteer research scientists interested in the area.

After the assistant director had developed an appropriate research team and designated a *Team Project Director* (TPD), the project team would then proceed on a time-limited plan of research. Members would be obligated to commit themselves to the project for an agreed-upon time period, and a clear designation of role responsibilities and duties would be established at the outset. Agreements about subsequent publication and involvement in dissemination would be completed. From the beginning until the end of the project, the project team would operate as a semi-autonomous research unit with only a moderate degree of monitoring by the assistant director who established its existence at the outset. It might also be pointed out that research scientists could conceivably be members of more than one project team. Thus, an individual might be a Team Project Director on a research in the area of youth employment, but might also be involved in a less extensive manner on project dealing with family planning. The intent here is, of course, to maximize the degree of cross-fertilization of ideas and disciplines throughout the entire center. Thus, at the research scientists level, there would be multiple involvements in researches and limited confinement to a single social problem area.

Considering the organizational diagram presented in Fig. 14.2 once again, we might now elaborate the role of the center director and his or her staff. Actually it is assumed that the role of this director will be in many ways analogous to those of his assistant directors. The director-assistant director relationship is one in which the director would be trying to encourage research in broad research areas. Thus, the center director might be involved with one or two assistant directors in encouraging specific researches in several areas. Attached to the director's office, there would be an associate director for administration. This person would not be involved in scientific matters to any significant degree but would control such auxiliary staff functions as accounting, legal aid, purchasing, and supervision of the clerical staff. The director's office would essentially service the entire organization with administrative-bureaucratic necessities.

One additional feature which we have not discussed up until now is the *Associate Director for Dissemination*, included in Fig. 14.2. As has been discussed in Chapter 3, the role of dissemination is crucial to the whole experimental social innovation process. In turn, it has been our experience that most experimentalists often neglect this highly important aspect of field research. In order to insure that this function is performed, the associate director for research dissemination has been added to the organization. He or she would have a small staff of researchers who are specialists in dissemination research and practice. They would perform two functions for the research unit. On the one hand they would provide expertise and consultation to those project teams who wanted to actually perform their own dissemination research. Related to this role would be the role as overall dissemination clearing house coordinator for the total research unit. Thus, this office would engage in a continuous search process for experimentally valid programs suitable for dissemination. Finally, it would be assumed that the office of dissemination would be involved in a number of different dissemination researches in its own right. These would include dissemination activities not done by individual project teams and other more theoretical issues that could be addressed through innovative research funds. In the organizational format shown in Fig. 14.2, this unit has been established as *superordinate* to the assistant directors of individual social program areas, since it is assumed that dissemination activities will often overlap many social problem areas. It was further assumed that it would be desirable to make the assistant director subordinate to the dissemination activity.

Some comments on other support personnel for the center are relevant at this point. In the section above, some of the support staff relevant to the administration of the center was discussed. It should be pointed out that there are other support staff of a more technical-scientific nature that would be appropriate. For example, it would be quite desirable to have at least one full-time staff person who is a specialist in statistical analyses and computer programming. Similarly, it would be desirable to have specialists in media development and communications. It is assumed that all of the professional staff positions would be established on a career basis because of the length of time required for longitudinal studies and because of the gradual accumulation of knowledge by experimentalists. The longitudinal nature of appointments to the center would be necessary because it may require several years of research before an experimentalist is sufficiently familiar with a particular social problem for him or her to create a meaningful social model as an alternative solution to the problem. Another type of staff position that might be desirable for the center is that of visiting professional persons. The positions might be designated as something akin to a *visiting scholar*. Such persons might be professors on sabbatical leave from a university, staff persons from government agencies or private foundations, legislators, or interested others. The length and the intensity of involvement of these people would need to be adjusted to their needs and interests. The inclusion of such staff positions, however, would be beneficial both for the cross-fertilization of ideas it would provide and for the legitimacy that academic communities across the nation would give to the center.

THE SPECIAL PROBLEM OF TRAINING

As has been implicitly or explicity stated throughout the discussion, it is assumed that many staff members, especially the director, will have training in experimental social innovative skills. Since there are so few people in the nation who have had experience in conducting experiments in field settings, the likelihood of staffing the center completely with such experienced people will be extremely small. As a result, the center should have a heavy involvement in training activities. These training activities should be twofold: the post-doctoral, in-service training of professional staff and the PhD-level training of students. Although these two levels of training would attract persons with educational sophistication, there are several common features of value and skill acquisition that both need to master. To provide trainees with such skills, the four central features of training would be: (1) its multidisciplinary nature, (2) its humanitarian values and democratic processes, (3) its methodological focus, and (4) its action orientation.

Multidisciplinary Training

It is assumed that problem-solving experimentalists cannot confine their interests to a single social problem or disciplinary focus and be totally effective. As has been discussed previously by Fairweather (1967), the nature of marginal man (and social problems) is such that no single disciplinary orientation is sufficient. Training in becoming a social innovative experimentalist must then involve the creation of a multidisciplinary approach to human problems. Thus, an individual must gain considerable awareness of a wide variety of social sciences and, to some degree, natural science disciplines. The typical university PhD program is deficient in such a broad-based level of content acquisition, since most are based exclusively in a single academic department. Thus, as part of both the pre- and post-doctoral level of training within the institute some type of pro-seminar dealing with a rapprochement among the appropriate disciplines, or its equivalent, would be a necessary feature of the curriculum. Although this fairly straightforward acquisition of content knowledge seems simple enough, the end goal would be far broader: to create a fairly eclectic type of "knowledge user." The goal of creating multidisciplinary thinking is not to reinforce dilettantism, but rather it is to insure that the functioning experimental social innovator knows where to get relevant background scientific information relative to any particular social problem.

Human Values and Democratic Processes

Although a complete multidisciplinary training would involve an understanding of different philosophies and ethics, this is so central to value-centered research that it is treated here as a separate area of training. It should also be clear by now that an essential ingredient of any successful training program for a new generation of socially conscious scientists will have to involve the continuous appraisal of humanitarian values in a democratic context. To accomplish this, a necessary ingredient of training procedures will be continuing seminars and discussions about ethical and moral values—their roots and changing nature. In addition, continuous discussions and field experiences with persons suffering from the different social problems—racism, aging, mental illness, and so on—would contribute to the scientists' understanding of the actual social conditions and feelings of those who are daily suffering from these difficulties. In this way it would be hoped that each social innovative scientist would gain an interest and dedication to eliminating unjust human suffering and would be an advocate for improving the human condition through his or her research. This essential information would clearly point out to the concerned researchers the injustices in social stratification and lack of participation so that they would further become advocates of participative democratic processes.

Methodology

It should be clear from reading this book that a strong component of experimental social innovation practice involves the acquisition of fairly sophisticated technical skills and scientific methods. The core of this methodology lies in using experimental design, statistics, and other evaluative techniques in field settings. Thus, trainees, both at a pre- and post-doctoral level, would receive formal classroom training and field center experience in social innovative design and evaluative techniques. A number of other subsidiary methodological skills would be useful to those presented in this book. These include systems analysis, survey research techniques, cost-benefit analysis, quasi-experimental techniques, to name a few. All of these specialized techniques when mastered would provide usable skills for the experimental social innovative researcher.

Action Training

All three of the above components would be useless without this crucial aspect of a complete training program. It is our contention that essential field experimental techniques can only be learned in the context of *doing* longitudinal field experimentation. Thus, either for in-service training of post-doctoral staff, or the pre-doctoral training of graduate students, actual involvement in an experiment in the community is both desirable and essential. How such involvement might operate in the context of a PhD training program has been discussed at length elsewhere (Tornatzky, Fairweather, & O'Kelly, 1970; Tornatzky *et al.*, 1975) but will be briefly summarized here. Early in the training program, a student would be expected to pick some social problem area in which to do research. After acquiring the necessary background content and methodological skills as described above, the student would attempt to define some or all of the specific parameters of the problem at hand. The key parameters would be included in the creation of two or more experimental social models which would be perceived as problem solutions when put into practice. These innovative models would be established and evaluated on a longitudinal experimental basis. Obviously, the structure of the research center as we have described it would lend itself quite nicely to this aspect of the training component. Thus, training would be fostered by first actually serving as a member of a project team and at a later point in training development as a team project director.

We have attempted, through the use of this field educational program, to train a person who is both multidisciplinary and multiproblem focused, who is able to use available scientific knowledge and personnel, and who can quickly define the parameters of a given social problem and create possible solutions for it. Additionally, the person would be sufficiently sophisticated in a wide variety of experimental and nonexperimental research techniques. Thus, even though they are "applied" researchers, their skill level would have to be at a par or considerably above the average of the traditionally trained PhD. Finally, the training we have outlined has a strong emphasis on actual tangible involvement in community problems and research. Only through this vehicle will the mettle of the trainee be truly tested in the arena where it really matters—the real world.

IMPLICATIONS OF THE PROPOSED CENTER FOR THE STRUCTURE OF A DEMOCRATIC SOCIETY

One of the reasons for writing this book was a sense of despair over the current crisis of confidence in our society. As was outlined in Chapter 1, problems of racism, poverty, violence, environmental deprivation, and the like, are so critical that as a society we are likely doing something wrong that could perhaps be done more beneficially. The question that will be addressed in this section is whether the proposed center for experimental social innovation (which might accrue great power and influence) is congruent with the principles of modern democracy. In other words, have we arranged institutional practices so that we have "thrown out the baby with the bath water"?

The crucial issue involves the extent to which the normal democratic processes would be replaced with a meritocracy or technocracy. Several writers in the political science area have commented on the dangers of legitimating power on the basis of knowledge or special qualities (Spitz, 1958). The danger is fairly simple. Knowledge or technical skills is not a guarantee that power will not be abused. Thus there are no inherent characteristics of the experimental social innovators that insure they will not redirect their accumulated power in such a way that it would be contrary to the wishes of the people. Since it seems accurate that "power corrupts and absolute power corrupts absolutely," the central issue becomes whether or not in the formulation presented here we have built in sufficient constraints to insure that this will not happen.

Since all organizations tend to become rigid and unchanging as their established roles and statuses become behaviorally defined and carried out over a long period of time, it is essential that a center devoted to social problem solutions and its inherent social change practices have a mechanism for changing itself. For this reason, the center must establish as part of its operating procedure continuous feedback about its functioning. Such feedback information should be used as the basis for organizational change when sufficient evidence is accumulated that operational changes are warranted.

It would be extremely important that some outside organization or group conduct the continuous monitoring of the center because of the difficulty that individuals and organizations have in perceiving the need for change when it exists within themselves and their organizations. And when outside evaluators recommend changes they should be established as experiments which are consistent with the philosophy and practice of the center. Thus, no changes would occur within the center until actual experimental evidence indicated that such changes would result in more desirable organizational practices. This form of change-monitoring would aid the center in making as certain as possible that its activities remained humane and democratically oriented as well as that its staff was utilizing the most advanced technical knowledge available. It would help prevent institutional stagnation and the development of self-serving norms of organizational behavior.

There are two additional aspects of the experimental research center that we have proposed which should insure that it will not abuse its power. We have attempted to accomplish this through the design and function of the center. In addition to training concerned scientists in humanitarian values and democratic principles, the organization itself must be established so that these values and principles become institutionalized through the rights and obligations of the researchers. The operational procedure that should help guarantee this is that the *control and funding* of the center is a direct reflection of a *sharing of power* among the different societal institutions. As was depicted in Fig. 14.1, both policy and administrative links are established between the center and the executive operational and legislative branches of government as well as the university. In addition, we have made allowance at the policy level and in the composition of the board for citizen involvement. It will also be recalled that in the actual development of specific research proposals, it is incumbent upon the researchers to involve members of the problem population in designing the innovative social models. Thus, at an institutional level of functioning the center has been established in such a way that it is subject to the institutional constraints of representative governance and in turn this democratic involvement is shared by different branches of government.

It can also be argued that the "products" of the research center will actually assist the democratic process. It has been pointed out by several individuals that a democratic government can only function well when information about public issues is maximized. Unfortunately, in this time of increasingly complex social processes, the level of both citizen and governmental official awareness of social issues has diminished considerably. The parameters of many social problems are so highly complex that often the excessively expanded reliance on expert opinion is indeed a real danger. It is for this reason that the methodology developed in this book might be particularly important. Most reliance on experts in the past has been on expert *opinion* and not data-based. While on the one hand citizens and officials may not understand all the conceptual idiosyncrasies of a social problem, they do understand from their daily lives the parameters of the problem from which social models can be generated and designed to meet their needs. Thus, for example, while the *average* legislators may not understand all the ramifications of psychological and correctional theory, they can readily appreciate that it might be useful to compare a community residential facility against a traditional correctional institution to see how they affect recidivism and other outcomes. To the extent that this *methodology can reduce complex issues to fairly straightforward tests of alternatives whose outcomes are public property, the net level of knowledge throughout the society will increase.* Hopefully, this will have a positive affect on the process of democratic decision making. As has been pointed out previously, a good portion of this proposed center's research should involve contracted research. Thus, either or both the executive and legislative branches of government would benefit from getting definitive *information* about our pressing social problem issues. The apparent complexity of social issues in our current society is often more a function of the way in which issues are phrased rather than of the inherent complexity involved. Hopefully, some improvement in the democratic process can be realized from the proposed methodology presented in this book.

Perhaps more appropriate to the issue at hand than the expected positive effect of this methodology on society is the understanding of the social issues and the improvement in the democratic processes that could occur through this approach. Throughout our history, this society has only intermittently been committed to a moral, just, and at the same time rational approach to solving its problems. Periods of strength have been interspersed with a more dominant process of inept decision making based mainly upon political trade-offs. The methodology of experimental social innovation can lend considerable strength to the democratic process as it *should* exist, because legislators would be deciding among alternatives whose outcomes would already be known—at least in a probabilistic sense. Verbal discussions could then center about deciding among *informed* alternative approaches to human problems.

In this chapter we have attempted to outline a hypothetical research center dedicated to experimental social innovation. We have pointed out how this center might be related administratively and organizationally to different units of government and the university and how such a unit might operate internally in the pursuit of research excellence. Finally, we have considered the relationship and implications of such a research center *vis-à-vis* the larger society. Hopefully, the case has been made for the development of such a unit and the resultant solving of the acute problems of our contemporary society.

References

Alcoholics Anonymous, (1955) *Alcoholics Anonymous: The story of how thousands of men and women have recovered from alcoholism* (Rev.), New York: Alcoholics Anonymous.

American Association for the Advancement of Science, (1965) *Air Conservation*, No. 80.

American Psychological Association, (1953) *Ethical standards of psychologists*, Washington, D.C.: American Psychological Association.

American Psychological Association, (1973) Ethical principles in the consent of research with human participation, Washington, D.C.: American Psychological Association.

Anastasi, A. (1961) *Psychological testing* (2nd ed.), New York: Macmillan.

Anderson, B. F. (1971) *The psychology experiment*, Belmont, Calif.: Brooks-Cole.

Asch, S. E. (1956) Studies of independence and conformity: A minority of one against a unanimous majority, *Psychological Monograph*, **70**, No. 9 (whole no. 416).

Barnett, H. D. (1953) *Innovation: The basis of cultural change*, New York: McGraw-Hill.

Beck, A. A. (1972) Marginal status of consumers in a voluntary planning agency, Unpublished master's thesis, Michigan State University.

Beck, A. A. (1973) The application of small group techniques to training in community participation: A field experiment, Unpublished dissertation, Michigan State University.

Bennis, W. G. (1966) *Changing organizations*, New York: McGraw-Hill.

Bennis, W. G., Benne, K. D., & Chin, R. (Eds.), (1969) *The planning of change* (2nd ed.), New York: Holt, Rinehart & Winston.

Berelson, B. (1952) *Content analysis in communication research*, New York: The Free Press of Glencoe.

Bienen, H. (1968) Violence and social change: A review of current literature, Chicago: University of Chicago Press.

Bishop, P. C. and Beck, A. A. (1973) The Consumer Support Group: An experimental innovation in community planning, Technical Report, Capitol Area Comprehensive Health Planning Association, Contract Number CS–P (D01) 552005–01–72, Health Services and Mental Health Administration.

Block, J. (1961) *The Q-sort method in personality assessment and psychiatric research*, Springfield, Ill.: Charles C. Thomas.

Blockberger, C. W., and Lewis, J. S. (1964) The social worker's role, Fairweather, G. W. (Ed.), *Social psychology in treating mental illness: an experimental approach*, New York: John Wiley, 258–270.

Borgstrom, G. A. (1969) *Too many*, New York: Macmillan.

Borouch, R., and Riecken, H. (1974) *Social experiments: A method for planning and evaluating social programs*, New York: Academic Press.

Borus, M. E., and Tash, W. R. (1976) *Measuring the impact of man-power programs: A primer*, Ann Arbor: Institute for Labor and Industrial Relations.

Burt, C. (1941) *The factors of the mind: An introduction to factor analysis in psychology*, New York: Macmillan.

California, State of, Department of Mental Hygiene (1965) *Cohort follow-up program reports*, Nos. 3 & 4, Sacramento, Calif: Dept. of Mental Hygiene.

Campbell, D. T., and Stanley, J. C. (1966) *Experimental and quasi-experimental designs for research*, Chicago: Rand McNally.

Campbell, D. T. and Ross, L. N. (1965) The Connecticut crackdown on speeding: Time series data on quasi-experimental analysis, *Law Society Review*, **3**, 33–53.

Caplow, T., and McGee, R. J. (1958) *The academic marketplace*, New York: Basic Books.

Cattell, R. B. (1946) *Description and measurement of personality*, Yonkers, N.Y.: World Books.

Caudill, W. A. (1958) *The psychiatric hospital as a small society*, Cambridge, Mass.: Harvard University Press.

Chein, I., Gerard, D. L., Lee, R. S., and Rosenfeld, Eva. (1963) *The road to H*, New York: Basic Books.

Coch, L., and French, J. (1948) Overcoming resistance to change, *Human Relations*, **1**, 512–532.

Cochran, W. G. (1963) *Sampling techniques*, New York: Wiley.

Cochran, W. G., and Cox, Gertrude, M. (1957) *Experimental designs* (2nd ed.), New York: Wiley.

Coleman, J. S., Campbell, E. Q., Hobson, C. J., McPartland, J., Mood, A. M., Weinfeld, F. D., and York, R. L. (1966) *Equality of educational opportunity*, Report from Office of Education, Washington, D.C.: U.S. Government Printing Office.

Coleman, J. S., Katz, E. and Menzel, H. (1966) *Medical innovation: A diffusion study*, New York: Bobbs-Merrill.

Commoner, B. (1963) *Science and survival*, New York: Viking Press.

Conant, J. B. (1959) *The American high school today*, New York: McGraw-Hill.

Conover, W. J. (1971) *Practical nonparametric statistics*, New York: Wiley.

Cressler, D. L. (1964) Amount and intensity of interpersonal choice, Fairweather, G. W. (Ed.), *Social psychology in treating mental illness: An experimental approach*, New York: Wiley, 103–121.

Cronbach, L. J. (1960) *Essentials of psychological testing* (2nd ed.), New York: Harper & Row.

Daniels, Robert S. (1969) Toward a new model of human service delivery, *Health Services Research*, Summer, 4, 91–95.

Deutscher, I. (1966) Words and deeds: Social science and social policy, *Social Problems,* 13 (3), 254–285.

Dixon, W. J. (Ed.), (1965) *BMD Biomedial computer programs* (Rev.), Los Angeles, Calif.: Health Sciences Computing Facility, University of California.

Dixon, W. J., and Massey, F. J., Jr. (1957) *Introduction to statistical analysis* (2nd ed.), New York: McGraw-Hill.

Dubos, R. (1970) *Reason awake*, New York: Columbia University Press.

Edgington, E. S. (1969) *Statistical inference: The distribution free approach*, New York: McGraw-Hill.

Edwards, A. L. (1960) *Experimental design in psychological research* (Rev.), New York: Holt, Rinehart & Winston.

Ehrlich, P. R. (1968) *The population bomb*, New York: Ballantine.

Eipper, A. W. (1970) Pollution problems, resource policy, and the scientist, *Science*, 11–15, copyright 1970 by the American Association for the Advancement of Science.

Etzioni, A. (1961) *Complex organizations: A sociological reader*, New York: Holt, Rinehart & Winston.

Etzioni, A., and Etzioni, Eva. (1964) *Social change*, New York: Basic Books.

Fairweather, G. W. (Ed.), (1964) *Social psychology in treating mental illness: An experimental approach*, New York: Wiley.

Fairweather, G. W. (1967) *Methods for experimental social innovation*, New York: Wiley.

Fairweather, G. W. (1972) *Social change: The challenge to survival*, New Jersey: General Learning Press.

Fairweather, G. W., Moran, L. J., and Morton, R. B. (1956) Efficiency of attitudes, fantasies, and life history data in predicting observed behavior, *J. consult. Psychol.*, **20**, 58.

Fairweather, G. W., Sanders, D. H., Maynard, H., and Cressler, D. L. (1969) *Community life for the mentally ill*, Chicago: Aldine.

Fairweather, G. W., Sanders, D. H., and Tornatzky, L. G. (1974) *Creating change in mental health organizations*, New York: Pergamon Press.

Fairweather, G. W., and Simon, R. (1963) A further follow-up comparison of psychotherapeutic programs, *J. Consult. Psychol.*, **27**, 186.

Fairweather, G. W., Simon, R., Gebhard, M. E., Weingarten, E., Holland, J. L., Sanders, R., Stone, G. B., and Reahl, G. E. (1960) Relative effectiveness of psychotherapeutic programs: A multicriteria comparison of four programs for three different groups, *Psychol. Monograph*, **74**, No. 5 (whole no. 492).

Fergus, Esther O. (1973) The role of telephonic consultations in creating innovation adoption in health organizations, Unpublished dissertation, Michigan State University.

Ferguson, J., McReynolds, P., and Ballachey, E. (1953) *Hospital adjustment scale*, Stanford: Stanford University Press.

Fiedler, F. E. (1967) *A theory of leadership effectiveness*, New York: McGraw-Hill.

Finney, B. C. (1954) A scale to measure inter-personal relationships in group psychotherapy, *Group Psychotherapy*, **7**, 52–56.

Flanagan, J. C. (1956) *Performance record for the personal and social development program*, Chicago: Sci. Res. Assoc.

Forsyth, R. P., and Fairweather, G. W. (1961) Psychotherapeutic and other hospital treatment criteria: The dilemma, *J. Abnormal Social Psychology*, **62**, 598–604.

Frank, J. D. (1961) *Persuasion and healing*, Baltimore: Johns Hopkins Press.

Fromm, Erich. (1968) *The revolution of hope*, New York: Harper & Row.

Fuchter, B. (1954) *Introduction to factor analysis*, Princeton: Van Nostrand.

Galbraith, J. K. (1958) *The affluent society*, Boston: Houghton Mifflin.

Galbraith, J. K. (1971) *New industrial state*, Boston: Houghton Mifflin.

Ghiselli, E. E. (1964) *Theory of psychological measurement*, New York: McGraw-Hill.

Giedt, F. H., and Schlosser, J. R. (1955) Movement of patients through a neuropsychiatric hospital, Unpublished manuscript, Medical Library, V. A. Hospital, Perry Point, Maryland.

Glass, G. V. (1968) Analysis of data on the Connecticut speeding crackdown as a time series experiment, *Law and Society Review*, **3**, 55–76.

Glass, G. V., and Stanley, J. C. (1970) *Statistical methods in education and psychology*. Englewood Cliffs: Prentice Hall.

Goffman, E. (1962) *Asylums* (Essays on the social situation of mental patients and other inmates), Chicago: Aldine.

Goldman, A. R. (1964) The recreational hour: An evaluation of behavior in an unstructured situation, in Fairweather, G. W. (Ed.), *Social psychology in treating mental illness: An experimental approach*, New York: Wiley, 45–76.

Goldsteen, Joel, (1974) Social change for neighborhoods: Empirical analysis of participation in planning, Unpublished dissertation, Michigan State University.

Gouldner, A. W. (1961) Anti-Minotaur: The myth of a value-free sociology, Bennis, W. G., Benne, K. D., and Chin, R. (Eds.), *The planning of change*, New York: Holt, Rinehart, & Winston.

Green, R. L., Tornatzky, L. G., Logan, G. W., Pachon, H. P., Schweitzer, J. H., Tenbrunsel, T. W., and Wisenbaker, J. M. (1976) *Process and planning evaluation, mini-station program, Detroit Police Department*, East Lansing: College of Urban Development, Michigan State University.

Guilford, J. P. (1954) *Psychometric methods* (2nd ed.), New York: McGraw-Hill.

Guilford, J. P. (1956) *Fundamental statistics in psychology and education*, New York: McGraw-Hill.

Gunn, C. F. (1973) The amazing Ralph Heintz: Portrait of an inventor, *The Stanford Magazine*, Fall-Winter.

Hage, J., and Aiken, M. (1970) *Social change in complex organizations*, New York: Random House.

Harrington, M. (1962) *The other America: Poverty in the United States*, New York: Macmillan.

Harrington, M. H. (1968) A conversation with Kenneth B. Clark, *Psychology Today*, Vol. 2, No. 1, 19–25.

Harris, R. N. (1973) The diffusion of the community lodge, Unpublished dissertation, Michigan State University.

Havelock, R. G. (1969) *Planning for innovation for dissemination and utilization of knowledge*, Ann Arbor, Michigan: Institute for Social Research.

Havelock, R. G. (1973) *The change agents guide to innovation in education*, Ann Arbor, Michigan: Institute for Social Research.

Havelock, R. G., and Havelock, M. C. (1973) *Educational innovation in the United States*, Ann Arbor, Michigan: Institute for Social Research.

Hawkridge, D. J., Chalupsky, A. B., and Roberts, A. O. H. (1968) A study of selected exemplary programs for the education of disadvantaged children, *Final Report on Project No. 089013*, U.S. Office of Education.

Heyns, R. W., and Lippitt, R. (1954) Systematic observational techniques, in Lindsey G. (Ed.), *Handbook of social psychology*, Vol. I, Reading, Mass.: Addison-Wesley, 370–404.

Hodgkinson, H. L., and Thelin, J. (1971) Survey of the applications and uses of unobtrusive measures in the fields of social service, Center for research and development in higher education, Unpublished manuscript, University of California.

Holland, J. L. (1961) Creative and academic performance among talented adolescents, *Journal of Educational Psychol.*, **52**, No. 3, 136–147.

Holland, J. L., and Richards, J. M., Jr. (1965) Academic and nonacademic accomplishment: Correlated or uncorrelated? *Journal of Educational Psychol.*, **56**, 165–174.

Hollander, M. B., and Wolfe, D. A. (1973) *Nonparametric statistical methods*, New York: Wiley Press.

Hollingshead, A. B., and Redlich, F. C. (1958) *Social class and mental illness: A community study*, New York: Wiley.

Holzinger, K. J., and Harman, H. H. (1941) *Factor analysis: A synthesis of factoral methods*, Chicago: University of Chicago Press.

Hotelling, H. (1933) *Analysis of a complex of statistical variables into principal components*, Baltimore: Warwick & York.

Hughes, C., Tremblay, M., Rappaport, R., and Lelghton, A. H. (1960) *People of Cove and Woodlot*, Vol. II, New York: Basic Books.

Hunter, M., Schooler, C., and Spohn, H. E. (1962) The measurement of characteristic patterns of ward behavior in chronic schizophrenics, *J. Consult. Psychol.*, **26**, 69–73.

Hyman, H. H. (1954) *Interviewing in social research*, Chicago: University of Chicago Press.

Ives, W. R. (1974) *An evaluation of two drug abuse programs in Lansing, Michigan*, Unpublished dissertation, Michigan State University.

Jackson, J. M., and Saltzstein, H. G. (1956) *Group membership and conformity processes*, Ann Arbor, Michigan: University of Michigan, Research Center for Group Dynamics, Institute for Social Research.

Jacokes, L. E. (1975) Coeducational and single sex residence halls: An experimental comparison, Unpublished dissertation, Michigan State University.

Jamison, Kent S. (1974) An evaluation of the effectiveness of a nutritional counseling program in alleviating certain health problems, Unpublished dissertation, Michigan State University.

Jones, L. V. (1952) Tests of hypotheses: One-sided vs. two-sided alternatives, *Psychol. Bull*, **49** (1), 43–46.

Jones, L. V., and Fiske, D. W. (1953) Models for testing the significance of combined results, *Psych. Bull.*, **56**, No. 5, 375–382.

Jones, M. (1953) *The therapeutic community: A new treatment method in psychiatry*, New York: Basic Books.

Katz, I. (1964) Review of evidence relative to the effects of desegregation on the intellectual performance of Negroes, *American Psycholo.*, **19**(6), 381–399.

Katz, I., and Benjamin, L. (1960) Effects of white authoritarianism in biracial work groups, *J. abnorm. Soc. Psychol.*, **61**, 448–456.

Katz, I., and Cohen, M. (1962) The effects of training Negroes upon cooperative problem solving in biracial terms, *J. abnorm. soc. Psychol.*, **64**, 319–325.

Keith, Lynn, (1974) Perceived interorganizational similarity-dissimilarity and the attraction paradigm. Unpublished dissertation, Michigan State University.

Keller, O. J., and Alper, B. S. (1970) *Halfway houses: Community centered correction and treatment*, Lexington, Mass.: Heath-Lexington.

Kelling, G. L., Pate, T., Dieckman, D., Brown, C. E. (1974) The Kansas City Prevention Patrol Experiment, Police Foundation.

Kempthorne, O. (1952) *Design and analysis of experiments*, New York: Wiley.

Kerlinger, F. N., and Pedhazur, J. E. (1973) *Multiple regression in behavioral research*, New York: Holt, Rinehart & Winston.

Knowles, L. L., and Prewitt, K. (1969) (Eds.), *Institutional racism in America*, Prentice-Hall.

Krech, D., Crutchfield, R. S., and Ballachey, E. L. (1962) *Individual in society*, New York: McGraw-Hill.

LaPiere, R. T. (1965) *Social change*, New York: McGraw-Hill.

Lehmann, E. L. (1959) *Testing statistical hypotheses*, New York: Wiley.

Lerner, M. J., and Fairweather, G. W. (1963) The social behavior of chronic schizophrenics in supervised and unsupervised work groups. *J. Abnorm. Soc. Psychol.*, **67**, 219–225.

Lewin, K., Lippit, R., and White, R. (1939) Patterns of aggressive behavior in experimentally created "social climate," *J. Soc. Psychol.*, **X**, 271–299.

Lindeblom, C. E. (1965) The science of muddling through, In Zald (Ed.), *Social welfare institutions*, New York: Wiley.

Lindemann, James E., Fairweather, G. W., Stone, G. B., and Smith, R. S. (1959) The use of demographic characteristics in predicting length of neuropsychiatric hospital stay. *J. consult. Psychol.*, **23**, 1, 1958, 85–89.

Lindholm, C. (1964) The science of muddling through, In Leavitt, H., and Pondy, L., *Readings in managerial psychology*, Chicago: University of Chicago Press, pp. 61–78.

Lindquist, E. F. (1953) *Design and analysis of experiments in psychology and education*, Boston: Houghton Mifflin.

Lippit, R., Watson, J., Westley, B. (1958) *The dynamics of planned change*, New York: Harcourt, Brace, & World.

Litwak, E. (September 1961) Models of bureaucracy that permit conflict. *American Journal of Psychol.*, **57,** pp. 173–183.

Litwak, E., and Hylton, L. (March 1962) Interorganizational analysis: A hypothesis on coordination. *Administrative Science Quarterly*, **6,** pp. 395–420.

Lounsbury, J. W. (1973) A community experiment is dissemination models for citizen environmental action, Unpublished dissertation, Michigan State University.

Luce, R. D., and Raiffa, H. (1957) *Games and decisions*, New York: Wiley.

Maccoby, Eleanor E., and Maccoby, N. (1954) The interview: A tool of social science, In G. Lindzey (Ed.), *Handbook of social psychol.*, Vol. I. Reading, Mass.: Addison-Wesley, 449–487.

MacDonald, W. S. (1964) The large group meeting hour: An evaluation of behavior in a structured situation, in Fairweather, G. W. (Ed.), *Social psychology in treating mental illness: An experimental approach*, New York: Wiley, 77–102.

Marascuilo, Leonard A. (1971) *Statistical methods for behavior science research*, New York: McGraw-Hill.

Marris, Peter and Rein, Martin. (1967) *Dilemmas of social reform*, New York: Atherton Press.

Maynard, H. (1966) Functional dimensions of small groups in a mental hospital treatment program, Unpublished doctoral dissertation, University of Oregon.

Maynard, H. (1964) The effect of group composition on task performance, Unpublished masters thesis, University of Oregon.

McGrath, J. E., and Altman, I. (1966) *Small group research*, New York: Holt, Rinehart & Winston.

McKenzie, G. (1976) Alternative Decision-Making Roles in a Learning Environment. Unpublished dissertation, Michigan State University.

McNemar, Q. (1962) *Psychological statistics* (3rd ed.), New York: Wiley.

Miller, D. C. (1964) *Handbook of research design and social measurement*, New York: McKay.

Mills, C. W. (1956) *The power élite*, New York: Oxford University Press.

Mischel, Walter (1968) *Personality and assessment*, New York: Wiley.

Moran, L. J., Fairweather, G. W., and Morton, R. B. (1956) Some determinants of successful and unsuccessful adaptation to hospital treatment of tuberculosis, *J. consult. Psychol.*, 20, 125–131.

Moroney, M. J. (1956) *Facts from figures* (3rd Rev.), Baltimore, Md.: Penguin Books.

Moses, L. E. (1952) Nonparametric statistics for psychological research, *Psychol. Bull.*, 49, 122–143.

Myrdal, G. (1944) *An American dilemma*, New York: Harper & Row.

National Academy of Sciences-National Research Council, (1969) *Resources and Man:* A study and recommendations, San Francisco: Freeman.

Nie, Norman A., Hull, C. H., Jenkins, Jean J., Steinbrenner, Karin, Bert, Dale H. (1975) *SPSS: Statistical package for the social sciences*, (2nd ed.), New York: McGraw-Hill.

Nunnally, J. (1967) *Psychometric theory*, New York: McGraw-Hill.

Olshansky, S. (1960) The transitional sheltered workshop: A survey, *J. soc. Issues*, 16, 33–39.

Oppenheimer, J. R. (1954) See U.S. Atomic Energy Commission, Personnel Security Board Hearing, Washington, D.C., p. 33.

Raven, B. H. (1961) *A bibliography of publications relating to the small group*, (2nd ed.), Los Angeles, Calif.: University of Calif.

Riley, M. W., Riley, J. W., Jr., and Toby, J. (1954) *Sociological studies in scale analysis*, New Brunswick, N.J.: Rutgers University Press.

Rogers, E. M. (1962) *Diffusion of innovations*, New York: The Free Press.

Rogers, E. M., and Shoemaker, F. F. (1971) *Communication of innovations: A cross cultural approach*, New York: The Free Press.

Rose, A. M. (1967) *The power structure*, New York: Oxford University Press.

Rossi, P. H., and Williams, W. (1972) *Evaluating social programs*, New York: Seminar Press.

Sakoda, James M., Cohen, Burton, H., and Beall, G. (1954) Tests of significance for a series of statistical tests, *Psych. Bull.*, 51, No. 2, 172–175.

Sanders, D. H., MacDonald, W. S., and Maynard, H. (1964) The effect of group composition on task performance and role differentiation, in Fairweather, G. W. (Ed.), *Social psychology in treating mental illness: An experimental approach*, New York: Wiley, 196–209.

Sanford, N. (1965) Will psychologists study human problems? *Amer. Psychol.*, 20, 192–202.

Sherif, Carolyn W. (1965) *Attitude and attitude change: The social judgment-involvement approach*, Philadelphia: Saunders.

Sherif, M., and Sherif, Carolyn W. (1964) *Reference groups*, New York: Harper & Row.

Siegel, S. (1956) *Nonparametric statistics for the behavioral sciences*, New York: McGraw-Hill.

Snedecor, G. W. (1956) *Statistical methods* (5th ed.), Ames, Iowa: Iowa State University Press.

Spearman, C. (1927) *The abilities of man*, London: Macmillan.

Spitz, David. (1958) *Democracy and the change in power*, New York: Columbia University.

Stanton, A. H., and Schwartz, M. S. (1954) *The mental hospital*, New York: Basic Books.

Stephenson, W. (1953) *The study of behavior: Q-technique and its methodology*, Chicago: University of Chicago Press.

Stevens, S. S. (1951) Mathematics, measurement and psychophysics, in Stevens, S. S. (Ed.), *Handbook of experimental psychology*, New York: Wiley.

Taylor, Jeffrey, R. (1975) A comparative experiment in voluntary birth planning, Unpublished dissertation, Michigan State University.

Thomson, G. W. (1940) *An analysis of performance test scores of a representative group of Scottish children*, London: University of London Press.

Thurstone, L. L. (1947) *Multiple factor analysis: A development and expansion of the vectors of mind*, Chicago: University of Chicago Press.

Tillman, I. (1976) A comparison of three intervention approaches aimed at improving the prenatal health of women of low socioeconomic status, Unpublished dissertation, Michigan State University.

Tipler, Doris L., and Rankin, Elizabeth A. (1964) The nurse's role, in Fairweather, G. W. (Ed.), *Social psychology in treating mental illness: An experimental approach*, New York: Wiley.

Torgerson, W. S. (1958) *Theory and methods of scaling*, New York: Wiley.

Tornatzky, L. G., Fairweather, G. W., and O'Kelley, L. I. (September 1970) A PhD program aimed at survival. *American Psychologist*, **25**, No. 9.

Tornatzky, L. G. Schweitzer, J. H., Green, R. L., Logan, G. W., Pachon, H., Tenbrunsel, T. W., Wisenbaker, J. M. (1975) A description of the evaluation for the Detroit mini police station program. Paper presented at 79th Annual Meeting of the Michigan Academy of Science, Arts and Letters, Ann Arbor, April 4, 1975.

Tornatzky, L. G., Taylor, J. R., Harris, R., Beck, A., McKenzie, D., and Nemon, B. (1970) Social, demographic and normative determinants of family size preferences—A preliminary report: The middle class, Unpublished manuscript, Michigan State University.

Tryon, R. C. (1958) Cumulative communality cluster analysis, *Educ. psychol. measmt.*, **18**, 3–35.

Tryon, R. C. (1959) Domain sampling formulation of cluster and factor analysis, *Psychometrika*, **24**, 113–135.

Tryon, R. C. (1963) Psychology in flux: The academic-professional bipolarity, *Amer. Psychol.*, **18**, 134–143.

Tryon, R. C. (1966) Unrestricted cluster and factor analysis with applications to the MMPI and Holzinger-Harman problems, *Multivar. Behav. Res.*, **2**, 229–244.

Tryon, R. C., and Bailey, D. E. (1966) The BC TRY computer system of cluster and factor analysis, *Multivar. Behav. Res.*, **1**, 95–111.

Tryon, R. C., and Bailey, D. E. (1970) *Cluster analysis*, New York: McGraw-Hill.

Tryon, R. C., Tryon, Caroline M., and Kuznets, G. (1941a) Studies in individual differences in maze ability, IX, Ratings of hiding, avoidance, escape, and vocalization responses, *J. comp. Psychol.*, **32**, 407–435.

Tryon, R. C., Tryon, Caroline M., and Kuznets, G. (1941b) Studies in individual differences in maze ability, X, Ratings and other measures of initial emotional responses of rats to novel inanimate objects, *J. comp. Psychol.*, **32**, 447–473.

Tucker, Charles. (1974) The role of reading, speaking dialects, and associative bridging in behavior achievement, Unpublished doctoral dissertation, Michigan State University.

Vitale, J. H. (1964) The impact of the study upon the hospital: opinions of administrative and staff personnel, in Fairweather, G. W., (Ed.), *Social psychology in treating mental illness: An experimental approach*, New York: Wiley, 213–244.

Walker, Helen, M., and Lev, Joseph. (1953) *Statistical inference*, New York: Holt.

Warner, W. S. (1960) *Social class in America*, New York: Harper & Row.

Webb, E. J., Campbell, D. T., Schwartz, R. D., and Sechrest, L. (1966) *Unobtrusive measures: Nonreactive research in the social sciences*, Chicago, Ill.: Rand-McNally.

Whitney, W. M. (1974) An evaluation of a community based delinquency prevention program on the basis of group and individual employment. Unpublished doctoral dissertation, Michigan State University.

Whyte, W. F. (1955) *Street corner society. The social structure of an Italian Slum* (2nd ed.), Chicago: University of Chicago Press.

Wicker, Allen J. (1969) Attitudes and action: The relationship of verbal and overt behavioral responses to attitude objects, *Journal of Social Issues*, **25**, 41–78.

Wilcoxon, F., and Wilcox, Roberta A. (1964) *Some rapid approximate statistical procedures*. (Rev. Ed.) Pearl River, N.Y.: Lederle Laboratories, American Cyanamid.

Winer, Ben J. (1962) *Statistical principles in experimental design*, New York: McGraw-Hill.

Wohl, S. A. (1964) Follow-up community adjustment, in Fairweather, G. W. (Ed.), *Social psychology in treating mental illness: An experimental approach*, New York: Wiley, 160–168.

Wright, P. (1966) Technology transfer and utilization: Active promotion or passive dissemination? *Research/Development*, Nov. 1966.

Yablonsky, L. (1964) *The tunnel back*, New York: Macmillan.

Yates, F. (1949) *Sampling methods for censuses and surveys*, London: Griffin.

Zimbardo, Philip, Haney, Craig, and Banks, W. C. (1975) A Pirandillian prison, in Edward Krapat (Ed.), *Psychology is social*, Glenville, Ill.: Scott Foresman.

Index